The Theory of Contract Law

Although the law of contract is largely settled, there is at present no widely accepted comprehensive theory either of its main principles and doctrines or of its normative basis. Contract law theory raises issues concerning the relation between law and morality, the role and the importance of rights, the connection between justice and economics, and the distinction between private and public law. This collection of six full-length original essays, written by some of the most eminent scholars in the field, explores the general theory of contract law from a variety of theoretical perspectives.

The volume addresses a wide range of issues, both methodological and substantive, in the theory and practice of contract law. While the essays build upon past theoretical contributions, they also attempt to take contract theory further and suggest new and promising ways to develop the theory of contract law.

The Theory of Contract Law represents one of the most ambitious attempts to date to advance the general theory of contract law. It will be of interest to professionals and students of law and philosophy.

Peter Benson is Professor of Law at the University of Toronto.

Cambridge Studies in Philosophy and Law

Other books in the series:

The Theory of Contract Law

New Essays

Edited by

Peter Benson

University of Toronto

CAMBRIDGE
UNIVERSITY PRESS

PUBLISHED BY THE PRESS SYNDICATE OF THE UNIVERSITY OF CAMBRIDGE
The Pitt Building, Trumpington Street, Cambridge, United Kingdom

CAMBRIDGE UNIVERSITY PRESS
The Edinburgh Building, Cambridge CB2 2RU, UK
40 West 20th Street, New York, NY 10011-4211, USA
10 Stamford Road, Oakleigh, VIC 3166, Australia
Ruiz de Alarcón 13, 28014 Madrid, Spain
Dock House, The Waterfront, Cape Town 8001, South Africa

http://www.cambridge.org

© Cambridge University Press 2001

First published 2001

Printed in the United States of America

Typeface Times Roman 10/12 pt.   *System* QuarkXPress 4.04 [AG]

A catalog record for this book is available from the British Library.

Library of Congress Cataloging in Publication Data
The theory of contract law : new essays / edited by Peter Benson.
p. cm. – (Cambridge studies in philosophy and law)
Includes bibliographical references.
ISBN 0-521-64038-5
1. Contracts. I. Benson, Peter, 1953- II. Series.
K840. T48 2001
346.02–dc21   00-033710

ISBN 0 521 64038 5 hardback

For My Parents

Contents

Acknowledgments

I would like to express my gratitude to Jules Coleman who, as former General Editor of the Cambridge Studies in Philosophy and Law, kindly invited me to be editor of this volume and provided crucial guidance and assistance in getting the project off the ground and firmly established. I have tried throughout to fulfill his conception of the goals and character of this series. To Gerald Postema, the present General Editor, my thanks for his help and advice in bringing the book to completion. I owe Terence Moore, Executive Editor of Humanities at Cambridge University Press and Editorial Assistant Alexis Ruda, Associate Editor Gwen Seznec, and Assistant Editor Robyn Wainner much thanks for cheerfully and patiently shepherding the preparation and the production of the book from start to finish.

I organized the project in a preliminary way while I was at the Faculty of Law, McGill University, to which I would like to express my sincere thanks. I executed and completed it as a member of the Faculty of Law at the University of Toronto. I am most grateful to this institution. In particular, I wish to thank my new colleagues who have made the transition a happy one and my Dean, Ronald Daniels, who by his untiring encouragement, support, and inspiring vision of what a law school can be has provided an intellectual and moral environment conducive to sustained and searching scholarly work. My thanks to my research assistants, Daniel Batista, for his invaluable help in editing all the contributions and for compiling the index and Katie Sykes, for proofreading and doing a final edit of the whole work; and to May Seto for her skillful and always cheerful secretarial assistance.

For my wife, Ann, gratitude deeper than words can express. And finally to my parents, Norma Betty and Robert Benson, I dedicate this book: for their unconditional love, all the opportunities they have given me, and their respect for human individuality.

Contributors

PETER BENSON is Professor of Law at the University of Toronto Faculty of Law, having previously taught at the Faculty of Law, McGill University.

RICHARD CRASWELL is Professor of Law at Stanford University, having previously taught at the University of Chicago and the University of Southern California law schools. He is also the co-editor (with Alan Schwartz) of *Foundations of Contract Law* (Oxford University Press, 1994).

MELVIN EISENBERG is the Koret Professor of Law at the School of Law of the University of California at Berkeley and Visiting Professor of Law at the Columbia Law School. He is the author of *The Nature of the Common Law* (Harvard University Press, 1988) and *The Structure of the Corporation* (Little, Brown & Co., 1976). He is also the co-editor (with Lon L. Fuller) of *Basic Contract Law, 6th Ed.* (1996) and the co-editor (with W. Cary) of *Cases and Materials on Corporations and Other Business Organizations, 8th Ed.* (2000). Professor Eisenberg is a Fellow of the American Academy of Arts and Sciences.

STEVEN ELLIOTT is a Lecturer at St. Catherine's College, Oxford University.

JAMES GORDLEY is Shannon Cecil Turner Professor of Jurisprudence at the School of Law of the University of California at Berkeley. He is the author of *The Philosophical Origins of Modern Contract Doctrine* (Clarendon Law Series, Oxford University Press, 1991) and *The Civil Law System: An Introduction to the Comparative Study of Law* (with Arthur von Mehren; Little, Brown & Co., 1977). He is a Fellow of the American Academy of Arts and Sciences.

T. M. SCANLON is Alford Professor of Natural Religion, Moral Philosophy, and Civil Polity at Harvard University. He is the author of *What We Owe to Each Other* (Harvard University Press, 1999).

MICHAEL J. TREBILCOCK is Professor of Law and Economics at the University of Toronto Faculty of Law and Director of its Law and Economics

Programme since 1976. He is the author of *The Limits of Freedom of Contract* (Harvard University Press, 1993). Professor Trebilcock is also the author of *The Common Law of Restraint of Trade: A Legal and Economic Analysis* (Carswell, 1986); *Exploring the Domain of Accident Law: Taking Facts Seriously* (with Dewees and Duff; Oxford University Press, 1996); *International Trade Regulation, 2nd Ed.* (with R. Howse; Routledge, London, 1999); and *The Making of the Mosaic: A History of Canadian Immigration Policy* (with N. Kelley; University of Toronto Press, 1998).
He is the recipient of the 1999 Molson Prize for contributions to the humanities and social sciences in Canada.

Introduction

PETER BENSON

Although the six essays that comprise the present collection may differ widely in approach, they are all animated by a shared belief in the possibility and in the importance of a theory of contract law that aims to be comprehensive in scope and normative in character. They are intended as contributions to the ongoing elaboration of such a theory. All the essays have been specifically prepared for this volume and appear now for the first time in print. In keeping with the goals of the Cambridge Law and Philosophy Series, the contributors have been encouraged to present their ideas and arguments in as fully developed and detailed a manner as possible. Each essay stands on its own as a sustained effort to explore a distinct theoretical point of view via an engagement with specific aspects of the law of contract. Before introducing the contents of the individual essays, however, I should say something about prior theoretical discussions that form their immediate intellectual backdrop. The following remarks are necessarily brief and selective.

In the twentieth century, it may be fairly said that theoretical writing about the common law of contract is inaugurated by one piece: Lon L. Fuller's 1936 article "The Reliance Interest in Contract Damages."[1] It is only a slight exaggeration to say that all subsequent efforts either take up and elaborate lines of argument suggested by this essay or attempt to forge an alternative approach in response to it. In one way or another, it has dominated the course of theoretical discussion since its publication.

What is the article's primary theoretical contribution on the basis of which it may be said to have inaugurated common law contract theory in the twentieth

---

1. (1936) 46 Yale L.J.52. I should say that although the article is co-authored by Fuller and his research assistant William Perdue, Jr., I take, as do others, Fuller to be the writer of the article and certainly of its theoretical parts. For recent discussions of the article, see T. Rakoff, "Fuller and Perdue's *The Reliance Interest* as a Work of Legal Scholarship" (1991) Wis. L. Rev. 203; D. Friedmann, "The Performance Interest in Contract Damages" (1995) 111 Law Q. R. 628; P. Benson, "Contract" in *A Companion to Philosophy of Law and Legal Theory*, ed. D. Patterson (Oxford: Blackwell); and R. Craswell, "Against Fuller and Perdue" (2000) 67 Univ. Chic. L. Rev. 99.

century? It is not, as one might think, Fuller's well-known specification of the three interests – expectation, reliance, and restitution – which, he argues, constitute the three principal purposes that may be pursued in awarding contract damages.[2] Nor is it his effort to show that courts protect the reliance interest in ways that are not ordinarily recognized or acknowledged. Although these aspects of the article undoubtedly have exercised wide influence, particularly in legal scholarship, they do not go beyond ordinary legal classification and analysis. In themselves, they do not pose a question that goes to the very basis and intelligibility of contractual obligation. The article's theoretical contribution lies elsewhere.

On the very first page of the article, Fuller refers to the basic, perhaps the most basic, principle of contract law that a plaintiff is entitled to receive as compensation for breach of contract the value of what he or she was promised and that in giving such damages the law aims to protect the "expectation interest," that is, to put the plaintiff in the position that he or she would have been in had the defendant performed as promised. It is not by chance that Fuller refers here to Samuel Williston's statement of the principle. Williston's *A Treatise on the Law of Contracts* represents the most systematically and carefully worked-out presentation of the legal point of view that culminates several decades of intensive and highly sophisticated efforts by such masters of the common law as Pollock, Holmes, Langdell, Ames, Holdsworth, Salmond, and Leake, to bring order and internal consistency to the law of contract.[3] These writers, and Williston in particular, were remarkably successful in achieving this aim. For all that, however, their work remains *un*theoretical: They simply presuppose the premise that the expectation remedy is a form of compensation without exploring its normative basis and they stipulate the existence of a deep connection between the expectation principle and the basic doctrines of contract formation without explaining its necessity.

The reason why twentieth-century contract *theory* begins with Fuller's article is precisely because it in contrast to the work of these other scholars, does not simply *take* the expectation principle as the fundamental principle of compensation but clearly and decisively questions it. In doing so, Fuller challenges the coherence of contract on a point that goes to its very core. For the first time in the twentieth century, contract scholarship *must* ask at a fundamental level what is the normative basis of contract.[4]

---

2. This division was already suggested by Fuller's contemporaries. See, for example, G. Gardner, "An Inquiry into the Principles of the Law of Contract" (1932) 46 Harv. L. Rev. 1.
3. Their writings are collected in one remarkable volume, *Selected Readings on the Law of Contracts,* The Association of American Law Schools, ed. (New York: The Macmillan Company, 1931). This monumental volume, which is more than one thousand three hundred pages in length, is, in the present writer's opinion, the single most important collection of essays ever published on the common law of contract.
4. In *The Death of Contract,* Grant Gilmore sees the work of Fuller, Corbin, and others as causing the "general theory of contract" developed by such jurists as Langdell, Holmes, Pollock, and

To elaborate a little, Fuller suggests that the expectation remedy "seems on its face a queer kind of compensation"[5] because it gives the promisee something that he or she never lost. Now if breach of an executory contract does not as such deprive the promisee of anything, it plainly follows that the promisee never had anything to lose in the first place. In other words, an executory contrat does not as such give the promisee anything that can count as a legally protected interest against the promisor. This must be Fuller's underlying premise. Yet, the idea of compensation in private law presupposes just that the defendant has injured something which belongs to the plantiff by exclusive right as against the defendant. On Fuller's view, the expectation remedy cannot be a form of compensation because contract is not a mode of acquiring such entitlements. This represents Fuller's theoretical challenge at its deepest level.

Accordingly, on Fuller's view, the expectation interest presents a lesser claim in justice to judicial intervention than do the reliance and restitution interests. Whereas protection of the latter interests restores a disturbed equilibrium and so exemplifies corrective justice, enforcement of the former "brings into being a new situation"[6] and represents an exercise of distributive justice. From the standpoint of corrective justice, Fuller contends, it is by no means clear "why a promise which has not been relied on [should] ever be enforced at all."[7] Thus the expectation remedy, the so-called normal measure of recovery for breach of contract, appears anomalous from the standpoint of private law itself. Yet it is precisely the availability of the expectation remedy for breach of a wholly executory contract that is the distinctive hallmark of contract law.

Despite Fuller's view that the expectation principle is "as a matter of fact no easy thing to explain" and a problem that "throws its shadow across our whole subject,"[8] he thinks himself obliged to provide a satisfactory rationale for this settled rule of law. Fuller's answer that expectation damages cure and prevent reliance losses as well as facilitate general reliance on business arrangements would appear to be the only justification available once breach of an

---

Williston to "come unstuck." G. Gilmore, *The Death of Contract* (Columbus: Ohio State University Press, 1974), p. 102. This assessment is wrong, I think, in at least two respects. First, it mistakenly attributes to these writers a general *theory* of contract, whereas, as I have already indicated in the text above, these jurists did not so much develop a theory as systematically present the legal point of view by clarifying the definitions of contract principles and doctrines and by exploring, within limits, their implications and their conceptual interconnections. Second, far from coming unstuck, their work still represents to date the most sophisticated and successful effort to present the legal point of view in one integrated compass. Of course, insofar as contract law has developed in certain ways since they wrote – I am thinking here primarily of the full reception of a doctrine of unconscionability – this presentation would have to be revised. Fuller's challenge does not so much undermine their work as require an elaboration and a defence of the conception of contract that informs it. And what we chiefly lack at present is just such a theory that attempts this. For an instructive and careful discussion of Gilmore's assessment of the work of these contract scholars, see J. Gordley, Review of Grant Gilmore *The Death of Contract*, in (1975) 89 Harv. L. Rev. 452, esp. pp. 457ff.

5. *Supra* note 1 at p. 53.   6. Ibid.   7. Ibid., at p.57.   8. Ibid.

unrelied-upon promise is seen as causing no injury to the plaintiff and the expectation remedy is characterized as an exercise of distributive justice. On this
rationale, reliance becomes the Archimedian point in the understanding of contractual liability and the instrumental relation between contract and economic
efficiency becomes a central consideration.

The first major wave of theorizing after Fuller, which takes place during the
late 1970s and early 1980s, consists of writers who, almost without exception,
either elaborate one or more facets of his answer or, where they propose an alternative vision of contract, do so in ways that attempt to answer his challenge.
Thus, the idea that protection of the reliance and restitution interests provides
a more secure normative foundation for contractual liability is developed with
subtlety and richness in the work of Patrick Atiyah.[9] Anthony Kronman, among
others, takes seriously Fuller's suggestion that the normal remedy for breach
of contract comes under distributive justice and proposes that contract law as a
whole, including its core notion of consent, can *only* be understood in terms of
distributive justice; if contract rules are to have any moral acceptability, they
must be framed, Kronman argues, so as to promote a fair division of wealth and
power among citizens.[10] Already during this first wave, the most detailed and
comprehensive theoretical approach is the economic theory of contract. With the
appearance in 1979 of *The Economics of Contract Law,*[11] a collection of previously published essays edited by Kronman and Richard Posner, the economic
approach takes up Fuller's embryonic thesis that contract law is explicable as a
means of facilitating and supporting efficient economic relations and demon-
strates that it can be developed with sophistication to illuminate an unprece-
dented range of substantive issues in contract law. With certain notable exceptions, economic analysis during this period focuses exclusively on the question
of the efficiency of carrying out the promises that form an agreement. Contract

---

9. The central theoretical works are his essay "Contracts, Promises, and the Law of Obligations"
    (1978) 94 Law Q. R. 193, reprinted with revisions and additions in P. Atiyah, *Essays on Con-
    tract* (Oxford: Clarendon Press, 1986), pp. 10–56, and P. Atiyah, *Promises, Morals, and Law*
    (Oxford: Clarendon Press, 1981).
10. See A. Kronman, "Contract Law and Distributive Justice" (1980) Yale Law J. 472 and A. Kron-
    man, "Paternalism and the Law of Contracts" (1983) 92 Yale Law J. 763.
11. A. Kronman and R. Posner, eds. *The Economics of Contract Law* (Boston: Little, Brown and
    Company, 1979). I should add here that, throughout the first and second waves of contract the-
    ory and even at present, the economic analysis of contract is the dominant theoretical approach
    and economic writing is by far the most prolific, although much of this writing is "normal sci-
    ence" rather than inquiry self-counsciously engaged in exploring and reshaping the theoretical
    premises and claims of the economic approach. I will not even attempt here to give an ex-
    haustive list of the articles and works that are of special theoretical interest. That being said, in
    addition to the economic writing to which I refer in the text, two recent collections might be
    noted: They are *Foundations of Contract Law,* R. Craswell and A. Schwartz, eds. (Oxford: Ox-
    ford University Press, 1994) and *The Fall and Rise of Freedom of Contract,* F. H. Buckley, ed.
    (Durham and London: Duke University Press, 1999).

law is to be judged in light of the principle that voluntary exchanges move resources toward their most valuable uses.[12]

Arguably the most important, and certainly the most discussed single work of this first wave of contract theorizing is, however, Charles Fried's *Contract as Promise*.[13] It is the only book-length presentation of a theory of contract that systematically explores the normative foundation of contract and that attempts to explain the main contract doctrines on a unified moral basis. Fried challenges all the previously discussed approaches on the ground that they do not provide a normative basis for contract that is morally acceptable and that brings out its unity. Invoking the distinction between the right and the good, Fried argues that if, as is generally supposed, contractual obligation is self-imposed as well as legally enforceable, it must not entail the imposition of a conception of the good, as this would violate individual autonomy. Fried proposes instead the "promise principle," which he presents as Kantian in inspiration, as the moral basis of contractual obligation. At the same time, he emphasizes that, while central aspects and doctrines of contract law may be understood on this basis, there are others that either require additional and distinct principles or that are flatly in tension with the promise principle and so must be rejected. For instance, in Fried's view, the law of implied terms and conditions cannot be explained on the basis of the promise principle alone but requires other principles, whether of fairness, risk allocation, or custom. Moreover, endorsement of the promise principle requires, he argues, rejection of the doctrine of consideration and the objective test for contract formation. To date, *Contract as Promise* remains the one systematic effort to explain contract on the basis of a conception of Kantian moral autonomy.

The second wave of contract theory, which dates from the late 1980s, begins with and builds upon a criticism of the principal first wave theories. Neither the autonomy-based nor the economic approach, this criticism maintains, is able by itself to provide a comprehensive theory of contract.

This second wave is firmly established with the appearance of Richard Craswell's influential piece, "Contract, Default Rules, and the Philosophy of Promising"[14] which argues that autonomy-based theories, and Fried's in particular,

12. Ibid., pp.1-2.
13. C. Fried, *Contract as Promise: A Theory of Contractual Obligation* (Cambridge, MA: Harvard University Press, 1981).
14. (1989) 88 Mich. L. Rev. 489. In connection with the start of the second wave, two earlier articles should be mentioned. First, there is Roberto Unger's essay "The Critical Legal Studies Movement" (1983) 96 Harv. L. Rev. 561, 616–648. Unger challenges globally the claims of first wave theorists – autonomy, reliance, and distributive justice theorists – by arguing that while each of their principles may be at work in contract law, none of them accounts for the whole of it. To the contrary, contract law, he contends, is a unstable conjunction of principle and counter-principle. The second is Randy Barnett's important article "A Consent Theory of Contract" (1986) 86 Col. L. Rev. 269. Barnett's piece may be viewed as part of this second

cannot explain the substance of a party's contractual obligations. Although the moral duty to keep a promise may be relevant in determining what Craswell calls "agreement rules," namely, those rules, such as offer and acceptance, that define the kind of voluntary assent that is necessary for contract formation, it has no implications for the content of "background rules" which, among other things, specify the conditions under which nonperformance is excused and determine the legal sanctions applicable in case of breach. Contract as promise, Craswell argues, is indeterminate with respect to these matters. To fill the gap, there must be recourse to substantive values, such as efficiency or distributive justice, in addition to the formal principle of individual autonomy. On this view, the promise principle is not the distinctive or principal normative basis of contract but merely one element – and not necessarily the most important – in the normative account.

James Gordley[15] takes this challenge to the self-sufficiency of the principle of autonomy one step further: The difficulty, he argues, lies in the fact that this principle seeks to ground obligation in human choice alone. Unless some reason is given other than the mere fact that a promisor has willed to be bound, we cannot explain why the law enforces certain choices or commitments and not others. Although contract is undoubtedly consensual, the promise principle is mistaken in attempting to conceive consent in detachment from the ends that give it point and value. It is only via an examination and a specification of those ends that we can account for the fundamental premise of contract law that only certain acts of consent give rise to a contractual obligation.

Gordley also challenges the economic approach on similar grounds.[16] The satisfaction of individual preferences, he says, cannot in and of itself be normatively compelling. In any case, the legal enforcement of contracts results in the satisfaction of only some preferences and not others. Preference satisfaction as such is therefore an insufficient normative basis upon which to found a theory of contract. We need to specify a set of purposes that determines which preferences are to be satisfied.

But it is Michael Trebilcock, himself a law and economics scholar, who perhaps poses the most fundamental challenge to the self-sufficiency of the economic theory of contract.[17] According to Trebilcock, the strongest welfare claim

wave, especially in view of the fact that it anticipates the kinds of criticisms of previous autonomy and welfare approaches that are characteristic of it. Barnett proposes an autonomy-based approach that, in contrast to Fried's, founds contractual obligation, not on the moral duty to keep one's promises, but rather on a rights-based analysis of contract as a voluntary transfer of entitlements.

15. In J. Gordley, *The Philosophical Origins of Modern Contract Doctrine* (Oxford: Clarendon Press, 1991). See in particular Chapter 9.

16. Ibid.

17. In M. Trebilcock, *The Limits of Freedom of Contract* (Cambridge, MA: Harvard University Press, 1993). See for example his discussion at pages 244–249. I should add that in this book Trebilcock critically evaluates in detail and in depth a range of theoretical approaches including autonomy theories such as Fried's and Kronman's distributive justice approach.

that can be made by the economic approach is that the enforcement of contracts is Pareto efficient. Pareto superiority holds only where a party has given actual consent. But every contract contains within itself the possibility of what Trebilcock calls the "Paretian dilemma,"[18] which arises in the following way. Suppose that a party regrets his or her initial decision to enter a transaction because, when the time for performance comes, new opportunities have arisen or for some reason the party's preferences have changed. Whether the transaction is Pareto superior will depend upon which of the two sets of preferences, the earlier or the later, is taken into account. If anything, it seems more rational to refer to the party's last revealed preferences. But, in any case, the Pareto criterion does not itself decide between them. On the contrary, it applies only on the premise that a selection has *already* been made. Trebilcock argues that on an economic approach this determination can only be made on the basis of Kaldor-Hicks efficiency. The latter, however, makes hypothetical not actual consent the relevant consideration and it requires a comprehensive assessment of the costs and benefits of a transaction for both contracting and third parties. In adopting this framework, the economic approach can no longer make a strong welfare claim on behalf of the enforcement of contractual transactions. The conclusions reached, Trebilcock contends, will typically be highly speculative and inconclusive, if not indeterminate. In light of the ever-present possibility of regret, the economic approach does not possess the normative resources to explain the general enforceability of contracts.

In light of this apparent insufficiency of either an autonomy or an economic approach to contract theory, the question becomes whether comprehensive normative theorizing about contract law is still possible. One response might be to try to combine the principles of autonomy and efficiency (or welfare) on the supposition that together they may be able to provide what each by itself cannot: a satisfactory comprehensive account of contract. But this is possible only if the two approaches can be suitably integrated. Whether they can be so combined or, if not, whether there can be an alternative normative framework that explains contract law becomes a central problem for contract theory. Henceforth, writing that does not take this problem seriously cannot hope to advance the theory of contract.

In this respect, the representative comprehensive work of this second wave is Trebilcock's *The Limits of Freedom of Contract*[19] which, after exploring the strengths and limits of autonomy and welfare approaches across a wide range of contract issues, concludes that only a pluralist conception of contract theory –

---

18. An illuminating earlier critique of the indeterminacy of efficiency, which proceeds on a basis that is similar to the Paretian dilemma but which develops and generalizes the argument so as to show the necessity of supposing the conceptual priority of rights, is provided by Jules Coleman. See J. Coleman, *Markets, Morals, and the Law* (New York: Cambridge University Press, 1988), Chapter 3.
19. *Supra* note 17.

one that makes reference to autonomy, welfare, and distributive justice values –
can hope to provide a satisfactory account. According to Trebilcock, the most
promising combination is that of welfare-maximizing background rules qualified by a right, rooted in autonomy, to contract around them. But even this, he
argues, is an unstable equilibrium. Conclusions dictated by efficiency unavoidably conflict with the implications of autonomy. Trebilcock concludes that on
various central normative issues pertaining to freedom of contract the claim of
convergence between autonomy and welfare is tenuous. Without attempting to
provide a meta-theory that weighs or ranks the different values, he nevertheless
proposes what he calls a pragmatic response at a lower level of abstraction that
identifies the institutions or mechanisms that are best fitted to vindicate them.
In keeping with this conclusion, he outlines an appropriate institutional division
of labour for advancing the values of autonomy and efficiency.

The other major work of the second wave, Gordley's *The Philosophical Origins of Modern Contract Doctrine,*[20] suggests a second kind of response to the
apparent insufficiencies of the autonomy and welfare approaches. Gordley argues that what is needed is a differently conceived teleological framework which
preserves the insights of the autonomy and efficiency approaches but which at
the same time corrects their deficiencies and is able to explain the content of
contract law on a morally satisfactory basis. He proposes a pluralist theory that
integrates conceptually, and not merely pragmatically, the distinct Aristotelian
values of liberality, commutative justice, and distributive justice. Gordley argues that the many aspects of contract doctrine, including the principles of contract formation, implied terms, mistake and frustration, and unconscionability,
can be suitably accounted for on this basis. I will leave further discussion of
Gordley's views, however, to my presentation of his essay along with the others that make up this collection – to which I now turn.

These six essays may be viewed as efforts to deepen the kind of contract theorizing that characterizes the second wave. Thus none of the essays assumes the
self-sufficiency of the earlier formulations of the autonomy and welfare theories.
To the contrary, all take seriously the criticisms of these approaches and, even
more important, they attempt constructively to advance theories of contract that
are not vulnerable to those criticisms. It is worth noting, finally, that three of
the essays (those by Gordley, Thomas Scanlon, and the present writer) expressly take up and try to answer Fuller's challenge to the expectation principle,
in this way coming full circle to the central question that inaugurates modern
contract theory.

For the purposes of presentation, I have placed the essays in the following
order. First, there are the two essays by Craswell and by Trebilcock and Steven
Elliott which explore the economic approach and are consequentialist in character. Following these are the two essays by Scanlon and myself which are

20. *Supra* note 15.

non-consequentialist in character and try to understand contract in terms of what one party owes another as a reasonable implication of their interaction. Finally, there are the two essays by Melvin Eisenberg and Gordley which advance two different pluralist theories that are teleological in character. I will now briefly discuss each essay in turn.

The essays by Craswell and by Trebilcock and Elliott explore the conceptual resources and the explanatory reach of the economic approach. Fully cognizant of the point that efficiency alone may not be able to provide a comprehensive account of contract, they nevertheless wish to bring out its conceptual richness and scope. Whereas Craswell explores the theoretical implications of two different approaches to the efficiency of contract enforcement, Trebilcock and Elliott show that the economic theory of contract can illumine a set of issues ordinarily thought to be particularly inhospitable to this approach.

In "Two Economic Theories of Enforcing Promises,"[21] Richard Craswell argues that it would be a mistake to equate the efficiency of enforcing promises with the efficiency of carrying out promised actions, as is largely presupposed during the first wave of contract theory. In contrast to this first approach, contemporary economic analysis, he notes, recognizes that legal enforceability triggers a much more complex set of effects. For example, enforceability may influence not only whether the promise is carried out, but also whether the promise gets made at all, how carefully the promisor thinks before making it, or how much the promisor spends on precautions to guard against accidents that might leave him or her unable to perform in the future (to list just a few of the possible effects). The efficiency of legal enforceability depends upon the combined or net efficiency of all these consequences. This is the conception of efficiency that underpins the second economic theory. This theory, Craswell contends, fits better with other non-economic approaches and provides a more complete and a more determinate account of contract.

More particularly, Craswell argues that there is a fit between the second economic theory and three other conceptual views of contract that are most often associated with non-economic perspectives. "Relational" contract theorists, for instance, recognize that there is more to most promises than just the eventual acts of performance and that the parties' actions leading up to that performance may be just as important as the performance itself. In this respect at least, this approach fits better with the second economic theory than with the first. The same is true of the view that contracts are a form of privately enacted regulation. On this view, by entering an enforceable contract, parties subject themselves to an entire set of rules that are provided by both the contract and the legal system and that will govern their relationship into the future. This view supposes, then, that every enforceable contract gives rise to an entire set of legal constraints that alter the parties' incentives. It calls for a full analysis of these

21. See pages 19–44 of this book.

incentives, which the second economic theory provides, and not an analysis limited just to eventual performance, as the first economic theory gives. Finally, Craswell notes that the second economic approach fits better with the view of contract as a transfer of property, which focuses on the entitlements that parties acquire at contract formation. Under the second economic theory, it is precisely the change in entitlements at the time of formation that gives rise to all of the interim incentives.

Craswell also shows in detail how the adoption of the second economic theory has important implications for a number of issues in contract law, altering the way these issues are viewed and changing the underlying argument of their appropriate analysis. For example, he argues that whereas the first economic theory (which justifies enforcement solely on the basis of the efficiency of performing the promised actions) cannot easily explain the enforcement of contracts in cases where changed circumstances have made performance no longer efficient, this is not true of the second approach: Even if performance itself is no longer efficient, it may still be efficient to hold the promisor liable, because in this way the promisor is given an incentive to decide whether it is still worthwhile to perform. Or take the question of paternalism, whether courts or the parties themselves should decide if enforcement of a promise would be efficient. Many of those who advocate efficiency believe that affected individuals are usually the best judges of their own welfare and that those individual judgments will usually be less imperfect than those of courts or of other third parties. Craswell contends that on the first economic theory, the correctness of this belief is debatable. Once, however, efficiency is taken to mean more than just the efficiency of the actual performance, and once there is the corresponding recognition that many effects must be considered in any assessment of efficiency, the case for judicial second-guessing becomes weaker.

A third set of issues which Craswell thinks is illumined by the second economic theory concerns the significance and role of detrimental reliance. Here, among other things, Craswell discusses the relation between the second economic approach and Atiyah's theoretical writing, casting interesting and novel light on the latter. Craswell argues that whereas the first economic approach is necessarily at odds with the reliance argument, the gap between reliance theory and the second economic theory, which takes into account the effect of enforceability on the promisee's incentives to rely, is much narrower. At the same time, he notes that the second economic theory, no less than the first, can answer the challenge that contracts should be enforced only in cases of detrimental reliance.

In "The Scope and Limits of Legal Paternalism: Altruism and Coercion in Family Financial Arrangements,"[22] Michael Trebilcock and Steven Elliott test the resources of the economic approach to illuminate and to resolve particularly

22. See pages 45–85 of this book.

intractable questions of legal paternalism that arise in family financial transactions. Commonwealth contract law already recognizes the need for a measure of paternalism in a number of ways. Family financial transactions, the authors argue, raise uniquely difficult questions about the scope and limits of legal paternalism. For they bring together two phenomena that have proven especially problematic in contract law: altruism and coercion. Many family commitments are motivated by altruism and characterized by high levels of trust. At the same time, the intimate and dependent nature of many family relationships raises risks that one family member has been coerced or misled by another. Tension between these polarities has been highlighted in the burgeoning Commonwealth case-law concerning family sureties. This case-law, however, exhibits sharply different and often inconsistent approaches to determining the validity of these transactions. This is an area of the law that calls out for a consistent and cogent ordering principle.

Trebilcock and Elliott argue that the economic method contains the resources to make sense of certain paternalistic interventions in the family financial setting. Building on the methodology of Trebilcock's *The Limits of Freedom of Contract,* they challenge the view that neo-classical economics must be antithetical to paternalism and they show that it can yield insights even with respect to transactions that are motivated at least in part by altruism. They do this by working out fully and in detail a principled analysis of the family surety cases – one that provides guidance in resolving the various particular issues that confront the courts – and they conclude that a requirement of independent legal advice in cases of what they call "suspect family financial transactions" is justified. A lender, in order to ensure the validity of the security that it is taking, must require that the family surety obtain such advice as to both the legal and business implications of the suspect transaction. Once this advice has been obtained, the paper argues, the preferences of the family member as to whether to enter the transaction should be respected.

At the same time, Trebilcock and Elliott highlight the limits of the economic approach. Whereas economic analysis takes individuals' revealed preferences as the basic normative reference point, paternalistic interventions are often necessitated by defects in those preferences. As economic analysis has no theory of how preferences are formed, it cannot justify overriding preferences that many would consider to be problematic. Still, where the reason for paternalistic intervention is not that a vulnerable contractor's preferences are defective but rather that some condition is causing the contractor to make choices that are inconsistent with those preferences, actual preferences remain the basic reference point and economic analysis applies. The authors argue that in any comprehensive approach to contract failure in the family setting – which must, they say, make reference not only to welfare but also to other values such as autonomy – an economic analysis along the lines they have proposed will play not merely an essential but also an organizing role.

In "Promises and Contracts,"[23] T. M. Scanlon uses the contractualist procedure he has developed for moral theory to provide distinct, albeit related, accounts of the moral principles that govern promises and of the legal principles
that govern the enforcement of contracts. Scanlon's presentation of his account
of moral principles for promises largely follows the approach taken in his earlier piece "Promises and Practices,"[24] although, it should be noted, he includes
here certain significant changes to and expansions of this argument as well as
responses to objections. His account of the moral permissibility of contractual
enforcement is, however, wholly novel. This is the first occasion on which
Scanlon has applied contractualism to justify principles of private law.

Scanlon's contention is that promise and contract arise in response to and are
shaped by some of the same underlying values, in this respect being parallel
ideas. Both the moral duty to keep promises and the moral permissibility of the
legal enforcement of contracts are to be justified on the basis of a set of principles that no one, suitably motivated, could reasonably reject. These are
principles that people have reason to want because they enshrine certain values;
for example, to name three of the most important, the values of reliance, of assurance, and of choice (discussed below). At the same time, promises and
contract respond to these values in different ways and are independent notions,
neither of which is properly seen as based on the other. Given limits of space,
I shall focus on Scanlon's discussion of the legal enforcement of contracts.

In taking up the questions of the enforceability of contracts and the legitimacy of certain remedies for breach, Scanlon declines to take an approach that
founds these either directly on moral requirements, such as the duty to keep one's
promises, or on the basis of a rights analysis, such as Randy Barnett's.[25] Instead,
Scanlon proposes a two-stage analysis: first, one shows that parties have good
reason(s) to want a certain principle entailing the moral permissibility of coercive legal enforcement through specified remedies; and second, one shows that
the parties – in particular, the defendant – could not reasonably reject or object
to that principle. On this basis, Scanlon justifies two main principles.

The first, Principle EL,[26] holds that it is morally permissible (*not* morally required) for a legal system to enforce compensation for reliance losses sustained
by one as a result of reliance upon expectations that another has intentionally
or negligently led the first to form about what the second is going to do. Scanlon identifies the reasons individuals have for accepting EL – such as the need
to rely on other's representations and reasons for wanting to avoid significant
reliance losses when these representations prove false – and shows that EL could
not be reasonably rejected from the point of view of those whom the law would

---

23. See pages 86–117 of this book.
24. (1990) 19 Philosophy and Public Affairs 199
25. See reference to Barnett in *supra* note 14.
26. "L" refers to a "Principle of Loss Prevention," "E" to the enforceability of this principle.

require to pay compensation. And although EL may certainly apply in cases of breach of contract, it also applies where no promise or contract is involved. Scanlon characterizes EL as a tort-like basis for recovery.

The second, Principle EF,[27] goes beyond a strictly reliance-based liability and holds that when certain conditions obtain it is morally permissible (*not* required) for a legal system to enforce a contract by way of expectation damages or specific performance. According to Scanlon, the justification for EF answers Fuller's question "Why should the law ever protect the expectation interest?" and provides a ground for recovery that is unique to contracts: an independent basis of purely contractual obligation. Scanlon anchors the first stage of this justification in the value of assurance, that is, in the value of being able to rely on agreements even when one has not actually relied on them. Promisees, he says, have reason to want to receive, and promisors to provide, such assurance; and both sides also have reason to want their agreements to be legally enforceable as a means of supporting this value. As for the second step, Scanlon argues that promisors could not reasonably reject EF because it incorporates a number of reasonable conditions: the remedy must not be excessive; promisors must indicate that they understand themselves to be undertaking a legal obligation to promisees and must be able to foresee at contract formation the remedy to which promisees would be entitled; and so forth. Scanlon discusses the implications of his two-part justification of EF for a number of basic issues in contract theory including the availability of non-default remedies and the legitimacy of default remedies, the necessity of a requirement of consideration, and Fuller's contention that the expectation remedy must be "quasi-punitive" in character and not compensatory.

In the concluding section, Scanlon develops an account of the moral significance of choice and voluntariness for contract. Scanlon's main point is that the relevant notion of voluntariness is not an idea specifiable independently of the argument for EF but, to the contrary, is given shape by being incorporated in that argument. Principle EF incorporates a notion of voluntariness by including specific conditions that reflect "the value of choice," that is, the value of having what happens to one (including the obligations one incurs) depend upon how one responds to a set of alternatives under certain conditions. Scanlon compares and contrasts this view with those of efficiency theorists such as Craswell and of distributive justice theorists like Kronman. The discussion is intended to address concerns raised by Atiyah, among others, that promise-based principles of liability take an exaggerated and absolutist view of the value of freedom of choice because they fail to recognize the case for paternalistic restrictions and ignore the fact that due to superior resources some are more able than others to take advantage of freedom choice. Scanlon argues that

---

27. "F" refers to a "Principle of Fidelity," "E" to the enforceability of this principle.

the understanding of voluntariness that informs his account of promissory liability under Principle EF avoids these difficulties.

In "The Unity of Contract Law,"[28] I develop an account of contract law that
is presented, in Rawls's terms, as part of a public basis of justification. I try to
show that the general idea of a public basis of justification, which Rawls has
specified for the particular case of political justice and public (constitutional)
law, also applies to what may be called "juridical" justice and to private law.
Although in general terms both instances of justification *qua* public will share
certain common elements, such as a conception of the person, an idea of a relevant form of social relation, notions of the reasonable and the rational, and so
forth, the contents of these elements will differ depending upon whether they
are specified for the domain of the political or for that of the juridical. My aim
in this essay is to present a public basis of justification for a particular part of
the juridical: the law of contract.

To this end, I try to bring out the conception of contract that is implicit in the
main doctrines of contract law and that is therefore latent in our public legal
culture. The overriding aim of the public justification is to show just how these
doctrines fit together in one conception and that this conception is reasonable
and plausible from a juridical point of view. In keeping with the general idea of
a public basis of justification, however, this account of the main doctrines of contract law does not attempt to provide, although it certainly does not deny the possibility of giving, a deeper moral foundation for them, whether the foundation
be Kantian autonomy, utility, welfare, or virtue. It leaves this question to a further stage of theoretical reflection that, strictly speaking, does not belong to the
public basis of justification. The justification of contract on a public basis is just
one step removed from the judicial formulations of the basic principles and doctrines of contract law. It elucidates the legal point of view, but at a higher level
of abstraction through the conception of contract that is implicit in them. This
conception of contract, I argue, must be the starting point for all other theoretical endeavours from whatever perspective. This is an essential condition of any
theory's being a theory *of law*.

More particularly, I argue that if, *contra* Fuller, the expectation principle is
indeed a principle of compensation as the law holds it to be, we must suppose
that contract formation itself gives parties entitlements of the kind reflected in
an award of expectation damages. Contract must be viewed as a mode by which
parties can acquire proprietary rights from and against each other. And crucially, this right must vest at formation, that is, prior to and independent of actual performance. This conception of contract I call "contract as a transfer of
rights." I explain why, from a juridical point of view, this conception is coherent and reasonable. In this connection, I discuss how the rights acquired by
contract, although they are "personal" as distinct from "real" and though they do

---

28. See pages 118–205 of this book.

not depend upon actual physical possession of the object of the right, are nevertheless fully proprietary in character. Moreover, I set out the basic logic, that is, the necessary and sufficient fundamental premises, of the conception of contract as a transfer of rights.

The main object of the essay is, however, to demonstrate that the logic of a transfer of rights is in fact reflected in the main doctrines of contract law. Thus, I argue at length and in detail that first with the doctrine of offer and acceptance, then with the requirement of consideration, and finally with the doctrine of unconscionability, one can show, step by step, how these doctrines are mutually complementary and how together they completely fill out a conception of contract that satisfies fully the logic of a transfer of rights. This conception of contract, it turns out, is entirely indifferent to considerations of distributive justice. Through this elucidation of contract as a transfer of right, I try to give interconnected answers to the three central issues of modern contract theory: first, the justification of expectation damages for breach of a wholly executory contract; second, the role of and the rationale for consideration; and third, the compatibility between contractual liberty, as embodied in the traditional principles of contract formation, and contractual fairness, as reflected in the more recently developed doctrine of unconscionability. I conclude the essay by noting three limits of the public justification as I have presented it and sketch how it might be brought to completion, culminating in a public justification of private law as a whole.

The last two essays, those by Eisenberg and Gordley, present systematic critiques of both autonomy and welfare theories of contract. Each sets out in detail an alternative pluralist theory that aims to be comprehensive in scope. They illustrate the reach of their theories by showing how they can generate and explain important parts of contract law.

In "The Theory of Contracts,"[29] Melvin Eisenberg begins with a comprehensive critical examination of the main kinds of theories of contract. He considers each of the following in detail and with a wide variety of illustrations: "axiomatic" theories which hold that fundamental doctrinal propositions are established on the ground that they are self-evident; "deductive" theories which view doctrinal propositions as logically deduced from other, more fundamental doctrinal propositions; "interpretative" theories that proceed by identifying principles that meet some standard of fit with and that best justify or rationalize doctrine as a whole or significant areas of doctrine; and "normative" theories that select a set of principles on the ground that they are desirable or morally compelling and determine what legal doctrines may be generated by those principles. After a detailed critical analysis of these theories that considers both their content and presuppositions as well as their power to explain contract law, Eisenberg concludes that a satisfactory theory of the best substantive content of contract law *must* be normative.

29. See pages 206–264 of this book.

Eisenberg then goes on to examine the two main kinds of normative theories that have been formulated thus far: single-value autonomy or welfare theories. Each of these approaches turns out to be unsatisfactory as a basis for understanding and justifying fundamental aspects of contract law. In this critical part of the essay, Eisenberg develops a wide range of objections against autonomy and welfare-based theories, including many of the objections raised during the second wave of modern contract theory. To my knowledge, this is among the most concentrated yet comprehensive presentation of such criticisms to date. He argues that in general a single-value theory cannot do justice to the phenomenon of contract law. Accordingly, a pluralist theory is needed.

The constructive portion of the essay outlines just such a pluralist theory. He proposes what he refers to as the "basic contracts principle" that should determine the content of contract law. This principle makes reference to diverse moral and policy principles and it is to be applied by a fully informed ideal Legislator (whose capacities and roles are defined and who differs from a judge in that he or she is not bound by precedent). The Legislator must give each principle proper weight and craft a rule that is the best vector of all such principles. Many kinds of choices must be made by the Legislator under the basic contracts principle. Among these are whether, when moral norms are relevant, the Legislator should choose norms on the basis of critical or social morality; whether the Legislator should assume that actors know the rules of contract law; whether the Legislator should base rules of contract law solely on rational-actor psychology or should also take into account limited-cognition psychology; and whether the rules of contract law should reflect considerations of distributive justice. Each of these issues is examined with references to different aspects of contract doctrine and practice. Eisenberg concludes by returning to Fuller's theme in a discussion of why, under the basic contracts principle, certain kinds of promises should be legally enforceable and the extent to which they should be enforced.

In "Contract Law in the Aristotelian Tradition,"[30] James Gordley presents comprehensively in one place both his criticisms of prevailing theories and his own proposed alternative. In this essay, he goes even more deeply into the roots of contemporary theories than he has done previously and he defends his own approach against a range of objections that have been raised from a variety of recent theoretical standpoints. This essay represents the most exhaustive and theoretically self-conscious defence and development of his views to date.

To begin, Gordley argues that despite their apparently marked differences, contemporary autonomy and efficiency theories rest on a common presupposition: Both are voluntaristic in the sense that they place a value on choice that is independent of the value of what is chosen. He contends that such theories are inherently unable to explain contract law. Gordley examines in some de-

---

30. See pages 265–334 of this book.

tail the deeper philosophical expressions of autonomy and welfare theories, namely the philosophies of Kant and Hegel on the one hand and utilitarianism on the other. More particularly, he considers whether these two philosophical approaches, either as originally formulated or as more recently interpreted, can satisfactorily account for the fact that the law in general respects the choice of contracting parties but in certain definite instances does not. He argues, in both cases, that they cannot. Gordley organizes his discussion around the need to resolve three basic problems in contract theory. The first problem is the normative justification for enforcing contracts. The second is explaining the content of a contractual obligation. A third problem concerns the consequences that should ensue when a contract is breached. In relation to each problem, Gordley investigates the normative and conceptual resources of the two main theoretical approaches and argues that they do not – and *cannot* – provide answers.

The constructive core of Gordley's argument is that, in contrast to the voluntaristic theories, an Aristotelian approach not only leads to satisfactory theoretical solutions to these problems but also explains the basic rules of modern contract law in both common law and civil law jurisdictions. Gordley's discussion is unusually rich and comprehensive in scope. He shows in detail how the Aristotelian tradition has the normative principles and resources to illumine both agreement and background rules, to use Craswell's terms. In doing so, he addresses a wide range of substantive aspects not only of the common law of contract but of the civil law as well. Moreover, here for the first time, Gordley expressly answers Fuller's challenge to the expectation measure. Interestingly, his solution – the idea of a transfer of right – is similar to the one proposed in my piece. A major difference is that, unlike my own, Gordley's analysis of transfer is embedded in a teleological theory, not a rights-based approach.

Gordley's theory is pluralist because it makes reference to and combines the different Aristotelian virtues of liberality, commutative justice, and distributive justice. According to Gordley, each of these elements is necessary because each is needed to resolve the three main problems of contract theory mentioned above. It is worth noting that in this paper that Gordley clarifies the role of distributive justice and its relation to commutative justice in the theory of contract. Moreover, he explains more fully why contract in both the common law and the civil law must presuppose a distinction between gift and exchange contracts. In this connection, Gordley revisits the views he first advanced in his seminal article, "Equality in Exchange."[31] Gordley takes pains to clarify certain aspects of the argument, answering objections to it and bringing out its strengths in relation to competing explanations.

It is now time to bring this Introduction to a close. At the end of *The Death of Contract,* Grant Gilmore famously muses that despite "the dismantling of the

---

31. (1981) 69 Cal. L. Rev. 1587.

formal system of the classical theorists,"[32] somewhere a contemporary Langdell may already be at work, raising a new general theory of contract out of the ashes of the old. Yet some twenty-five years later and notwithstanding the range and richness of the efforts to theorize the common law of contract, it is difficult to disagree with Gordley that "[t]oday, we have no generally recognized theory of contract."[33] This failure stands in sharp contrast with the fact that the basic doctrines and principles of contract law are now well settled and contract law is now widely viewed as complete. Indeed, it is increasingly recognized that the organization of the law of contract and its larger concepts are now similar throughout nearly the entire world. But perhaps this very contrast gives grounds for optimism. For now, probably for the first time, the law of contract, being a fully articulated and generally accepted body of doctrines, is suitable for formulation in terms of a general theory. The public legal culture itself invites this elaboration. As well, the very existence of a multiplicity of richly developed yet competing theoretical accounts calls out for a general theory to order their different perspectives and to settle their various claims. These six essays are offered with the hope that they will contribute to and hasten the establishment of such a theory. If they stimulate and assist further efforts in that direction, their appearance will be amply justified.[34]

---

32. *Supra,* note 4 at p. 103.   33. *Supra,* note 15 at p. 230.
34. I wish to thank Daniel Batista and Sophia Reibetanz for their help with editing this Introduction.

1

Two Economic Theories
of Enforcing Promises

RICHARD CRASWELL

The question, "Why should promises be enforced?" has received many different philosophical answers. One set of answers, of course, comes from the utilitarian tradition. In legal scholarship, these are the answers most often advanced (or presupposed) in the subfield of law and economics.

The purpose of this essay is to distinguish two rather different economic theories (or possible theories) within that tradition. The first theory treats enforcement as equivalent to the eventual *performance* of the promised actions. On this theory, enforcing the promise is efficient just in case performing the promised actions would be efficient. By contrast, the second theory treats enforcement as altering the parties' *incentives,* by changing the relevant payoffs from those the parties would face in the absence of an enforceable obligation. Under the second theory, enforcing the promise is efficient just in case the new set of incentives is, on balance, efficient.

Although the second of these theories is the one held by most economists today, the first theory (or some version of it) is sometimes attributed to economists in the noneconomic literature. Accordingly, Sections II and III of this essay set out the two theories and explain the differences between them. The fourth and final section discusses the implications these differences could have for several issues of interest to contract theory: (1) whether to enforce a promise even if circumstances have changed, so that performance would no longer be efficient; (2) whether to presume the efficiency of enforcement simply from the fact that the promise was agreed to voluntarily; (3) whether to enforce a promise if nobody has yet relied on the promise; and (4) whether (or when) to impute a promise to a party who has not promised explicitly.

I. Preliminary Matters

Any theory that turns on efficiency – either the efficiency of performing the promised action, or the efficiency of creating some larger set of incentives – must have a definition of "efficiency" by which those effects can be evaluated.

Indeed, many criticisms of economic criteria for legal rules have focused on the shortcomings of one or more of the possible definitions. As is well known, the choice of any particular definition can have significant normative consequences.

In this essay, however, my goal is not to defend any particular definition of "efficiency," or even to take up the criticisms that might be raised. Instead, my analysis is entirely internal – internal, that is, to some definition of efficiency. My focus, thus, is not on the propriety of taking efficiency (however defined) as a goal; but merely on the difference between assessing the efficiency (however defined) of carrying out a promised action, on the one hand, and the efficiency of creating a broad set of incentives, on the other. To be sure, some of what I have to say about this difference may have implications for external critiques of economic analysis, and I will note those implications as they arise (especially in Section IV). But in order to focus on the narrower or internal distinction, I will remain deliberately agnostic on most of the questions about how "efficiency" ought to be defined.

For example, I take no position on the question of how one party's well-being is to be balanced against another's, in any case where one party would gain and the other would lose from actually carrying out the promise. In many contractual settings, this issue does not even arise, for often both parties will gain from the promised actions. For instance, if A has promised to sell her car to B for $6,000, A may be better off with the money and without the car, and B may be better off with the car and without the money. But it is easy to imagine situations where one party would lose from carrying out the promise (e.g., A's position has changed and she would now be better off keeping her car), so any overall assessment of efficiency would have to somehow balance B's gains against A's losses.

One way of making this balance invokes the Kaldor-Hicks test, which asks if B would still gain if he paid A enough that she would no longer lose. However, the Kaldor-Hicks test is not universally accepted (even among economists), and there are many other methods of balancing B's gains against A's losses that could also be used.[1] And though the conclusions about which exchanges are efficient may well change depending on which method of interpersonal comparison is used, for purposes of this paper it is unnecessary to specify any particular method. In effect, I am really considering an entire class of theories that vary in how they make interpersonal trade-offs, but that are otherwise similar in their rationale for enforcement. The theories in the first section of this paper all hold that the efficiency of enforcing a promise depends on whether the promised actions will increase overall welfare under *some* method of balancing gains to one party and losses to another.

---

1. For a discussion of possible methods see, for example, A. Sen, *Choice, Welfare, and Measurement* (Cambridge, MA: MIT Press, 1982).

For similar reasons, it is also unnecessary to specify here how any individual's welfare is to be judged. Most theories of efficiency do not limit themselves to monetary values, so we can still speak of the efficiency of exchanging a car for a beautiful painting, or for anything else that contributes to a party's nonmonetary well-being. Nor are these theories limited to cases of *exchange,* at least as that concept is ordinarily understood. If A promises her car to a favorite nephew without asking him to give anything in return, we can still ask whether having the car will improve the nephew's welfare, and whether this improvement of her nephew's welfare is more important to A than is her own continued ownership of the car. All that is required to make such judgments is that there be *some* metric by which the welfare of A and her nephew can be judged. But that metric does not need to be money: It could just as easily be subjective utility, or (indeed) any other criterion of well-being. And although any conclusions as to which exchanges are efficient could again vary depending on which criterion of well-being is chosen, in this paper I abstract from that choice as well.

Indeed, for much of the paper I will not even limit my focus to subjectivist theories, or theories that equate individual well-being with a party's own assessments of his or her welfare. Instead, much of my analysis would apply equally to theories that use *any* method of assessing an individual's welfare, including assessments based entirely on external or paternalistic criteria. For example, it would be possible to judge the efficiency of the sale of A's car by asking whether A *in fact* would be better off having $6,000 but no car (according to some objective criterion), and whether B *in fact* would be better off with a car but no $6,000. It would then be possible to argue that the promise should be enforced if and only if this transfer would be efficient, in the sense of increasing A's and B's welfare, with their welfare assessed according to these external or objective criteria.[2] In other words, the hallmark of this class of theories is simply that they rest the case for enforcing a promise on *some* method of assessing the efficiency of the promised actions – as opposed, say, to some deontological commitment that did not depend on the effects on individual welfare.

II. Enforcement as Performance

I can now turn to the distinction that interests me, between two distinct kinds of theories that might both justify the enforcement of promises on efficiency grounds. The first theory, discussed in this section, derives the efficiency of enforcing a promise from the efficiency of the promised behavior. For example, if A has promised to sell her car to B for $6,000, this theory rests the efficiency of enforcing the promise on the efficiency (or likely efficiency) of actually exchanging A's car for B's $6,000.

---

2. The potential administrative problems with external criteria of welfare will be discussed below in Section III.A.

I should emphasize that, as far as I know, no economist actually holds this theory, at least today. However, there are passages in some of the early literature that are not inconsistent with this theory, so the resulting confusion about what economists believed is entirely understandable. Indeed, the early development of the economic theories played a large role in creating this impression, so it may be useful to trace that history here.

A. *The Theory of Efficient Breach*

Briefly, the modern economic analysis began in the early 1970s, with articles that did indeed focus on the efficiency of the promised actions.[3] These articles emphasized two points. First, there were some circumstances in which it might not be efficient to perform a contract. Second, contract law could be seen as encouraging nonperformance in precisely those circumstances, by allowing a nonperforming party to choose to breach and pay damages (rather than trying to compel performance by injunctive remedies, or by the threat of more punitive sanctions).

The idea that nonperformance might be justified on grounds of inefficiency was, of course, controversial. Although traditional scholars had always acknowledged that sufficiently *extreme* difficulties might justify nonperformance, it was quite another matter to assert that nonperformance might be justified merely by an increase in the cost of performance, or by any other change that made performance inefficient. As a result, this "theory of efficient breach" (as it came to be known) was attacked on a number of different grounds. In part because of the resulting controversy, this theory came to be associated – at least in the minds of many noneconomists – as the essence of what economics had to say to contract theory.

Although many of the criticisms that were raised are only tangential to my concerns here, one criticism does deserve further mention. If, as the economists said, the inefficiency of performance could *justify* a party who chose not to perform, it might be wondered why such a party should be liable for any damages at all? In other words, if the inefficiency of performance could be established in court, why shouldn't that constitute a complete defense to any liability for breach of contract? If the defendant's behavior was justified, why should she have to pay any damages at all?

To be sure, the economists had not themselves argued that the inefficiency of performance should be a complete defense. Instead, the economists had argued for something closer to strict liability, in which a breaching party would have to pay damages whether or not her nonperformance was justified. Their

---

3. The earliest expositions of this theory were R. L. Birmingham, "Breach of Contract, Damage Measures, and Economic Efficiency" (1980) 24 Rutgers L. Rev. 273; and J. H. Barton, "The Economic Basis of Damages for Breach of Contract" (1972) 1 J. Legal Stud. 277.

argument was that the threat of having to pay such damages – especially if those damages were set at the proper level – would give the nonperforming party the proper incentive to *choose* between performance and breach. For example, under this system the nonperforming party would not have any incentive to breach unless doing so would save her more than she would have to pay out in damages to the nonbreaching party. But this is precisely the situation in which a breach would be efficient (or so the argument ran): when the savings from not performing exceeded any damages that nonperformance could inflict on the other party. Thus, the economists did not need to argue that breaching parties should be excused from liability entirely. In their model, breachers could be held strictly liable for all breaches and still have the correct incentives.[4]

Nevertheless, even though the economists themselves were recommending that breaching parties should have to pay damages, this recommendation was not strictly required by the theory of efficient breach. In that theory, proper incentives to perform or breach could also have been attained by something closer to a negligence rule, in which breachers (a) were made to pay damages if their breach was found to be unreasonable (i.e., inefficient), but (b) were excused from liability if their breach was found to be reasonable (i.e., efficient). Under this rule, too, breachers would gain by breaching if and only if their breach was efficient, so this would have been another way to give breachers the correct incentive.

Indeed, it is not entirely clear why economists of the time did not consider the possibility of a "complete excuse" or "negligence" type of rule. Granted, a "complete excuse" rule would require a court to decide, in every case, whether the breach was efficient; and it might have been objected that this would add unreasonably to the cost of trying each case. But that same objection had also been raised in the debate between strict liability and negligence in tort law, where there was already a thriving (though inconclusive) economic analysis of both of the competing rules.[5] For some reason, though, it was only much later that economists began to see the fundamental correspondence between the choice of liability rules in contract law and the choice of liability rules in tort.[6]

In any event, to noneconomists during this early period – and especially to those noneconomists who believed that behavior that was justified normally should not incur legal liability – it could easily have seemed that the economists'

---

4. The summary in the text ignores the possibility – extensively canvassed in the earlier literature – that the parties might renegotiate to bribe the promisor to perform when she might otherwise choose to breach, or to bribe the promisee to accept nonperformance when the promisor might otherwise feel compelled to perform. For purposes of the discussion here, though, the possibility of renegotiation is largely irrelevant. For a survey and critique of the earlier literature on renegotiation, see R. Craswell, "Contract Remedies, Renegotiation, and the Theory of Efficient Breach" (1988) 61 S. Cal. L. Rev. 629.

5. See, for example, G. Calabresi, *The Cost of Accidents* (New Haven: Yale University Press, 1970); J. P. Brown, "Toward an Economic Theory of Liability" (1973) 2 J. Legal Stud. 323.

6. See, for example, R. Cooter, "Unity in Tort, Contract, and Property: The Model of Precaution" (1985) 73 Cal. L. Rev. 1.

theories should lead to a complete excuse for any efficient breach.[7] More important, this debate seemed to confirm the impression that economists were concerned only with whether it was efficient actually to carry out the promised actions, and that an analysis of this issue was all that economics had to contribute to contract law. Moreover, this impression may have been further confirmed by other arguments I discuss below.

B. The Presumptive Efficiency of Voluntary Promises

The economists' analysis of the efficiency of performance might also have had implications for another debate, about which promises ought to be enforced. For example, if most promisors are capable of assessing their own interests properly, then it might be argued that any promise that was voluntarily entered into must necessarily be one whose performance will be efficient. After all, if A and B have freely agreed to the sale of A's car, it would normally follow that carrying out that promise would (at least presumptively) improve both parties' welfare. Similarly, if A has promised to make a gift of her car to her nephew, it could usually be presumed that the gift's contribution to A's own welfare must exceed the value of the car to her: otherwise, why would she have made the promise? Thus, if the only concern of economic analysis is whether performance itself will improve the parties' welfare, this might seem to imply that all voluntary promises ought to be enforced.

Indeed, this analysis might seem to justify not just the positive conclusion that most voluntary promises should be enforced, but also the negative conclusion that most promises induced by fraud or duress should *not* be enforced. That is, if A or B did not consent knowingly or voluntarily, the inference of an improvement to that party's welfare would no longer be as strong, so the case for enforcing the promise would (on this theory) be weaker. As Richard Posner once put it:

Even when nothing has happened since the signing of the contract to make performance uneconomical, discharge may be permitted where *the presumption that performance would produce a value increasing exchange* is rebutted, as when it is shown that the promisee induced the promise by a lie.[8]

In this debate, too, then, the economists' focus on whether performance would be efficient (or whether it would produce a "value-increasing exchange") seemed to justify an important conclusion about which promises should be enforced. Passages such as these thus provided further support for the impression

---

7. For an example of this criticism, see R. E. Barnett, "A Consent Theory of Contract" (1986) 86 Colum. L. Rev. 269, 277–81. As I discuss below, the second economic theory is much more consistent with Barnett's own position (see the text *infra* at note 34).
8. R. A. Posner, *Economic Analysis of Law* (Boston, MA: Little, Brown & Co., 4th ed. 1986), 109 (emphasis added).

that economic analysis made every issue turn on the efficiency, or likely efficiency, of actually carrying out the promised actions.

C. The Effect of Changed Circumstances

Finally, a focus on the efficiency of the promised actions might also justify an economic analysis of the various legal doctrines (such as impracticability, mistake, and frustration) that excuse promisors in severely altered circumstances. Although this connection is more tenuous, and does not at all correspond to what economists were actually writing at the time,[9] it could help explain the persistence of the belief that economists care only about the efficiency of the eventual performance.

Briefly, circumstances other than force or fraud can also alter the efficiency of the promised actions. For example, if *B* promised to buy *A*'s car, but now *B* has taken a job in another city and no longer needs a car, it might not be efficient (under any definition of efficiency) for the sale to be consummated. Thus, changes in circumstances, no less than fraud or duress, can also negate any conclusion that "performance would produce a value increasing exchange." If the promised exchange was no longer efficient, then the simple theory under consideration here would appear to hold that the promise should not be enforced.

Of course, the introduction of administrative costs might alter this conclusion. As noted earlier, it will often be difficult for a court to decide whether performance would be efficient in any given case. Indeed, this was one of the potential arguments for a system of strict liability, in which all breachers must pay damages no matter how inefficient performance has become.[10] If individuals are *usually* the best judges of their own welfare, and if conditions do *not very often* change so drastically as to make an efficient transfer inefficient, it might even be possible to defend a fixed rule of *always* enforcing voluntary promises. Although a fixed rule would admittedly err by enforcing some transfers that were no longer efficient, the costs of the occasional error of this type might be less than the costs of requiring courts to evaluate the efficiency of every transfer on a case-by-case basis. In effect, a fixed rule ("always enforce voluntary promises") could be seen as the rule-utilitarian analog of the simpler act-utilitarian regime ("enforce promises if and only if performance is found to be efficient") described above.[11]

However, a more refined analysis might support an even more refined rule-utilitarian regime, while still focusing only on the efficiency of the eventual

---

9. See, for example, R. A. Posner and A. M. Rosenfield, "Impossibility and Related Doctrines in Contract Law: An Economic Analysis" (1977), 6 J. Legal Stud. 83.
10. See the discussion *supra* in Section II.A.
11. Note that, since we are talking about rules to be followed by courts and other legal decision-makers, many of the usual objections to rule-utilitarianism do not apply. For a further discussion of this point, see C. Fried, *Contract as Promise: A Theory of Contractual Obligation* (Cambridge, MA: Harvard University Press, 1981), 16.

performance. That is, if courts are at least sometimes able to judge the efficiency of the promised actions, the best rule might be to "enforce all voluntary promises *unless* conditions have changed in a way that is both dramatic and easily verifiable by the courts."[12] Indeed, such a rule might at least roughly approximate the current legal defenses, which excuse a nonperforming party not whenever performance seems inefficient, but only in cases of *extreme* impracticability or frustration of purpose. Seen in this way, a simple focus on the efficiency of performing the promised actions (when combined with suitable assumptions about administrative costs) might seem to support the implied excuse doctrines as well.

In short, there are a number of simple economic arguments that can be developed in connection with a very simple theory, in which the only goal is to encourage the performance of efficient actions and the nonperformance of inefficient ones. Because these arguments are so simple, they are easily reproduced (and also easily criticized), so it is not surprising that they continue to loom large in much of contracts scholarship. In the first-year casebook that I teach from, for instance, the *only* discussion of economic arguments comes in a chapter dealing with the theory of efficient breach.[13]

In point of fact, though, most economists have long since moved on to a much more complex analysis of efficiency and contract law. The remaining sections of the paper will summarize this theory and discuss some of its possible implications.

II. Enforcement as Incentives

As noted earlier, even those economists who developed the "theory of efficient breach" were not recommending that promises be enforced only when performance was still efficient. Instead, they analyzed a form of strict liability in which promises would be enforced in all cases, regardless of the efficiency of actual performance. Their argument was that enforcing a promise would not necessarily lead to actual performance, for the promisor could always choose to breach and pay damages. Instead, they argued, enforcing the promise in all such cases (even those in which the promisor chose not to perform) would give promisors the right incentive to *choose* whether to perform or breach.

Put slightly differently, the early economists exploited the fact that "enforcing" a promise need not entail carrying out the promised actions. Instead, "enforcing" can take the form of inflicting a monetary penalty, whose main sig-

---

12. For a defense of a somewhat similar rule (though not on exactly the lines discussed here), see A. Schwartz (1992) "Relational Contracts in the Courts: An Analysis of Incomplete Agreements and Judicial Strategies," 21 J. Legal Stud. 271.
13. C. M. Knapp, N. L. Crystal and H. G. Prince, *Problems in Contract Law: Cases and Materials* (Boston, MA: Little, Brown & Co., 4th ed. 1999), 1078–85.

nificance is that it represents a threat that alters the promisor's incentives in various ways. Significantly, this form of enforcement is rarely considered in the philosophical literature on promising, which usually assumes that promises must either (1) oblige the promisor to perform the promised actions, or (2) have no moral force at all.[14]

The form of liability considered here thus represents an intermediate level of moral force, in which a promisor can choose not to perform but cannot escape her liability for damages. The classic statement of this view is, of course, Oliver Wendell Holmes:

> The only universal consequence of a legally binding promise is, that the law makes the promisor pay damages if the promised event does not come to pass. In every case, it leaves him free from interference until the time for fulfilment has gone by, and therefore free to break his contract if he chooses.[15]

To be sure, this intermediate form of obligation has often been criticized in the legal literature, on the grounds (among others) that this is not how the concept of a "promise" ought to be understood.[16] Significantly, though, no critic has argued that the intermediate form of obligation would be positively immoral, or that nobody in our society would ever wish to create such an intermediate obligation. A more defensible position is the one taken by Thomas Scanlon, who suggests that many people would be better served by an obligation to perform (rather than an obligation to perform-or-pay-damages), but who does not claim that the stronger form of obligation is the only morally legitimate one.[17] Indeed, in his contribution to this volume, Scanlon is quite explicit in his position that parties could also accept an obligation either to perform or to pay some other agreed-upon measure of damages.[18] On this view (which I share), we could still reserve the word "promise" for the stronger obligation to perform absolutely, but that would be merely a stipulation about terminology. At most, it would show that we need some other term to describe the perfectly legitimate commitment to an intermediate obligation to perform-or-pay-damages.[19]

In any event, my purpose here is not to defend this theory of monetary damages, but to show how far it has taken economists beyond the simple theory

---

14. A noteworthy exception in the prior literature is T. M. Scanlon, "Promises and Practices" (1990) 19 Phil. & Pub. Aff. 199, 205 (discussed *infra* at note 17). See also T. M. Scanlon, "Promises and Contracts" (elsewhere in this book).

15. O. W. Holmes, *The Common Law,* ed. by M. deWolfe Howe (Boston, MA: Little, Brown & Co., 1963), 236.

16. See, for example, D. Friedmann, "The Efficient Breach Fallacy" (1989) 18 J. Legal Stud. 1; P. Linzer, "On the Amorality of Contract Remedies – Efficiency, Equity, and the *Second Restatement*" (1981) 81 Colum. L. Rev. 111, 138–9.

17. Scanlon, "Promises and Practices," *supra* note 14 at 205.

18. Scanlon, "Promises and Contracts," *supra* note 14 at 107.

19. I develop this argument at more length in R. Craswell, "Contract Law, Default Rules, and the Philosophy of Promising" (1989) 88 Mich. L. Rev. 489, 506–8. See also R. Craswell and A. Schwartz, eds., *Foundations of Contract Law* (New York: Oxford University Press, 1994), 54–5.

discussed earlier. Once it is recognized that the threat of having to pay damages can alter a promisor's incentive to perform or breach, it is a short step to realize that the threat of having to pay damages can also alter a good many other incentives. Indeed, most of the history of contract economics since around 1980 has consisted of a gradual adding to the list of incentives that might be affected by remedies for breach. As the following sections will discuss, economists are now concerned with far more than the effect on the promisor's incentives actually to carry out the promised actions. In a nutshell, whenever a party to a contract must make a decision about something, there will be a corresponding economic analysis of how the incentive to make that decision might be altered by various remedies for breach.

A. *The Incentive to Rely*

For example, often one or both of the parties must decide how heavily to rely on the promised performance. If *A* has promised to give *B* her car, *B* may have various steps he could take before the car is delivered (taking driving lessons, leasing parking space, and so on). If *B* is confident that the car will be delivered, taking those steps in advance may increase the benefit he derives from the car – but if he takes those steps and *A* fails to perform, then some of his effort or expenses may be wasted (e.g., a nonrefundable deposit on the lease of a parking space). Of course, *B*'s reliance could also take the form of refraining from certain actions. For example, if *B* is confident that *A* will deliver the car he might refrain from making alternative plans (buying a season-long bus pass) – but this decision, too, could have negative consequences if *A* fails to perform her promise.

As these steps in reliance on the promise all involve potential benefits as well as potential harms, we can speak of the efficiency or inefficiency of each step. Roughly speaking, the efficiency of any step depends on the balance between its potential upside (its enhancement to *B*'s welfare if *A* does perform) and its potential downside (the loss if *B* relies and *A* fails to perform), with each factor weighted in some fashion by the probability that *A* will or will not perform. To be sure, at this point the theory must be combined with a particular conception of efficiency in order to evaluate the potential gains and losses, and to decide how to balance the risks (e.g., should *B* be assumed to be risk-averse?). For my purposes, however, the particular concept of efficiency that is used is less important than the actions whose efficiency is being assessed. In the more complex theory under consideration now, we have moved from assessing the efficiency of the ultimate *performance* of the promise (the delivery or nondelivery of the car) to assessing the efficiency of *B*'s *reliance* on *A*'s promise, at a time when he is still awaiting delivery.

Significantly, much of the recent economics literature has focused on just this issue: on how enforceability affects the efficiency of the parties' reliance.[20] Clearly, making *A*'s promise enforceable will increase *B*'s incentive to rely in one respect, since enforceability will usually increase the probability that *A* will perform (thereby reducing the probability that *B* will be left in the lurch). But the exact effect on *B*'s reliance incentives may depend not only on enforceability *vel non,* but also on the exact nature of the enforceability, including the measure of damages *B* will collect if *A* fails to perform. For example, if *B* knows that he is guaranteed compensation for all of his reliance expenses (lease deposits, driving lessons, etc.), he will clearly have more of an incentive to rely than if *A*'s promise is "enforceable" but *B* is guaranteed only some token payment in compensation. In other words, enforceability is really a matter of degree rather than an all-or-nothing matter – and the effect on *B*'s reliance incentives may depend on the exact form that enforceability takes.

Indeed, this reliance argument has long been part of the instrumental case for enforcing promises. An early version of the argument can be traced to Thomas Hobbes, who emphasized the importance of enforceability whenever performance was to take place in sequence. Under Hobbes's account, enforceability might be unnecessary if the goods or services could be exchanged simultaneously, but without enforceability nobody would be willing to perform first, for fear that the other party would not give whatever he or she had promised in return.[21] But advance performance is simply one particular form of reliance on a promise, so the modern economists' treatment of reliance is really a generalization of Hobbes's concern. For example, even if the actual *performance* of the promise is to take place simultaneously by both parties (so Hobbes's concern would be satisfied), one party might still have to rely on the promise by making specialized investments in advance, in order to be in a position to carry out her end of the deal. If the promise is legally enforceable, that party will be much

---

20. Relatively accessible, nontechnical discussions include A. M. Polinsky, *An Introduction to Law and Economics,* 2nd ed. (Boston: Little, Brown & Co., 1989), 34–7; C. J. Goetz and R. E. Scott, "Enforcing Promises: An Examination of the Basis of Contract" (1980); 89 Yale Law J. 1261; Cooter, *supra* note 6, at 11–19; L. A. Kornhauser, "An Introduction to the Economic Analysis of Contract Remedies" (1986), 57 U. Colo. L. Rev. 683, 700–02. Goetz and Scott anticipated one theme of the present paper when they said, ibid. at 1264: "It is critically important to realize that a promise is conceptually distinct from the actual transfer that it announces."

For a sampling of the more technical economic literature on the incentives for efficient reliance see, for example, S. Shavell, "Damage Measures for Breach of Contract" (1980), 11 Bell J. Econ. 466; W. P. Rogerson, "Efficient Reliance and Damage Measures for Breach of Contract" (1984); 15 Rand J. Econ. 39 (1984); T. Chung, "Incomplete Contracts, Specific Investments, and Risk Sharing" (1991) 58 Rev. Econ. Stud. 1031; and A. S. Edlin and S. Reichelstein, "Holdups, Standard Breach Remedies, and Optimal Investment" (1996) 86 Am. Econ. Rev. 478.

21. T. Hobbes, *Leviathan,* ed. by E. Curley (Indianapolis: Hackett Publishing Co., 1994), 84–5. For a modern restatement of this argument, see Posner, *supra* note 8, at 89–90.

more willing to make such an investment, just as (in Hobbes's example) enforceability will make one party willing to perform first.

Of course, the goal of the modern economic theory is not to encourage the
greatest possible amount of reliance, but rather to encourage an *efficient* amount.
Even promisors with the best of intentions will occasionally find themselves
unable to perform, so (under any conception of efficiency) there will usually be
some acts of reliance whose combination of upside and downside potential
makes them clearly inefficient. For example, even if A has promised to deliver
her car exactly at noon on the first of next month, it would normally be inefficient for B to depend on that promise so heavily that several lives would be lost
if the car were to be delivered an hour late. One goal of an economic analysis,
then – and one focus of the recent economic literature – is to identify those
forms of enforceability that will give parties an incentive to rely efficiently, but
no further.[22]

In addition, once the incentives for reliance are added into the calculus, it is
possible for conflicts to arise between the form of enforceability that would
optimize the incentives to perform and the form of enforceability that would optimize the incentive to rely.[23] In that case, the efficiency of any given form of
enforceability will depend on its combined effect on each of the two relevant
incentives, so some trade-off may have to be made between slightly better effects on the incentive to perform and slightly worse effects on the incentive to
rely (or vice versa). In that event, the exact concept of efficiency being used would
no doubt be crucial in determining how the offsetting effects should be balanced.

Still, all that matters for my purposes is that – whatever concept of efficiency
is used – the resulting assessment rests the efficiency of any form of enforcement on the efficiency of the resulting *incentives*. In effect, we have now moved
even further away from the simpler theory discussed above, which held that the
efficiency of enforcement depended solely on the effect of enforcement on the
decision to perform or breach.

---

22. Since the efficiency of any reliance decision depends in part on the probability that A will per-
    form, and since that probability in turn depends partly on whether A's promise is enforceable,
    it might be thought that the efficiency of any reliance decision cannot be assessed without *first*
    deciding whether the promise is enforceable or not, thus making it circular to decide the en-
    forceability question by reference to the efficiency of the resulting reliance. (For an analogous
    argument that it is circular to decide the enforceability question by reference to the *reasonable-
    ness* of any reliance decision, see L. L. Fuller and W. R. R. Perdue Jr., "The Reliance Interest
    in Contract Damages" (1936) 46 Yale Law J. 52, 85.) However, this circularity can usually be
    avoided by solving both issues simultaneously – that is, by comparing the combined or total
    efficiency of (1) the likely probability that A would perform, and the level of reliance B would
    likely choose, if A's promise *were* enforceable; with (2) the likely probability that A would per-
    form, and the level of reliance B would likely choose, if A's promise were *not* enforceable. For
    a discussion of this point in economic terms, see Jim Leitzel, "Reliance and Contract Breach"
    (1989) 52 L. & Contemp. Prob. 87.
23. Much of the technical literature cited *supra* in note 20 deals with exactly this conflict.

B. Other Interim Incentives

Moreover, once we have broadened our focus from one set of incentives to two, we might just as well proceed to three and beyond. For one thing, enforceability can also affect each side's incentives to take various precautions that might affect their ability to perform. For example, if *A* has promised to deliver the car in good condition, her ability to do so might depend on how well she treats the car in the weeks before she is due to deliver it to *B*. If she parks the car in construction zones, or fails to perform even the most routine maintenance, then the odds that the car will still be in good condition will be much lower than if she is assiduous in taking care of the car. Moreover, her incentive to take these precautions may depend in part on whether her promise is enforceable – as well as on the extent of its enforceability, including how much she will have to pay if the car is not in good condition when she delivers it.[24]

Once this effect is recognized, we can expand the economic theory in a manner exactly analogous to the expansion discussed in the preceding subsection. Just as in the case of reliance, it is possible to have too many precautions (changing the oil three times a day), so one goal of an economic theory is to induce an *efficient* level of precautions. But since enforceability can affect the level of precautions that the parties choose, this means that the efficiency of enforcing promises must now depend on three effects: (1) the effect on the incentive to perform, (2) the effect on the incentive to rely, and (3) the effect on the incentive to take interim precautions. As before, it is entirely possible for some of these effects to be positive and others negative, so the concept of efficiency that is used will have to balance the offsetting effects to come up with an overall assessment. However that balancing is accomplished, though, it is clear that the efficiency of enforcing promises will now depend on the combined effect of three sets of incentives.

Nor is there any reason to stop here. The parties may also have decisions to make at any of several stages before the promise is ever made – for example, decisions about which parties to transact with (and at what price),[25] or about how much time and effort to spend searching for better transacting partners,[26]

---

24. For discussions of this effect see, for example, Cooter, *supra* note 6; Craswell, *supra* note 4, 61 S. Cal. L. Rev. at 646–50; L. A. Kornhauser, "Reliance, Reputation, and Breach of Contract" (1983), 26 J. L. & Econ. 691. As Cooter's article emphasizes, this effect is closely analogous to the effect of tort law in creating incentives to take precautions against accidental injury.
25. This is an important aspect of many recent game-theoretic models involving pooling and separating equilibria. See, for example, P. Aghion and B. Hermalin, "Legal Restrictions on Private Contracts Can Enhance Efficiency" (1990) 6 J. L., Econ., & Org. 381; I. Ayres and R. Gertner, "Filling Gaps in Incomplete Contracts: An Economic Theory of Default Rules" (1989) 99 Yale Law J. 87, 108–132; Lucian Ayre Bebchuk and Steven Shavell, "Information and the Scope of Liability for Breach of Contract: The Rule of *Hadley* v. *Baxendale*" (1991) 7 J. L., Econ., & Org. 284.
26. See P. A. Diamond and E. Maskin, "An Equilibrium Analysis of Search and Breach of Contract,

or how carefully to evaluate the proposed transaction (including their own potential inability to perform) before committing themselves to a promise,[27] or how much to tell the other party prior to the contract.[28] Each of these decisions can either promote or reduce efficiency – for example, it is possible to spend either too much or too little time investigating the proposed transaction – and the enforceability of the promise (including the potential penalties for breach) may well affect the parties' incentives on each of these decisions. But once we add these four effects to the three identified in the preceding paragraph, the desirability of enforcement must now be seen to turn on the combined effect of seven different incentives. And even this list is not complete, for other items could be added for every possible decision that parties to a transaction might conceivably have to make.

Indeed, there is at least one other effect that should be mentioned, which is the effect of enforceability on the allocation of risk. If the risk of nonperformance cannot be completely eliminated – that is, if even promisors who have taken all reasonable precautions will at least occasionally be unable to perform – then the losses resulting from nonperformance must (under a system of private litigation) fall on one or the other of the two parties to the promise. Roughly speaking, a rule of non-enforceability puts all of those losses on the promisee, while a rule of enforceability shifts some of the losses to the promisor, with the amount of the shift depending on the measure of damages that enforcement entails. This shifting of losses might seem to be a pure transfer from one party to the other, with no consequences for overall efficiency. However, if either of the parties is risk-averse, that party's interim welfare can be reduced simply by bearing the *risk* of an eventual loss. And if the two parties differ in their degree of risk-aversion, there may be net gains from a regime of enforceability (or nonenforceability) that puts more of the losses on the party who is least risk-averse.[29] This adds an eighth item to the list of possible effects that must be considered under the broader economic theory sketched here.

C. Some Noneconomic Analogies

The final section of the paper will discuss the significance of this broader economic theory for various philosophical issues of interest to contract law. Before

I: Steady States" (1979) 10 Bell J. Econ. 282; P. A. Diamond and E. Maskin, "An Equilibrium Analysis of Search and Breach of Contract, II: A Non-Steady State Example" (1981) 25 J. Econ. Theory 165; D. T. Mortensen, "Property Rights and Efficiency in Mating and Racing Games" (1981) 72 Am. Econ. Rev. 968.

27. See R. Craswell, "Precontractual Investigation as an Optimal Precaution Problem" (1988) 17 J. Legal Stud. 401.
28. See R. Craswell, "Performance, Reliance, and One-Sided Information" (1989) 18 J. Legal Stud. 365.
29. See, for example, A. M. Polinsky, "Risk Sharing Through Breach of Contract Remedies" (1983) 12 J. Legal Stud. 427.

doing that, however, it may help to see how this broader theory fits with three other conceptual views of contracts – views that are more often associated with noneconomic perspectives, but which cohere quite nicely with the second economic theory presented here.

The first view sees most contracts as essentially "relational," in that they involve an entire set of relationships rather than a single discrete transaction.[30] Relational analysis thus recognizes that there is more to most promises than just the eventual acts of performance, and that the parties' actions leading up to that performance may be just as important as the performance itself. To be sure, relational theorists often adopt normative goals other than efficiency, and thus could in theory differ from economists in their conclusions about what forms of enforceability are best.[31] Still, since relational analysis focuses on more than just the ultimate act of performance, it clearly fits better with the second economic theory than with the first.

A second theoretical approach views contracts as a form of privately enacted regulation.[32] After all, by entering into a legally enforceable contract, the parties subject themselves to an entire set of rules – some spelled out in the contract; others supplied by the legal system – that will govern their relationship in the future. Moreover, violations of those rules can be punished by the coercive power of the state, in much the same way as violations of any public law. To be sure, many of those who adopt this view do so to argue for greater state control over this "private regulation,"[33] but the accuracy of the metaphor can be separated from this alleged normative implication. (The normative implication would be inseparable from the metaphor only if one believed that describing something as "regulation" automatically justified greater state control.) For present purposes, what is important about this metaphor is its insistence that every enforceable contract gives rise to an entire *set* of legal constraints, and that these constraints then alter the parties' incentives in the same way as any other regulatory regime. A full analysis of these incentives – as opposed to merely analyzing the eventual performance of the contract – is also what is emphasized by the second economic theory.

Indeed, the same could be said of a third view, which sees contracts not as precursors of some action to take place in the future, but rather as instantly

---

30. See, for example, I. R. Macneil, "Economic Analysis of Contract Law: Its Shortfalls and the Need for a 'Rich Classificatory Apparatus'" (1981) 75 Nw. U. L. Rev. 1018; I. R. Macneil, "Contracts: Adjustment of Long-Term Economic Relations Under Classical, Neoclassical, and Relational Contract Law" (1978) 72 Nw. U. L. Rev. 854; R. W. Gordon, "Macaulay, Macneil, and the Discovery of Solidarity and Power in Contract Law" (1985) Wis. L. Rev. 565.
31. I say "in theory" because relational theorists sometimes endorse something close to efficiency as their goal. See R. Craswell, "The Relational Move: Some Questions from Law and Economics" (1994) 3 S. Cal. Interdisc. L.J. 91, 99–108.
32. W. D. Slawson, "Standard Form Contracts and Democratic Control of Lawmaking Power" (1971) 84 Harv. L. Rev. 529; see also T. D. Rakoff, "Contracts of Adhesion: An Essay in Reconstruction" (1983) 96 Harv. L. Rev. 1174, 1206–1215.
33. For example, Slawson, ibid.

effective transfers of a set of legal entitlements. On this view, if *A* promises to sell *B* her car then *A* has *as of that date* transferred certain rights in her car to *B*. Of course, many of the rights thus transferred will be contingent ones, which may not spring to life until a certain date has arrived, or until *B* first tenders the price of the car, or until some other condition of the contract has been satisfied. But if all of the contingencies are met, *A*'s subsequent delivery of the car can be seen not merely as the performance of a promise, but as the handing over of what is now *B*'s car. On this view, then, the obligation to perform a promise can be seen as one aspect of the obligation to respect others' property rights.[34]

This property-rights perspective might seem to fit slightly less well with the second of the theories discussed here, since it emphasizes an instantaneous transfer of rights rather than an ongoing set of relationships. But the "property rights" perspective does at least shift the focus away from the very last step in the process – the eventual consummation of the promise – to the change in legal relations that is effected the very day the contract is made. Moreover, the "property rights" metaphor (like the "private regulation" metaphor discussed above) makes it easier to see that it is a *bundle* of rights that has been transferred: that more has changed hands than just the good or service that will eventually be bought or sold. In this respect, both metaphors fit much better with the second or more complete economic theory than they do with the first. Under the second economic theory, it is precisely the change in entitlements at the time the promise becomes binding that gives rise to all of the interim incentives.

IV. Implications of the Distinction

For some purposes, very little turns on the distinction I have drawn here. That is, if we judge the efficiency of enforcement not simply by the efficiency of the promised actions, but rather by the efficiency of the set of incentives that are created by the promise, many of the same questions arise in an only slightly altered form. For example, those who believe that individuals are the best judges of their own welfare could still argue that most voluntary promises ought to be enforced, on the ground that any set of incentives chosen by the individual parties will probably be an efficient one. Similarly, it can still be argued that this presumption should be reversed in the case of promises induced by fraud or duress, on the ground that it can no longer be presumed that the incentives created by the promise must have been efficient. Thus, although the earlier quotation from Richard Posner questioned whether *performance* should be presumed to be ef-

---

34. For two (very different) recent statements of this view, see Barnett, *supra* note 7, at 291–300; and Peter Benson, "The Unity of Contract Law" (elsewhere in this book). Some commentators have traced this view back to medieval law; for a discussion and critique of these historical claims, see A. W. B. Simpson, *A History of the Common Law of Contract* (Oxford: Clarendon Press, 1975), 75–80.

ficient (if the promise was induced by fraud),[35] he could just as well have questioned whether *the entire package of incentives* created by the promise can be presumed to be efficient in cases of fraud. In short, once we view the effect of a promise as transferring an entire set of entitlements, not just the ultimate performance, many of the same arguments can still be made.

In some cases, though, a switch to the broader economic theory alters the issue or changes the underlying argument. In the remainder of this essay I discuss the implications of the broader theory for several issues that have interested contracts scholars: (1) whether to enforce a promise even if circumstances have changed, so that performance would no longer be efficient; (2) whether to presume the efficiency of enforcement simply from the fact that the promise was agreed to voluntarily; (3) whether to enforce a promise if nobody has yet relied on the promise; and (4) when to impute a promise to a party who has not made any sort of explicit commitment.

A. The Problem of Changed Circumstances

As noted earlier, the first economic theory, which justified enforcement by the presumed efficiency of the promised actions, had difficulty with cases where circumstances had changed so that performance was no longer efficient. If the promised actions were no longer efficient, the first theory could imply that the promise should no longer be enforceable, so the promisor should be released with no liability at all.[36]

By contrast, the second or broader economic theory has a much easier time with this sort of case. Even if performance itself would no longer be efficient, it could still be efficient to hold the promisor liable, to give her an incentive to *decide* whether it was still worthwhile to perform. It might also be efficient to hold her liable to preserve her incentives to take the optimal level of precautions against just this sort of mistake, or to optimize the other party's incentive to rely on these contracts, or to allocate the consequences of this sort of mistake in accordance with the parties' relative risk-bearing abilities (to list just three of the possible reasons). In short, the fact that *performance* is no longer efficient does not in itself give any reason for believing that the combination of *incentives* created by the promise is no longer likely to be efficient.[37] This is why the second economic theory has much less difficulty justifying enforcement of a promise even after circumstances have changed.

---

35. See *supra* note 8 and accompanying text.
36. See the discussion above in Section I.B.
37. As Michael Trebilcock puts it, "an exchange of contractual rights may be Pareto superior (including agreed risk allocations) even if the subsequent exchange of the promised performance is not." M. J. Trebilcock, *The Limits of Freedom of Contract* (Cambridge, MA: Harvard University Press, 1993), 127.

To be sure, the second economic theory is not completely immune from the problem of changed circumstances. That is, there might still be cases in which circumstances had changed so drastically that *the entire set* of incentives created by the promise, though perfectly efficient at the time the promise was made, is no longer efficient – for example, if there were a dramatic change in the parties' relative risk-aversion, or in their relative ability to take precautions to minimize certain risks. After all, even when the efficiency of enforcement is seen to turn on an entire set of incentives (as the second theory holds), it is always possible for the circumstances relevant to those incentives to change after the promise was made. At some level, then, the switch to the second theory does not free us from having to deal with the problem of changed circumstances.

There are, however, two reasons why this problem is quantitatively different under the second theory. First, the number of cases in which circumstances change enough to upset the entire balance of incentives is likely to be small, at least in comparison to the number of cases that could arise under the first theory, where all that needed to change was the efficiency of the promised actions. Indeed, if the circumstances change sufficiently to upset the entire balance of incentives, the promisor may well be excused under existing law – either completely excused, as in cases of impracticability or frustration;[38] or partially relieved from responsibility, as under the various mitigation doctrines.[39] In this respect, the second economic theory may provide a closer fit with current doctrine than the first.

Second, courts may also be less able to recognize cases where the entire balance of incentives is no longer efficient.[40] Under the first theory, where the only concern was whether it was still efficient to perform the promise, it was easy to imagine situations where even a judge (acting with the benefit of perfect hindsight) could see that performance was no longer efficient. Consider, for example, cases in which the promisor has made a slight mistake that would now be hugely expensive to correct (e.g., a building that is built one foot smaller than it should have been), and where the cost of correcting the mistake exceeds any plausible estimate of the importance of the problem to the promisee. Although it might be hard to measure the damage award needed to compensate the promisee, few would argue that such a promise should be completely unenforceable (implying that damages should automatically be zero), especially if the mistake that led to the increased cost was the promisor's own fault, thus negating any defense

---

38. For analyses of the impracticability defense that are broadly in keeping with this approach, see Posner and Rosenfield, *supra* note 9; M. J. White, "Contract Breach and Contract Discharge Due to Impossibility: A Unified Theory" (1988) 17 J. Legal Stud. 353; A. O. Sykes, "The Doctrine of Commercial Impracticability in a Second-Best World" (1990) 19 J. Legal Stud. 43.

39. See, for example, C. J. Goetz and R. E. Scott, "The Mitigation Principle: Toward a General Theory of Contractual Obligations" (1983) 69 Va. L. Rev. 967.

40. This drawback of impracticability and the other excuse doctrines was emphasized by Schwartz, *supra* note 12, and by Sykes, *supra* note 38. See also A. Kull, "Mistake, Frustration, and the Windfall Principle of Contract Remedies" (1991) 43 Hastings L.J. 1.

of impracticability. Significantly, though, liability in such a case is harder to defend under the first economic theory. If performance is clearly and verifiably inefficient, and if the the only justification for enforcing the promise is to make sure the performance decision is efficient (as the first theory would hold), why should a clearly inefficient performance ever be enforced?

Under the second theory, though, where the relevant question is whether the entire set of contractual incentives is still efficient, it is less likely that there will be many cases where courts can easily tell that the efficiency of those incentives has been reversed. As this point is closely related to the issue of whether individuals or courts should be deemed to be the best judge of individual welfare, I turn now to that issue.

B. The Problem of Paternalism

Section II.B introduced the question of whether the efficiency of enforcement can be inferred from the fact that a promise was made knowingly and voluntarily. The concept of efficiency, standing alone, does not imply anything about how efficiency should be identified in any given case, or about what institution should be charged with that task. Still, many of those who advocate efficiency do believe that the affected individuals are usually the best judges of their own welfare, and that those individual judgments will usually be less imperfect than the judgments of courts or of other third parties. If this belief is correct, it might make sense to adopt an absolute rule barring courts from ever second-guessing the knowing and voluntary judgments of the contracting parties.[41]

The key question, of course, is whether this belief is correct. I suggest that, if the only dimension of efficiency that is relevant is the efficiency of performing the promise (as the first economic theory would have it), the correctness of that belief is at least debatable. Even if individuals have better knowledge of their own wants and needs, courts sometimes have the advantage (as noted earlier) of better knowledge of events subsequent to the promise. And even when nothing has changed since the promise was made, there also may be cases where one of the individuals simply was not very good at evaluating the promised performance, and where this mistake or error will be obvious to a more competent court. If an expensive English-language encyclopedia has been sold to a childless couple that does not even speak English, or if fifty years' worth of dance lessons have been sold to an eighty-year-old widow, it is difficult to argue that –

---

41. I abstract here from the admittedly difficult question of how one ought to define "knowing" and "voluntary" for purposes of this argument. For a thoughtful discussion of the latter issue, together with a survey of the extensive literature, see A. Wertheimer, *Coercion* (Princeton: Princeton University Press, 1987). My own views are set forth in R. Craswell, "Property Rules and Liability Rules in Unconscionability and Related Doctrines" (1993) 60 U. Chi. L. Rev. 1; and R. Craswell, "Remedies When Contracts Lack Consent: Autonomy and Institutional Competence" (1995) 33 Osgoode Hall L.J. 209.

at least in these cases – a court could not make a better judgment than that made by the individuals involved.

To be sure, granting courts the power to block such exchanges is not a foolproof solution, for the courts themselves will at least occasionally err. And if courts were never (or hardly ever) better at judging such matters than were the parties themselves, a flat rule prohibiting this sort of second-guessing might well be justified on the grounds that it would minimize the total number of likely errors. But as long as the only relevant issue concerns the efficiency of actually performing the promise (as the first theory would have it), it simply is not clear that courts are hardly ever good at making such judgments, so it is at least a close question whether we might get more efficient results by allowing a defence to enforceability in any case where the inefficiency of performance were extreme and obvious. In effect, such a defence would correspond to a purely substantive version of the unconscionability doctrine, in which the unfairness or inefficiency of the terms themselves could be ground for setting the contract aside.

Indeed, even Richard Epstein – a staunch defender of freedom of contract – once defended a functionally equivalent role for the unconscionability doctrine.[42] To be sure, Epstein argued that obviously inefficient contracts should be taken as presumptive evidence of some underlying problem such as incapacity or fraud, so technically Epstein was urging that enforcement be blocked because of the (likely) underlying problem, not because of the inefficiency of the contract itself. But since Epstein did not require any direct evidence of the underlying incapacity or fraud – indeed, his argument was precisely that incapacity and fraud are sometimes too hard to prove directly – the practical effect of his proposal would have been to justify courts in refusing to enforce contracts whenever the contracts themselves seemed clearly and obviously inefficient. Such a rule is defensible only if we think the courts are reasonably good at recognizing such cases.

Once it is seen that there is more to efficiency than the efficiency of the actual performance, however, the case for judicial second-guessing becomes weaker. Even in cases where it is obvious that actually selling the product or service would be inefficient, allowing a defense to enforcement would also have a number of other effects, and these may be harder for a court to evaluate. For example, denying enforceability in such cases might also change sellers' incentives to seek out certain kinds of customers, or to raise the price charged to an entire class of customers who might later be released by the courts.[43] And though it is possible for these combined effects still to be positive on balance, that judgment is obviously more complicated, and therefore harder for courts

42. R. A. Epstein, "Unconscionability: A Critical Reappraisal" (1975) 18 J. L. & Econ. 293, 293–301.
43. As Epstein himself recognized (ibid.). For another discussion of this aspect of the unconscionability doctrine see A. Schwartz, "A Reexamination of Nonsubstantive Unconscionability" (1977) 63 Va. L. Rev. 1053, 1076–82.

to get right. Admittedly, these additional effects of an enforceable promise may also make it harder for individuals to judge whether a given promise is in their own interests, so it might be thought that there would be no net effect on the *relative* abilities of courts and individuals. But to the extent that the attraction of judicial second-guessing depends on there being clear or easy cases where enforcement would obviously be inefficient, that attraction can no longer be claimed once the full range of efficiency consequences is recognized.

C. The Problem of Detrimental Reliance

The broader economic theory also sheds some light on the relationship between the enforceability of a promise and the promisee's reliance. Some philosophers and some lawyers have argued that the case for enforcement is weaker, or perhaps even nonexistent, if a promisor changes her mind before the other party has relied on her promise in any way. In essence, these authors see the obligation to keep a promise as simply a specific instance of the obligation not to cause harm. And if the promise is withdrawn before anyone has changed his or her position, they argue, then the promise can be broken without harming anyone, and so the obligation to keep the promise loses its force.[44]

Of course, on one view of this reliance argument, the economic theories discussed here have nothing to say to it. The reliance theory starts from the premise that one should not cause harm, and if this principle is taken to be an absolute, nonconsequentialist command, then nothing that economics can say will be of any relevance. Many advocates of the reliance theory, however, do not attempt to ground the harm principle in any particular moral theory, and thus are not necessarily opposed to any form of consequential analysis. Indeed, since the goal of not causing harm fits very easily into any consequentialist framework, it should not be surprising that some of the conclusions of the reliance theory appear in the second economic theory as well.

In particular, we have already seen that the second economic theory counts, as one of the factors that could justify enforceability, the effect of enforceability on the promisee's incentives to rely.[45] To be sure, this factor played no role in the first economic theory (whose only goal was ensuring that the choice between performance and breach was made efficiently), so that theory would indeed be at odds with the arguments of the reliance theorists. But because the

---

44. In the legal literature, examples of this position include P. S. Atiyah, *Promises, Morals, and Law* (Oxford: Clarendon Press, 1981) [hereinafter Atiyah, *Promises, Morals, and Law*]; and Fuller and Perdue, *supra* note 22 at 53–7. Examples in the philosophical literature include N. Mac-Cormick, "Voluntary Obligations and Normative Powers" (1972) 46 (Supp. Vol.) Proc. Aristotelian Soc'y 59 at 62–7; and O. Hanfling, "Promises, Games and Institutions" (1975) 75 Proc. Aristotelian Soc'y 13 at 15–18. For criticisms of the reliance argument see, for example, Fried, *supra* note 11, at 10–11; Barnett, *supra* note 7, at 274–7; J. Raz, "Promises in Morality and Law" (1982) 95 Harv. L. Rev. 916, 924–5; T. M. Scanlon, *Promises and Contract.*

45. See Section III.B above.

second economic theory counts the effect on reliance as one of the principal reasons for the enforcement, the gap between the reliance argument and this second economic theory is much narrower.

Of course, this does not mean there is no gap at all. For one thing, the goal of the second economic theory (insofar as reliance is concerned) is to induce an *efficient* level of reliance, and the reliance theorists do not necessarily accept efficiency as their goal. Indeed, some of the reliance theorists seem to take the promisee's level of reliance as given – that is, they frame the question, "Should we enforce this promise?" at a time when the promisee already has (or has not) relied, and thus do not even address the effect of their answer on the promisee's ex-ante reliance incentives.

Nevertheless, most reliance theorists recognize that they do not want to encourage any and all forms of reliance on a promise, and that some method must therefore be found for separating legitimate from illegitimate reliance. Patrick Atiyah, for example, regarded the question of whether a promisor should be responsible for any particular act of reliance as a complex question of social policy, which must ultimately depend on a social judgment about what kinds of reliance ought to be encouraged.[46] But Atiyah did not make it his goal to spell out the exact social policy that ought to be employed, so his position is at least potentially consistent with the economists' social policy of encouraging only efficient reliance.

In short, it is a mistake to assume that there is any necessary or inherent conflict between reliance theories, on the one hand, and the second economic theory, on the other. Individual reliance theorists may of course differ – both with economists, and with each other – but the extent of their differences will depend on how each answers Atiyah's more specific policy question, about just which kinds of reliance ought to be encouraged. And any differences that do result should be attributed to their different stance on this policy question, not to their initial choice of a "reliance" or an "economic" perspective. On this issue, then, the devil really is in the details, and the choice of initial perspectives determines much less than is usually supposed.

The same might be said of another possible conflict, concerning which promises ought *not* to be enforced. As noted earlier, some reliance theorists believe that, if a promise has not yet been relied upon, the promise should not be enforceable. This conclusion does seem to be at odds with the second economic theory, for under that theory reliance was merely one of several factors that might bear on the efficiency of enforcement. Thus, under the second economic theory, it might still be efficient to enforce a promise that had not yet been relied upon if enforcement would induce a more efficient level of precautions

---

46. Atiyah, *Promises, Morals, and Law, supra* note 44, at 65–69. The need for some kind of social or policy judgment is also emphasized by J. M. Feinman, "Promissory Estoppel and Judicial Method" (1984) 97 Harv. L. Rev. 678, 712–716.

against accidents (for example), or if enforcement would make for a more efficient allocation of risks.

On closer examination, though, there is no reason for a reliance theorist to be committed to the idea that protecting reasonable reliance is the *only* possible justification for enforcement. Again, Patrick Atiyah can serve as a convenient counterexample. Atiyah discussed only one of the other possible economic effects of enforcement – the effect of enforceability on the allocation of risk – but he was quite explicit that a contract designed to shift risks could justifiably be enforced, even if it had not been relied upon.[47] For Atiyah, then, the effect of enforceability on reliance is one possible reason for enforcing promises, but it is not the only one. Exactly the same is true under the second economic theory discussed here. If reliance theorists differ with economists on this issue, then, it will be because of how they answer this secondary question (what other grounds for enforcing promises are justifiable?), and not because of anything inherent in reliance theory itself.

Still another possible conflict concerns the role of freedom of contract. The economic theory discussed here accords a relatively large weight to the individual parties' own judgments about efficiency, on the ground (as discussed in the preceding subsections) that individuals usually know their own circumstances better than judges will. By contrast, Atiyah is usually identified with a position that is much less supportive of freedom of contract.[48]

On this issue too, however, Atiyah's actual position does not diverge from the economic theory nearly as much as might be expected. As noted earlier, Atiyah believes that the question of whether any particular promisor ought to be liable is a question of social policy, which may require a balance between any number of conflicting factors.[49] But once he has framed the issue in terms of the balance of social policy, Atiyah then suggests that an explicit promise by a promisor should often be treated as an admission that the balance of social policy, at least in this case, justifies enforcement. Since this is an admission against the promisor's own interests (assuming that the promisor is now in court contesting enforcement), Atiyah argues that the admission ought at least to be presumptive on the question of enforceability, and in many cases ought to be conclusive.[50] Thus, in the end Atiyah is willing to give priority to the individual's own knowledge of her own circumstances, rather than to allow courts to second-guess the desirability of enforceability in every case. Of course, other reliance theorists might take a different position on this issue, which would lead

---

47. Atiyah, *Promises, Morals, and Law, supra* note 44, at 208–9 (discussing contracts of insurance, and other pure risk-shifting contracts).
48. See especially P. S. Atiyah, *The Rise and Fall of Freedom of Contract* (Oxford: Clarendon Press, 1979) at 5–6 [hereinafter Atiyah, *Freedom of Contract*]. See also the discussion below in Section IV.D.
49. See *supra* note 46 and accompanying text.
50. Atiyah, *Promises, Morals, and Law, supra* note 44, at 184–202.

them into more of a conflict with economists. My point is simply that differences of this sort will stem from their answers to this narrower institutional issue – whose decision should decide whether enforcement is justified on social grounds? – and not from anything required by reliance theory itself. Here, too, the choice of initial perspective determines much less than is usually supposed.

D. The Problem of Imputed Promises

The popular view of reliance theory as somehow hostile to freedom of contract may stem from the views of some reliance theorists on the question of when the law should *infer* an enforceable promise. For example, Atiyah points out that the law often infers such promises when the other party has relied in some way on the putative promisor's behavior. In these cases, he suggests, it is really the reliance itself that justifies the imposition of liability, and the implied "promise" is merely a legal fiction that could easily be dispensed with.[51] He then argues that this sort of imputed promise is at least potentially in conflict with the idea of freedom of contract:

As soon as liabilities come to be placed upon a person in whom another has reposed trust or reliance, even though there is no explicit promise or agreement to bear that liability, the door is opened to a species of liability which does not depend upon a belief in individual responsibility and free choice. Not only is the party relied upon held liable without his promise, but the party relying is relieved from the consequences of his own actions. The values involved in this type of liability are therefore closely associated with a paternalist social philosophy, and a redistributive economic system.[52]

Although this view might seem to be quite at odds with the economic arguments, here, too, the divergence is more apparent than real. The key to the reconciliation is that, in the cases now at issue, the putative promisor has not clearly said whether she has or has not made a binding promise. That is, if one party were to explicitly disclaim any responsibility – "I think I will probably do *x*, and you may well want to rely on my doing so, but I warn you that I'm not actually *promising* that I'll do it, so you should rely only if you're willing to accept the risk of being disappointed" – if the speaker has made such an explicit disclaimer, few if any reliance theorists would hold the speaker liable.[53] The hard case,

---

51. Ibid. at 173–176.
52. Atiyah, *Freedom of Contract, supra* note 48, at 6–7. The view that reliance-based liability is inconsistent with freedom of contract can also be found in G. Gilmore, *The Death of Contract* (Columbus: Ohio State University Press, 1974) at 88–103. This view has also been accepted by some critics of the reliance doctrine – for example, R. E. Barnett, "Contract Scholarship and the Reemergence of Legal Philosophy" (1984) 97 Harv. L. Rev. 1223, 1240–41.
53. Scanlon, "Promises and Practices," *supra* note 14 at 209, 211 note 9, considers just such a case and takes it as obvious that the speaker has discharged any responsibility by such a warning at the time he makes the promise. His argument (and mine) assumes, of course, that the disclaimer

then, is when the speaker has neither expressly assumed nor expressly denied any sort of obligation. To decide such cases, the law must perforce adopt a default rule or default interpretation.

There is, of course, a large and growing literature on the choice of default rules, which I will not try to summarize here.[54] Still, as long as whatever rule the law adopts is merely a *default* rule – that is, as long as the speaker is free to opt out of the rule by clearly specifying an intention to do so – it is hard to argue that the rule interferes in any way with the speaker's freedom of contract. True, any such rule may to some extent burden the speaker's freedom, since any default rule will require at least some parties (those who would prefer a different rule) to take whatever steps are required to opt out of the default. But if this is enough to count as an infringement of freedom of contract, then freedom of contract is doomed from the start, since the law must always have *some* default rule (to have no default rule at all would mean the case could not be decided), and thus will always impose such a burden on at least some contracting parties. As long as the steps required to opt out of the default are not unduly burdensome, I would argue that every possible default rule (including Atiyah's) is just as consistent with freedom of contract as any other.[55]

Indeed, even if one believes instead that freedom of contract requires default rules that match whatever most parties intend,[56] it may still be the case that Atiyah's default rule meets this test. Default rules that correspond with what most parties intend (sometimes called "majoritarian" default rules) do at least reduce the number of parties who will have to opt out of the default, so they might be thought desirable whether or not they are seen as more consistent with freedom of contract. But if we ask when most parties would want their tentative or potential plans to be legally enforceable, one answer is: Whenever enforceability would increase the total expected value of the project, by encouraging the other party to choose an efficient level of reliance.[57] If this is correct, then it is not surprising that the law often imputes an enforceable obligation in just those

---

is obvious (e.g., not buried in the fine print of a long document), that the other party is capable of understanding the disclaimer, and that there are no other imperfections of the sort that would invalidate any mutual agreement regardless of its terms. Compare M. Pettit Jr., "Modern Unilateral Contracts" (1983) 63 Boston U. L. Rev. 551, 574–81 (discussing cases where disclaimers that had not been adequately brought to the other party's attention were not given legal effect).

54. See, for example, Ayres and Gertner, *supra* note 25; and the symposium published at 3 S. Cal. Interdisc. L. J. 1 (1993).

55. I develop this argument at more length in R. Craswell, "Philosophy of Promising" *supra* note 19 at 514–28.

56. See, for example, R. E. Barnett, "The Sound of Silence: Default Rules and Contractual Consent" (1992) 78 Va. L. Rev. 821, 875–85.

57. See, for example, R. Craswell, "Offer, Acceptance, and Efficient Reliance" (1996), 48 Stan. L. Rev. 481; A. Katz, "When Should an Offer Stick? The Economics of Promissory Estoppel in Preliminary Negotiations" (1996) 105 Yale Law J. 1249; Y. Che and D. Hausch, "Cooperative Investments and the Value of Contracting" (2000) Am. Econ. Rev., forthcoming.

cases where it is desirable for the other party to rely. Far from indicating that the law has rejected freedom of contract, it may simply show that the law is selecting (or trying to select) the most efficient default rule.

Again, there is room for differences on this point – either differences about what default rule most people in fact would want, or differences about whether default rules should even be selected on that basis. My claim is simply that differences on issues such as these do not depend, in any necessary way, on whether one starts with some version of reliance theory or with the second economic theory discussed here. On this issue, too, there is no inherent conflict between reliance theory and economics.

V. CONCLUSION

There are, of course, many other grounds for disagreeing with the economic theory described here. There are many disagreements that are entirely internal to the theory ("all things considered, which measure of damages is in fact the most efficient?"), or about the issues I have elided here (how should individual welfare be judged? how should interpersonal comparisons be made?). There is also room for external disagreement about whether efficiency should be the goal of contract law. Nothing I have said in this essay even begins to address these other, more interesting disagreements.

Instead, my goal here has been the more modest one of clarifying just what the economic theory is (and is not). Although some authors occasionally speak as though efficiency, as applied to contract law, meant nothing more than enforcing all contracts whose performance is still efficient – a theory that would indeed be starkly opposed to most other perspectives – most modern economic writers hold a theory that is much richer and more complex. It is this theory, and not the simpler one-dimensional version, that should be on the table in future debates.[58]

58. I am grateful to Peter Benson, Barbara H. Fried, Martha C. Nussbaum, Eric A. Posner, and participants at a Stanford workshop for helpful comments; and to the Lynde and Harry Bradley Foundation and the Sarah Scaife Foundation for financial support when I was a faculty member at the University of Chicago Law School.

2

The Scope and Limits
of Legal Paternalism

Altruism and Coercion in
Family Financial Arrangements

MICHAEL J. TREBILCOCK AND STEVEN ELLIOTT

I. Introduction

A. *The Analytical Problem*

The regulation of family business financial arrangements has become a major problem for contract lawyers in Commonwealth jurisdictions. While the communality of family life and the informality and trust that it engenders are often rightly celebrated, they can also permit dominant family members to impose financial risks on other members that they would not otherwise choose. A recurrent example involves family homes being used as security for business ventures being undertaken by family members. Wives are sometimes induced by their husbands, who operate small businesses that are in financial difficulties, to enter into a mortgage of the jointly owned family home to secure the business's line of credit. The business subsequently fails and the bank moves to foreclose on the mortgage. Similarly, parents are sometimes induced by adult children to enter into security transactions to obtain credit for the child's business. Not understanding the legal implications of the transaction or appreciating the risks of the venture, wives and elderly parents can be led to stake their interest in their home in what they ought to view as a poor investment. When these risks materialize, courts are asked to allocate the loss from the venture as between the unsophisticated family members and the lender holding the security. The principles upon which courts make these allocations determine the terms upon which lenders will advance credit to many small businesses. Lord Browne-Wilkinson has articulated a dilemma raised by these facts:

... it is important to keep a sense of balance when approaching these cases. It is easy to allow sympathy for the wife who is threatened with the loss of her home at the suit of a rich bank to obscure an important public interest viz., the need to ensure that the wealth currently tied up in a matrimonial home does not become economically sterile. If the rights secured to wives by the law render vulnerable loans granted on the security of matrimonial homes, institutions will be unwilling to accept such security, thereby reducing the flow of loan capital to business enterprises.[1]

The volume of litigation raising variants on the basic family home fact pattern evinces the difficulties Commonwealth courts have had in articulating a fair and efficient governing regime.[2] Markedly different approaches have been taken to delineating the legal relationships of the parties to these arrangements. In recent years English courts have been especially active in developing the law in this area. The House of Lords has treated the problem in a trilogy of cases culminating in *Barclays Bank plc* v. *O'Brien* in 1993.[3] Their lordships pressed the slumbering doctrines of undue influence and constructive notice into service in protecting the interests of vulnerable transactors. *Barclays Bank plc* v. *O'Brien* marks a trend towards increasingly paternalistic regulation of family surety transactions. The English Court of Appeal has now in *Royal Bank of Scotland* v. *Etridge* issued a major restatement of the law, which is of particular interest for its detailed discussion of the independent advice requirement.[4] The same year saw major decisions by the Australian High Court and the New Zealand Court of Appeal in *Garcia* v. *National Australia Bank Limited* and *Wilkinson* v. *ASB Bank Ltd.* respectively.[5] Underlying these legal doctrines are important questions about the limits of private ordering in the family setting. The communality, informality, and trust characteristic of family life can generate agency costs that subvert or outweigh the conventional benefits of free contracting. This poses special problems for designers of legal regimes intended to regulate the behaviour of family members and financial institutions.

This paper explores the nature of family financial contracting in an attempt to clarify the regulatory issues that arise out of the basic family home fact pattern and its variants. The primary focus is on the contractual relationship between family sureties and lenders. Several possible legal regimes are examined in light of a proposed analysis of the typical contract failures they ought to address. The aim is to specify the inefficiencies associated with each possibility in order to make comparative evaluations. While each of the possible regimes we examine entails error and transaction costs, there are better and worse contenders. For expository purposes this study concentrates on spousal and parent

---

1. *Barclays Bank plc* v. *O'Brien* [1994] 1 AC 180 at 188 [hereinafter *Barclays Bank*].
2. See the *Table of Cases* in B. Fehlberg, *Sexually Transmitted Debt: Surety Experience and English Law* (Oxford: Clarendon Press, 1997) at xv–xxii [hereinafter *Sexually Transmitted Debt*].
3. *National Westminster Bank plc* v. *Morgan* [1985] 1 AC 686 [hereinafter *Morgan*]; *CIBC Mortgages plc* v. *Pitt* [1994] 1 A.C. 200 [hereinafter *Pitt*]; *O'Brien, supra* note 1.
4. *Royal Bank of Scotland* v. *Etridge (No 2)* [1998] 4 All ER 705 (CA) [hereinafter *Etridge*]; *Etridge* is curently under appeal to the House of Lords and is scheduled to be heard in summer 2000. See also *Barclays Bank* v. *Boulter* [1999] 1 W.L.R. 1919 (H.L.).
5. *Garcia* v. *National Australia Bank Limited* (1998) 72 A.L.R. 1243 (H.C.) [hereinafter *Garcia*]; *Wilkinson* v. *ASB Bank Ltd* [1998] 1 N.Z.L.R. 674 (C.A.) [hereinafter *Wilkinson*].

surety cases.[6] Similar problems sometimes arise between cohabitants, siblings, and even friends, and the analysis applies *mutatis mutandis* in these cases.

We argue that the optimal approach is to insist that vulnerable contractors proposing to enter potentially disadvantageous arrangements be independently advised as to their nature and risks. Vulnerable contractors who have been properly advised should be held to their bargains. The enforceability of a lender's security ought to be contingent on its ensuring that vulnerable contractors are so advised. While protecting wives and elderly parents from being taken advantage of in certain ways, this proposed rule respects their ultimate choices and enables them to organize their affairs according to their own best judgment and inclinations, including altruistic inclinations. In view of the potential for exploitation in family life, we argue that not stipulating that vulnerable contractors be independently advised when they are proposing to enter into potentially disadvantageous arrangements foregoes real welfare gains. Independent advice in these circumstances increases the likelihood that agreements will be Pareto superior. We also reject more interventionist and paternalistic regulation as working against the best interests of the very people it is intended to protect. In this respect we take issue with those who hold that the risks of exploitation in the family setting call for governance with a heavy judicial hand.[7] The approach we propose is also sensitive to the importance of credit to family-centred businesses.[8]

B. *Theoretical Orientation*

John Stuart Mill famously argues in his essay, *On Liberty,* that people should be free to make choices concerning their own lives subject to their not harming others. He writes that there is no basis for interfering with a person's conduct:

6. The usual fact pattern considered in this study involves a lender, a primary borrower, and a surety. In most cases the primary borrower is male and the surety is female. In the interest of clarity we have elected to use the female pronoun to identify all sureties and similarly placed persons, and the male pronoun to identify lenders and primary borrowers.
7. For example, D. Otto, "A Barren Future? Equity's Conscience and Women's Inequality" (1992) 18 Melbourne U. L. Rev. 809; although not discussing the family setting, P. Burrows makes a similar call for greater judicial intervention in contractual relations: "Contract Discipline: In Search of Principles in the Control of Contracting Power" (1995) 2 Eur. J. L. & Econ. 127 [hereinafter Burrows, "Contract Discipline"]; see also M. Richardson, "Protecting Women Who Provide Security for a Husband's, Partner's, or Child's Debts: The Value and Limits of an Economic Perspective" (1996) 16 Legal Stud. 368.
8. Compare *Sexually Transmitted Debt, supra* note 2 at 281. Special mention needs to be made to two books that form the intellectual backdrop to this study and are referred to extensively. The first is M. Trebilcock, *The Limits of Freedom of Contract* (Cambridge, MA: Harvard University Press, 1993) [hereinafter *Limits*], in which one of us explores at a general level some of the theoretical problems engaged in this study. The second is Fehlberg's valuable study, *Sexually Transmitted Debt, supra* note 2. Our evaluations draw on empirical evidence Fehlberg gathered on the experiences of spousal sureties in England.

... when that conduct affects the conduct of no persons beside himself or need not affect them unless they like (all the persons concerned being of full age, and the ordinary amount of understanding). In all such cases there should be perfect freedom, legal and social, to do the action and stand the consequences.[9]

Despite the strong terms in which Mill states this anti-paternalist doctrine, he acknowledges early in his essay that "it is, perhaps, hardly necessary to say that this doctrine is meant to apply only to human beings in the maturity of their faculties."[10] In the quoted passage he confines the proposition to persons of full age and the ordinary amount of understanding. Moreover, Mill contends that voluntary enslavement contracts are inconsistent with basic notions of individual self-fulfilment – an individual should not be free to agree not to be free.[11] These are notable qualifications to Mill's anti-paternalism. There is no denying the necessity of qualifications such as these. Even the committed laissez-faire liberal Milton Friedman is forced to concede that "there is no use pretending that problems are simpler than in fact they are. There is no avoiding the need for some measure of paternalism."[12]

Legal restrictions on contractual capacity of minors and mental incompetents reflect Mill's qualifications on the anti-paternalism principle. These are complicating restrictions, as the legal categories of minors and mental incompetents can be arbitrary. Law makers may choose a particular age of capacity for pragmatic reasons, but maturity of judgment is not a discontinuous or binary state, completely absent at one moment in time and fully realized in the next. The legal category of minors is consequently both over and under-inclusive. Mental incompetence is also distributed unevenly. Individuals display different degrees of mental competence in relation to different kinds of interactions with others. In extreme cases of infancy or insanity individuals may lack the capacity to form a stable or coherent preference structure as their wills are unformed or paralysed, but many other cases are not so clear.[13]

Individuals with stable and coherent preference sets may nonetheless make choices that are inconsistent with those preferences. Coercion or information failure are both conditions under which this may occur. In these circumstances the individual's existing preferences remain the basic reference point. Some scholars favour a broader scope for paternalistic intervention. For example, Sunstein argues for a substantial role for legal paternalism, reflecting a majority of the population's preferences about preferences, or second order preferences at the expense of first order preferences, by way of analogy with the story of Ulysses and the Sirens, in which Ulysses asked to be bound to the mast in or-

9. J. S. Mill, *On Liberty* (Northbrook, IL: AHM Pub. Corp., 1947) at 76 [hereinafter *On Liberty*].
10. Ibid. at 10.   11. Ibid. at 104.
12. M. Friedman, *Capitalism and Freedom* (Chicago: University of Chicago Press, 1962) at 33–34.
13. See *Limits, supra* note 8 at c. 7 ("Paternalism").

der to avoid momentary temptations to succumb to the entreaties of the Sirens.[14] Sunstein gives examples including addiction, habit, and myopia.[15]

Others argue that many preferences are endogenous or contingent and lead to choices that individuals would make differently absent the social, economic, legal, ideological, and other influences that have determined them. This view has the potential to subvert traditional autonomy values. Sunstein acknowledges that "if the ideas of endogenous preferences and cognitive distortions are carried sufficiently far, it may be impossible to describe a truly autonomous preference."[16] In order to avoid this implication, Sunstein argues that "there is a substantial difference between a preference that results from the absence of available opportunities, or a lack of information about alternatives, and a preference that is formed in the face of numerous opportunities and all relevant information."[17] While this qualification perhaps puts some constraints on the scope of legitimate paternalistic intervention, when a preference is formed in the face of numerous "opportunities" and "all relevant" information raises far from axiomatic issues, and moreover does not directly address the mental or emotional capacity of given individuals to evaluate available opportunities, even if numerous, or all relevant information, even if available to them.

Family financial transactions raise particularly difficult questions about the scope and limits of legal paternalism. This context brings together two phenomena that have proven particularly intractable in the law of contract: altruism and coercion. Many family commitments are at least partially motivated by altruism. These commitments exist in the penumbra of arms-length commercial contracts, but have always been accorded an exceptional status in the law of contract. Family commitments are often taken by the courts as not having been intended or understood to be legally enforceable.[18] Even where family commitments are otherwise legally enforceable – for example, completed gifts, clear reciprocal commitments, or arrangements involving non-familial third parties – the intimate or dependent nature of many familial relationships may provide a basis for arguing that one family member was coerced by another. While altruism is an exalted quality, in some cases it may be symptomatic of invidious features of family relations – domination and subjugation. The tension between

---

14. See J. Elster, *Ulysses and the Sirens: Studies in Rationality and Irrationality,* rev. ed. (Cambridge: Cambridge University Press, 1985).
15. See for example C. Sunstein, "Legal Interference with Private Preferences" (1986) 53 U. Chi. L. Rev. 1129 [hereinafter Sunstein, "Private Preferences"]; C. Sunstein, "Preferences and Politics" (1991) 20 Philosophy and Public Affairs 3.
16. Sunstein, "Private Preferences," *supra* note 15 at 1170
17. See C. Sunstein, "Disrupting Voluntary Transactions" in J. Chapman and R. Pennock, eds., *Markets and Justice* (New York: New York University Press, 1989) at 275.
18. See *Limits, supra* note 8 at c. 8 ("Consideration"); E. A. Posner, "Altruism, Status, and Trust in the Law of Gifts and Gratuitous Promises" (1997) Wis. L. Rev. 567.

these polarities has been dramatically highlighted in the burgeoning case law concerning family financial transactions, typically also involving third party financial institutions. While family financial transactions and arrangements are often viewed as falling outside the scope of mainstream contract law, they provide a signal opportunity to re-evaluate the scope and limits of legal paternalism in contract law generally.

In this paper, we largely adopt a law and economics perspective on legal paternalism, while attempting to be sensitive to the implications of other normative perspectives. Our approach accords primacy to the task of uncovering and respecting transactors' real preferences, and is sceptical about legal interventions that over-ride or disregard those preferences. In addition, a law and economics perspective on contract theory in general, probably reflecting its utilitarian foundations, tends to the view that theorizing for theorizing's sake has little value. Useful theorizing illuminates real-world problems that have otherwise proven intractable. We are for this reason unapologetic in motivating our analysis of the scope and limits of legal paternalism in contract law with a real-world problem.

This is a study of the scope and limits of legal paternalism in a salient and difficult context. Courts adopt a paternalistic stance when they interfere with contractual relations in order to protect vulnerable family members from transactions not in their best interests that they may choose or be induced to enter. There is a growing literature addressing the theoretical challenges posed by paternalistic state intervention in contractual relations.[19] Scholars have noted that practically useful analysis can only occur in close relation to the facts of particular contracting contexts.[20] We would note at the outset that even factually specific analysis of this sort cannot, as a matter of principle, yield determinate solutions to real world problems. Theoretical analysis can only provide the forms of arguments that might justify or discredit particular paternalistic interventions. Judgment and evidence are also needed, and judgments of this sort are inherently contestable. In the last section of this paper we assess several possible governing rules in order to determine which, in our judgment, best vindicates the welfare and autonomy values that frame our analysis.

---

19. G. Dworkin, "Paternalism" in R. A. Wasserstrom, ed., *Morality and the Law* (Belmont: Wadsworth Pub. Co., 1971); D. Kennedy, "Distributive and Paternalist Motives in Contract and Tort Law, with Special Reference to Compulsory Terms and Unequal Bargaining Power" (1982) 41 Maryland L. Rev. 563; A Kronman, "Paternalism and the Law of Contracts" (1983) 92 Yale Law J. 763 [hereinafter Kronman, "Paternalism"]; R. Spergel, "Paternalism and Contract: A Critique of Anthony Kronman" (1988) 10 Cardozo L. Rev. 593; Sunstein, "Private Preferences," *supra* note 15; P. Burrows, "Analyzing Legal Paternalism" (1995) 15 Int'l Rev. L. & Econ. 489 [hereinafter Burrows, "Legal Paternalism"]; S. A. Smith, "Future Freedom and Freedom of Contract" (1996) 59 Modern L. Rev. 167; E. Zamir, "The Efficiency of Paternalism" (1998) 84 Va. L. Rev. 229. There is a substantial philosophical literature on paternalism that is reviewed in *Limits, supra* note 8 at c. 7.

20. For example, Burrows "Analyzing Legal Paternalism," *supra* note 19 at 506–507.

C. Organization of Paper

In Section II, we look generally at the role of private ordering in the family setting. We contrast the benefits of free contracting with concomitant risks, and point to features of family life that give rise to a need for paternalistic regulation of family financial arrangements. In Section III, we define certain terms and taxonomize the contracting problems that are prevalent in the family setting. In Section IV, we consider the role of independent legal advice as a device that is often employed to correct some of those contracting problems. We outline three possible functions of independent advice and assess their potential efficacy. In Section V, we detail the gatekeeper role that lenders play in detecting and correcting contract failure in the family setting. In so doing, we specify the parameters of the gatekeeping duty that lenders ought to be under. We conclude, in Section VI, with a general discussion of the scope and limits of legal paternalism in this contractual setting.

II. Private Ordering and Family Financial Arrangements

Private ordering holds out the possibility for individuals to fashion life plans for themselves and with those with whom they share intimate relationships that meet their aspirations in a way that no standardized legal norms or expansive judicial discretion exercised by others who are not privy to those life plans or aspirations is likely to achieve.[21] A properly structured legal regime that is respectful of private contractual ordering can serve as a support for the personal autonomy of those that it governs, and can promote their welfare by enabling them to arrange their affairs as they see fit. Amongst family members, contractual freedom can permit the furtherance of their mutual and several ends in accord with their own judgments and inclinations. In relation to their financial affairs the benefits of freedom of contract are obvious. Families often need to accumulate assets in order to realize their mutual and several life plans. Particularly where their skills lie in business, families need access to credit if they are to accumulate those assets. As credit often requires collateral it is important to many families that they be free to borrow on the strength of their current assets, including their family home.

Communality is a cardinal feature of family life. Whereas self-interest may be an appropriate general characterization of motivation in the broader social world, the presumption is reversed in familial interactions. Family members often display interdependent utility functions. The happiness of each is to some extent contingent on the happiness of the others. From a contracting perspective, this feature of family relations can be the source of important benefits to

---

21. See M. Trebilcock and R. Keshvani, "The Role of Private Ordering in Family Law: A Law and Economics Perspective" (1991) 41 U. Toronto L. J. 533.

family members. Apart from the mutual goods that family members may pursue, such as child rearing, and the common goods that they may participate in, such as companionship and emotional well-being, the interdependent utility functions that family members display also help members to achieve their several ends efficiently. Joint arrangements that promote the projects of some members only will be willingly made if other members are confident that their happiness is also important. There is no need to specify consideration for the contributions of the others – what comes around, goes around. Where there is a community of interdependent interests, members can trust that they will receive a share of the benefits in due course. This trust or implicit reciprocity allows arrangements to be structured informally and therefore more flexibly. Funds are made available for the education of children, and their time is in turn made available to care for their parents when they age. Homecare is provided to enable a spouse to devote himself or herself to a career, and the proceeds of that career in turn secure the economic future of the homecare worker. Countless smaller advances are routinely made on the credit of a loving bond. The informality engendered by familial trust can yield savings in the transaction costs of negotiating formal complete contingent claims contracts and legal enforcement. At the limit, the unity of families is itself a costless enforcement device; or rather, it obviates the need for enforcement.[22]

Although families can be of the first importance in enabling members to develop and realize mutual and several life plans, feminist scholarship alerts us to the risks of oppression and exploitation that can inhere in family relationships. It is enough to state the communal ideal of family life to recognize that it is rarely achieved. Particularly where families are characterized by a sharp division of labour and a high degree of dependency between members, family financial contracting can be rife with abuse. The law reports are replete with cases in which a vulnerable spouse, parent, or child claims to have been taken advantage of financially by another family member concerned primarily with personal gain. It may seem rational for a family member to delegate financial decision making to another family member as an efficient division of labour. Unfortunately, having placed her financial affairs in the hands of that family member, she may find that her interests are detrimentally ignored.

The difficulties of family contract regulation arise out of the fact that no family is a perfect unity. Even the members of the most harmonious households have several as well as mutual ends. These differences of interest are accentuated by the possibility of family breakdown. The high incidence of divorce in most Western societies and the prevalence of elder abandonment mean that the prospect of breakdown should often weigh in making family financial arrangements. Prudent family members will want to protect their personal positions in

---

22. See A. Kronman, "Contract Law and the State of Nature" (1985) 1 J. L., Econ. & Org. 5 at 30–31.

light of this contingency. The trust and informality that result from family communality can be easily abused by a member seeking to favour his own severable interests at the expense of his family. The purpose of regulating family arrangements is to put safeguards in place to reduce this risk.

The limited communality of family life raises a special problem for the designers of a legal regime intended to regulate family financial affairs. Limited communality means that family agreements differ categorically from arms-length commercial contracts. Whereas commercial actors can be assumed for interpretive purposes to be actuated by self-oriented motives, family members cannot be. Family financial arrangements should not therefore be thought of as bargains in the strict sense. In assessing the equity of commercial agreements courts can and variously do consider both the fairness of the substantive terms and the process leading up to their execution.[23] There is a long-standing debate about which type of factor or combination of factors should be sufficient to justify intervention.[24] In the pre-breakdown family setting it is not possible to assess the fairness of substantive terms without doing violence to the interdependent preferences of participants. Family arrangements are opaque in that apparent one-sidedness is not a reliable indicator of inequity. There is no probable basis for inferring that gifts are disadvantageous from the point of view of the donor because participants are as likely to be motivated by familial altruism as by self-interest.

Judicial interference with family guarantees is sometimes said to depend in part on whether the surety consented out of genuine familial altruism or out of submission. Stuart-Smith LJ wrote this in *Royal Bank of Scotland* v. *Etridge:*

> Legitimate commercial pressure brought by a creditor, however strong, coupled with proper feelings of family loyalty and a laudable desire to help a husband or son in financial difficulty, may be difficult to resist. They may be sufficient to induce a reluctant wife or mother to agree to charge her home by way of collateral security, particularly if they are accompanied by family pressure and emotional scenes. But they are not enough to justify the setting aside of the transaction unless they go beyond what is permissible and lead the complainant to execute the charge not because, however reluctantly, she is persuaded that it is the right thing to do, but because the wrongdoer's importunity has left her with no will of her own.[25]

This is reasonable in principle but in practice difficult to apply directly because of the difficulty a court would face in trying to assess the surety wife's psychological state when she agreed to the security obligation. What evidence there may be is likely unreliable. The difficulty stems in part from a moral hazard endemic to many family surety cases. At the time the security is given the husband

---

23. See P. S. Atiyah, "Contract and Fair Exchange" (1985) 35 U. Toronto L. J. 1.
24. See for example Burrows "Contract Discipline," *supra* note 7; A. A. Leff, "Unconsionability and the Code – The Emperor's New Clause" (1967) 115 U. Penn. L. Rev. 485.
25. *Etridge, supra* note 4 at para 10.

and wife may have divergent interests as the husband seeks finance for a business that it is not in the wife's best interests to promote.[26] If the business fails, however, and the bank moves to enforce its security, then the husband's and the wife's interests will converge. At this time it will be in both of their interests to defeat the bank's claim and retain possession of their home. Both the husband and the wife have a strong incentive in these cases to misrepresent the wife's psychological dependence and the indicia of pressure.[27] They will often be the only witnesses to important events leading up to the wife's execution of the bank's security. For this and other reasons external observers after the fact are poorly positioned to examine whether vulnerable sureties were motivated by genuine familial altruism or by psychological submission.

A regulatory strategy is driven by the practical difficulty of distinguishing altruism from psychological submission to focus on the procedure by which arrangements are made. The challenge is to specify procedural safeguards that minimize the likelihood that Pareto inferior arrangements will be consummated. These safeguards must not actually prevent people from acting on their own better judgment or inclination, nor must they drive the costs of small business finance up to unacceptable levels. Transparent and objective criteria need to be found to trigger extraordinary protective measures, and these measures themselves must be carefully crafted. While ostensibly one-sided transactions may be the legitimate product of familial altruism, the adequacy of consideration may nonetheless serve an important purpose in flagging transactions that call for these special measures. In Section V, we return to the details and justification of a procedural regulatory strategy.

III. Contract Failure in the Family Setting

The primary welfarist justification of private ordering is that in free cooperation all participants maximize the satisfaction of their utility functions. Contracts that are not mutually maximizing are to that extent inefficient. Just as free markets can be afflicted by various forms of market failure, free contracting can be afflicted by contract failure.[28] A contract failure is a condition that causes a particular agreement to be other than mutually welfare maximizing. Prominent examples are coercion and information failure. A contract failure is then a *prima facie* reason why a particular contract should not be enforced. Not every contract failure is, however, sufficiently serious to justify judicial interference. The notion of contract failure embraces many minor shortcomings that ought to be tolerated as not undermining the essence of a beneficial exchange. Weak coer-

---

26. See discussion at pages 60–62 below.
27. This phenomenon is vividly illustrated by the facts of *Goldberg* v. *Barnett Alexander Chart* (English Ch. D, 30 July 1998).
28. Sunstein, "Private Preferences," *supra* note 15.

cion may cause an agreement to be less than mutually welfare maximizing while there may still be good reason to believe that it is mutually welfare enhancing. As well, courts are ill-equipped to identify certain forms of contract failure on a case-by-case basis. Rough justice consists in minimizing transaction costs by selecting rules and setting standards that will uphold welfare-enhancing agreements most of the time, while varying or setting aside agreements that are afflicted by more egregious forms of contract failure.

In this section, we identify the forms of contract failure that are commonly associated with family contracting. Family arrangements are interesting in part because they can implicate a complicated set of contracting problems. Before proceeding to set out the taxonomy of common contract failures, we briefly explain the normative terminology in which our discussion is cast.

A. Welfare and Autonomy

The principal normative measure that we employ in our analysis is utility or welfare as conventionally understood by economists. In our conceptual schema it is analytically true that preference satisfaction conduces to welfare maximization. For the purposes of our study it is necessary, however, to go beyond the economist's reliance on revealed preferences. As we elaborate below, cognitive incapacities may cause people to try to satisfy preferences that do not form part of a stable or coherent preference structure. This may be because the actor's immaturity or mental incompetence prevents her from having such a preference structure. It may also be because the actor has not reflected on her preferences in such a manner as to form a settled view about her own best interests and the extent to which those interests are bound up with the interests of others. In either case, where the preferences of an actor are not stable and coherent it cannot confidently be said that her choices are welfare enhancing. It is important to look both at the extent to which agreements satisfy the preferences of participants and at the quality of those preferences.

Autonomy is a second concept we use in assessing regulatory regimes. We distinguish internal from external autonomy.[29] Internal autonomy involves constraints on free action internal to the person. Cognitive incapacities such as immaturity and mental incompetence are commonly thought to limit the sense in which action can be said to be fully autonomous. A lack of internal autonomy might be described as an inability to act in a fully purposive manner; it might also be described by saying that the actor lacks a stable or coherent utility function.[30] Some people may even lack an independent utility function of any sort. Internal autonomy is not a quality that humans simply have; it is found

---

29. Compare A. Wertheimer, *Exploitation* (Princeton: Princeton University Press, 1996) at 64–65.
30. See discussions in Kronman, "Paternalism," *supra* note 19; Burrows, "Legal Paternalism," *supra* note 19; and Burrows, "Contract Discipline," *supra* note 7.

in differing degrees, and can be both damaged and fostered.[31] Internal autonomy is helpfully thought of as a continuum, with fully mature and thoughtful action at one end, and immature or mentally incompetent action at the other. The law must of course find a point on the continuum at which it is satisfied that action is sufficiently internally autonomous to be legally efficacious.

External autonomy is the freedom of the actor to do things in the world without impediment. It is an amalgam, embracing three relevant types of external constraint on free action.[32] A first type is lack of resources such as capital or information which can prevent an actor from freely realizing her life plans. A second constraint is laws backed by the coercive power of the state that curtail free action. Legal incapacities interfere with autonomy in this external sense. Specifically, the refusal of courts to uphold agreements made by certain types of actors (for example, dependent housewives) would interfere with their external autonomy. This second type of constraint overlaps with the first because a person's lack of resources may be perpetuated by state enforcement of property rights. That is to say, a person's lack of resources may be dependent upon the existence of coercive laws. A third constraint is private coercion which limits choice by imposing undesirable consequences on actions that would otherwise be preference satisfying. While each of these three types of constraint operates in a different manner upon the freedom of the actor to maximize his or her preference satisfaction, and while normative questions about their justified limits may differ, for the purposes of our analysis the three types are helpfully gathered together into the concept of external autonomy.

B. Forms of Contract Failure

In this section we taxonomize several forms of contract failure that are prevalent in the family setting. The causes of contract failure do not always yield to discrete classification. Often the same behaviour can give rise to more than one type of failure, or to different failures in different circumstances, that is to say, there is overlapping and shading. For example, physical or emotional abuse may have a direct coercive effect on a victimized spouse; abuse may also go beyond coercion and damage the abused spouse's psychological health to such an extent that he or she is unable to make considered and rational decisions even absent an immediate threat. The differences between the forms of contract failure that we identify are nonetheless significant and worth highlighting.

I. COGNITIVE INCAPACITY. Cognitive incapacity occurs whenever a person lacks the capacity to form a stable or coherent preference structure. Paradig-

---

31. See J. Nedelsky, "Reconceiving Autonomy" (1989) 1 Yale J. L. & Fem. 7.
32. A fourth type of external constraint that is not relevant for present purposes is actual physical barriers.

matic examples of cognitive incapacity are immaturity and mental incompetence. These conditions are conventionally recognized as preventing the actor from achieving the standard of internal autonomy the law expects of transactional participants. There is reason to doubt that an agreement entered into by a cognitively incapacitated actor will promote her welfare, and as such there is reason for the law to restrict her contractual freedom. Cases decided on the basis of undue influence often invoke notions of immaturity and mental incompetence to justify setting agreements aside, particularly where young persons or aging parents are participants.[33]

TEMPORARY DISTORTING STATES. Some cognitively distorting states are temporary. Powerful emotions, for example, may prevent a person from acting on a stable and coherent preference structure, and a person in a state of high emotion may be thought to be incapable of rationally deciding whether to enter into contractual relations. This may be the basis of laws requiring prospective marriage partners to wait a period of time after the issuance of a marriage licence before marrying as well as laws that require spouses on marriage break-up to remain separated for a minimum period before divorcing.[34] These laws are attempts to mute powerful passions that can cloud judgment. Impulsiveness, fatigue, excessive agitation, and intoxication are other temporarily distorting states.[35] Family financial arrangements are often made in emotionally charged circumstances. Particularly when family finances are in trouble and stress levels run high, the intimate relations that exist between spouses and between parents and children can give rise to ill-considered decisions. In the course of deciding whether to enforce family financial agreements courts have often noted the emotional state of participants at the time of execution.[36]

ABSENCE OF REFLECTION. A further and important head of cognitive incapacity is lack of reflection. People may have the intellectual resources needed to understand the nature and implications of a transaction, but nonetheless act against their best interests because they do not give their own preferences adequate thought. These decisions cannot be said to spring from stable and coherent preference structures. This is because the actor's preferences are not rooted in an appreciation of their identity and a durable life plan, and are consequently

---

33. For example, *Powell* v. *Powell* [1900] 1 Ch 243 [hereinafter *Powell*] (immaturity); *Canadian Kawasaki Motors Ltd* v. *McKenzie* (1981) 126 D. L. R. (3d) 253 (Ont Co Ct) [hereinafter *Kawasaki Motors*] (immaturity); *Contractors Bonding Ltd* v. *Snee* [1992] 2 N.Z.L.R. 157 (C.A.) [hereinafter *Snee*] (senility); *Geffen* v. *Goodman Estate* (1991) 81 D. L. R. (4th) 211 (SCC) [hereinafter *Geffen*] (mental illness).
34. Kronman, "Paternalism," *supra* note 19.
35. Compare J. Feinberg, *Harm to Self* (1986) at 113.
36. For example, *Morgan, supra* note 3; *Kawasaki Motors, supra* note 33; *Bank of Credit and Commerce International SA* v. *Aboody* [1992] 4 All ER 955 (CA) [hereinafter *Aboody*]; *Etridge, supra* note 4.

prone to being altered by relatively contingent influences. A recurrent theme in feminist analysis is that many women are conditioned to defer to the projects and needs of their parents, husbands, and children.[37] Not only are interdependent utility functions inculcated, but it is commonly said that women are encouraged not to give much thought to their own independent interests.[38] Parents are also prone to this form of contract failure in dealings with their children.[39] A failure to reflect on one's own interests must be distinguished in principle from deliberate and reflective altruism arising out of familial love. Altruism is not a form of contract failure. As we have noted, the designer of a legal regime governing family arrangements must contend with the practical difficulty faced by external evaluators in drawing this principled distinction.[40]

PSYCHOLOGICAL DAMAGE. A more insidious and hopefully less common form of cognitive incapacity observed in family life is the psychological damage that can be done by physical and emotional abuse. There has been considerable research into the psychological effects of spousal, child, and elder abuse.[41] It seems clear that abused persons may become incapable of evaluating their own preferences independently of the context of abuse, of imagining acts that might free them from that pattern of abuse, and of anticipating a life outside of that context.[42] Victims of abuse may also have a feeling of powerlessness that prompts them not to reflect on their preferences.[43] They may also come to experience themselves as increasingly dependent on the person who exerts control over them, this in turn causing heightened or continuing attachment and loyalty (a form of cognitive dissonance).[44] Severe distress, depression, and

---

37. See, for example, C. MacKinnon, *Feminism Unmodified: Discourses on Life and Law* (Cambridge, MaA: Harvard University Press, 1987) at 39; L. McClain, "'Atomistic Man' Revisited: Liberalism, Connection, and Feminist Jurisprudence" (1992) 65 Cal. L. Rev. 1171; G. Greer, *The Female Eunuch* (London: MacGibbon & Kee, 1970) at 149–152; J. S. Mill, *The Subjection of Women,* 2nd ed. (London: Longmans, Green, Reader, and Dyer, 1869).
38. *Bank of Montreal* v. *Stuart* [1911] A.C. 120 (PC-Canada) at 136–137 [hereinafter *Stuart*] is a striking example.
39. *MacKay* v. *Bank of Nova Scotia* (1994) 20 OR (3d) 698 (Gen. Div.) [hereinafter *Mackay*]; *Avon Finance Co Ltd* v. *Bridger* [1985] 2 All ER 281 (CA) [hereinafter *Avon Finance*]; *Lloyds Bank* v. *Bundy* [1975] 1 QB 326 (CA) [hereinafter *Bundy*].
40. See discussion at pages 53–54 above.
41. See M. A. Dutton, *Empowering and Healing the Battered Woman* (New York: Springer Pub. Co., 1992) at 51–71.
42. J. Blackman, *Intimate Violence: A Study of Injustice* (New York: Columbia University Press, 1989).
43. L. E. Walker, *The Battered Woman Syndrome* (New York: Springer Pub. Co., 1984); C. Peterson and M. Seligman, "Learned Helplessness and Victimization" (1983) 2 J. Soc. Issues 103; M. Seligman, *Helplessness: On Depression, Development and Death* (San Francisco: W. H. Freeman, 1975).
44. D. Dutton, *The Domestic Assault of Women* (Boston: Allyn and Bacon, 1988); D. Dutton & S. Painter, "Traumatic Bonding: The Development of Emotional Attachment in Battered Women and Other Relationships of Intermittent Abuse" (1981) 6 Victimology: Int'l J. 139; see also F. M. Ochberg, *Post-traumatic Therapy and Victims of Violence* (New York: Brunner/Mazel, 1988).

anger may preoccupy victims to such an extent that they are unable to function in basic social roles. Abuse-related difficulty in concentrating may prevent victims from bringing their minds to bear on complex financial affairs. These are judgment-impairing incapacities that reduce the internal autonomy of the victim and constitute a form of contract failure.

II. CHOICES THAT DO NOT REFLECT UNDERLYING PREFERENCES. Grounds for judicial contract regulation may exist where an actor has a stable and coherent preference structure but the choices that they make in particular circumstances are inconsistent with that structure. This inconsistency may be due to either coercion or information failure. Information failure consists in problems of either availability or processing ability.

COERCION. Coercion connotes force, but a moment of reflection tells us that coerced people generally comply willingly because of their alternatives. This, the focus of a normative theory of coercion should not be on the psychological state of the coerced person, but rather on the status of the decision she faces. A person's decision may be said to be coerced where it is structured by another person's threat to perform a wrongful or otherwise illegitimate act. The coerced person's decision to comply is determined by the risk of this illegitimate alternative. Absent the threat, the coerced person would have a more attractive third option. The question is, what sorts of choices are such that no one should have to make them? In *The Limits of Freedom of Contract,* one of us explores the philosophical debate about coercion, and we do not intend to revisit it here.[45] For reasons that will become clear, it is sufficient to observe that threatening to breach a contract may have a coercive effect if the contract cannot be effectively enforced.

Family relations are often characterized by both overt and covert coercion. In extreme circumstances family financial arrangements may be made under the explicit threat of immediate physical harm.[46] This is a classic duress scenario. More commonly perhaps, relationships may be underwritten by implicit threats of violence, perhaps made credible by periodic actualization.[47] Where this is so, the lack of an articulated threat of immediate violence if certain arrangements are not made does not detract from the operation of the threat on the decision faced by the threatened spouse, parent, or child. Psychological abuse may also be coercive, as the threat of harm may be no less real to the victim.[48] A pattern of violence supporting an implied threat of abuse or comparable

---

45. *Limits, supra* note 8 at c. 4.
46. *E & R Distributors* v. *Atlas Drywall Ltd* (1980) 118 D.L.R. (3d) 339 (B.C.C.A.).
47. *Bank of Nova Scotia* v. *MacLellan* (1980) 70 APR 596 (N.B.C.A.); *Farmers' Co-operative Executors & Trustees Ltd* v. *Perks* (1989) 52 S.A.S.R. 299 (S.C.); *Shoppers Trust Co* v. *Dynamic Homes Ltd* (1992) 10 O.R. (3d) 361 (Gen. Div).
48. *Aboody, supra* note 36.

psychological abuse may be coercive; as noted above, it may also go beyond coercion and strip the abused of her capacity to identify her own best interests.

The spousal relationship also can give rise to coercion of a more subtle but possibly more widespread variety. Where the well-being of a marriage is more important to one spouse than the other, the spouse for whom the relationship is less important can use it in bargaining to extract rents.[49] Consider a marriage characterized by a sharp division of labour. Assume that the wife is unable to achieve the level of financial well-being alone that she can in the marriage, while pursuing her other objectives, such as child rearing. The implicit marriage agreement might be summarized in this way: the husband will pursue a career and earn money for the benefit of the family; the husband will provide the wife with financial security in her old age; the wife will not pursue a career, but will work in the home caring for the husband and raising the couple's children. The wife is in the position of a first mover in this relationship and risks a defection strategy by the husband in later stages of the relationship which will typically impose greater costs on her than him.[50]

Husbands and wives in the basic family home fact pattern often have divergent interests. This point that has not always been appreciated by the courts.[51] Wives can be expected to have a greater aversion to financial risk because of the contingency of marriage breakdown. The most recent United States data suggest that after divorce the average standard of living of women declines by 27 percent and the standard of living of men rises by 10 percent.[52] This is largely due to the fact that during marriage it has been traditional for men to concentrate their energies on acquiring marketable human capital and for women to acquire less marketable homemaking and child rearing skills. The post-divorce financial security of many women is therefore more dependent on their interest in assets accumulated during the marriage than is the security of men. Married women who are concerned about their future well-being and alert to the possibility of marital breakdown will choose in light of this to invest their share of family assets more conservatively than their husbands will. The magnitude of this divergence of interests in any particular case depends on how stable the marriage is, taking into account the strains that financial crises may put the relationship under.[53] A further divergence of interests may occur where the husband operates the business venture in question and derives greater psychic benefits from it than his wife because his identity and self-esteem are more closely

49. See generally A. Wax, "Bargaining in the Shadow of the Market: Is There a Future for Egalitarian Marriage?" (1998) 84 Va. L. Rev. 509, especially at 544–551.
50. See N. Duclos, "Breaking the Dependency Circle: *The Family Law Act* Reconsidered" (1987) 45 U. Toronto Fac. L. Rev. 1; Trebilcock & Keshvani, *supra* note 21.
51. See *Aboody, supra* note 36; *Etridge, supra* note 4 at para. 23, but compare para. 25; *Akins* v. *National Australia Bank* (1994) 34 N.S.W.L.R. 155 (CA) at 173 [hereinafter *Akins*].
52. R. Peterson, "A Re-evaluation of the Economic Consequences of Divorce" (1996) 61 Am. Soc. Rev. 528.
53. *Sexually Transmitted Debt, supra* note 2.

bound up with the business's success. Empirical evidence gathered by Fehlberg confirms the reality of these divergences of interest. She notes a "distinction between entrepreneurial debtors and financially more cautious sureties."[54] Fehlberg found that female sureties tended to act out of motivations which prioritize economic and relationship preservation above any expectation of direct financial benefit from providing security; "sureties supported debtors out of loyalty, love and economic necessity, but generally expressed a preference for a lower but more reliable income."[55]

The fact that the husband captures most of the financial and psychic benefits if a family business succeeds but bears only half of the financial costs if it fails creates an agency cost problem. This is analogous to the agency costs of debt in a corporation where equity-holders derive all the upside gains from a risky investment while sharing the down-side losses with debt-holders, and to the agency costs of free cash flow where managers can employ uncommitted cash for purposes at variance with the interests of shareholders.[56] The husband in family home cases has a differential incentive to convert a specific asset into more liquid form.

Imagine then a traditional couple in middle life, the husband wishing to embark on a business venture that puts the family assets at substantial risk. The husband makes an explicit or implicit threat to leave his wife if she will not contribute her share of the family assets to the venture as security.[57] It is a credible threat for in the event of divorce the husband's standard of living may rise as he would no longer be responsible for supporting his wife into retirement. Taking into account the limited financial settlement she can expect in the event of divorce, the wife is faced with a coercive choice. She can refuse to participate in the venture and risk a divorce which would deprive her of the considerable financial and other benefits afforded by the marriage. Alternatively, she can choose to participate and place herself in a financial position that, while better than it would be in the event of divorce, is worse than the position she was in before the venture was proposed as her assets would now be invested less conservatively. Fehlberg found that "most sureties considered that by signing they could benefit to the extent that their pre-signing position would be maintained, both financially and in terms of the relationship. Most, however, viewed it as a neutral or negative benefit, because they were in effect sacrificing in order to maintain their pre-security position."[58] The pressure on the wife can be emotional

---

54. Ibid. at 267.   55. Ibid.
56. See M. Jensen and W. H. Meckling, "Theory of the Firm: Managerial Behaviour, Agency Costs and Ownership Structure" (1976) 3 J. Finan. Econ. 305; M. Jensen, "Agency Costs of Free Cash Flow, Corporate Finance and Takeovers" (1986) 76 Am. Econ. Rev. 323.
57. The threat was explicit in *Bank of Scotland* v. *Bennett* (English CA, 21 December 1998) [hereinafter *Bennett*] and in *Teachers Health Investments Pty Ltd* v. *Wynne* (1996) A.S.C. 56–356 (N.S.W.C.A.) [hereinafter *Teachers Health Investments*], to give two examples.
58. *Sexually Transmitted Debt, supra* note 2 at 188.

as well as financial because of the relatively low prospects of middle-aged women remarrying.[59] Lord Browne-Wilkinson observed that "the sexual and emotional ties between the parties provide a ready weapon for undue influence: a wife's true wishes can easily be overborne because of her fear of destroying or damaging the wider relationship between her and her husband if she opposes his wishes."[60] The reason that the choice in all of these cases is coercive is that the husband is in effect structuring it by the threat of a wrongful act. He is opportunistically threatening not to perform his second mover obligations under the implicit marriage agreement. These are obligations that the wife cannot effectively enforce.[61]

The prevalence of opportunistic breach in the marital setting has been noted before.[62] Our purpose here is to draw attention to the fact that its availability can enable husbands to structure coercive choices for their wives that are designed to extract financial benefits. In our view this basic fact pattern and variations on it are widespread and deserve serious attention.

INFORMATION FAILURE. Information failure occurs where a transactor either lacks information about a proposed arrangement or lacks the ability to process it. Information failure is a form of contract failure because agreements that are subject to it may not be Pareto superior. The best agreements made on the basis of limited information will differ systematically from agreements made on the basis of perfect information. By processing information we refer both to the comprehension of complex legal and business facts and to the sorting and sifting of alternatives that people perform in an effort to decide which arrangement will best satisfy their utility functions. The lack of an ability to process information is in a sense a form of incapacity, as some people lack the intellectual or experiential resources needed to synthesize and make sense of financial affairs. We treat this inability under the rubric of information failure rather than cognitive incapacity because we use that term in relation to preferences and preference structures. It is analytically and realistically possible that a person would be able to formulate and act on a stable and coherent preference structure, and so not have a cognitive incapacity, and yet not be able to appreciate the legal and financial implications of a mortgage or to identify which of a range of complex choices best satisfies their considered preferences.

Three primary types of information failure afflict family financial arrangements. First, parties may not understand the legal nature and effect of these transactions. This could be because they have been misled. A recent example is

59. See, for example, *Teachers Health Investments, supra* note 57; more generally, see Wax, *supra* note 49.
60. *Barclays Bank, supra* note 1 at 190–191.
61. See M. F. Brinig and S.M. Crafton, "Marriage and Opportunism" (1994) 23 J. Leg. Stud. 869.
62. L. Cohen, "Marriage, Divorce, and Quasi-Rents; Or I Gave Him the Best Years of My Life" (1987) 16 Leg. Stud. 267.

Barclays Bank plc v. *O'Brien*, where Mrs. O'Brien was misled by her husband about the extent of her liability under the guarantee that she signed.[63] Lord Browne-Wilkinson warned that the informality of business dealings between spouses raises a substantial risk that the husband has not accurately stated to the wife the nature of the liability she is undertaking, that is, that he has misrepresented the position, albeit negligently.[64] Alternately, the surety may have had the transaction explained to her but nonetheless lacks comprehension. Many of the reported cases involve sureties who speak English poorly or not at all, and who would therefore find legal details particularly impenetrable.[65] Alternatively, the surety may have made no effort to understand the transaction because she routinely delegates responsibility for her financial affairs to a spouse or a child.[66] Whatever the reason, if a proposed transaction is not properly understood by the actor, to that extent she will be unable to bring her mind to bear on whether or not the transaction accords with her utility function.

Second, information failure occurs when a party appreciates the nature and effect of a transaction, but is not aware of alternatives that might achieve her ends at a lower cost. This form of information failure influenced the Privy Council's advice in *Inche Noriah* v. *Shaik Allie Bin Omar,* a case involving an elderly woman who gave her entire wealth to her nephew.[67] Lord Hailsham emphasised that the woman's solicitor did not bring home to her mind "the fact that she could more prudently, and equally effectively, have benefited the donee without undue risk to herself by retaining the property in her own possession during her life and bestowing it upon him by her will."[68] In surety scenarios this form of information failure is salient because vulnerable sureties are often not involved in negotiations with lenders. All too often familial sureties are brought in once the details have been settled and faced with a choice of either signing or not.[69] This procedure supports the illusion that affairs cannot be structured in another manner that may be more accommodating of the interests of the vulnerable surety.

---

63. *O'Brien, supra* note 1; see also *Avon Finance, supra* note 39; *Kawasaki Motors, supra* note 33; *McKenzie* v. *Bank of Montreal* (1975) 55 D. L. R. (3d) 641 (Ont HC); *Cox* v. *Adams* (1904) 35 S. C. R. 393; *Cornish* v. *Midland Bank plc* [1988] 3 All E. R. 513 (C.A.); *Kingsnorth Trust Ltd* v. *Bell* [1986] 1 All E. R. 423 (C.A.); *Bank of Baroda* v. *Shah* [1988] 3 All E. R. 24 (C.A.).
64. *O'Brien, supra* note 1 at 196.
65. For example *Royal Bank* v. *Domingues* (1995) 21 B. L. R. (2d) 79 (Ont. Gen. Div.) [hereinafter *Domingues*]; *Bank of Baroda* v. *Rayarel* [1995] 2 F. L. R. 376 (C.A.) [hereinafter *Rayarel*].
66. For example *Akins, supra* note 51 at 166; *Aboody, supra* note 36; *Kawasaki Motors, supra* note 33.
67. *Inche Noriah* v. *Shaik Allie Bin Omar* [1929] A. C. 127 (PC-Singapore) [hereinafter *Inche Noriah*].
68. Ibid. at 136; see also *Powell, supra* note 33; *MacKay, supra* note 39; *Cheese* v. *Thomas* [1994] 1 All E. R. 34.
69. See discussions in *Etridge, supra* note 4 at para. 20; and in B. Fehlberg, "The Husband, The Bank, The Wife and her Signature" (1996) 56 Modern L. Rev. 675 [hereinafter "The Wife and her Signature"].

Third, information failure can consist in a lack of appreciation of business risks. It frequently happens that a spouse or aging parent has little knowledge of the viability of the business venture they are being asked to support. *Lloyds Bank* v. *Bundy* is a famous example of a court acting on concerns about this type of information failure. In the court's view Mr. Bundy agreed to secure his son's overdraft against his farm without any real understanding of the likelihood that this security would be called upon.[70]

IV. The Functions and Efficacy of Independent Advice

Independent advice is a major device the law uses to correct contract failure in family financial dealings. It is thought to be a salutary antidote for some of the forms of contract failure that commonly afflict these contracts. Independent advice most obviously serves an informational function in helping sureties to understand proposed transactions. Independent advice also can enhance the internal autonomy of sureties in helping them to exercise their judgment in a more careful and considered manner. Furthermore, under one possible legal regime the independent advisor could screen misconduct, effectively vetoing transactions thought to be afflicted by egregious contract failures. The law employs this device by conditioning the validity of suspect transactions on whether vulnerable participants are encouraged or required to meet with an independent advisor.

In this section, we review the functions that independent advice can perform, and assess its efficacy in correcting the forms of contract failure that often afflict family financial agreements. In practice the efficacy of independent advice in alleviating different contract failures depends on the detailed content of the advice and the circumstances in which it is given. These matters are examined in greater depth in Section V.d below. The present Section outlines and assesses the functions of advice at a general level.

A. *Information*

The most important function of independent advice consists in informing advisees of the nature and consequences of proposed financial arrangements. Requiring vulnerable transactors to become informed about proposed arrangements and realistic alternatives interferes minimally with their external autonomy, and may yield substantial welfare gains by optimizing financial arrangements. Not only does independent advice ensure that transactors will be in a superior position to evaluate the merits of agreements but it also prevents them from being misled by other family members. Independent advice may also prevent contract

---

70. *Bundy, supra* note 39; see also *Teachers Health Investments, supra* note 57; *Snee, supra* note 33; *Commercial Bank of Australia Ltd* v. *Amadio* (1983) 46 A. L. R. 402 (H.C.) [hereinafter *Amadio*]; *Royal Bank of Canada* v. *Hinds* (1978) 20 O. R. (2d) 613; *Buchanan* v.*CIBC* (1980) 125 D. L. R. (3d) 394 (B.C.C.A.).

failure arising out of an inability to process information. The delegation of financial decision-making responsibility within a family often occurs because the delegator lacks the intellectual or experiential resources needed to make sense of business affairs. Professional advisors should have the communication skills needed to reduce complicated legal and business matters to comprehensible basics. Independent advice can be expected therefore to correct for a substantial range of information availability and processing failures.

The emphasis in the leading cases is on independent *legal* advice. While it is certainly important that transactors understand the legal implications of their actions, it can be equally important for them to understand the financial implications of such actions. In *Lloyds Bank Ltd.* v. *Bundy,* the Court of Appeal held that Mr. Bundy should have received independent advice about the viability of his son's business before agreeing to commit his remaining property to it.[71] Their Lordships did not explain why his solicitor would be competent to give this advice. Although lawyers will often be more experienced in the business world than their non-specialist clients, they rarely have professional training in evaluating business risks. The assistance of an accountant or investment advisor may be more appropriate.[72] It must be borne in mind, however, that increasing the number of advisors consulted before transactions can be consummated increases the cost of those transactions.

B. Internal Autonomy Enhancement

Independent advice can enhance the internal autonomy of the advisee for the purposes of a proposed transaction. The advisor serves as a disinterested interlocutor who may help the advisee to sort through her own thoughts, options, emotions, and preferences. The advisor can assist her in overcoming certain forms of cognitive incapacity by challenging her assumptions and encouraging deliberation. An advisee who is provoked by a detached perspective may reach a more considered judgment.

The first type of incapacity that may be amenable to this treatment is emotional disturbance. An advisor can help a vulnerable transactor to regain an equilibrium where powerful emotions are leading her to execute an agreement or gift. Simply sitting down with a professional advisor may impress upon the advisee the seriousness of her affairs and encourage her to take a broader and more dispassionate view.

The second type of incapacity that may be ameliorated by independent advice is absence of reflection. In giving advice the lawyer takes on a role akin to that

---

71. *Bundy, supra* note 39.
72. Each of the justices in *Swindle* v. *Harrison* [1997] 4 All E. R. 705 (C.A.) noted that Mrs. Harrison did not receive independent advice on a loan transaction despite the fact that she was advised throughout by an accountant.

of a friend, guiding the advisee through her own thoughts and provoking changes of heart by asking difficult questions. Aristotle tells us that "with friends men are more able both to think and to act."[73] Jennifer Nedelsky's work illuminates the extent to which internal autonomy grows out of interactions with other persons.[74] Nedelsky urges us to look at the "social forms, relationships, and personal practices that foster [autonomy]"; she writes that "if we ask ourselves what actually enables people to be autonomous, the answer is not isolation, but relationships – with parents, teachers, friends, loved ones – that provide the support and guidance necessary for the development and experience of autonomy."[75] Legal advisors may enhance the internal autonomy of their clients by inviting them to emerge from the closed confines of their own cogitations and to engage in reasoned interaction.[76] Professional advisors are more and less able to serve as effective catalysts for reflection. The advice of trusted friends would often be more helpful, but not everyone has reliable and thoughtful friends. Housewives and the elderly are especially prone to social isolation.

C. Screening Contract Failure

Under a possible legal regime the independent advisor could have a role in blocking arrangements that are not Pareto superior. That is, the law could give the advisor a practical veto over proposed transactions, to be exercised when he believes the vulnerable advisee's participation is prompted by a salient contract failure. Farwell J. advocated this rule in *Powell* v. *Powell:*

> [I]t is not sufficient that the donor should have an independent advisor unless he acts on his advice. If this were not so, the same influence that produced the desire to make the settlement would produce disregard of the advice to refrain from executing it, and so defeat the rule; but the stronger the influence the greater the need for protection.[77]

A rule along these lines would effectively place advisees in the hands of their advisors. The exercise of any advisor veto would have to be tightly circumscribed because of the potential that would exist for interference with the external autonomy of advisees. Legal advisors may often recommend sub-optimal arrange-

---

73. Aristotle, *The Nichomachean Ethics,* trans. D. Ross (Oxford: Oxford University Press, 1980) at 192. See also C. Fried, "The Lawyer as Friend: The Moral Foundations of the Lawyer-Client Relation" (1976) 85 Yale Law J. 1060. In the course of articulating an ethical justification for favouring the interests of a particular client over those of other persons, Fried provocatively analogizes the role of the lawyer to that of a friend, and links this role to supporting the client's autonomy.
74. Nedelsky, *supra* note 31.   75. Ibid. at 12.
76. See also A. Kronman, *The Lost Lawyer: Failing Ideals of the Legal Profession* (Cambridge MA.: Harvard University Press, 1993).
77. *Powell, supra* note 33; see also *Etridge, supra* note 4; *Wright* v. *Carter* [1901] 1 Ch 27 [hereinafter *Wright*]; Richardson, *supra* note 7; Otto, *supra* note 7 at 826.

ments because they are not privy to the preferences of advisees. This rule is also infantilizing as it treats vulnerable transactors as wards of the legal system. Nonetheless, it might be argued that the impact of certain forms of contract failure is sufficiently egregious to justify interference in some cases.

D. Summary

It has sometimes been argued that independent advice is a formal gesture that does not address the deeper relationships of subordination that often characterize family life.[78] It is no doubt true that family financial arrangements can be afflicted by contract failures such as coercion that independent advice alone cannot correct. There are nonetheless real efficiencies to be gained through the provision of independent advice. First, it can remedy information failures, including both availability and processing problems. Second, independent advice may help advisees to overcome cognitive incapacities such as failures to reflect and temporary distorting emotional states. Independent advice can in this way enhance the internal autonomy of vulnerable actors and help them to exercise sounder judgment than they otherwise would.

V. Specifying the Gatekeeper Duties of Lenders

The law adopts a gatekeeper strategy by pressing lenders into service to protect vulnerable family members from exploitation. The essence of a gatekeeper strategy is to impose liability on a party who is not the cause of misconduct nor a primary beneficiary, but who is in a position to prevent wrongdoing by refusing cooperation or support.[79] Familiar examples of gatekeeper strategies include holding accountants and lawyers liable for the frauds of their clients, and holding taverns and social hosts liable for serving alcohol to impaired individuals who subsequently injure third parties. The law gives lenders a liability incentive to ensure that vulnerable sureties are not imposed upon by their relatives by invalidating a lender's security in the event that it was obtained by a tainted process. Lenders may be efficient detectors and correctors of some forms of contract failure because of their direct contractual relationship with potentially vulnerable transactors. This Section is concerned with the details and justification of such a strategy. As with all other enforcement strategies, the advisability of imposing gatekeeping duties on a particular relationship depends upon the balance between the strategy's efficacy in averting targeted conduct – for our purposes, contract failure – and its various costs. The emphasis falls on specifying the parameters of the gatekeeper's duties to avert anticipated contract failure at the lowest cost.

---

78. See, for example, Otto, *supra* note 7 at 826.
79. R. Kraakman, "Gatekeepers: The Anatomy of a Third-Party Enforcement Strategy" (1986) 2 J. L. Econ. & Organization 53.

In Section V.a, "Normative Criteria," we explain the considerations that weigh on either side of the balance in the context of the relationship between lenders and familial borrowers. In Section V.b, "Triggering Protective Measures," we discuss the factors that lenders should be alert for and that should trigger measures that protect vulnerable transactors. In Section V.c, "Immunizing the Lender's Security," we discuss the measures that should be taken once the trigger has been caught – measures that must be taken to immunize the lender's security. We discuss several possibilities, the most important of which are requiring lenders to recommend or insist that vulnerable transactors be independently advised. These possibilities are assessed in the light of the normative considerations described in Section V.a. In Section V.d, "Enhancing the Efficacy of Independent Advice," we look at ways in which the efficacy of independent advice in averting contract failure might be enhanced.

A. Normative Criteria

A socially optimal gatekeeping duty will be calibrated to achieve a welfare maximizing balance between the avoidance of contract failure and the costs of monitoring. As Lord Browne-Wilkinson observed in *Barclays Bank plc v. O'Brien,* our inclination to relieve vulnerable family members threatened with the loss of their homes at the suit of rich banks should not lead us to lose sight of the economic and social importance of credit being available to small businesses.[80] Highly interventionist gatekeeping duties may be expected to prevent a wide range of salient contract failures, but the cost may be overcorrection by blocking welfare-enhancing arrangements as well as excessive transaction costs. Similarly, timid gatekeeping duties may undercorrect by allowing harmful arrangements to be made that could be efficiently detected.

The conventional benefits of private ordering make out a *prima facie* case in favour of non-interference. Countervailing justification is needed for any legal rule that limits the external autonomy of willing contractors because lawmakers and legal administrators are not privy to the preferences and deliberations of the people they govern, and may consequently make sub-optimal decisions for them in many cases. This is an acute problem in the context of intimate relationships because it is difficult for someone external to the relationship to distinguish acts of genuine altruism from acts motivated by coercion or unreflective self-sacrifice. This is one argument against judicial review of the substantive fairness of family transactions.[81] People with sufficiently robust internal autonomy are efficient choosers of their own actions due to the privileged knowledge they have of their own interests and desires. A complementary argument against legal interference is that paternalistic laws can infantilize their

---

80. *O'Brien, supra* note 1 at 188.
81. See pages 53–54 above.

wards. The weight of this argument must not be underestimated as denial of the law's respect can lead to a damaging loss of self-respect.

Two types of distinctively paternalistic argument may justify a legal rule that limits the external autonomy of willing contractors. The first relates to internal autonomy. Paternalistic intervention may be justified where significant internal autonomy deficiencies are common in a particular transacting context if it can remedy those deficiencies. For example, statutory "cooling off" periods in consumer law following door-to-door sales may allow purchasers to regain their composure before being fixed with liability. These laws interfere with external autonomy by preventing purchasers from making immediate purchases. This restriction is thought to be justified by the fact that it leads consumers to make better decisions. In the family setting, a law requiring that a party wishing to enter a particular financial transaction be independently advised would restrict the external autonomy of that party by imposing a condition on the transaction she might not otherwise choose. One of the justifications of such a rule is that the advisor may enhance her internal autonomy and in so doing assist her in reaching a more considered decision.

The second paternalistic argument justifying intervention relates to the external autonomy of willing contractors. Freedom from legal incapacities may be counter-productive under conditions of coercion or information failure. Where the structure of a coercive choice forces a person to agree to unfavourable terms, a decision to override her freedom of contract may generate a better result. Similarly, a person who lacks critical information may make a choice that runs against her true preferences. John Stuart Mill famously wrote that preventing a person from crossing a bridge that she mistakenly believes to be safe is not a real interference with her autonomy.[82] Paternalistic intervention may lead to outcomes that the contractor would have chosen if she had not been coerced or ignorant of critical facts. In these circumstances paternalism is paradoxically respectful of true preferences and therefore utility maximizing.

The gatekeeper duty imposed on lenders can affect the cost of credit to many small businesses and so it is important that the duty be circumscribed with the highest possible degree of precision.[83] The cost of ambiguity will generally be passed on to borrowers as lenders incorporate a risk premium into their charges to cover contingent liabilities. At the limit this cost may be prohibitive. A second factor that affects the cost of credit are the transaction costs of a proposed gatekeeper duty. Lenders may generally be expected to pass along the costs of resources devoted to monitoring and detection activities. Similarly, an independent advice stipulation would impose non-trivial transaction costs on proposing contractors. For lower income transactors this cost could be particularly

---

82. *On Liberty, supra* note 9 at 89.
83. This point was emphasized by the English Court of Appeal in *Etridge, supra* note 4 at para. 42; compare *Massey* v. *Midland Bank plc* [1995] 1 All E.R. 929 at 934 (C.A.) [hereinafter *Massey*].

onerous.[84] Anecdotal evidence from Australia suggests that the costs of independent advice on guarantees ranges from \$A100 to \$A400.[85]

B. Triggering Protective Measures

Lenders ordinarily owe no duty to proffer explanations of proposed transactions or to recommend independent advice to persons, including family members, wishing to sign securities.[86] Arrangements that have an unusually high likelihood of being afflicted by contract failure fall outside of the ordinary course and lenders ought to be given incentives to screen for them. The lender's gatekeeper duty first requires it to determine whether in a given case there is a potential for serious contract failure. If there is then this ought to trigger protective measures designed to minimize that likelihood.

The definition of the trigger was set out with some care in *Barclays Bank plc* v. *O'Brien* and further refined in *Royal Bank of Scotland* v. *Etridge*.[87] According to these cases, whether the lender's concern should be triggered depends on whether it is aware of facts indicating a possibility that the surety's consent has been procured by illegitimate means. If the lender is actually aware that the borrower has exerted undue pressure or misrepresented material facts, or where a suspect relationship is coupled with a suspect transaction, the definition of the trigger as set out in the cases is met.[88] A relationship is suspect where the surety implicitly trusts the debtor and as such may be expected to have delegated financial decision making to them. Cohabitation should be taken as a presumptive signal that the surety ordinarily delegates decision making.[89] A transaction is suspect where it is "on its face not to the financial advantage" of the surety or where the lender knows that the true purpose of the loan is some benefit to the proposing family member alone.[90] A joint loan might be superficially beneficial to both parties but still engage the trigger because the lender knows that the true purpose was some benefit to the proposing debtor alone, such as payment of his personal debts.[91] The Court of Appeal held in *Royal Bank of*

---

84. See, for example, *MacKay, supra* note 39 (older woman declining independent advice on the ground of cost, being \$150–\$200; \$45, 000 security).
85. M. Sneddon, "Lenders and Independent Solicitors' Certificates for Guarantors and Borrowers: Risk Minimization or Loss Sharing?" (1996) 24 Aus. Bus. L. Rev. 5 at 34.
86. *O'Brien, supra* note 1 at 193; *Barclays Bank plc* v. *Khaira* [1992] 1 W. L. R. 623 at 637.
87. *O'Brien, supra* note 1 at 195–197; *Etridge, supra* note 4 at paras. 34–36.
88. There is an exception for certain relationships which are automatically suspect. These include the relationship between solicitor and client, and between medical advisor and patient. Special measures need to be taken in these cases regardless of whether the transaction is also suspect. The relationships between husband and wife, cohabitants, and parents and children are not automatically suspect, for "it cannot be said that every wife or cohabitee places implicit trust in her husband or partner, though many do." *Etridge, supra* note 4 at 719. The relationship between fiancé and fiancée is presumptively suspect: *Zamet* v. *Hyman* [1961] 1 W.L.R. 1442 (C.A.).
89. *Etridge, supra* note 4 at para 36.
90. *O'Brien, supra* note 1 at 196.
91. For example, *Allied Irish Bank plc* v. *Byrne* [1995] 2 F. L. R. 325 [hereinafter *Byrne*].

Scotland v. *Etridge* that the financial disadvantage test will only be met where "the transaction is so extravagantly improvident that it is difficult to explain in the absence of some impropriety".[92] In the typical case, "the transaction by which a wife is asked to provide a guarantee or collateral security for the debts of the business from which the family derives its income cannot be said to be extravagant or even necessarily improvident."[93] This is because the wife stands to gain from the business's success. Whether the trigger is caught depends upon facts known to the lender, and the lender has no business inquiring into the nature of the relationship between the parties or their motives.[94] For reasons that follow, the test articulated by the English Courts is too cautious and foregoes welfare gains in the efficient aversion of contract failure.

In practice the suspect relationship part of the *Barclays Bank plc* v. *O'Brien* trigger largely turns on whether the borrower and surety cohabit. If the borrower and surety cohabit, as virtually all spouses do, then this part of the trigger obtains regardless of whether the surety in fact ordinarily delegates financial decision making to the borrower. The *Barclays Bank plc* v. *O'Brien* trigger is over-inclusive as it bears on cohabitants for it would catch, amongst others, relationships between sophisticated partners who ordinarily take financial decisions together. The test is under-inclusive as it bears on non-cohabiting family relationships, such as the relation between parents and children or between siblings. Because the test depends on whether the lender actually knows facts indicating that the surety habitually reposes trust in the borrower in financial matters, and because the lender is said to have no business asking about the specific relation between the parties, very few non-cohabiting family relations will meet it, and then only accidentally. A deeper problem consists in the difficulty that lending officials face in identifying relationships that involve a sufficient degree of implicit trust. There is no bright line separating family sureties who habitually trust and those who do not habitually trust their husbands or children. Familial trust is a matter of degree and takes many forms. An external observer such as a lending official or a court is poorly positioned to discern the special dynamics of any particular family relationship. The *Barclays Bank plc* v. *O'Brien* test for suspect relationships is then insensitive and unworkably difficult to apply in many cases. These problems seem intractable and it would be simpler to rely on the suspect transactions part of the test alone.

The suspect transactions part of the *Barclays Bank plc* v. *O'Brien* test turns on whether the dealing is financially disadvantageous to the surety. This part of the test may be over-inclusive in one respect and is under-inclusive in another. The test may be over-inclusive by catching relatively small transactions that do not proportionally benefit the surety, imposing costly protective measures

---

92. *Etridge, supra* note 4 at para. 34.
93. Ibid. at para. 35.
94. *Banco Exterior Internacional SA* v. *Thomas* [1997] 1 All E. R. 46 (C.A.) [hereinafter *Thomas*].

on them. Although the risks of contract failure are the same in transactions involving small and large sums, liabilities that are small relative to the personal wealth of the vulnerable surety do not provoke the same depth of concern. The Court of Appeal appears to have been aiming to exclude relatively small transactions from the trigger in *Royal Bank of Scotland* v. *Etridge* when it described suspect transactions as those that are "extravagantly improvident."

The *Barclays Bank plc* v. *O'Brien* test is under-inclusive in that many transactions will be financially advantageous to the vulnerable surety on their face while the underlying reality is that the primary beneficiary is the proposing family member.[95] In the typical case finance is sought for a business primarily controlled by the husband proposing the loan. The surety spouse may be a shareholder or officer of the company.[96] The Court of Appeal held in *Royal Bank of Scotland* v. *Etridge* that in this typical case the surety spouse is benefited by the secured loan facilities. If the financed venture succeeds then the spouse shares in the augmented family wealth and may also benefit personally because of the increased value of the company's shares.[97] This view is rooted in two unstable assumptions. First, Fehlberg's empirical work suggests that when family businesses are successful husbands are more likely to be in a position to decide who will enjoy the fruits of success. Fehlberg concludes that:

> . . . the discretionary nature of surety benefit was revealed in cases where profit was being taken out of the business: debtors in practical terms controlled access and flow, and felt most comfortable about doing so, even where the surety was an officeholder (for example, a company director) in, or worked for, the family business. In fact, where businesses were profitable, families often lived modestly while profit was poured back into the business by debtors who were often described as having an emotional investment in the success of the enterprise which went beyond the welfare of the family.[98]

These findings weaken the assumption that family sureties benefit proportionally from business success. Second, where the investment payoff would benefit the family as a unit, the risks may nonetheless be greater than the vulnerable surety would rationally choose to bear. We have argued above that in light of the risk of family breakdown, family members with relatively fewer marketable skills should be more risk averse than family members more able to recover from the loss of assets.[99] Fehlberg's evidence supports this contention. She found that "sureties supported debtors out of loyalty, love and economic necessity, but generally expressed a preference for a lower but more reliable income."[100]

95. See Fehlberg, "The Wife and her Signature," *supra* note 69 at 473.
96. For example, *Aboody, supra* note 36 and *National Australia Bank Ltd* v. *Garcia* (N.S.W.C.A., 1996); *Nightingale Finance Ltd* v. *Scott* (Eng. Ch. D, 18 November 1997).
97. See *Etridge, supra* note 4 at para. 23; *Aboody, supra* note 36 at 966; see also *Akins, supra* note 51 at 174.
98. *Sexually Transmitted Debt, supra* note 2; see also Fehlberg, "The Wife and her Signature," *supra* note 69.
99. See discussion at pages 60–62 above.
100. Ibid.

While these arguments do not refute the proposition that family business investments generally benefit vulnerable sureties, they are sufficiently destabilizing that for the purposes of the trigger the presumption should be against surety benefit. The financial disadvantage specification in *Barclays Bank plc* v. *O'Brien* is in these respects superficial and formalistic. Suspect transactions should be those by virtue of which a surety commits a substantial proportion of her personal wealth either (a) in a transaction that is on its face not financially advantageous to her; (b) in a transaction the true purpose of which is not financially advantageous to her; or (c) as security for a business or investment largely controlled by the family member proposing the commitment. A transaction is financially disadvantageous to the surety on its face where she receives no direct and material quid pro quo. A burden falls on lenders to determine whether transactions are in fact disadvantageous in particular cases. Lenders should hold interviews with family sureties at which proposing family members are not present. At these interviews lenders should ask sureties (a) what proportion of their personal and family wealth is being committed to the venture; (b) what the true purposes of the loan are; (c) if the loan is being used for business purposes, what the surety's level of involvement in that business is.[101]

This specification of the trigger catches gifts and other transactions whereby the benefit, if any, to the vulnerable surety is some advantage to another family member, perhaps a child or a spouse. It does not interfere, however, with routine transactions that alter the pattern of a person's liabilities without substantially altering her liability-asset ratio,[102] and it does not interfere with transactions involving a relatively small proportion of the surety's wealth. This test does not catch joint loans on their face beneficial to both co-signors unless the lender becomes aware that the true purpose of the loan is primarily advantageous to only one of them. This result is consonant with the ruling in *CIBC Mortgages plc* v. *Pitt*.[103] Their Lordships there held that the lender was not fixed with constructive notice of wrongdoing where a joint loan was taken by a couple for the ostensible purpose of purchasing a recreational property when in fact and unknown to the lender the husband intended to use the proceeds for stock market speculations, which proved disastrous.

Two of the questions lenders would need to answer in order to determine whether the trigger has been caught are not susceptible to sharp definition. These are, first, whether a surety is committing a substantial proportion of her wealth to a venture, and second, whether she exercises significant control over the business for which finance is sought. Lenders may err on the side of caution in deciding to proceed as if the trigger has been caught. This trigger may be expected to generate higher transaction costs than the simple *Barclays Bank plc*

---

101. See *Goode Durante Administration* v. *Biddulph* [1994] 2 F. L. R. 551 at 554–555; but see *Equity and Law Life Assurance Society plc* v. *McGrath* (Eng. C.A., 9 May 1995).
102. See *Dunbar Bank plc* v. *Nadeem* [1998] 3 All E. R. 876 (C.A.).
103. *Pitt, supra* note 3; compare *Byrne, supra* note 91 at 350.

v. *O'Brien* test of facial financial disadvantage. This is because lenders may need to meet with family sureties even where dealings are ostensibly advantageous to them, and because protective measures would be required in a greater number of cases. In practice this may not generate many more costs because the facial financial disadvantage criterion will often be met and so the lender will not need to inquire into the true purposes of the loan nor the extent of the surety's involvement in the business. Some costs would be saved relative to the *Barclays Bank plc* v. *O'Brien* test by allowing relatively minor transactions to slip through the net. Whether any increased costs would be offset by efficiency gains in averting contract failure depends on one's judgment about the prevalence of risk in this context. In our view the *Barclays Bank plc* v. *O'Brien* test fails to take sufficient advantage of the lender's potential as a gatekeeper to detect and correct salient types of contract failure, most importantly information failure and forms of cognitive incapacity.

C. Immunizing the Lender's Security

Once the trigger is caught, the question becomes, what must a lender do to immunize its security? Immunization protects the lender's security from the risk of being invalidated on the basis that the surety's participation was prompted by a salient contract failure. A lender that fails to take adequate precautions will nonetheless be safe if the surety's participation was not actually tainted by contract failure. In legal terminology, the surety's right to avoid the security depends in part upon whether she was induced to sign by undue influence, unconscionability, or misrepresentation. In practice lenders should rarely hope to rely on this line of argument. As noted above, the husband and wife will often be the only witnesses to relevant events, and they will both have an interest *ex post* in exaggerating or misstating the indicia of contract failure.[104] A lender should also be safe if a potentially vulnerable surety approaches the lender through a lawyer, for the lawyer is then responsible for ensuring that the surety is adequately advised.[105]

There are a range of protective measures that the law could require lenders to adopt once the trigger has been caught. At one extreme lenders could be forbidden from proceeding on pain of risking their security. This rule would in effect require that any arrangement involving a vulnerable transactor be substantively fair and not for the purposes of a business controlled by the proposing debtor. In Section II, we explained why this rule must be rejected in the family setting. Family members display interdependent utility functions and there may be legitimate reasons why people willingly enter apparently one-sided transactions. This rule would also dramatically restrict the availability of loan finance

---

104. See discussion at pages 53–54 above.
105. *Rayarel, supra* note 65.

to family businesses. The other extreme would be to require no special protective measures, treating signatures as sacrosanct and enforcing any agreement regardless of the possibility of contract failure. This rule is crassly respectful of private ordering but fails to take advantage of the gatekeeping potential of lenders. Between these two unattractive poles lie several plausible measures. Each of these alternatives must be reviewed for under- or over-correction of contract failure with special attention paid to differences in likely transaction costs.

First, lenders could be obliged to ensure that vulnerable transactors understand the basic legal nature and effect of proposed arrangements by explaining these aspects in a separate interview, and to ensure that at the time documents are executed vulnerable transactors are not labouring under obviously apparent temporary cognitive incapacities such as emotional disturbance, intoxication, or distraction. The corrective potential of this measure is slight. It can be expected to overcome certain information failures, primarily failures to appreciate the legal nature and effect of transactions. However, because point of execution explanation will rarely be wide ranging, it may fail to correct for information processing problems that cause a lack of comprehension despite appreciation of key primary facts. Furthermore, the lender's explanation may not correct failures to understand the business risk of investments, which is a most important category of information failure.[106] The explanation offered by the lender cannot be expected to give the transactor a sense of her alternatives. As well, this measure holds out no possibility of correcting for cognitive incapacities other than temporary ones. A vulnerable transactor's internal autonomy will not be enhanced by a lender's explanation because the transactor will not be encouraged to deliberate in a detached manner. Vulnerable transactors can be expected to make judgments about their own interests and desires as poorly as they would absent the point of execution explanation. This measure is also unable to block coercion of any sort. An important reason why point of execution explanation can be expected to correct for such a small set of contract failures is that the lender is often in a conflict of interest position. The lender cannot be expected to provide an objective and assiduous explanation where it hopes to benefit from the proposed security arrangement. This condition will ordinarily hold when the security is being used to secure capital to revitalize an insolvent business.

Second, the lender could be fixed with the additional obligation of recommending to the vulnerable transactor that she seek independent advice. This approximates the law in England in cases where the facts known to the lender indicate that undue influence or misrepresentation is possible.[107] This measure

---

106. See, for example, *Bundy, supra* note 39; *Amadio, supra* note 70.
107. Where undue influence is probable, the validity of the lender's security depends in England on independent legal advice actually being taken: *O'Brien, supra* note 1 at 197; *Massey, supra* note 83; *Banco Exterior Internacional* v. *Mann* [1995] 1 All E. R. 936 (C.A.) [hereinafter *Mann*]; *Midland Bank plc* v. *Kidwai* (Eng. C.A., 28 April 1995) [hereinafter *Kidwai*]; J. R. F. Lehane, "Undue Influence, Misrepresentation and Third Parties" (1994) 110 L. Q. Rev. 167.

improves on the corrective potential of point of execution explanation by impressing on the vulnerable transactor the seriousness of the commitment that she is undertaking, and hopefully by raising the possibility that she may have interests implicated in the transaction that are distinct from the interests of the family member promoting the arrangement. Whether she has divergent interests is ultimately for the vulnerable transactor to determine; the recommendation will be beneficial if it encourages reflection along these lines. We are sympathetic to Burrows' criticism of this measure that "the way the recommendation is made can minimize the likelihood of the independent advice actually being sought, and when it is clear to the influential party that the other is not going to follow the 'recommendation' the way is open again for him to indulge in persuasion."[108]

Third, lenders could be required to insist that vulnerable transactors be independently advised by lawyers on the arrangements they are proposing to make. This rule was favoured by the Ontario Court – General Division in *Mackay* v. *Bank of Nova Scotia*.[109] This more interventionist measure holds out the possibility of correcting for contract failures that are not caught by the first measure discussed, and may not be caught by the second. The independent advisor is in a better position than a lending official to inform the vulnerable transactor about the elements of a proposed arrangement and to broaden her understanding. Good advice will also inform the transactor about the alternatives that are open to her, including possibilities that will achieve her perhaps altruistic ends while better protecting her personal financial position. If advice is based upon knowledge of the advisee's financial affairs and those of the family member proposing the transaction then it should also give them an awareness of the business risks they are undertaking. This is a function that explanation by a lender official cannot easily perform given the conflict of interest.[110] The advisor may also avert fraud or innocent misrepresentation by carefully examining and explaining the documents. Independent advice may also correct for some cognitive incapacities. Certainly most temporary incapacities such as high emotion or distraction would be addressed by a meeting with a professional advisor. More importantly, the advisor may enhance the surety's internal autonomy by engaging her in a deliberative dialogue about her reasons for assenting to a proposed arrangement and in examining the extent to which that arrangement can be expected to meet her goals. In requiring that advice be independent this measure promotes more candid and objective explanation and discussion.

---

108. Burrows, "Contract Discipline," *supra* note 7 at 140.
109. *MacKay, supra* note 39 at 709; but see *Domingues, supra* note 65. Several Canadian family law statutes governing separation agreements, which are afflicted by similar forms of contract failure to the family financial arrangements that we are studying, make independent legal advice a condition of their validity: see J. G. McLeod and A. A. Mamo, eds., *Annual Review of Family Law* (Toronto: Carswell, 1995) at 314.
110. *Kidwai, supra* note 107.

To be weighed against the value of independent advice in averting some of the foregoing varieties of contract failure are transaction costs in the form of professional fees. These fees would increase the cost of credit to many family-centred businesses, and would be particularly onerous to prospective low income transactors. In another way this third rule may not go far enough. Independent advice alone cannot be expected to alter the structure of a coercive choice. A coerced transactor may fully understand the proposed transaction, recognize that it does not meet her aspirations, but nonetheless be led into it by virtue of a wrongful threat that the advisor cannot prevent. A possible exception is the limiting case where the threat is to commit an overt crime or tort. If the advisee admits the threat to the advisor, the advisor may be able to recommend avenues of recourse. For instance, an abused spouse may be advised about the availability of women's shelters and about her rights under the law to a share in the matrimonial assets.

A variation on the second and third measures would be to recommend or insist additionally that willing transactors seek the advice of professional financial advisors.[111] As we noted in Section IV, in many cases it will be easier for the advisee to understand the nature of the legal liability they are proposing to accept than it will be for them to appreciate the transaction's risks. Financial advisors are better qualified than lawyers to determine whether a given business venture is likely to yield positive net returns, and to recommend alternative uses for capital. For this reason financial advisors may be better able than lawyers to alleviate certain forms of information failure. On the other hand, insisting that willing contractors seek financial as well as legal advice would impose a substantial additional cost on numerous transactions.

Fourth, lenders could be required to insist that vulnerable transactors be independently advised and that they not enter into arrangements they are advised against.[112] In *Royal Bank of Scotland* v. *Etridge,* the English Court of Appeal held that where a lawyer considers that his client is induced to stand as surety by an "improper influence" and that the transaction is not one she could "sensibly be advised to enter if free from such influence," he must advise her not to enter it.[113] If the client insists on proceeding then he must decline to act for her any further and must notify the other parties, including the lender, that he has given the proposing surety certain advice and that as a result he has ended the

---

111. Fehlberg argues that the law should force lenders to insist that vulnerable sureties obtain both legal and financial information on proposed transactions: *Sexually Transmitted Debt, supra* note 2 at 277. The Australian Law Reform Commission also has recommended that sureties receive both legal and financial advice: *Equality Before the Law: Women's Equality* (1994) Report No 69, Recommendation 13.4. See also A. Chandler, "Undue Influence and the Function of Independent Advice" (1995) 111 L. Q. Rev. 51 at 53; R. Hasson, "Darkness at Noon – A Comment on the Consumer Guarantee Law in Ontario" (1994) 11 B. F. L. R. 141; *Teachers Health Investments, supra* note 57.

112. See Section IV.c above.

113. *Etridge, supra* note 4 at para. 19.

retainer. Though the advisor must not tell the lender what the content of the advice was or his reason for ending the retainer, the lender should ordinarily infer that the proposed surety is ignoring warnings about the transaction. Stuart-Smith LJ wrote that "the bank cannot afford the risk of taking a security which it knows the wife's solicitor has advised her she should not take.[114]

On the one hand, a requirement that advice be both taken and followed would substantially interfere with the external autonomy of vulnerable family members as it effectively imposes a lawyer's view of their best interests on them. This point was emphasized by the English Court of Appeal in *Banco Exterior Internacional SA* v. *Thomas*.[115] As advisors are not privy to the surety's preferences they may over-correct by vetoing arrangements participants legitimately judge to best satisfy their utility functions (including altruistic motivations). On the other hand, this measure may reduce the incidence of cognitive incapacity as well as the likelihood of information failure. It would also protect vulnerable family members from coercion. Threats are futile where the ultimate decision lies with the advisor. In particular, the opportunistic threat of divorce if the other spouse does not commit her resources to an imprudent venture would be neutralized. If a wife is legally unable to commit her personal wealth as security to finance a venture proposed by her husband, he will have no reason to ask her to do so.

On balance we favour the third alternative, a requirement of independent legal advice but not that it be followed. The first and second alternatives fail in our view to take sufficient advantage of the potential of independent advice to correct for common forms of contract failure in the family setting. We judge the increased transaction costs associated with an independent advice stipulation to be outweighed by the reduction of important forms of information failure and cognitive incapacity. In this we go beyond the rule established by the House of Lords in *Barclays Bank plc* v. *O'Brien,* which only requires that lenders insist on independent advice in exceptional cases.[116] The rule that we propose is instead in line with the position taken by the Ontario Court – General Division in *MacKay* v. *Bank of Nova Scotia*.[117] The fourth alternative would be attractive if error costs were zero, but in practice the risk of over-correction is probably too high. The scope of a veto rule would have to be restricted to cases of coercion, prior abuse and extreme forms of unreflective altruism in order to minimize this effect. These categories are not susceptible to bright line definition and so there would be major uncertainties in the operation of a veto rule. These uncertainties would translate into higher risk premiums and greater transaction

114. Ibid. at para. 20; see also Richardson, *supra* note 7.
115. See *Thomas, supra* note 94.
116. *O'Brien, supra* note 1. It is worth noting that while the *Barclays Bank* v. *O'Brien* rule only requires lenders to recommend independent advice in most cases, the risk is such that in practice many lenders routinely insist that advice be taken: *Etridge, supra* note 4.
117. *Mackay, supra* note 39.

costs. Under our proposed rule a transaction would be immunized from challenge on this basis once independent legal advice has been obtained whether the advice is followed or not. With the assistance of an advisor people should be free to arbitrate their own preferences.

In our assessment lenders should not be required to insist that sureties obtain both legal and financial advice.[118] Credit availability is not only in the greater social interest, but also in the interests of families that need capital in order to realize their mutual and several life plans. Families whose primary human assets are business skills may find it difficult to take advantage of them without affordable credit. These benefits accrue to dependent wives as well as to entrepreneurial husbands, though not always in the same proportion. The cost of credit is an impediment to the external autonomy of vulnerable transactors that must be given due weight. In complex cases the legal advisor may recommend that a proposing surety take separate financial advice, but it should be their decision whether to follow that suggestion.

D. Enhancing the Efficacy of Independent Advice

While we do not consider that it would be efficient to insist that vulnerable sureties receive both legal and financial advice, greater attention to the quality of the advice that is given may yield real gains. Advice is too often given in a manner that fails to capitalize on its potential to correct salient contract failures. Stuart-Smith L.J. lamented the practices of the United Kingdom banking industry in *Royal Bank of Scotland* v. *Etridge:*

> The advice which the wife has received has often been perfunctory, limited to an explanation of the documents and yet inadequate to dispel her misunderstanding of the real extent of the liability which she is undertaking, and not directed to ensure that she was entering into the transaction of her own free will rather than the result of illegitimate pressure from her husband or blind trust.[119]

This passage shows the Court of Appeal's sensitivity to the potential of independent advice both to correct information failure and to enhance internal autonomy. In order to ensure that independent advice is as efficacious as possible, certain standards and rules should be in place to ensure that legal advice is efficacious.

First, lenders should be under a duty to disclose to advisors any information they have about the financial status and viability of business ventures in respect of which security is sought.[120] While legal advisors often lack the specialized skills needed to assess complex business risks, experienced counsel should be

---

118. Contrast Fehlberg, "The Wife and her Signature," *supra* note 69.
119. *Etridge, supra* note 4 at para. 3.
120. See *Sexually Transmitted Debt, supra* note 2 at 277.

able to spot outlier transactions, especially in the relatively straightforward small business transactions that are typically involved in these cases.[121] If the matter is complicated the lawyer should consider recommending that the surety take independent financial advice.[122]

Second, advisors should attempt to engage vulnerable sureties in cooperative deliberation about their preferences and hopes for transactions. Advisors should express opinions about whether or not sureties should sign. Advisors should be particularly careful to bring home to sureties the consequences for them of business failure in the event of family breakdown.

Third, advisors should discuss alternative arrangements with proposing sureties, encouraging them to negotiate with proposing borrowers and lenders for an arrangement that they are more comfortable with. Sureties are often brought into deals after they have been negotiated, and faced with a stark choice of either signing or not.[123] Advisors should communicate to them the fact that their participation is sufficiently important that these other parties might be willing to adjust arrangements to accommodate the surety's interests.[124] Stuart-Smith L.J. in *Royal Bank of Scotland* v. *Etridge* wrote that the advisor

... should not assume that the bank's request is on a 'take it or leave it' basis, or that it has an impregnable negotiating position. In fact, its position vis-a-vis the wife is relatively weak, since (i) she is not obliged to give security (ii) any security is better than none and (iii) the bank cannot afford the risk of taking a security which it knows the wife's solicitor has advised her she should not give.[125]

Fourth, the interview should not be attended by the proposing borrower or any representative of the lender.

Fifth, where possible surety agreements should not be executed, for example, for one week after advice is given. This would allow sureties to "cool off" if need be and to reflect on the advice they have received. This should bolster the internal autonomy enhancement function of independent advice. Exceptions may need to be made in emergencies, but the heightened pressure on the surety in these situations would highlight the lawyer's responsibility to give a thorough and careful explanation.

Sixth, legal advisors should meet a high standard of independence.[126] Vulnerable sureties should not be advised by the proposing borrower's lawyer nor by his partners. The possibility of marital breakdown, especially in view of the strains a financial crisis may add to the relationship, means that there will al-

---

121. For example, *Teachers Health Investments, supra* note 57.
122. *Etridge, supra* note 4 at para. 25
123. Fehlberg, "The Wife and her Signature," *supra* note 69.
124. See *Credit Lyonnais Bank Nederland NV* v. *Burch* [1997] 1 All E. R. 144.
125. *Etridge, supra* note 4.
126. See *Bertolo* v. *Bank of Montreal* (1986) 57 O. R. (2d) 577 (C.A.) [hereinafter *Bertolo*]; *Guardian Assurance plc* v. *Burbridge* (Eng. C.A., 31 July 1995) [hereinafter *Burbridge*]; *Byrne, supra* note 91; *Massey, supra* note 83; *Mann, supra* note 107; *Rayarel, supra* note 65.

most always be a potential conflict of interest between the husband and wife.[127] Advice should also not be given by the lender's lawyer or a "tame" lawyer whose practice substantially consists in servicing the clients of the lender and who depends on the lender's goodwill for continued business. There can be no objection, though, to the surety's lawyer's being instructed by the lender to perform routine tasks associated with the transaction such as checking title.[128]

Meeting these six criteria will necessarily drive up the cost of advice and thus the real cost of credit, but in our judgment this increase should be offset by efficient gains in the aversion of contract failure. If advice is effectively to alleviate information failure and enhance internal autonomy, safeguards must be in place to ensure that it is more than a hollow gesture. It is more important for vulnerable advisees to receive quality advice from one advisor than thumbnail advice from two. A final point needs to be made about the consequences of advice not meeting these standards. Defective advice should not ordinarily afford the surety a basis for setting aside the lender's security.[129] The lender's security should be immune once a lawyer has certified that independent advice has been taken. Attributing the lawyer's failings to the lender would generate unacceptable uncertainty, and the surety has recourse against the solicitor in a negligence suit.

VI. Conclusion: The Scope and Limits of Legal Paternalism

The sample is certainly skewed, but reading the large volume of reported cases and reviewing the empirical evidence it is tempting (but no doubt unjustified) to conclude that vulnerable sureties are systematically deprived of their personal wealth by a conspiracy of self-interested family members and studiously inattentive lenders. Contract failure is nevertheless prevalent in intimate relationships because of the trust that family communality engenders and because of economic and emotional dependence. Family trust often leads wives and elderly parents to delegate financial decision-making to other family members, who may not give their interests sufficient weight. Because they often do not understand the details of loan transactions nor the risks they entail, and because they are rarely involved in negotiations, vulnerable sureties find themselves unable to assess independently whether proposed agreements promote their own best interests. In more extreme cases vulnerable sureties are economically and

---

127. Compare *Etridge, supra* note 4 at para. 24.
128. See, for example, *Halifax Mortgage Services* v. *Stepsky* [1996] Ch 207 (C.A.); *Midland Bank* v. *Serter* [1995] 1 F. L. R. 1034 (C.A.) [hereinafter *Serter*]; *Barclays Bank plc* v. *Thompson* [1997] 4 All E. R. 816 (C.A.).
129. *National Bank of Abu Dhabi* v. *Mohamed* (Eng. C.A., 21 March 1997); *Serter, supra* note 128; *Barclays Bank* v. *Thompson, supra* note 128. There is an exception where the lender knew that the advising solicitor would not appreciate critical features of the transaction: for example, *Northern Rock Building Society* v. *Archer* (Eng. C.A., 31 July 1998).

emotionally pressured to take risks that they should eschew. In the event of family breakdown, which has a heightened likelihood of occurring in the wake of business failure, vulnerable sureties find that their personal wealth has been depleted and that they are fixed with the consequences of these risks materializing. Vulnerable sureties tragically tend to have less of the human capital needed to regain financial security than the family members who have led them into the position of financial risk.

There has been considerable interest over the past fifteen years in the possibility of using contract law to temper some of the inequalities that give rise to contract failures in the family financial setting. Before this period the gatekeeping duties of lenders were relatively circumscribed. The prevailing view was that people ought to be responsible for their own signatures. Banking law was thought to hold little potential for addressing deeper imbalances between men and women. Family sureties differ from the ideal model of arm's length responsibility imagined by classical contract law, however, and in the 1980s the courts began to see that lender gatekeeper duties might be efficiently expanded. The decision in *Barclays Bank plc* v. *O'Brien* effected a significant shift in this direction.[130] The House of Lords mandated procedural protections designed to minimize the incidence of certain common information failures and cognitive incapacities. Other commentators have since urged even more paternalistic and onerous lending procedures. There are, however, important limits to the scope of paternalistic regulation in this context. The benefits of procedural protection need to be balanced against the increased cost of finance that those protections entail. The cost of credit is an important constraint on the external autonomy of vulnerable contractors because it can impede them in the realization of their life plans, both as individuals and as families. More onerous lending procedures, such as advisor vetos of proposed transactions that are not thought to be in the interests of advisees, may block genuinely welfare-enhancing transactions.

We have concluded that there is greater scope for efficient paternalistic aversion of contract failure in this context that has commonly been thought by the courts. The procedures mandated by *Barclay Bank plc* v. *O'Brien* constitute an improvement over previous practice, but explanations by lender officials have limited efficacy in correcting for common information failures and cannot be expected to enhance the internal autonomy of vulnerable sureties. Where the six criteria that we have set out in Section V.d are met, the advice of an independent lawyer has a much greater likelihood of alleviating information failures, particularly failures to appreciate the nature and risks of transactions and failures to consider alternatives, and holds out the possibility of appreciably enhancing the internal autonomy of advisees. Vulnerable sureties who have had the benefit of advice should be better at deciding whether proposed transactions

---

130. *O'Brien, supra* note 1; on previous English banking practice, see *Sexually Transmitted Debt, supra* note 2 at pp. 206–209.

accord with their utility functions. This in turn increases the likelihood that resulting transactions will be Pareto superior. While insisting that independent advice be obtained in a substantial number of cases will increase the cost of credit for family businesses, we judge the prevalence of contract failure in this setting to be such that the efficiency gains of paternalism offset these costs.

While our study has found that there is a greater scope for efficient paternalistic intervention in family financial dealings than is sometimes thought, it has also clarified the limits of efficient intervention. Contract law is not institutionally suited to resolving some of the underlying inequalities that give rise to contract failure in this setting. Coercion is a notable difficulty. Independent advice cannot be expected to prevent vulnerable transactors from entering surety agreements where they are pressured to do so either by physical threats or by threats of economically and emotionally harmful abandonment. A vulnerable transactor might fully understand her position and the proposed transaction, recognize that it runs against her best interests, and still rationally choose to comply because of the coercive alternative. Similarly, a propensity to unreflective self-sacrifice may not yield to the cooperative deliberation that an independent advisor should try to provoke. Family members may legitimately undertake onerous obligations out of family altruism, but the same result may be illegitimately caused by an unreflective failure to consider and promote their own interests. The tools of contract law and banking regulation are inadequate to the task of counteracting the causes of coercion and of unreflective self-sacrifice.

Extra-contractual policy instruments may be better suited to reducing the prevalence of contract failure in the family context. Family law reform may be an appropriate response to the extent that divergences of interest and hence of risk preference caused by the possibility of family breakdown are a source of agency costs in committing jointly owned family assets to secure the indebtedness of a family business. Equal division in the event of divorce of all business assets acquired both before and during the marriage would better align the interests of wives and husbands in decisions to commit family assets to business investments. It would do so by enhancing the sharing of upside as well as downside risks, although it would raise its own set of problems. Putting these problems aside, unequal distribution of returns during marriage, the frequent divergence between husband and wife in the psychic returns of family businesses, and the differential market value of their human rather than financial capital and remarriage prospects may still yield a real difference in their risk aversion. These difficulties would leave the agency cost problem to some extent unresolved.[131] Family law reform might also favour alimony awards designed to compensate the wife for the opportunity costs of marriage in the form of her reduced labour market prospects.[132] Other extra-contractual avenues of reform

131. See Wax, *supra* note 49.
132. See discussions in Trebilcock and Keshvani, *supra* note 21; E. Scott and R. Scott, "Marriage

might include a variety of social policy measures intended to reduce the economic dependence of women on male breadwinners. Economically independent women are more able to escape from abusive relationships and to resist threats of abandonment. They may also be less prone to the emotional dependence that can induce unreflective compliance. A further avenue might be public education about the risks of family financial arrangements. Public education should encourage caution and involvement in family affairs.[133]

There are also lessons to be drawn from this study about the scope and limits of the economic analysis of law. Neo-classical economic analysis is often criticized for its reliance on revealed preferences. Liberal confidence in the veracity of revealed preferences is a principal support of a more general confidence in the efficiency of free contracting. Choices do not always reflect underlying preferences, however, and at other times the preferences reflected in choices are suspect. A theory of efficient contracting entails a theory of contract breakdown, and consequently an account of legal paternalism. Relatively few economists have examined this necessary corollary to the positive theory of the free market. An economic theory of legal paternalism justifies public interferences with private ordering by their capacity to prevent or rectify inefficient contracting. Paternalistic analysis starts by identifying the forms of contract failure that prevail in a given transactional setting, and moves to designing legal rules that efficiently respond to these shortcomings.

Economic analysis brings two principal strengths to bear on the study of complex contracting problems. First, it assists in drawing out the pathologies of contract failure. The economic method leads its practitioner to disagreggate the infirmities afflicting transactions of any particular variety, mapping and sorting the contract failures that motivate legal regulation. Legal decisions in the family contracting area rarely distinguish the types of information failure we identify, nor do they demonstrate an appreciation of the subtle forms of coercion that characterize family life. Careful disagreggation of these contract failures is a necessary first step in designing a responsive regulatory scheme.

Economic analysis has a second strength, in assisting evaluation of regulatory prescriptions for identified transactional infirmities. In tandem with empirical assessment and normative judgment, economic analysis assists us in comparing and choosing between possible legal rules. As a corollary, economic analysis helps us to appreciate the institutional limits of contract law in redressing inequality and in protecting vulnerable contractors. While other nor-

---

as Relational Contract" (1998) 84 Va. L. Rev. 1225; E. Scott and R. Scott, " A Contract Theory of Marriage," in F. H. Buckley, ed., *The Fall and Rise of Freedom of Contract* Durham N.C.: Duke University Press, 1999).

133. B. Fehlberg advocates public education about the dangers of family surety arrangements in "The Wife and her Signature," *supra* note 69. She notes that such a campaign has been conducted in Australia by the Consumer Credit Legal Service.

mative perspectives must be given their due, the contracting failure and transaction cost concepts comprise a sophisticated evaluative framework.

These strengths of economic analysis highlight its own limits, one of which is its narrowly utilitarian moral foundation. Welfare values need to be supplemented by considerations of equality and autonomy. Few would argue that the economic approach contains the moral resources needed to plot a comprehensive system of laws. However, even with respect to non-utilitarian values, economic analysis can helpfully illuminate the choice of instrument in attempting to vindicate those values. Economic analysis leads its practitioner to probe whether a given instrument in fact advances these values and at what private and social costs, so that trade-offs between values and instruments can be more rigorously specified.[134]

134. We are indebted to Richard Craswell, Alan Wertheimer, Belinda Fehlberg, Megan Richardson, Rick Bigwood, Tony Duggan, Amy Wax, Clay Gillette, George Triantis, Michelle Oliver, Martin Zelder, and participants at the Australian Law and Economics Association Annual Conference, May, 1996, the Canadian Law and Economics Association Annual Conference, September 1996, and a Faculty Workshop at the University of Virginia Law School, September 1996, for helpful comments on earlier drafts of this paper.

3

Promises and Contracts

T. M. SCANLON

I. Introduction

The similarity between a promise and a contract is so obvious that it is natural to suppose that there is much to be learned about one of these notions by studying the other, or even that the legal notion of a contract can be understood by seeing it as based on the moral idea of a promise.[1] This article will examine some of the similarities between these two notions. These similarities are due to the fact that contract and promise arise in response to, and are consequently shaped by, some of the same underlying values. They are in this respect parallel ideas. But they respond to these values in different ways and are independent notions, neither of which is properly seen as based on the other.

The law of contracts is clearly a social institution, backed by the coercive power of the state and subject to modification through judicial decisions and legislative enactments. Promising is also often seen as a social institution of a more informal kind, defined by certain rules which are not enacted but rather backed by moral argument and enforced through the informal sanction of moral disapproval. Many have argued that the wrong involved in breaking a promise depends essentially on the existence of a social practice of this kind. Hume,[2] for example, maintains that fidelity to promises is "an artificial virtue," dependent on the existence of a convention of keeping agreements, and other accounts of this kind have been advanced in our own day by Rawls[3] and others.

These analyses do not seem to me to be convincing. I do not doubt that there is such a thing as a social practice of promising, which consists in the fact that people accept certain norms, which they often invoke by using the words "I promise." I do not believe, however, that either the obligation generated by a

---

1. As suggested by Charles Fried in C. Fried, *Contract as Promise: A Theory of Contractual Obligation* (Cambridge, Mass: Harvard University Press, 1981).
2. In D. Hume, *A Treatise of Human Nature,* ed. by L. A. Selby-Bigge (Oxford: Clarendon Press, 1960) at Book III, Pt. II, Ch. V.
3. See J. Rawls, *A Theory of Justice* (Cambridge, MA: Harvard University Press, 1971) at 344–350.

promise or the wrong involved in breaking one depends on the existence of this practice. I will argue that the wrong of breaking a promise and the wrong of making a lying promise are instances of a more general family of moral wrongs which are not concerned with social practices but rather with what we owe to other people when we have led them to form expectations about our future conduct.[4] Social practices of agreement-making, when they exist, may provide the means for creating such expectations, and hence for committing such wrongs. But I will argue that these practices play no essential role in explaining why these actions are wrongs.

In Section II, I will present some examples of one class of wrongs that I have in mind, formulate principles that would explain why they are wrongs, and argue for the validity of these principles within the contractualist account of right and wrong that I have defended elsewhere.[5] These principles all deal, in one way or another, with one's responsibility for harms that others suffer as a result of relying on expectations one has led them to form about one's future conduct. The task of Section III is to extend these principles to one that explains the obligation to keep a promise. In Section IV, I will take up the question of the moral permissibility of laws that enforce obligations of the kind that these principles describe. The two main questions to be addressed here are, first, the relation between the existence of a moral obligation and the moral justifiability of laws that require those who violate this obligation to compensate those to whom it was owed, and, second, the justifiability of requiring those who violate a contract to

4. Neil MacCormick expressed similar misgivings in N. MacCormick, "Voluntary Obligations and Normative Powers I" (1972) 46 (Supp. Vol.) Proc. Aristotelian Soc'y 59. He goes on to offer an account based on a general obligation not to disappoint the expectations of others whom we have knowingly induced to rely upon us (ibid. at 68). I will set out the moral foundations of a similar account that I hope will avoid objections such as those raised by Joseph Raz in his contribution to that same symposium ("Voluntary Obligations and Normative Powers II" (1972) 46 (Supp. Vol.) Proc. Aristotelian Soc'y 79) and in J. Raz, "Promises and Obligations" in P. M. S. Hacker and J. Raz, eds., *Law, Morality and Society: Essays in Honour of H. L. A. Hart* (Oxford: Oxford University Press, 1977) 210. In the latter article, Raz distinguishes between the "intention" conception of promises, according to which the essence of a promise lies in the communication, under the proper circumstances, of a firm intention to act in a certain way, and the "obligation" conception, according to which the essence of a promise lies in the intention to undertake, by that very act of communication, an obligation to perform a certain action. In my view, which lies in the common ground between MacCormick's account and Raz's, the elements of intention and obligation are interdependent: promises are distinguished by the fact that the intention expressed is supposed to be made credible by appeal to a shared conception of obligation, but the grounds of this obligation lie in a principle very close to the one which MacCormick states. Judith Thomson presents an account of promises that is similar to mine in Chapter 12 of J. Thomson, *The Realm of Rights* (Cambridge, MA: Harvard University Press, 1990).
5. In T. Scanlon, "Contractualism and Utilitarianism," in A. Sen and Bernard Williams, eds., *Utilitarianism and Beyond* (Cambridge: Cambridge University Press, 1982) 103, and in T. Scanlon, *What We Owe to Each Other* (Cambridge, MA: Harvard University Press, 1998). This account is commonly called "contractualist" because of its appeal to the idea of people trying to reach agreement on standards of conduct. But since it does not rely on the idea that there is an obligation to keep the agreements one has entered into, it does not presuppose a notion of contract that would make it viciously circular for present purposes.

pay "expectation damages." Finally, in Section V, I will consider how the requirement that a valid promise or contract must be voluntary arises and is justified within the moral framework I am employing.

II. Manipulation and Regard for Expectations[6]

As a first step toward understanding the morality of promising let me consider the wrong of making a "lying promise" – a promise that one has no intention of fulfilling. I maintain that this is a instance of a more general class of wrongs that do not depend on the existence of a social institution of promising and need not involve the making of a promise at all. Consider the following examples.

Suppose that you and I are farmers who own adjacent pieces of land, and that I would like to get you to help me build up the banks of the stream that runs through my property in order to prevent it from overflowing each spring. I could get you to help me by leading you to believe that if you help me then I will help you build up the banks of *your* stream. There are several ways I might do this. First, I might persuade you that if my stream is kept within its banks, then it will be worth my while to see to it that yours is too, because the runoff from the flooding of your field will then be the only obstacle to profitable planting of mine. If my stream were contained, then, simply as *homo economicus,* I would have sufficient reason to help you build up the banks of your stream. Alternatively, I might lead you to believe that I am a very sentimental person and that I would be so touched by your neighborly willingness to help me that I would be eager to respond in kind, both out of gratitude and out of a desire to keep alive that wonderful spirit of neighborly solidarity. A third alternative would be to persuade you that I am a devoted member of the Sacred Brotherhood of Reindeer, and then say, "I swear to you on my honor as a Reindeer that if you help me with my stream I will help you with yours." (It is assumed here that you are not yourself a Reindeer, and it is left open whether I am or not and whether the Sacred Brotherhood of Reindeer even exists.) Fourth, and finally, having led you to believe that I am a stern Kantian moralist, I might offer you a solemn promise that if you help me, I will help you in return.

Assume for the moment that in all of these cases my intentions are purely cynical. My only concern is how to get you to help me, and I have no intention of helping you in return. Given this assumption, it seems to me that these four cases involve exactly the same wrong, which I will refer to as "unjustified manipulation." The principle forbidding it might be stated as follows.

Principle M: In the absence of special justification, it is not permissible for one person, *A,* in order to get another person, *B,* to do some act, *X* (which *A* wants *B* to do and which

---

6. Most of what I say in this section and the next is taken, with a few significant changes, from T. Scanlon "Promises and Practices" (1990) 19 Phil. & Pub. Aff. 199.

B is morally free to do or not do but would otherwise not do) to lead *B* to expect that if he or she does *X* then *A* will do *Y* (which *B* wants but believes that *A* will otherwise not do) when in fact *A* has no intention of doing *Y* if *B* does *X*, and *A* can reasonably foresee that *B* will suffer significant loss if he or she does *X* and *A* does not reciprocate by doing Y.

I take this to be a valid moral principle; that is to say, a correct statement about which acts are wrong. Let me take a moment to explain what I mean by this and why I think it is so. In my view, an action is wrong if any principle that permitted it would be one that, for that reason, someone could reasonably reject even if that person were moved to find principles for the general regulation of behavior that others, similarly motivated, also could not reasonably reject.[7] This general account applies to the present case in the following way. Potential victims of manipulation have strong reason to want to be able to direct their efforts and resources toward aims that they have chosen, and not to have their planning co-opted in the way Principle *M* forbids whenever this suits someone else's purposes. So they have strong *prima facie* reason to reject a principle offering any less protection against manipulation than *M* would provide. Whether it would be reasonable in the sense in question for them to reject such principles depends on the strength of the reasons that others have to want the opportunities that these principles would provide. The perfectly general reasons that people may have for wanting to be able to manipulate others whenever it would be convenient to do so are not strong enough to make it unreasonable to insist on the protection that *M* provides. These general reasons are weaker than the reasons people have to want to avoid being manipulated in part because manipulation would undermine expectations about others' behavior that it would be very difficult to avoid relying on. By contrast, we generally have many means other than manipulation of the kind *M* rules out to pursue the ends it might be used for.

Of course, there are special situations in which one has particularly strong reasons for manipulating someone (and no alternative to doing so) or in which the normally strong reasons for rejecting a principle that would permit manipulation are weakened (because manipulation would not be contrary to the interests of the person who is manipulated). The existence of such situations is recognized by the limiting clause, "in the absence of special justification," and it would be reasonable to reject a principle that did not include such a clause. Situations covered by this clause include at least the following: (1) *emergency cases,* in which *A,* or someone else, is in danger and *A* cannot communicate with *B* directly but can make it appear that it would be in *B*'s interest to do something that will help the endangered person (or will bring *B* closer so that *A* can ask for help); (2) *threat cases,* such as when *A* (or someone else) has been kidnapped by *B* and *A* needs to mislead *B* in order for the victim to have a chance

---

7. I elaborate and defend this account of wrongness in the works cited at *supra* note 5.

to escape; (3) *paternalistic cases,* such as when *B*'s capacities for rational choice are significantly diminished and misleading *B* is the least intrusive way to prevent him or her from suffering serious loss or harm; (4) *permission cases,* such as when *A* and *B* have entered, by mutual consent, into a game or other activity which involves the kind of deception that is in question.

It would be misleading to say that these are cases in which special justifications "override" or "outweigh" the obligation specified by Principle *M*. Rather, they are cases in which *M* does not apply because the reasons that support it in normal cases are modified in important respects. A stricter version of *M,* which did not recognize these exceptions, could therefore reasonably be rejected. In emergency cases, for example, *A*'s legitimate reasons for needing to mislead *B* are much stronger than normal. In threat cases, these reasons are also particularly strong and, in addition, the force of *B*'s reasons for objecting to being manipulated is undermined by the fact that the course of action that he is pursuing is itself wrong – any principle that permitted it would be one that *A* could reasonably reject. In paternalistic cases and permission cases, *B*'s reasons for objecting to manipulation are also weakened, but for different reasons. In paternalistic cases it is because incapacities undermine the value for *B* of being able to make his or her own choices. In permission cases it is because being vulnerable to certain restricted forms of manipulation is an essential part of practices that we have good reason to want to engage in.

Principle *M* clearly does not depend on the existence of a social practice of agreement-making. When such a practice exists, it provides one way of committing the wrong of unjustified manipulation, because it provides one kind of basis for a person's expectation that another person will respond to his or her action in a certain way. But, as the above examples show, these expectations can have other bases, and manipulating others by creating such an expectation is open to the same moral objection whatever the basis of the expectation may be.

The examples I have described all involve wrongful deception, but this similarity should not be allowed to obscure other respects in which these examples are morally different from one another. I have in mind here, in particular, differences in the degree and nature of the obligation to fulfill the expectation one has created, and differences in the degree to which the person who forms the expectation can be said to have a "right to rely" on it. So let me change the examples I have given by assuming that when I set out to make you expect reciprocal help I have every intention of fulfilling this expectation. Why would it be wrong for me to change my mind and fail to perform once you had done your part? To answer this question we need to appeal to a richer set of underlying moral principles.

Principle *M* states one moral constraint governing the creation of expectations about one's behavior. There are other principles of this kind, one of which is what I will call the principle of Due Care.

Principle D: One must exercise due care not to lead others to form reasonable but false expectations about what one will do when there is reason to believe that they would suffer significant loss as a result of relying on these expectations.

This principle is more demanding than Principle *M* since it requires a degree of vigilance beyond mere avoidance of intentional manipulation. In contrast to *M*, which prohibits a specific class of actions, *D* does not state explicitly what actions it requires. Its validity consists just in the fact that one can reasonably refuse to grant others license to ignore the costs of the expectations they lead one to form, though there is no obvious way to specify the exact nature and extent of the "due care" that is required. The following principle of Loss Prevention is slightly more specific, and extends beyond mere care in the creation of expectations.

Principle L: If one has intentionally or negligently (that is to say, in violation of Principle *D*) led someone to expect that one is going to follow a certain course of action *X*, and one has reason to believe that that person will suffer significant loss as a result of this expectation if one does not follow *X*, then one must take reasonable steps to prevent that loss.

The idea of "reasonable steps" incorporates a notion of proportionality between the steps taken and the magnitude of the threatened loss, as well as sensitivity to the degree of negligence involved in creating the expectation. I take Principle *L* to be valid on the same grounds as *M* and *D:* It is reasonable to refuse to grant others the freedom to ignore significant losses caused by the expectations they intentionally or negligently lead one to form.

Principle *L* does not require one always to prevent others from suffering loss in such cases, and even when it does require this, the choice of means is left open. One way of satisfying *L* would obviously be to fulfill the expectation once one realized that the other person was relying on it. But this is not required. *L* can also be satisfied by warning the other person before he or she has taken any action based on this expectation.

If no such warning has been given, and the expectation has not been fulfilled, Principle *L* can still be satisfied by compensating the person who was misled. What level of compensation is required? It would obviously be *sufficient* for *A* to compensate *B* for any loss suffered as a result of relying on this expectation. Given that all *A* has done is to create an expectation in *B* that *A* will do a certain thing, it would be reasonable for someone in *A*'s position to reject a principle requiring him or her to do more than restore *B* to as good a position as he or she would have been in if the expectation had never been created. But this may not always be required. In many cases, the benefits *B* would have reaped if his or her expectations about *A*'s conduct had been fulfilled would have been greater than the costs to *B* of relying on this expectation. But this is not always the case. Suppose, for example, that *B* had highly unrealistic plans about how he or she might benefit if *A* did *X,* and that *B* has expended great sums either in furtherance of this plan or in anticipation of its benefits. Most of these funds would have been lost even if *A* had acted as *B* expected. It would be reasonable for *A* to reject a principle that required *A* to make *B* as well off as he or she would have been if none of this had occurred, that is to say, to bear the cost, no matter how great, of *B*'s schemes, no matter how foolish they may have been. It would be reasonable to reject a principle that required *A,* in such a situation, to do more than make *B* as well off as *B* would have been if *A* had done *X,* as *B* expected him to.

As I have said, *A* can satisfy the requirements of Principle *L* just as fully by giving *B* a timely warning that *A* is not going to do *X* as by fulfilling this expectation. But the obligation to fulfill a promise is not neutral in this way between warning and fulfillment. Suppose, for example, that I promise to drive you to work if you will mow my lawn, and that you accept this arrangement. Then, a day or so later (but before the time has come for either of us to begin fulfilling the bargain) I think better of the deal and want to back out. On most people's understanding of promising, I am not free to do this. I am obligated to drive you to work unless you "release" me, even if I warn you before you have undertaken any action based on our arrangement. If I am not going to drive you to work then it is better to warn you than not to do so, but even if I do this I am breaking a promise.

The same can be said of compensation. If one fails to fulfill a promise, one should compensate the promisee if one can, but the obligation one undertakes when one makes a promise is an obligation to do the thing promised, not simply to do it or compensate the promisee accordingly. The difference between fulfillment and compensation is made particularly salient by the fact that in personal life, as opposed to the commercial transactions with which the law of contracts is centrally concerned, our main interest is likely to be in the actual performance of actions that have no obvious monetary or other equivalents, and by the fact that in the domain of informal personal morality (in contrast to the domain of law) there is no designated third party, presumed to be impartial, who is assigned the authority to make judgments of equivalence. The central concern of the morality of promises is therefore with the obligation to perform; the idea of compensation is of at most secondary interest.

Moreover, when compensation is in order for failure to fulfill a promise, the considerations bearing on the level of compensation that is required are different than in the case of *L.* When a person has failed to keep a promise, and not merely disappointed an expectation, it is plausible to say that the appropriate compensation must take the form of making the promisee as well off as he or she would have been had the promise been kept, even if doing this is more costly than compensating the promisee for reliance losses.

So in order to explain the obligations arising from promises it will be necessary to move beyond Principle *L* to a principle stating a duty specifically to fulfill the expectations one has created under certain conditions. How might such a principle be formulated and defended?

III. Fidelity and the Value of Assurance

The difficulty can be stated as follows. The arguments I offered for Principles *M, D,* and *L* appealed to the reasons individuals have to want to avoid losses that they would incur by acting on other people's false or misleading representations about what they will do. The problem is how to extend these arguments to support a principle that requires agents to do what they have promised even when (as in the car and lawn example above) no "reliance loss" would result from one's failure to do so, since the promisee has not yet made any decision relying on the assurance given. The key to the problem lies in noticing the narrowness of the idea of reliance that I have just used in stating it. The reliance losses that are normally thought of in this context (and those that I invoked in arguing for Principles *M, D,* and *L*) are of two kinds: First, time, energy, and resources that have been expended and are wasted or lost because the other party fails to perform as expected; and, second, opportunities to make or look for alternative arrangements that are passed up because of this expectation. Considerations of these two kinds do provide reason to reject principles that would permit others to act in the ways that *M, D,* and *L* forbid. But they do not exhaust the reasons we have for wanting to be able to make stable agreements with others about what they will do. There are good reasons for wanting to have reliable assurance about what others will do that do not concern the consequences of acting on these assurances.

Suppose, for example, that George has, quite accidentally, come into possession of information about you, or about your firm, which would be damaging if revealed. (I will assume that it is not information that he is under any obligation to reveal, such as evidence of a crime, or of a danger that people need to be warned against, and that he would violate no duty to you by revealing it.) In such a case you might well ask him to promise not to tell anyone what he has learned. If there is nothing else you could do to prevent George from revealing this information, and nothing you can do to mitigate the effects of his doing so, then your reasons for rejecting a principle that would permit him to reveal the information after promising not to cannot depend on reliance losses of the two kinds I have mentioned.

As described, this is a unilateral "executory" promise, but the same point could be made by an example of bilateral exchange. If it would be advantageous for George to use this information in a way that would reveal it to others, you might make a reciprocal promise to reward him in some way after five years if he has kept his promise by not revealing the secret. Your willingness to make this promise indicates the interest you have in his keeping the one he makes, but the reason you would have for rejecting a principle permitting him to break his promise remains the same as before: Your interest in being able to make it the case that he will not reveal the information. Reliance losses of the two kinds mentioned above are still not an issue, since if he breaks his promise, and reveals the information, you will be under no obligation to reward him. This may seem to be a special case, but I believe that it illustrates a general point: One reason we have for wanting to be able to rely on what others tell us about what they will do is in order to avoid losses resulting from decisions that we may take on the basis of this information, but this is not our only reason.[8] I will call this more general reason the value of assurance.

In the examples I have just discussed, your reason for wanting the other person not to behave in a certain way is that this would make you worse off than you would have been in the absence of any interaction with that person at all (although he or she is under no duty not to injure you in this way.) The value of assurance is equally well illustrated, however, in cases involving benefits rather than injury.[9] Suppose, for example, that you want to buy my horse, and that no other horse is as desirable to you. You make me an offer, and I promise to sell it to you at the end of the season. In this case there is no threat of your being made worse off than you were before I came along, but the crucial elements of the value of assurance are nonetheless present: You have reason to want me to do a certain thing; I am free to do this and would violate no duty by not doing it; and you thus have reason to want to make an arrangement with me that provides assurance that I will act in the way in question. Unless you had some reason to want me to do this thing you would have no interest in having this assurance. But since, despite this reason, I am morally free to do it or not, an analysis that bases promissory obligation on the value of assurance does not reduce promise breaking to some independently explainable wrong.

In their influential discussion of why the law of contracts should be concerned with what they call "the expectation interest" – that is, with making promisees as well-off as they would have been had the promise or contract been fulfilled – rather than merely with compensating promisees for losses suffered

---

8. Dennis Patterson has suggested that my argument mixes ideas of expectation and reliance that are in fact incompatible. See D. Patterson, "The Value of a Promise" (1992) 11 L. & Phil. 385 at 400. I do not believe this to be the case, but some confusion may result from the fact that I employ these notions in a different way than is common in the legal literature. "Expectation" and "reliance" can refer to incompatible standards of remedy for breach of promise, and to incompatible criteria for determining whether a promise is binding (is it binding if it leads someone to form an expectation or only if it has been relied on?) But as I am using these terms here they are not incompatible. The question I am addressing is the reasons people have for accepting or rejecting principles of conduct regarding the expectations we lead others to form about what we will do. The most general reason is that we want to be able to form expectations about what others will do that we can be confident are correct. One important special case of this reason is that we may need to rely on these expectations in action, and we want to avoid losses from so acting. So our interest in reliance is one reason for caring about the expectations others lead us to form. But it is not, as I have just argued, the only such reason.

9. I am indebted to Peter Benson for prompting me to clarify this point.

as a result of reliance on a promise or contract that was broken, Fuller and Perdue consider, as "perhaps the most obvious answer," one which they label as "psychological."[10] They refer here to promisees' "sense of injury," to their "degree of resentment," and to "the impulse to assuage disappointment."[11]

The value that I am calling the value of assurance is intended to answer a moral analog of the question Fuller and Perdue are addressing: To explain why morality should be concerned with "the expectation interest." (Although what I am presently concerned with is why our moral obligations should reflect this interest, not with whether it should figure in determining compensation that is owed when those obligations are breached.) The value of assurance, as I have described it, might be called "psychological," since one thing the people I describe have a reason to want is a certain confident state of mind about what is going to happen. But the value I have in mind is not *merely* psychological. What you have reason to want is not merely the peace of mind of believing that someone will not reveal damaging information about you, or that I will sell you my horse; you have reason to want these things actually to be the case. What I am calling the value of assurance reflects reasons of both of these kinds, but it is the latter that are primary.

Given the reasons that potential promisees have for wanting assurance about what others will do, potential promisors have reason to want to be able to provide this assurance.[12] In a situation in which both parties know that they have these reasons, promisors may seek to provide assurance by saying that they will do the thing in question unless the other person gives them permission not to. From the point of view of both potential promisees and potential promisors, then, there is reason to reject any principle that would permit a person who has given such assurance to fail to perform in the way in question (in the absence of special justification for not doing so.) If it would be reasonable to reject any such principle, then the acts that they would permit are wrong. This result is summed up in the following Principle of Fidelity:

Principle F: If (1) in the absence of objectionable constraint, and with adequate understanding (or the ability to acquire such understanding) of his or her situation, *A* intentionally leads *B* to expect that *A* will do *X* unless *B* consents to *A*'s not doing so; (2) *A* knows that *B* wants to be assured of this; (3) *A* acts with the aim of providing this assurance, and has good reason to believe that he or she has done so; (4) *B* knows that *A* has the beliefs and intentions just described; (5) *A* intends for *B* to know this, and knows that *B* does know it; and (6) *B* knows that *A* has this knowledge and intent; then, in the absence of special justification, *A* must do *X* unless *B* consents to *X*'s not being done.

---

10. L. L. Fuller and W. R. Perdue Jr., "The Reliance Interest in Contract Damages" (1936) 46 Yale Law J. 52.
11. Ibid. at 57, 58.
12. The importance of promisors' interests in being able to bind themselves is pointed out by Joseph Raz. See J. Raz, *The Morality of Freedom* (Oxford: Clarendon Press, 1986) at 173.

This is a principle of the kind we have been seeking: One that goes beyond Principle *L* in requiring performance rather than compensation or warning. The reasons that potential promisees and promisors have to reject principles that would permit the actions that Principle *F* rules out are sufficient to make it reasonable to reject these principles, and hence to establish Principle *F* as correct, unless it would be reasonable to object to this principle because of the burden it would impose on those who create expectations in others. So we need to consider what these burdens might be and whether they could easily be avoided. One could, of course, avoid bearing any burden at all simply by refraining from voluntarily and intentionally creating any expectations about one's future conduct. But the availability of this option would not, by itself, be enough to rule out reasonable objections. A principle according to which the only way to avoid obligations that are as binding as those specified by Principle *F* is to avoid voluntarily creating any expectations at all about one's future conduct would be too limiting. It would mean, for example, that we could never tell people what we intend to do without being bound to seek their permission before taking a different course of action.

Principle *F* does not have this effect, however, since it applies only when *A* has acted with the aim of assuring *B* that *A* will do *X* unless *B* consents to *A*'s not doing so, when *A* knows that *B* wants this assurance, and when this and other features of the situation are mutual knowledge.[13] No one could reasonably object to a principle that, when these conditions are fulfilled, imposes a duty to provide a warning at the time of creating the expectation if one does not intend to be bound – to say, "This is my present intention, but of course I may change my mind," or to make this clear in some other way if it is not already clear in the context. Since the burden of such a duty to warn is so slight, and the advantages of being able to enter into binding obligations are significant, one can hardly complain if failure to give such a warning under these conditions leaves one open to the more stringent duty to perform or seek permission not to. But this is just the duty stated by Principle *F*, since condition (1) of that principle entails that no such warning has been given.[14] Indeed, quite the opposite has occurred, since *A* has acted with the aim of providing assurance that he or she will do *X* that is not hedged in this way in a situation in which he or she knows

---

13. In the absence of these conditions, *A* might still have some obligations to B, including at least obligations of the weaker kinds specified by Principles *D* and *L*. Since my aim is to show how full-fledged promises can be accounted for on a noninstitutional basis, I leave aside the question of whether *F* might be supplemented by a principle specifying that *A* has a stronger obligation of the kind provided by *F* if *A* has unintentionally given *B* good reason to believe that conditions of *F* are fulfilled.

14. They entail this since *A* has led *B* to believe that he or she will do *X unless* B *consents to* A*'s not doing* X. This is the assurance that *A* is said to know that *B* wants and that *A* intends to provide. But *A* would not have provided this assurance if *A* added the rider, "But of course I may change my mind and reserve the right to do so."

that the difference between an expectation qualified by such a warning and one without that qualification is important to B.

I conclude that when the conditions of Principle F are fulfilled it would be wrong, in the absence of special justification, for the party in A's position not to do X. As in the case of Principle M, this justification need not take the form of considerations that *override* the obligation specified by Principle F. But there are cases in which this term may seem more appropriate than in the four examples I listed in discussing manipulation. For example, if it turns out that the thing one has promised to do would be improper or wrong because of the harm it would cause to third parties, then one should not do it despite having promised to do so.[15] In such cases there might remain an obligation, of the kind specified by Principle L, to warn the promisee that one will not perform or, if he has performed first, to compensate by repaying the cost of that performance.

When the conditions of F are fulfilled, in addition to its being wrong for the person in A's position not to do X, the party in B's position has "a right to rely" on this performance: that is to say, the second party has grounds for insisting that the first party fulfill the expectation he or she has created. This right differentiates the case of promising (though not only that case) from some of the other examples of expectation-creation that I have been discussing. For example, in the first version of the story about the farmers, I spoke of one farmer persuading the other that if the first farmer's stream were contained then it would be in that farmer's economic interest to help contain the neighbor's stream as well. We could imagine this persuasion taking place in a face-to-face encounter, although it is not necessary to suppose that the encounter culminates in anything one would call an agreement. Alternatively – and this is the possibility I want to focus on – we might suppose that when the first farmer sets out to get the second farmer to believe that he or she will reciprocate, this is done without ever speaking to the second farmer directly. (The first farmer might drop broad hints at the feed store about the problem of the stream, and give the loquacious county agent a detailed version of the story the neighbor is supposed to hear.) In this case it would be wrong of the first farmer to fail to perform after the second had done so but all right to fail to perform after warning the neighbor before any reliance had occurred. We would not say in this case that the second farmer had

---

15. A principle that did not recognize such a limitation would be one that third parties could reasonably reject. Under the form of contractualist moral argument that I am employing, however, these objections are to be considered one by one, not as an aggregate. That is, the question is whether any particular third party could reasonably reject the principle in question. At least in the first instance, then, only the harms to each individual are weighed, not the sum of such harms. This individualistic character is a significant difference between the moral framework I am employing and the ideas of efficiency typically employed in law and economics approaches. See, for example, the discussion of incentives in Richard Craswell's contribution to this volume. The question of how aggregative harms or benefits can become morally significant is discussed in *What We Owe to Each Other, supra* note 5 at c. 5 sec. 9.

any right to rely on his neighbor's reciprocation. In performing first, he or she "goes out on a limb" morally speaking. But in order for this not to be the case – in order for the second farmer to have "the right to rely" – it is not necessary for the first farmer to have used the words "I promise." It is enough that the conditions of intention and mutual knowledge specified in Principle F be fulfilled.

Principle F is not just the social institution of promising under another name. To begin with, the principle is not itself a social institution – its validity does not depend on its being generally recognized or adhered to. The moral force of undertakings of the kind described by Principle F depend only on the expectations, intentions, and knowledge of the parties involved, and these can be created *ad hoc,* without the help of standing background expectations of the kind that would constitute an institution. Second, the conditions of expectation and knowledge that Principle F specifies can be fulfilled in many ways other than by making a promise. As the examples of the farmers indicate, this can be done without invoking a social institution (or by invoking a fictitious one). Promising is a special case, distinguished in part by the kind of reason that the promisee has for believing that the promisor will perform.

An established social practice or "convention" can play either of two roles in the creation of obligations of the kind described by Principle F, but neither of these is essential. First, a linguistic convention governing the use of the words "I promise" can provide an easy way for speakers to indicate their understanding that they are in a situation of the kind described in F and that they intend to be offering the kind of assurance described there. But this can be conveyed in other ways, without using these words, such as by saying "You can count on me to do it." Second, where a social practice of promising exists and promise-breakers are subject to social sanctions, this can provide the promisee with reason to believe that the promisor will behave as promised. But this incentive is not necessary. In what I take to be the central cases of promising, saying "I promise" expresses the speaker's intention to offer assurance of the kind described in Principle F and indicates that he or she is aware of and takes seriously the fact that if this assurance is accepted then it would be wrong to fail to do the thing promised.[16] So understood, promissory obligations are instances of Principle F in which the first party's awareness of

---

16. Insofar as it holds that saying "I promise" involves this acknowledgement that one is in a situation in which offering assurance involves undertaking an obligation, my account resembles P. S. Atiyah's view that a promise is an admission that an obligation exists. See P. S. Atiyah, *Promises, Morals, and Law* (Oxford: Clarendon Press, 1981) at c. 7, esp. 192–193 [hereinafter *Promises*]. But I would not say, as Atiyah does, that the obligation in question is independent of the promise and that the function of the promise is thus primarily evidentiary. In my view, by saying "I promise" one can simultaneously create a new obligation and acknowledge that one is doing so. Indeed, one can do the former in part by doing the latter.

that principle itself is invoked as the source of motivation that gives the second party reason to believe that the assurance offered can be relied upon. Not every instance of Principle *F* operates in this way, however. Some may appeal to other sources of motivation such as those mentioned above in my examples of the two farmers.

The idea that a social practice of promising involves certain rules that are conventionally established suggests another function that such a practice might serve but I believe does not. It might be that when we are deciding whether a given promise is binding or whether, for example, certain factors excuse the promisor from his obligation, what we are doing is trying to determine what the rules of our social practice are. But it seems clear to me at least that this is not what we are doing: Whether a promise binds and what it requires are determined entirely by the combination of general moral requirements (such as the principles I have stated) and the content of the particular promise in question. Facts about particular social practices are relevant only insofar as they are made relevant by considerations of these primary kinds (that is to say, only insofar as they are part of the content of the promise, or are morally relevant because, say, they affect the costs or the significance of performance, or non-performance, for the parties in question.)

IV. Contracts and Enforceability

Even if, as I said at the outset, there are obvious similarities between the idea of a promise and that of a legal contract, important differences between the two notions are also apparent. While promises do not, I have argued, presuppose a social institution of agreement-making, the law of contracts obviously is such an institution. Moreover, it is an institution backed by the coercive power of the state, and one that, unlike the morality of promises, is centrally concerned with what is to be done when contracts have not been fulfilled. In this section I will shift my attention from promises to legal contracts, and will therefore take up both of these questions: the question of enforceability and the question of remedy. I will also address the question of how the moral permissibility of using the power of the state to enforce contracts (or to require those who break them to pay compensation) depends on, or is related to, moral conclusions of the kind discussed above about what individuals should do.

This dependence might be thought to be quite direct: Because individuals are morally required to keep their promises (Principle *F*), and are morally required to compensate promisees if they do not (Principle *L*), the power of the state can be legitimately used to force them to do these things. But the fact that some action is morally required is not, in general, a sufficient justification for legal intervention to force people to do it; and the rationale for the law of contracts does not seem to be, as this account would make it, an instance of the legal enforcement of morality.[17] There is, I believe, a connection between the morality of promises and the legitimacy of the law of contracts, but it is not this direct.

A second account of the enforceability of promises would appeal to the idea that while the power of the state is not legitimately used to enforce just any moral requirement, it is properly used to enforce individuals' rights, and it is legitimately used when individuals have consented to its use. The enforcement of compensation for breach of contract might then be justified on the grounds that promisees have a right to compensation, and promisors, by entering into legal contracts, have consented to their enforcement.[18]

I will take a different approach. Rather than beginning with specific moral elements, such as rights and consent, I will apply the general moral framework that I have employed above. On this view, the use of state power to enforce contracts, or to require compensation when they are breached, is morally permissible if a principle licensing this use is one that no one, suitably motivated, could reasonably reject.

I will consider first the permissibility of enforcing the compensation portion of Principle L. That principle specified that one must take reasonable steps to prevent others from suffering significant losses as a result of relying on expectations that one has intentionally or negligently led them to form about what one is going to do. These reasonable steps could take the form of a timely warning, or performance as expected, or compensation for the loss that the person incurred as a result of one's failure to act as expected. Now consider a principle that says that if a person has led another to form expectations in the way L describes, and has neither warned this person nor performed as expected, and the person has suffered significant loss as a result of relying on the expected performance, then the coercive power of the state may be used to force him or her to compensate the other person for this loss, provided that a law authorizing this is established and applied in a system of law that is tolerably fair and efficient. Call this Principle EL (since it concerns the enforceability of L). As I mentioned above, what Principle L normally requires is compensation for the person's reliance loss – as measured by the degree to which his or her situation has worsened as a result of relying on the expectation in question. This constitutes an upper bound on what L can require but, as I pointed out above, the limit of compensation is even lower than this in some cases. I will understand EL, in the light of this earlier discussion, as licensing the legal enforcement of compensation up to but not exceeding that required by L.

The argument for EL has two stages. The task of the first stage is to identify the reasons for having such a principle (or, alternatively, the reasons for rejecting

---

17. As Joseph Raz points out in J. Raz, "Promises in Morality and Law" (1982) 95 Harv. L. Rev. 917 at 937.
18. For an account of this kind, see R. E. Barnett, "A Consent Theory of Contract" (1986) 86 Colum. L. Rev. 269.

a principle which prohibited state enforcement of compensation in such cases.) The second task is to consider whether, despite these reasons in favor of it, *EL* could nonetheless reasonably be rejected. The prima facie reasons for accepting *EL* are clear. They consist of our need to rely on others' representations about what they are going to do, and the reasons we have for wanting to avoid significant losses that can result when these representations prove false. These constitute reasons for *EL* because most of us would be more likely to have to bear such costs if we were denied legal recourse of the kind that *EL* would permit.

The next question is whether this principle could reasonably be rejected from the point of view of those whom such laws would require to pay compensation. If the law were perfectly administered, and unjustified suits for damages were never brought, then laws of the kind licensed by *EL* would not impinge on anyone who complied with the noncompensation parts of Principle *L*: that is to say, on people who, whenever they had reason to believe that others would suffer significant losses as a result of relying on expectations about their behavior that they had intentionally or negligently created, either fulfilled these expectations or gave timely warning that they were not going to do so. One cost of laws of the kind *EL* would permit (I will call it the compliance cost) would thus be the cost of constraining one's behavior in this way. Since legal systems are imperfect, however, and unjustified suits are bound to occur, even a person who complied with the noncompensation parts of *L* would still be vulnerable to the risk of bearing the cost of defending himself against unjustified suits and perhaps paying the damages required by mistaken verdicts. Call these the error costs of *EL*.

If the law is administered with reasonable efficiency, these error costs will be much lower than the cost of being left defenseless against losses imposed on one by violators of Principle *L*, as one would be in the absence of laws of the kind described in *EL*. Error costs therefore do not provide grounds for reasonably rejecting *EL*. What then of the claim that compliance costs alone make it reasonable to reject *EL*, even given the reasons in its favor? I argued above that the costs of complying with *L* do not provide grounds for reasonably rejecting that principle, given the burdens that its violations impose on others. The compliance costs of *EL* are like those of *L*, with the slight modification that what one will be forced to comply with, under threat of legal sanctions, will be an interpretation of *L* that is the outcome of some legislative and judicial process. Given the need people have for the protection that can only be provided through such a process, this additional cost does not make *EL* reasonably rejectable.

This argument for Principle *EL* has elements in common with the two arguments mentioned at the beginning of this section, the argument involving the legal enforcement of morality and the argument appealing to rights and consent. But it does not coincide with either of these. The argument just given relies on the conclusion of the argument for Principle *L* – that is to say, the conclusion that the loss of the opportunities that *L* rules out does not constitute sufficient grounds for reasonably rejecting L given the reasons people have to want the protection it offers. But it does not rely on the conclusion that actions violating L are morally wrong (nor on the idea that because these actions are wrong it is permissible to make them illegal, or to legally require people who commit them to compensate their victims). So the case for EL is not an instance of the legal enforcement of morality.

But even if the argument for EL does not depend on the general thesis that if an action is immoral then it can be made illegal, it may seem to imply this thesis. If the fact that actions of certain type are immoral means that the compliance costs of a principle, P, forbidding these actions do not provide grounds for reasonably rejecting such a principle, then, just as the argument for L led to a defense of EL, it might seem to follow that the costs of complying with a principle EP that permitted the legal prohibition of these acts would not provide grounds for rejecting such a principle.

This argument is mistaken on at least two counts. First, it cannot be reasonable to reject a principle permitting actions of a certain kind unless there are individuals on whom these actions would impose burdens, and these burdens must be appealed to in order to make even a *prima facie* case for the permissibility of legally prohibiting a class of actions. But the notion of wrongness that is characterized by this idea of reasonable rejection does not capture the full range of actions commonly called immoral, since this term is commonly applied to actions, such as certain forms of sexual behavior, that have no victims.[19] Objections to the legal enforcement of morality are strongest in just such cases, in which it is plausible to say that because there are no victims with claims to be protected, there is no need to have a mechanism for collectively defining these forms of immorality and enforcing legal prohibitions against them. Second, even when actions do impose costs on certain individuals, these costs may not be great enough to justify having such a mechanism. So the argument I have offered for EL does not entail a general conclusion about the legal enforcement of morality.

The argument for EL depends on the assumption that people have good reason to want to avoid uncompensated reliance losses, and that such losses are in this sense a morally relevant consideration. But it does not presuppose the idea of a *right* to compensation. Not every morally significant interest is a right. My argument also takes into account the fact that (errors aside) people can avoid the costs of EL by making the appropriate choices, and it considers the costs to them of so choosing. But it does not rely on the idea of consent as part of the justification for legally enforced compensation. (I will consider the difference between these two forms of argument in more detail in Section V.)

Like L, Principle EL applies to cases in which no promise or contract is involved. It would, for example, support the decision in *Hoffman* v. *Red Owl*

---

19. I discuss this distinction between broader and narrower notions of morality in Chapter 4 of *What We Owe to Each Other, supra* note 5.

Stores,[20] in which Red Owl was required to compensate Hoffman for losses resulting from actions that they knew he was taking in the expectation, which they knew to be unrealistic, that he was going to get a Red Owl franchise. Principle *EL* explains why compensation can be required in such cases without appealing to the idea of an "imputed contract."[21] But it also explains why appeal to the idea of contract might seem appropriate: Even when they do not involve contracts, situations falling under *EL* are *like* breaches of contract in involving responsibility for the expectations one has led others to form about one's future conduct.

EL also allows for legal remedies in most cases of breach of contract. If recovery for breach of contract were confined to compensation for reliance losses, and hence also to cases in which reliance has occurred, the moral permissibility of contract law would be fully accounted for by *EL*. But there seem to be at least some cases in which legal enforcement of compensation for breach of contract is permissible even though no reliance has occurred, and other cases in which it is permissible to require specific performance or compensation for expectation damages that go beyond reliance losses. So I want to consider whether there is a stronger principle, analogous to Principle *F,* that provides for these remedies. Identifying the moral basis for such a principle will put us in a better position to respond to doubts about expectation-based remedies (and distinctively contractual forms of liability) such as those expressed by Fuller and Perdue and by Patrick Atiyah, among others.[22]

The principle in question would be one that, under certain conditions, permitted the use of state power to enforce contracts by such means as requiring specific performance or the payment of expectation damages even when these go beyond losses incurred in reliance. As in the case of *EL,* I will proceed by first identifying the reasons for having such a principle and then considering possible grounds for objecting to it. Considering these grounds will help us to formulate the principle by identifying the conditions that it must contain in order not to be reasonably rejectable.

The situations the principle would deal with are ones like those described in Principle *F,* in which one person, *A,* offers another, *B,* assurance that *A* will do *X* unless *B* consents to *A*'s not doing it, where *A* has reason to believe that *B* wants such assurance. As I pointed out in discussing the argument for Principle *F,* the reasons that people in *B*'s position have for wanting assurance include the interests they have in avoiding reliance loss but are not limited to these interests. *A* promise can provide assurance insofar as *B* believes that *A* will be moved to

20. 133 N. W. 2d 267, 26 Wis. 2d 683 (1965)
21. Principles *L* and *EL* thus account for the phenomena Atiyah describes when he writes, ". . . whenever promises are implied from conduct, it is often, perhaps always, the case that the conduct itself justifies the creation of the obligation." *Promises, supra* note 16 at 174.
22. Fuller and Perdue, *supra* note 10; P. S. Atiyah, *The Rise and Fall of Freedom of Contract* (Oxford: Clarendon Press, 1979) [hereinafter *Freedom of Contract*], and other writings.

do X either by a sense of obligation or by a desire to avoid social sanctions such as loss of reputation and the withdrawal of future cooperation. Since these motives may prove inadequate, however, people in B's position may have reason to want to have them supplemented by legal remedies, and when this is so A may thus have reason to want to offer additional assurance of this kind.

On the other hand, people have good reason to want to be able to make promises, even about things that matter a great deal to them, without making legally binding agreements, and it would therefore be reasonable to reject a principle that permitted a legal system to make every significant promise legally enforceable in the ways we are now discussing. The principle I propose will avoid this objection by requiring that A must indicate that he understands himself to be undertaking a legal obligation to do X.[23]

This is part of the more general requirement, which any nonrejectable principle must include, that a person in A's position must have adequate opportunity to avoid legal liability of the kind being discussed. This means, first, that A's understanding of his situation must not be unacceptably restricted. Obviously, perfect knowledge is not required: A certain amount of uncertainty is an unavoidable fact of life and an essential aspect of many situations in which contracts are made. But it would be reasonable to reject a principle that allowed the law to enforce contracts that were entered into only because of trickery or because information that A was entitled to have was withheld. Second, a non-rejectable principle must require that A's alternatives not be unacceptably constrained. Again, ideal conditions cannot be required: The point of making a contract may well be to obtain the means for extricating oneself from a situation one would rather not be in. But an acceptable principle must not allow the force of law to be brought to bear to enforce agreements obtained through coercion. I will say more in the next section about how this condition is to be understood. In stating these requirements I have used explicitly normative terms – "adequate opportunity to avoid," "not unacceptably restricted," and "not unacceptably constrained" – the application of which requires moral judgment. For reasons I will discuss more fully in the next section, I believe that this is unavoidable. (In particular, it cannot be avoided by saying that enforceable agreements must be "voluntary.")

The requirement that A indicate the intention to be undertaking a legal obligation to do X leaves it quite open what A takes this to involve, but A can hardly

23. Since my present aim is just to establish a conclusion about the possible legal enforceability of contracts, I leave aside the question of whether this might be replaced by the weaker requirement that A do something which he knows or should know will create a legal obligation unless he disclaims this intent, and A does not issue such a disclaimer. For similar reasons, I will not explore the extension of the principle I am formulating to cover cases in which one party negligently gives the other good reason to believe that a contract is being entered into. Even in cases that do not fall under this principle or its extensions, however, recovery for reliance losses may be allowed by Principle *EL*. (compare note 13 *supra*). I am grateful to Richard Craswell and Jody Kraus for calling these issues to my attention.

be said to have had adequate opportunity to avoid legal penalties for breach of contract if *A* could not fairly easily have found out what these penalties are likely to be. *B* also must be able to find this out: Someone in *B*'s position could reasonably object to a law that provided a remedy that was much lower than the one he or she had reason to expect and on which *B*'s willingness to accept the terms *A* offered was predicated.

Finally, the remedies for breach of contract that a non-rejectable principle allows must not be excessive. "Excessive" is, again, an undeniably moral notion. It cannot be eliminated, but the contractualist framework provides a structure that guides us in interpreting it. The general idea is that a penalty is excessive if it is one that contracting parties do not have good reason to want to have available given the costs of having it. The requirement that contracting parties have adequate opportunity to avoid being bound, and thus to avoid whatever remedy is prescribed, provides a significant degree of protection against this cost. But this protection is not absolute. People need to make contracts, and they may fail to keep them. We are all prone to errors in judgment, some of us more than others, and even given "adequate opportunity" to avoid the penalties for breach of contract, people will sometimes have to pay these penalties. A remedy is excessive if it is grossly out of proportion to the costs and benefits that are at stake in the contract itself. (Imprisonment for defaulting on small debts would be a case in point.) This disproportion means that the penalties are much greater than what is likely to be needed to overcome the conflicting motivations that the contracts give rise to. Any advantages in assurance that they bring are therefore slight, and not sufficient to justify the cost of incurring them: If the threat of a serious harm can be avoided altogether at slight cost, then arranging that it will befall only those who choose badly does not constitute adequate protection against it.

Bringing these considerations together, the principle we are looking for might be formulated as follows:

Principle EF: It is permissible legally to enforce remedies for breach of contract that go beyond compensation for reliance losses, provided that these remedies are not excessive and that they apply only in cases in which the following conditions hold: (1) *A,* the party against whom the remedy is enforced, has, in the absence of objectionable constraint and with adequate understanding (or the ability to acquire such understanding) of his or her situation, intentionally led *B* to expect that *A* would do *X* unless *B* consented to *A*'s not doing so; (2) *A* had reason to believe that *B* wanted to be assured of this; (3) *A* acted with the aim of providing this assurance, by indicating to *B* that he or she was undertaking a legal obligation to do *X*; (4) *B* indicated that he or she understood *A* to have undertaken such an obligation; (5) *A* and *B* knew, or could easily determine, what kind of remedy *B* would be legally entitled to if *A* breached this obligation; and (6) *A* failed to do *X* without being released from this obligation by *B,* and without special justification for doing so.

EF supports the permissibility of remedies such as specific performance and the payment of expectation damages (if these damages could reasonably have been foreseen at the time the contract was made) as long as these remedies are not "excessive" in the sense just discussed. (And they will in general not be excessive since they are, by definition, not disproportionate to the costs and benefits dealt with in the contract in question.) Like *EL,* however, *EF* is a principle about what it is morally permissible for a legal system to do, not a claim about what such a system must do or a claim about how the law of any particular system should be understood. There may, for example, be good reasons of policy for taking expectation as the measure of damages in some kinds of cases and reliance losses as the standard in others. The point of considering *EF* is to establish that the former is at least permissible in some cases in which the expectation value of a contract exceeds any reliance loss.

EF allows for the legal enforcement of merely executory contracts, but it avoids a common objection to such contracts because it is restricted to cases in which *A* has indicated the intention to undertake a legal obligation. It does not seem appropriate for the law to enforce every personal promise, such as a parent's promise to a child, even when the amount involved is significant. But the objection to such enforcement is undermined when the promisor has specifically indicated the intent to be making a legally binding commitment, and something important is gained by allowing parties to make such a commitment when they wish to do so.

Principle *EF* does not include any requirement of consideration: It does not require that *B* have given *A* anything or made any reciprocal promise in return for *A*'s undertaking an obligation to do *X.* My account does, however, identify several functions that consideration might be taken to serve. Consideration might, like a seal, serve to signal the parties' understanding that *A* is making a legal contract, not merely a promise. For this purpose, however, what *B* gives *A* need not be anything of value. A peppercorn would suffice. Alternatively, *B*'s giving *A* something (even a token) in return for his promise might be a way of indicating that the conditions of *EF* (or for that matter the corresponding conditions of F) are fulfilled: that *B* does want assurance that *A* will do *X* and takes *A* to be providing it by undertaking a legal obligation. Requiring consideration for this reason would be a way of making certain that "threat-promises" and other forms of unwanted assurance are excluded from the realm of enforceable contracts. Third, consideration might be a sign that the matters at stake in a given agreement are of sufficient importance to the parties to warrant the law's attention. For this purpose, if not for the first two, what *B* gives *A* in return for his or her undertaking to do *X* would have to be something of significant value.

These are three functions that consideration *could* serve, but each could also be served in other ways. It can be perfectly clear in a given context, even without any consideration being given, that parties understood themselves to be making a legal contract, that the assurance offered was in fact desired, and that the subject matter of the agreement should not be dismissed as trivial. So, although the account I have offered explains why consideration might sometimes be relevant, it provides no moral basis for the idea that it is always required.

Principle *EF* requires that *A* indicate an intent to be undertaking a legal obligation, and that both parties know, or can easily find out, what remedies for breach this entails. In addition to having fair notice of the remedies they are leaving themselves open to or relying upon, however, parties to a contract may have reason to want to be able to choose what these remedies will be. This flexibility can be provided in at least two ways. If the remedy that the law provides is the enforcement of specific performance where this is possible or, failing that, expectation damages, then the parties can achieve the effect of *A* having different remedy *R* if *A*, instead of contracting to do *X*, contracts to provide *R* if he does not do *X*.

Alternatively, the law might allow parties to specify, within certain limits, what the penalty for breach will be, perhaps by setting a "default" remedy which parties can modify (within these limits) if they wish to.[24] In this case then, whether it is the default remedy or some alternative that applies in a given case, this will apply only because the parties have chosen it, or at least have failed to object to it, given adequate notice that it will apply.[25]

Given this fact, it is tempting to say that in such a system the remedy is also based on a contract: that in addition to their primary contract the parties make a second "remedy contract" specifying what is to happen if *A* fails to fulfill this primary agreement. In my view, however, this is not a satisfactory description of the situation. First, if the remedy contract is just another contract then the question arises what is to be done in the event that it, in turn, is breached. (Specific performance seems to be presupposed.) Second, while a second contract could specify additional penalties that are to apply if the first contract is breached, it is not clear how such a contract could lower the remedy that would be appropriate in this event. To do this the parties would have to exercise some legal power other than merely making another contract.

I turn now to the argument for *EF.* Principle *F* itself provides no direct support for *EF,* since *F* deals only with what individuals should morally do, and says nothing either about enforcement or about remedy. But, as in the case of

---

24. For an example of this approach, and a discussion of such remedies, see R. Craswell, "Contract Law, Default Rules, and the Philosophy of Promising" (1989) 88 Mich. L. Rev. 489.
25. It might seem that there is a difference here between default and nondefault remedies, since the latter must be consciously chosen while the former may hold even though one or both of the parties has failed to consider what the remedy will be. But on the view I am presenting there is in principle no difference here. Just as default remedies may (or may not) be arrived at by conscious choice and deliberation, even when a nondefault remedy is specified in a written agreement, one party may have failed to notice this. Just as in the default case, conscious choice is not required: It is enough that both parties had fair notice that this remedy would apply. For helpful discussion of this point, see J. Coleman, *Risks and Wrongs* (Cambridge: Cambridge University Press, 1992) at 166–173.

L and *EL,* an argument for a principle authorizing the enforcement of expectation damages may be constructed by both tracking and relying on the argument for *F.*

As explained in that argument, people have good reason to want to be able to make agreements that they can rely on even when they have taken no action in reliance on these agreements (perhaps because there is no way for them to do so.) This is what I called above the value of assurance. Given that promisees have reason to want assurance of the kind I have described, promisors have reason to want to be able to provide it. Since the moral motives on which promises rely often fail to move people to keep promises they have made, both promisors and promisees have good reason to want to be able to make legally binding agreements that are enforced in some way that provides this kind of assurance, and there is thus good *prima facie* reason to permit the state to do this. The question, then, is whether this use of state power is something that those against whom it may be used could reasonably object to.

As in the case of *EL,* the costs of *EF* are of two kinds: error costs and compliance costs. Error costs, the costs of wrongful accusation and wrongful judgment, will be lower than in the case of *EL,* since the line between making and not making an agreement of the kind described by *EF* is clearer than the line drawn by Principle *EL.* So if *EF* can reasonably be rejected it would seem to be on the basis of compliance costs.

If the law is correctly applied, would-be contractors can avoid having state power used against them in the way that Principle *EF* would allow by taking either of two courses of action: They can refrain from offering the particular kind of assurance that the principle describes, or they can fulfill the assurances they offer. What *EF* allows a state to do is to deprive them of the opportunity to offer such assurances and then not fulfill them, even in the absence of special justification, without fear of legal intervention.

People in *A*'s position may have reasons for regretting a contract and wishing to be free of it. They may simply decide that they made a bad deal, or they may have discovered a better one. But *EF* cannot be reasonably rejected on such grounds. First, the main point of making a contract in the first place, both from the point of view of the promisee and that of the promisor, is to provide assurance against this kind of reconsideration, so a principle that recognized these conditions as justifying nonfulfillment would undermine the main purpose of contracts. Second, parties in *A*'s position are adequately protected against the cost of being bound in this way by the fact that they know, or have access to, the facts of their situation and the agreement they are making, and can if they choose refuse to enter into this agreement. (One of the justifications for nonfulfillment that an acceptable principle must recognize is that special features of *A*'s situation may deprive *A* of this protection.)

A number of writers have expressed doubts about the basis for legal enforcement of expectation damages that go beyond reliance losses and, in particular, doubts about the rationale for enforcing any remedy in cases in which there has been no reliance. Fuller and Perdue, in their classic article, maintain that what they call "the expectation interest" is much weaker than "the reliance interest" as a basis for contractual liability and that this interest in turn is weaker than "the restitution interest." They go on to ask the not merely rhetorical question, "Why should the law ever protect the expectation interest?"[26] In a similar vein, Atiyah observes that the grounds for the imposition of promise-based obligations "are, by the standards of modern values, very weak compared with the grounds for the creation of benefit-based and reliance-based obligations."[27]

The view I have been presenting responds to these doubts in two ways. First, the distinction between principles *EL* and *EF* acknowledges that there are

---

26. Fuller and Perdue, *supra* note 10 at 56–57. Although they regard the restitution interest as a stronger ground for remedy than the reliance interest, they observe that the two "coincide" in many cases. They write, "If, as we shall assume, the gain involved in the restitution interest results from and is identical with the plaintiff's loss through reliance, then the restitution interest is merely a special case of the reliance interest . . ." (Ibid. at 54) This involves a non-sequitur. It may be true that the cases in which the restitution interest supports recovery will be a subset of those in which the reliance interest does so, and the form of damages they recommend in those cases may coincide. But this does not make the restitution interest a special case of the reliance interest, since the two interests provide different rationales for recovery even when they recommend the same thing.

The restitution interest applies in cases in which the defendant has received something as advance payment for goods or services he has contracted to provide but then fails to deliver. The rationale for recovery which this interest picks out is the idea that the defendant's claim to the payment received is undermined by his breach of contract, or, alternatively, the idea that it is not a good thing for people to be allowed to keep goods they have obtained unjustly, and better that they should be forced to return them to their rightful owners. The former interpretation seems to me a stronger one but, whichever way the underlying rationale for state action supported by the restitution interest is understood, this rationale depends crucially on the rightfulness or wrongfulness of the defendant's gain. The aim of restitution may be like the reliance interest in being concerned to "make the plaintiff whole," but the reliance interest is concerned exclusively with this aim and is quite independent of the rightfulness of the defendant's claim to any benefits he has received or even to whether he has received any benefit at all. This explains why the range of cases covered by the reliance interest is broader, but also indicates that where the two both apply they stem from different reasons. This also may explain why Fuller and Perdue believe that the restitution interest gives rise to a stronger claim for judicial intervention (*Ibid.* at 56). In cases in which the reliance interest alone applies, the defendant is to be asked to give up goods to which he otherwise has a perfectly valid claim. So there is something that needs to be overcome by a reason for compensating the plaintiff's loss. In restitution cases, however, the defendant's claim to possession is itself invalid, and the goods in question in fact already belong to the plaintiff. This is what makes the name "restitution" appropriate: the judge acts with the aim of restoring to plaintiffs what is already rightfully theirs. For this reason, it is misleading to use the term "compensation" to cover what is done when acting in service of all three of these interests. The reliance interest is an interest in compensating plaintiffs for the losses they have suffered. This is true as well in expectancy cases where what is required is not specific performance but "compensation" for the failure to provide what was promised. Specific performance, however, is fulfillment of a promise rather than compensation for not fulfilling it, and restitution is, as I have said, a matter of giving back what rightfully belongs to plaintiff rather than compensating for the loss of it.

27. *Freedom of Contract, supra* note 22 at 4. By benefit-based obligations, he means ones arising from some benefit received.

different bases for legal remedy in breach of contract cases, and offers a characterization of this difference. The argument for *EL* provides a basis for reliance damages in breach of contract cases that is continuous with the grounds for similar recovery in cases in which there is no contract (and even no promise.) It expresses what might be called the underlying tort-like basis for such damages. By contrast, *EF* provides a ground for recovery that is unique to contracts and could fairly be called "promise-based."

Second, the argument for *EF* responds to doubts about this form of liability by providing it with a rationale, based on the value of assurance. As I argued in Section III, our reasons for caring about assurance are related to our reasons for wanting to avoid reliance losses, but are not reducible to these reasons. Assurance is something that people have reason to care about, quite independent of what the law may be, but it is also something that legal institutions can support and protect. As I pointed out earlier, assurance is not merely a "psychological" notion. What people have reason to want is not only a certain state of mind – confident belief that certain things will happen – they also want to make it more likely that these things will in fact occur.

Laws of the kind licensed by *EF* help to provide assurance partly because the threat of legal enforcement of specific performance or expectation damages provides people with an incentive to fulfill the contracts they make. This rationale for these remedies thus has what Fuller and Perdue call a "quasi-criminal aspect." They go on to say that this makes a policy of enforcing expectation damages analogous to "an ordinance that fines a man for driving through a stop light when no other vehicle is in sight."[28] But this analogy will seem apt only if one supposes that the only interest in assurance is the interest in avoiding loss due to actions taken in reliance. I as I have argued in section III, this does not seem to me to be the case.[29] The rationale that the idea of assurance provides for requiring specific performance or expectation damages is not merely "quasi-criminal," since these remedies do not merely serve to deter promisors from breaching contracts but also, in each of the cases in which they are applied, give promisees what they have wanted to be assured of (or come as close to doing this as is practically possible.)

One reason that Atiyah cites for resisting the idea of purely promissory liability is that he sees it as an expression of the emphasis on freedom of choice that is part of the classical *laissez faire* moral and political outlook. Part of this outlook, as he understands it, is the idea that there is liability for another per-

---

28. Fuller and Perdue, *supra* note 10 at 61. See also Atiyah, *Freedom of Contract, supra* note 22 at 3.
29. Atiyah (loc. cit.) says, in regard to the idea that a promisee whose expectations are disappointed is thereby made worse off, that "Psychologically this may be true; but it a pecuniary sense, it is not." The assumption, which I am contesting, is that if the promisee is not worse off "in a pecuniary sense" then any reason he may have for objecting to what has happened must be a matter of psychology.

son's reliance loss only where the agent has chosen to accept responsibility for this loss by giving a promise and that "if I have given no promise, you act at your peril, not mine."[30] On this point, the view I have offered represents an intermediate position between Atiyah's view (very nearly rejecting purely promissory liability) and the view he takes himself to be attacking (nearly limiting liability to cases where it has been consented to.) On the one hand, Principle *EL* authorizes legal liability in cases where there is no contract, or even promise. On the other, Principle *EF* recognizes an independent basis of purely contractual obligation.

A second ground for Atiyah's concern about promissory liability is that the classical *laissez faire* view that he associates with it takes an exaggerated and absolutist view of the value of freedom of choice. This view, as he understands it, fails to recognize the case for paternalistic restrictions and ignores the fact that, due to "material resources, skill, foresight, or temperament," some people are more able than others to take advantage of freedom of choice.[31] I believe that my account of promissory liability avoids these difficulties. In order to see why, we need to consider in more detail how ideas of voluntariness and choice figure in the arguments I have offered. This is the task of the next section.

V. Voluntariness

It is generally agreed that promises and contracts are binding only if they are entered into voluntarily. Principles *F* and *EF* endorse this truism, since the obligations they support and allow to be enforced must be entered into intentionally, with adequate understanding, and without objectionable constraint. Taken together, these conditions amount to what would ordinarily be called a requirement of voluntariness. In this section I want to examine in more detail how this requirement arises, and what it involves.

There are a number of different ways of classifying actions as voluntary or involuntary, and these classifications have different kinds of moral significance and involve different conditions. According to one familiar conception of voluntariness, an action is voluntary if it is a reflection of the agent's will, that is, of his or her judgment about what to do in the situation in question. It is this notion of voluntariness (or something close to it) that is the most basic precondition for the applicability of moral praise and blame.[32] But this idea of voluntariness is considerably weaker than one that is commonly invoked when we say, for example, that a coerced promise was not made voluntarily. Even a coerced promise can be voluntary in this basic sense. Moreover, it can be true that

---

30. P. S. Atiyah, Book Review of *Contract as Promise* by C. Fried (1981) 95 Harv. L. Rev. 509 at 521.
31. Ibid. at 526.
32. I discuss this claim in Chapter 6 of *What We Owe to Each Other, supra* note 5.

people acted voluntarily in this sense (true that what they did can be attributed to them in the sense relevant to moral praise and blame) even though much of what they believed about their actions and circumstances was mistaken. What matters for the moral assessment of agents is how they understood their situation and what they took to be a sufficient reason for acting in a certain way in that situation as they understood it.

A different way of assessing the conditions under which an agent acts is involved in the idea that individuals are likely to be the best judges of their own welfare, and that a person's choices, as long as they are informed and not constrained, are therefore likely to be a good indication of the outcomes that are best from that person's point of view. It follows from this idea that if efficiency is a morally significant goal, then it will matter morally whether agents' choices are voluntary in this stronger sense – that is to say, informed and unconstrained – since it will be a good thing morally speaking to let individuals make their own choices when these conditions are fulfilled, but not necessarily a good thing (at least not for this reason) when they are not.[33]

It is obvious why it should matter, from this efficiency-based point of view, whether an agent is well-informed. People are likely to make better choices among outcomes if they have the relevant information about these outcomes. Duress, however, is another matter. The requirement that there be no duress means that no penalties can be attached to choosing any of the alternatives. Since attaching such penalties amounts to changing what the alternative outcomes are, the assumption that agents are the best judges of their own welfare would indicate that they would also be the best judges of these changed alternatives. But the latter choice, insofar as it was affected by these penalties, might not be a good indication as to which of the original alternatives was best for the agent. So the reason for ruling out duress comes down to the idea that in order for an agent's choice to indicate which, among a given set of alternative outcomes, is best for him, it must be a choice among *those* alternatives, not some altered set.

The account that I am offering of the moral significance of choice and voluntariness is similar to this efficiency-based rationale but differs from it in starting from the point of view of the agent. The basic idea of my account is what I call the value of choice: that is to say, the value for an agent of having what happens (including what obligations are incurred) depend on how he or she responds when presented with a set of alternatives under certain conditions.[34] Many dif-

---

33. This idea is invoked in Richard Craswell's contribution to this volume. See R. Craswell "Two Economic Theories of Enforcing Promises" in this book, pp. 24, 37–39.

34. I develop this account in more detail in T. M. Scanlon, "The Significance of Choice" in S. McMurrin, ed., *The Tanner Lectures on Human Values* Vol. 8 (Salt Lake City: University of Utah Press, 1988), and in Chapter 6 of *What We Owe to Each Other, supra* note 5. The strategy I follow was laid out by Hart in H. L. A. Hart, "Legal Responsibility and Excuses," in *Punishment and Responsibility: Essays in the Philosophy of Law by H.L.A. Hart* (Oxford: Oxford University Press, 1968).

ferent factors go into determining this value. These include, but are not limited to, the values of the alternatives the agent can choose and the significance of having these outcomes occur by virtue of his or her having chosen them. The value of a choice also depends on whether, under the conditions in question, the agent would be able to think clearly, and would have, or know how to get easily, the information necessary to make a reliable choice. Usually, but not invariably, the value of a choice is enhanced by the addition of alternatives, provided that they are ones that the agent might want to realize. Often, the value of having a certain choice is decreased by having alternatives removed, or by duress (that is, by the addition of penalties that make certain alternatives less attractive.) But this is not always so: Given that we are imperfect choosers, we may have good reason to prefer choosing in a situation in which certain alternatives with long-range bad consequences have been made unavailable, or more immediately unattractive. Thus, when paternalism is justified – when it is legitimate to restrict choices "for the agent's own good" or to treat choices as lacking their usual moral significance – this is so because in these cases unconstrained choices lack their normal value for the agent rather than simply because this value is overridden by other considerations.

The value of choice is not a conception of voluntariness. Nor have I appealed to the notion of voluntariness to explain what makes a choice more or less valuable from an agent's point of view. Rather, I have appealed to such things as the value and significance of the alternatives and the influence of various conditions on the choice one is likely to make. Since these are factors that play a role in various ideas of voluntariness, a moral argument based on them may reach the same conclusion that would be reached by appealing to one of these notions. But, as I will now explain, it need not proceed by way of any such appeal.

So far, I have not described the value of choice in moral terms, but rather in terms of what an individual has reasons to want. But these reasons take on moral significance within the kind of moral argument I have been presenting because they figure in determining the strength of the reasons that various individuals may have for rejecting or not rejecting principles of the kinds I have listed above. This happens in two ways.

First, because people have reason to want certain alternatives to be available to them (under the right conditions) they have *prima facie* reason to favor principles that provide these alternatives (as Principle *F* does, for example), and *prima facie* reason to reject principles that would deny them the opportunity to make these choices or would permit others to interfere with this opportunity. Recognizing the value of choice in this way does not involve singling out "freedom of choice," or "freedom of contract" as a paramount value that is never, or almost never, to be interfered with. The value of choice as I understand it is highly variable, depending on the choice in question and the alternatives under which it is to be made. (Some choices have negative value.) Moreover, this value is only one kind of reason among the many that figure in determining whether a principle can reasonably be rejected.

Second, the value of choice as a protection against unwanted outcomes can reduce the force of individuals' reasons to reject a principle. If a person has good reason not to want a certain thing to occur, and a given principle would allow others to behave in ways that would bring that thing about, then this gives that person *prima facie* reason to reject that principle. But if the outcome in question is one that the person could easily avoid by choosing appropriately (or if the principle would license others to bring it about only if that person, chose, under favorable conditions, to permit them to do so), then the force of this objection may be reduced or even eliminated.[35] It is generally worse to be faced with having an unwanted outcome occur whatever one does than to be faced with having it occur only if one does not choose to prevent it.

The value of choice figured in both of these ways in the arguments I gave above for Principles *F* and *EF.* On the one hand, positively, potential promisors and promisees have reason to favor these principles because they provide opportunities to choose to give and receive assurance that they have reason to want. On the other hand, potential promisors' objections to being bound in ways they would not like are greatly weakened by the fact that they will be bound only if they choose to be so under the appropriate conditions. The value of choice also figured in this second way in the arguments for Principles *L* and *EL,* since it was an important part of those arguments that individuals could avoid being obligated to compensate others by taking due care about the expectations they create or by giving timely warnings. Thus, in one important way, the idea of choice plays the same role in the case for the "tort-like" principle *EL* and the case for the "promissory" principle *EF.* In this respect, the difference between the arguments for the two principles is a matter of degree rather than a sharp difference in kind, although the value of choice does also play a second, "positive" role in the case for *EF.*

As I said at the beginning of this section, this line of argument supports the familiar conclusion that promises are binding, and can be enforced, only if they are entered into voluntarily. But if we ask what "voluntariness" amounts to here, it turns out that a choice is voluntary in the relevant sense just in case the circumstances under which it was made are ones such that no one could reasonably reject a principle that took choices made under those conditions to create binding (or enforceable) obligations. The relevant notion of voluntariness is thus given its shape by the argument for the principle in question rather than being an independently specifiable notion that is appealed to in that argument. What is appealed to in the argument, and shapes its conclusion, is not voluntariness but the value of choice.

---

35. I say "may be," since it depends on the choice in question and the conditions under which it would be made. As we saw above in discussing "excessive" penalties for breach of contract, the fact that an agent could avoid a certain outcome by choosing appropriately does not necessarily eliminate his objection to a principle that makes it available. Given the imperfections of choice, one may have good reason to prefer that an outcome not be available at all.

An alternative approach would begin with a conception of when a choice is voluntary – for example, with the idea that a choice is voluntary if it expresses the agent's genuine will – and with the moral principle that if a choice is voluntary in that sense then it confers moral legitimacy on its outcome. We might say, for example, that a choice is voluntary in the relevant sense if it is voluntary in the basic sense required for moral responsibility and is made under conditions in which the agent has, and is aware of, acceptable alternatives to so choosing. But this runs into familiar difficulties. If we say that a promise to pay a robber is not voluntary, because the only alternative to making it was immediate, painful death, what are we to say about a promise to pay a surgeon for an operation, the only alternative to which is equally grim?[36] (A similar question might be raised about a treaty entered into at the end of a war by the defeated nation.)

On the view I am proposing, we address these questions by asking, for example, whether it would be reasonable to reject a principle requiring one to keep a promise to a robber, made under threat of death. The idea of the value of choice enters into the answers to these questions in two ways. First, part of the case for the nonrejectability of Principle F, for example, lay in the fact that the obligations it imposes on promisors are ones that they can avoid by refusing to promise. In this case, the robber's threat makes that option much less attractive, so a principle requiring one to keep the promise to the robber would in this respect be more open to objection. But, second, such a principle, by making it possible to enter into a binding commitment under such conditions, also makes available an option one might very much want to have (or might want not to have, since it gives robbers incentive to ask for such promises). It may be unclear how these considerations balance out.[37] In the case of the promise to the surgeon, however, the result is clear: One has reason to want to be able to make such a promise, and to have it be binding, even though when one makes it one will "have no other choice."

But the reasonableness (from the point of view of the promisor) of rejecting a principle that would require one to keep either of these promises also depends on whether potential promisees have forceful objections to the alternative principle, which would permit these promises to be broken. Here a clear difference between the two cases emerges. The robber has no reasonable objection to such a principle. Since his threat violates other valid principles, he cannot object to a principle that prevents him from gaining by making it. The surgeon, on the other hand, could object to such a principle (at least if the fee in question is something the surgeon is entitled to demand.)

---

36. The example given by Hume, *supra* note 2 at Book III, Part II, Sec. V., esp. at 525.
37. Deciding how they balance out is a matter of assessing the relative strength of reasons for wanting to have certain options be available. It is not a question about the "will" or preferences of any particular promisor: whether I am or am not bound by such a promise does not depend on whether I in particular would prefer to be able to make it or not.

There are, then, at least three considerations at work in these cases: the interest of promisors in being able to avoid an obligation by having an acceptable alternative course of action; the interest of promisors in being able to make binding commitments in some cases even when they lack such alternatives; and the varying strength of the interests of promisees in being able to rely on assurances they are given. The first two considerations may cancel each other out in some cases. Whether or not they do this in the cases we have been considering, these cases are distinguished by a decisive difference of the third kind.[38]

If this analysis is correct, then it is not mistaken but nonetheless somewhat misleading to say that what we should ask in such cases is whether the promise was or was not made voluntarily. Because this same term is also used to denote the basic condition of moral attributability, its use in this context suggests that what is at issue here is simply whether the promisor's action reflected his or her will, and whether this will was or was not constrained by lack of knowledge or absence of acceptable alternatives. But if voluntariness were a matter of the agent's will and the degree to which it is constrained by the unavailability of alternatives then we would have to say either that the promise to the robber and the promise to the surgeon are both voluntary (although the first may be invalid for other reasons) or that neither is voluntary (but the second is valid nonetheless.) But "voluntariness" is commonly used to distinguish between such cases: a promise is called voluntary if and only if the circumstances under which it was made do not constitute a decisive objection to taking it to be binding. I have no objection to this way of speaking as long as it is understood that when "voluntary" is used in this way an action is voluntary just in case it was made under conditions such that a person could not reasonably reject a principle according to which actions made under those conditions have moral consequences of the kind in question.

This is why, in stating principles F and EF, I have specified that A acts intentionally, in the absence of objectionable constraint, and with adequate understanding of his situation (or the ability to acquire such understanding) rather than saying that what A does is voluntary. As the examples I have just discussed indicate, there is no simple way to spell out which limits of an agent's options are objectionable. Similar difficulties prevent us from specifying, in non-normative terms, what constitutes "adequate" access to information about one's situation. Thus, in order to defend a particular law of contracts as legitimate under EF,

---

38. On the account I am proposing, the "voluntariness" of an action under given conditions depends on whether it would be reasonable to reject a principle that attached certain moral consequences to a choice under those circumstances, and this depends in turn on the claims of others as well as those of the agent in question. I am thus in general agreement with the view proposed by Anthony Kronman in A. Kronman, "Contract Law and Distributive Justice" (1980) 89 Yale Law J. 472. I would not say, however, that assessing whether an action is "voluntary" in this sense (e.g., whether it can be taken to create a binding or enforceable commitment) is in general a question of distributive justice.

one must argue that the exceptions it recognizes insure that the contracts it would hold to be binding would not include ones made under objectionable constraint or ones in which a person's lack of information or impaired capacity to deliberate was being taken advantage of in unacceptable ways. This illustrates how the idea of the value of choice can explain the positive value and moral significance of having a choice in a way that does not lead to absolutist conclusions of the kind that Atiyah rightly objects to.

VI. Conclusion

In this paper I have tried to do the following things. I have presented a series of principles governing our behavior toward others whom we have led to form expectations about what we are going to do, and have argued for the validity of these principles within a contractualist conception of right and wrong. The principles I argued for explain how promises can be morally binding, and show that promissory obligations do not require the existence of a social practice of agreement-making. I then went on to argue, within this same framework, for the validity of principles permitting the legal enforcement of promises and other related obligations. Finally, I tried to explain how the requirement that promises and contracts must be voluntary in order to be binding arises, within the contractualist framework I have been presupposing, from what I have called the value of choice. The idea of choice is often given special moral status – both in the form of the licensing power of consent, which is often taken as a basic moral axiom, and in the form of the idea of freedom of contract, which is taken as a value deserving special protection. I have tried to show how the value of choice can account for the moral significance that these notions actually have without giving them the special status often claimed for them.[39]

39. A draft of this paper was presented at the third Drum Moir conference on philosophy of law. I am grateful to participants in the conference for their many helpful suggestions, and especially to Jody Kraus, for his comments at that session and for subsequent correspondence and discussion, which has been extremely valuable. I also am indebted to Richard Craswell for extensive comments, and to Peter Benson for help at many stages in the process.

4

The Unity of Contract Law

PETER BENSON

I. Introduction

At the close of the twentieth century, the situation of contract law presents the following contrast. On the one hand, in both the common law and civil law the definitions of and mutual connections between the various principles of contract law are for the most part well-settled and no longer subject to controversy. Indeed, despite differences in formulation, the main elements of the law of contract are strikingly similar in both legal systems, and these systems, whether directly or by derivation, prevail throughout most of the contemporary world. The authoritative public articulation of the law of contract has achieved a certain apparent completeness and acceptability. The same cannot be said, however, of efforts to understand the law at a reflective level. In common law jurisdictions at least, there is at present no generally accepted theory or even family of theories of contract. To the contrary, there exist only a multiplicity of competing theoretical approaches, each of which, by its very terms, purports to provide a comprehensive yet distinctive understanding of contract but which, precisely for this reason, is incompatible with the others. Moreover, we seem to lack a suitable criterion by which to adjudicate among them, let alone to combine them in an ordered and integrated whole. The point has come when we appear to doubt the value and indeed the very possibility of a coherent and morally plausible general theory of contract, one that could gain wide acceptance. Yet, in the absence of such a theory, how can we vouchsafe the internal consistency and reasonableness which the law claims for its doctrines and principles? Unless we are able to make explicit the conception of contract that underlies these doctrines and principles, we do not fully understand them and whatever understanding we may have of them must of necessity be partial and deficient. At a time when the public authoritative articulation of the main elements of contract is relatively settled and complete, this failure is particularly unsatisfactory.

Despite the wide differences in approach taken by the competing theories of contract, it is nevertheless possible to identify at least three fundamental questions that have preoccupied common law contract theory as a whole during the twentieth century. Each question refers to basic features of contract law. The questions constitute the data, as it were, for which these theories or, for that matter, any fresh attempt at theory, must provide an account. If contract theorizing is to move beyond its present impasse, it will have to be on a basis that can gain wide acceptance. And this can be achieved, if at all, only if we are able to provide a set of interconnected and satisfactory answers to the three questions.

The first question asks why expectation damages and specific performance, the so-called "normal" contract remedies, should be given for breach of a wholly executory and unrelied-upon agreement. The second focuses on the necessity and the centrality of the doctrine of consideration: what might be the rationale for this long-established condition of contract formation? And the third question asks whether contractual liberty, as embodied in the traditional principles of contract formation, is compatible with contractual fairness, as reflected in, say, the more recently developed doctrine of unconscionability. Let us consider each question a little more closely.

The first question received its clearest and certainly its most influential formulation in Fuller's seminal article "The Reliance Interest in Contract Damages."[1] In the article, Fuller places this question at the center of contract theory by challenging what was and continues to be the prevailing legal point of view: namely, that in giving damages for breach of contract, the aim is to put the promisee in the position he or she would have been had the promisor performed as promised. According to the law, this is a ruling and a just principle of compensation.[2] Its purpose is fulfilled by giving the promisee either money damages equal to the value of what was promised or a specific thing where no substitute is available on the market for purchase. Following Fuller, we shall refer to this remedy as the expectation measure of recovery and the aim it serves as the expectation principle. Fuller objects that the expectation measure in fact gives the promisee something that he or she never lost, with the consequence that the remedy cannot qualify as compensatory in character.

A basic premise of Fuller's objection is the accepted idea of compensation. Compensation presupposes, first, that something belongs to the plaintiff by exclusive right as against the defendant and, second, that the defendant injures or otherwise interferes with this entitlement, thereby causing the plaintiff loss. Damages given to repair the loss are compensatory. Compensation thus postulates

1. (1936) 46 Yale Law J. 52. I discuss Fuller's treatment of the expectation principle in P. Benson, "Contract" in D. Patterson, ed., *A Companion to Philosophy of Law and Legal Theory* (Oxford: Blackwell, 1996), pp. 24–56.
2. See, for example, the speech of Lord Atkinson in *Sally Wertheim* v. *Chicoutimi Pulp Co.* [1911] A.C. 301 at 307 (P.C.). This is arguably the most influential judicial statement of the expectation principle in English and Commonwealth law. For an historical account of the availability of the expectation remedy, see A. W. B. Simpson, "The Horwitz Thesis and the History of Contracts" (1979) 46 U. Chicago L. Rev. 533.

in general that the plaintiff has an entitlement which exists prior to and independent of the defendant's wrong. In the particular case of the expectation measure, this remedy can be compensatory if, but only if, the thing promised,[3] including its value, is itself part of the promisee's entitlements prior to the breach. But, Fuller objects, the promisee in an executory contract does not have the thing promised or its value prior to performance. Fuller's view[4] appears to be that a contractually enforceable promise does not as such add anything to the promisee's legally protected assets and is not in itself a source of entitlements; at most it creates in the promisee the expectation of something to come (whence the term "expectation interest") which may be either fulfilled by performance or disappointed by breach. Since the thing promised, including its value, does not in any sense already belong to the promisee prior to performance, he or she cannot lose it as a result of breach. Hence Fuller's conclusion that the expectation measure "seems on the face of things a queer kind of 'compensation'."[5]

By contrast, Fuller argues that the conditions for compensation *are* met where a promisee reasonably relies on another's promise by foregoing some advantage or by making some expenditure and sustains a loss as a result of the latter's breach. In his view, protection of the reliance interest is not merely intelligible as a form of compensation; it also provides a more clearly defensible basis for the enforcement of promises. On Fuller's view, an unrelied-upon promise should be in principle unenforceable, at least insofar as the aim is compensation, not punishment. Expectation losses should be recovered only insofar as they can be analysed as reliance losses or as surrogates for such losses. The aim in giving expectation damages or specific performance cannot be, as the law proposes, the protection of the promisee's expectation interest in the fulfilment of the agreement *per se*. Rather, it must be the protection of the promisee's reliance interest in not being made worse off as a result of relying on the promise. The law should try to place the promisee in the position in which he or she was *prior* to making the agreement. Reliance, not expectation, should henceforth supply the archimedean point for understanding contract.

This argued-for displacement of expectation in favour of reliance leads naturally to the second fundamental question of modern contract theory, which

3. "Thing promised" is intended to be as inclusive as possible: It may be an external object or service and either unique or substitutable as I explain more fully in Part II. It does not favour specific performance over an award of expectation damages or vice versa. It is what the expectation remedy gives the promisee in the form of compensation. I have borrowed the term "thing promised" from Williston who thinks that the definition of consideration must be formulated in this substantive way to avoid a definition that is question-begging or unreasonable. See, S. Williston, "Sucessive Promises of the Same Performance" (1894) 8 Harv. L. Rev. 27 reprinted in *Selected Readings on the Law of Contracts* [hereinafter *Selected Readings*] (New York: The Macmillan Company, 1931), pp. 452–461 at pp. 458–459.
4. While Fuller does not explicitly state this view, it is expressed in extracts from Durkheim and Tourtoulon which Fuller quotes with approval. See Fuller, *supra* note 1 at p. 56, footnote 7.
5. *Supra* note 1 at 53. A similar objection had been made earlier by Salmond. See J. W. Salmond, *Essays in Jurisprudence and Legal History* (London: Stevens & Haynes, 1891) at pp. 200–201.

concerns the necessity for and the centrality of the doctrine of consideration. Traditionally, the existence of consideration has been assumed to be an essential prerequisite for the enforcement of promises in accordance with the expectation principle. The link between consideration and the availability of the expectation measure is taken to be the central and distinguishing feature of contractual liability, in contrast to liability in tort. The upshot of Fuller's criticism is, however, that liability for breach of promise should be reliance-based. And reliance, as a substantive basis of liability, is part of tort law. Thus Fuller prepares the way for the subsumption of contract under tort as later advocated by Patrick Atiyah,[6] among others. On this view, contract is just one form of reliance-based promissory liability. Thus, promissory estoppel, for example, is treated as a competing alternative basis of contractual liability. Consideration becomes evidence of reliance, nothing more. It is the existence of reliance that is the crucial factor in establishing liability, whether or not consideration has been given. The absence of consideration should not defeat expectations generated through reasonable reliance. Consideration is no longer a necessary or a central condition of contractual liability.

The doctrine of consideration is also problematic from the perspective of theories such as Charles Fried's[7] which, precisely in reaction to the threatened collapse of contract into tort, attempt to reinstate autonomy and voluntary intention – and with these the expectation principle – as the fundamental and distinctive basis of contractual liability. According to this view, contract is to be founded upon the moral obligation to keep one's promises, and this obligation is conceived as arising independently of reliance. The crucial factor is said to be the intentional assumption of promissory responsibility. But this need not depend upon or be evidenced by the existence of a consideration. Here again, consideration is neither a necessary nor a central feature of contractual obligation.

Both the reliance and promise-based challenges to the traditional understanding of the role of consideration call for a fresh examination of its possible rationale. The question is whether there is a necessary relation between the availability of expectation damages and consideration, and if so, whether this relation makes contract irreducible to tort. In undertaking this examination, we must see whether, *contra* Fuller, a link of this kind can be established within a conception of contract in which the expectation principle functions as a principle of compensation, in keeping with the legal point of view.

---

6. P. S. Atiyah, *Essays on Contract* (Oxford: Clarendon Press, 1986), Ch.1 at pp. 40–42. For the sake of completeness, I should add that, for Atiyah, contractual liability can be either reliance- or benefit-based. Consideration is thus evidence either of reliance or of the receipt of a benefit. Tort and unjust enrichment become the substantive bases of contractual liability. I discuss Atiyah's account of the basis of contractual obligation in Benson, *supra* note 1 at pp. 29–32.
7. C. Fried, *Contract as Promise: A Theory of Contractual Obligation* (Cambridge, MA: Harvard University Press, 1981). The discussion of consideration is at pp. 28–39.

In challenging the centrality and the compensatory character of the expectation principle, Fuller also raises the question of its justice.[8] Invoking Aristotle's distinction between corrective and distributive justice, Fuller argues that because damages given in accordance with the expectation principle do not heal a disturbed status quo but rather bring into existence a new situation, they come under distributive justice. Fuller's characterization of the expectation interest in terms of distributive justice directly challenges the traditional understanding. For traditionally it was always supposed, even if only rarely stated explicitly, that contract law, like other parts of private law, comes under corrective justice, not distributive justice. Indeed, even on Fuller's view, the characterization of the expectation interest as coming under distributive justice makes it anomalous, as evidenced by the fact that he takes both the reliance and restitution interests to be corrective. Now given that certain basic doctrines of contract law – I am thinking here of the principles of contract formation, for example – seem on their face to be non-distributive in character, Fuller's distributive turn raises the specter of a basic tension at the very core of contract law between such apparently corrective features and those which are viewed as coming under distributive justice: How can contract law be conceived as a coherent and integrated whole?

This challenge lies at the heart of the third fundamental question of modern contract theory, namely, the relation between contractual liberty and contractual fairness. For, with very few exceptions, writers have assumed that notions of contractual fairness as embodied in, say, the doctrine of substantive unconscionability, come under distributive justice, not corrective justice. The prevailing view among scholars is that the non-enforcement of agreements on a basis that goes beyond the traditional procedural defences of duress, mistake, misrepresentation, or fraud *must* be grounded on considerations of distributive justice. In the face of this assumed link between substantive contractual fairness and distributive justice, two sorts of theoretical responses have emerged.

One approach is to banish from contract proper considerations of fairness that go further than the traditional contract defences.[9] On this view, the moral basis of contract does not itself incorporate such concerns about substantive fairness. Contract law is the realm of liberty, possibly limited but not constituted by norms of substantive fairness which themselves derive from some other moral basis. This approach is, however, in tension with the legal standpoint which treats the principle of unconscionability as part of contract law and which views a finding of unconscionability as preventing a contractual obligation from arising unless the transaction is affirmed by the disadvantaged party.

8. *Supra* note 1 at p. 56.
9. See, for example, Fried, *supra* note 7 at pp. 103–111. According to Fried, non-enforcement of certain transactions on the basis of substantive unfairness reflects a "duty of humanity" – distinct from the promise principle that underlies contractual obligation – which is owed others in circumstances where the ordinary established institutions of justice and of civil society are impaired or broken down.

Other writers, endorsing the idea that principles of substantive fairness are indeed part of contract, have sought to generalize the assumption that such considerations are distributive by suggesting that other aspects of contract law – and perhaps contract law as a whole – should also be understood as distributive. On this view, contract is a mode of ordering that is indistinct from public law institutions of distributive justice such as taxation.[10] The very legitimacy of contract is thought to depend directly on whether it promotes, and is part of, a just distribution of resources and power. The difficulty with this approach, however, is that it is achieved at the cost of forcing an interpretation on certain essential aspects of contract that either distorts, or simply fails to preserve, the way these are understood at law and even according to common intuition. Thus, the analysis of consent – and, in particular, the principles of contract formation, the liberty to contract or not as one sees fit, and so forth – do not seem immediately amenable to characterization in terms of distributive justice. These aspects seem to reflect, rather, a conception of liberty that is indifferent to distributive concerns.

The perceived failure of both of the above approaches has encouraged the more far-reaching conclusion that contract law is riddled with unresolvable yet basic antinomies that invite the fundamental transformation of contract law as it now exists, however widely accepted and well established its main doctrines may be.[11] Yet, precisely because these doctrines are so widely recognized, we should not too readily dismiss the possibility that there is in fact latent in the law an intelligible and integrated conception of contract, one which unifies its main doctrines. A first task of theory must be to see whether it can uncover such a conception. In particular, it should also investigate whether there is an interpretation of contractual fairness that fits with the apparently non-distributive aspects of contract. And this may require questioning the assumption that any substantive notion of fairness going beyond the traditional defences of duress, fraud, and so forth, must be distributive. The possibility of a non-distributive conception of unconscionability must be explored.

The principal aim of this essay is to work out in detail a conception of contract that is latent in the main contract doctrines. In so doing, I hope to provide consistent and interconnected answers to the three questions of modern contract theory. The mode of justification employed will be public and non-foundational, in a sense that I will now briefly explain. In virtue of its being public, the justification can provide, I argue, the first step in advancing contract theory beyond its present impasse.

A theory or, more specifically, a basis of justification is public[12] insofar as it presents and elucidates its unifying conception as *implicit in the public legal*

10. This is the view proposed in A. Kronman, "Contract Law and Distributive Justice" (1980) 89 Yale Law J. 472.
11. A systematic presentation of this view is R. Unger, "The Critical Legal Studies Movement" (1983) 96 Harv. L. Rev. 561 at pp. 616–633.
12. As used here, "public" does not refer to public law as opposed to private law. Indeed, the par-

and political culture. In the particular case of a public justification of contract, the relevant public legal culture is the domain of private law principally constituted by the doctrines, principles, and rules that are articulated in authoritative judicial opinions and that are analysed and interpreted in certain widely accepted works of legal scholarship. First and foremost, a public justification of contract tries to show that there is a conception of contractual obligation that is implied by, and that in turn holds together in one whole, the basic doctrines of contract law. Which doctrines are basic, and what the definition of their content is, will be provisionally suggested by the law itself. Ideally, the selection of these doctrines and the specification of their content should be as uncontroversial as possible, at least from a legal point of view. The doctrines should also have been the focus of extensive judicial and scholarly discussion. The main doctrines selected for the purposes of this essay are four: the expectation remedy, offer and acceptance, consideration, and unconscionability.

A public theory begins, therefore, with what is widely settled in the public legal culture. It seeks the public reason latent in the law. The fact that the authoritative public articulation of the doctrines and principles of contract is now settled and appears complete makes possible for the first time a public basis of justification. Moreover, this same fact gives rise to the need for a theory that elaborates a conception of contract on this basis. For in articulating the conception of contract that is latent in the public legal culture, such a theory simply attempts to bring out explicitly the systematic and complete character which the legal point of view purports to have.

It should be noted here that however much competing contract theories may differ among themselves, they all purport to be theories *of contract law.* They presuppose, therefore, the existence of the legal point of view. Indeed if a theory were to ignore and not to take up, even provisionally, the standpoint of the law, the law would rightly dismiss it as extraneous and hence irrelevant to its own concerns and analysis – however internally coherent, sophisticated, or otherwise valid that theory might be. The theory that I outline here attempts to take the legal point of view seriously. It does so by making explicit the conception of contract that informs this standpoint and by answering the three questions of contract theory via the systematic elucidation of this conception. The concep-

---

ticular public basis of justification that I present here is worked out for, and is intrinsic to, an area of private law, namely, the common law of contract. Rather, "public" qualifies the mode of justification and reasoning that is appropriate to settle the fair terms (enforceable by coercive law) of interaction and cooperation among persons. A public justification is framed to address these persons viewed solely as reasonable participants in such interaction or cooperation. The modern *locus classicus* of this idea as applied to constitutional law and political justice is Rawls. See, in particular, J. Rawls, *Political Liberalism* (New York: Columbia University Press, 1993) and J. Rawls, "The Idea of Public Reason Revisited" (1997) 64 U. Chicago L. Rev. 765, reprinted in J. Rawls, *Collected Papers* (Cambridge, MA: Harvard University Press, 1999), Ch. 26. I discuss more fully the general character and features that make a justification of contract law public in "The Idea of a Public Justification for Contract" (1995) 33 Osgoode Hall L. J. 273 at pp. 305–334 ([hereinafter *Public Justification*].

tion of contract that it articulates is but one step removed from the formulations of the positive law. Because the conception makes explicit what the legal point of view implies, it must be presupposed, even if only provisionally, by anything that purports to be a theory of contract law. A public theory therefore represents the first step in working out a philosophically satisfactory and complete account of contract. A philosophical account – one that presumably relates contract law to utility, to Kantian freedom, or to some other more fundamental grounding – must take the conception of contract as its provisional starting point and justify its proposed grounding via an exploration of this conception – or else be open to the charge of irrelevance from the legal point of view.

Accordingly, in contrast to a philosophical account of contract, a public theory is *non-foundational* in the sense that it does not present the conception of contract and its organizing idea as founded upon or as part of a more comprehensive normative principle or framework, such as freedom or maximum utility. As public, the theory does not try to go beyond or under the conception itself. While it certainly does not deny the possibility of doing so, it limits itself to seeing whether the basic doctrines of contract law fit together within – and through – this conception. Doctrines "fit together" if each can be shown to belong to the same organizing idea and to contribute in an essential way to its full articulation. Viewed from within the conception of contract, the doctrines are both individually necessary and mutually supportive. Accordingly, the role of any one doctrine cannot, strictly speaking, be defined or even understood in isolation from the others. No single doctrine, taken by itself, is treated as foundational in relation to the others. At the same time, a public basis of justification views these doctrines, when understood in this way, as capable of having a certain intrinsic acceptability and reasonableness, even if provisionally.[13] It should be emphasized that in this public theory, the conception of contract, like the doctrines it informs, will be thoroughly juridical in character, even where it is presented in somewhat abstract terms and does not coincide with the explicit formulations in judicial decisions. Such abstraction is unavoidable and results from the effort to bring out the unity implicit in the legal formulations.

I present the public justification of contract in two steps. In Part II, I set out the logic, that is, the necessary conceptual premises, of a transfer of ownership or of right[14] from one person to another. Briefly stated, the need for and the role

---

13. I take the term " intrinsic reasonableness" from Rawls who writes: "Intrinsic reasonableness . . . means that a judgment or conviction strikes us as reasonable, or acceptable, without our deriving it from, or basing it on, other judgments. Of course, that a conviction strikes us as reasonable may indeed turn out to depend on our other beliefs or convictions, but that is not how it strikes us. On due reflection we may affirm the conviction as having a certain reasonableness, or acceptability, on its own." J. Rawls, *Justice as Fairness: A Briefer Restatement* (unpublished manuscript, 1990), p. 25, footnote 14.
14. As I will explain in Part II, the entitlements or rights that are transferred by contract are essentially proprietary in character. Thus, as I understand them, "transfer of right," "transfer of entitlements," and "transfer of ownership" are all equivalents.

of this logic in my argument are as follows. Once we take the expectation principle as a principle of compensation (as is contemplated by law), it is necessary, as I have already intimated and will more fully explain in Part II, to suppose that parties acquire entitlements at and through contract formation. It must be possible to think of contract formation as effecting and embodying a transfer of entitlements from one party to the other. The logic of a transfer of right represents the essential premises that allow us to conceive of such a transfer. Now while this logic does not exist apart from, and is actual only as it animates, a variety of definite legal relations (including, we shall see, contract), it can be presented at an abstract level without reference to doctrines and principles of contract law. And this is what I do in Part II. In Part III, I try to show in detail how, from the legal point of view, the main doctrines of the common law of contract actually fit together in one single conception of contract and I argue that this conception of contract embodies the logic of a transfer of ownership set out in Part II. By first examining the idea of a transfer of ownership on its own and in terms of its necessary character, we are enabled to see that the conception of contract that informs the common law is more than merely internally consistent. It also possesses a certain intrinsic reasonableness and plausibility, and indeed necessity, from a juridical point of view.

To close this Introduction, I should say something about the relation between the account of contract presented here and other writing on this topic. My overriding aim in this essay is positive and constructive: to lay out as carefully as possible a definite conception of contract rather than critically to evaluate alternative accounts.[15] Where I do discuss other approaches, this is only to clarify, by way of contrast, the one that I am trying to elaborate. This being said, the present theory attempts to complete as well as articulate at a higher level of abstraction the analysis of modern contract law that is elaborated (albeit with differences in formulation and detail) in the writings of Langdell, Pollock, Holmes, Leake, and, perhaps most satisfactorily, Williston. Their analysis of contract suffers, however, from two main deficiencies which I have attempted to correct. First, it lacks a distinct account of contractual fairness. This is not surprising since, at the time they wrote, the modern doctrine of unconscionability had yet to be explicitly articulated and incorporated into the law of contract. Secondly, while these writers treat the expectation principle as both fundamental to and distinctive of contract law, they do not make explicit the understanding of the contractual relation which this principle implies. To vindicate the idea that the expectation principle is a ruling and a just principle, it is necessary to make explicit this conception of contract and to show that it

15. In several earlier pieces, I discuss the main alternative views in some detail. See, for example, "Public Justification," *supra* note 12 at pp. 274–314; "Contract," *supra* note 1; and "Abstract Right and the Possibility of a Nondistributive Conception of Contract: Hegel and Contemporary Contract Theory" (1989) 10 Cardozo L. Rev. 1077 at pp. 1092–1147 [hereinafter *Abstract Right*].

indeed holds together the main doctrines of contract law, including unconscionability. This essay attempts to complete their work by outlining the chief structural features of the conception of contract that is implicit in it. It is this conception that best accords with the principal doctrines of the law and that provides consistent and interconnected answers to the three main questions of modern contract theory.

II. The Logic of a Transfer of Ownership

A. *The Need for a Logic of Transfer: The Expectation Principle as a Principle of Compensation*

Our starting point is the long and well-settled rule that expectation damages, or, in the alternative, specific performance, are available for breach of contract. The plaintiff is given the thing promised, including its value, either by money damages where the thing is available on a market or by receipt of a specified thing where it is unique. We provisionally assume with the law that the purpose of this remedy is to realize the expectation principle and that the latter is a principle of compensation. We also suppose that a wholly executory and unrelied-upon agreement can be so enforced. We do this so that we can see clearly whether there is in fact an intelligible principle of compensation that is independent of reliance. What we are seeking is a conception of contract that is coherent with this principle.

Taking Fuller's challenge to heart, we say that there can be a conception of contract in which the expectation principle functions as a principle of compensation if, but only if, prior to the breach and therefore before the time for performance, the promisee has an entitlement to the thing promised, including its value,[16] whether or not the latter also figures as a reliance loss. This is the interest that must be legally protected by the expectation principle if the latter is to qualify as a principle of compensation. It provides the baseline against which expectation loss is both conceived and measured. Specifying a little more exactly the manner in which the promisee must have this pre-performance entitlement, we say that the promised thing, including its value, must belong to the promisee as a matter of exclusive right vis-à-vis the promisor and, for this reason, must count as the exclusive property of the promisee as against the promisor. This is a necessary condition of the expectation principle's being a principle of compensation.

---

16. The law distinguishes three aspects of the entitlement: possession, use, and value. So far as the law of contract damages goes, loss of possession as such is reflected in *nominal* damages; impaired use is rectified by damages for so-called *consequential* loss; and lost value is remedied by *expectation* damages which give the plaintiff the difference between the contract price and the market price at the time of breach.

If we must suppose that prior to performance the substance of the promise belongs to the promisee by exclusive right, the next question is how he or she can acquire it. To begin, it is clear where we must locate the source of this entitlement: It must be in the contract itself, effected by contract formation. Contract formation, therefore, must itself constitute a mode of acquisition; it must give the promisee the requisite entitlement. More specifically, at and through formation, the promisee must acquire this entitlement from the promisor with his or her consent. Unless this is so, the expectation principle cannot qualify as a principle of compensation. Contract, then, must be intelligible as a transfer of ownership from one party to the other. The possibility of the idea of a transfer of right is presupposed. To achieve clarity of view, we should therefore try to elucidate the essential and necessary premises, that is, the logic, of a tranfer of right. To bring out this logic, which I have already said does not exist apart from the legal relations it animates, I will first consider its operation in an uncontroversial example of acquisition through another's consent, namely, in a present, fully executed transfer of property, and then show that this logic can apply in principle to contract as well.[17]

B. The Logic of Transfer in a Simple Case: A Present Physical Transfer of Property

Take, then, a present transfer of property whereby I physically give you my watch which you in turn physically take. I may do so either *gratis* or for a stipulated equivalent which you physically transfer to me. Before the transfer, I own the watch; at the end, you do. No one doubts that persons can acquire ownership from each other in this way. Since we suppose in such cases that ownership is transferred with delivery of the object or objects, there is no agreement to be performed, no temporal gap between agreement and performance, and so no contractual obligation as such. What are the essential premises of such a present transfer of ownership?[18]

First, the transfer must embody or express the decision of the initial owner to part with his or her property. A *merely* physical transfer cannot as such produce any juridical effects. In particular, the first party must, without reservation, give up ownership and confer it upon the second. Unless the first party alienates his or her property, it is not available for appropriation by the second.

The first condition of a transfer is, then, the initial owner's consent. But, while this condition is absolutely necessary, it is not by itself sufficient to trans-

17. This strategy is suggested and pursued by Grotius, among others. See H. Grotius, *De Jure Belli ac Pacis* (trans. F.W. Kelsey, 1925) Bk. II, Ch. XI, i & iv. Corbin discusses the differences between a present transfer of property and contract in A. Corbin, *Corbin on Contracts: One Volume Edition* (St. Paul: West, 1952), Ch.1, sect. 4 at pp. 6–8.
18. The following discussion of the necessary conditions of a transfer of ownership draws from previous accounts of contract in the philosophical tradition, particularly those of Duns Scotus, Grotius, Hobbes, Kant, and Hegel.

fer property. Its immediate juridical consequence is simply the cessation of the first party's ownership, not a *transfer* of ownership to the second. To confer ownership, a second decision is also necessary. The second party must express without reservation a decision to take up or to accept the object as his or her own. In the circumstances of an immediate transfer of property, this decision is expressed in (physically) taking the property. Thus, in addition to alienation by the first party, there must be appropriation by the second. To be compatible with the rights of ownership of the first party, the second decision must come *after* and must be *in response to* the decision to alienate. Only in this way can the second party acknowledge and respect the first's initial right of property in the thing.

A transfer of ownership requires, then, two temporally sequenced assents. Moreover, since this double assent consists in acts of alienation and appropriation, there can be, in formal terms, but two fundamental categories of transfer: first, where the acts of alienation and appropriation are apportioned between the parties – so that only one alienates and the other appropriates – there is gift; where, by contrast, each of the parties both alienates and appropriates, there is exchange. A transfer of ownership must be either a gift or an exchange and both require temporally sequenced double assents.

The foregoing conditions of a transfer of ownership are straightforward. There is, however, a further requirement which is not so obvious but which nevertheless is absolutely crucial to the very possibility of a transfer of ownership. Following Kant, I shall refer to this further requirement as the "principle of continuity."[19]

A transfer of ownership implies that the second party's acquisition is not only with the first party's consent, but also *through* it: The acquisition of one is *from* the other. Now suppose we were to conceive of a transfer as composed of two wholly separate acts: abandonment of ownership by the first party followed in time by appropriation by the second. The instant the property is abandoned by the first but before it is taken up by the second, it becomes ownerless. In this condition, the thing belongs to no one and may be appropriated by anyone. Consequently, at that moment both the first party's initial entitlement to the thing and his or her decision to confer it on the second party (and not on someone else) are irrelevant. If the second party appropriates it, it will not be through the first party's consent and entitlement; rather, it will be on the basis of a principle such as the right of first possession which holds that one who with the requisite intention brings a presently *unowned* thing under his or her physical control is its owner, relative to all others who come afterward.

19. It is Kant who first sets out this third requirement. See I. Kant, *The Metaphysics of Morals* in *Practical Philosophy,* M. Gregor, ed. and trans. (Cambridge: Cambridge University Press, 1996) at p. 424. In the following discussion, I draw on Kant but, in addition, I interpret the requirement in light of Hegel's account of contract in *The Philosophy of Right,* trans. T. M. Knox (London: Oxford University Press, 1967) at paras. 71–80. At certain points, my presentation departs from that of Kant.

Accordingly, for there to be a transfer of ownership from one person to another, the second party must appropriate the object *in the condition of being owned* by the first party. This is the fundamental import of the requirement of continuity. Now alienation is an aspect of ownership, in that property can be alienated only by its owner; by alienating his or her property, an owner exercises his or her right of ownership over it. Appropriation by the second party in accordance with continuity implies, therefore, that the thing is appropriated *at the same time* the owner exercises his or her right of ownership by alienating it. For both gifts as well as exchanges, it must be possible to represent the two acts of alienation and appropriation as absolutely co-present and simultaneous. Quite literally, the first party's exercise of the power of alienation is taken to be accomplished in, and identified with, the second party's appropriation: The latter's appropriation is the mode by which the former alienates, hence exercises ownership over, his or her thing. In Hegel's words, "my will as alienated is at the same time another's will."[20]

In addition to this identification between and simultaneity of acts of will, the requirement of continuity implies that these acts of will have as their object *one identical thing* which belongs to both parties at the same time. This follows from the fact that the object of transfer cannot cease to be the first party's without *already* belonging to the second. It must be possible to represent both gift and exchange as entailing an object of this kind if they are to qualify as transfers of ownership between the parties.

This third condition of a transfer of ownership – the requirement of continuity – may seem, however, paradoxical in light of the previously discussed need for temporally successive assents: How can the parties' assents be construed as *both* successive and simultaneous? Moreover, keeping in mind that the only kind of ownership contemplated here is individual, exclusive ownership of single things which therefore presupposes the distinction between mine and thine, how can the parties have one object at the same time? In both gift and exchange, when one party owns the particular object of the transfer, the other party does not, and vice versa. And even though parties to an exchange own something both at the start and at the end of the transaction, it is not the same thing. Given the requirement of temporal sequence, parties own the same particular thing only at *different* times, not at one and the same instant. What, then, can this "identical thing" be and how can simultaneity be satisfied consistently with the requirement of temporal sequence? I shall postpone further discussion of this important question until Part III. There, an analysis of the main common law contract doctrines will reveal the object that satisfies continuity compatibly with the requirement of sequence.

The idea of a transfer of ownership also implies a certain conception of the person, which I shall call a "juridical conception of the person." The legal analy-

20. Ibid. at para. 73.

sis of a transfer is concerned solely with the acts (as well as the relationship between these acts) that are necessary and sufficient to constitute a transfer of ownership. The corresponding juridical conception of the person views individuals just in their role and capacity as authors of the required acts. From this perspective, individuals count simply as persons who have exercised juridical powers to alienate or appropriate property. Their legal capacity to accomplish these acts is presupposed.

Negatively, this conception of the parties abstracts from whatever is not integral to the actual exercise of these powers. Now while appropriation and alienation are instances of purposive conduct and therefore presuppose in the one who appropriates or alienates some reason or end which the act is intended to realize, the question of whether one has appropriated or alienated is not decided by, and does not depend upon, whether this reason or purpose is of a certain particular kind. The juridical analysis of these acts thus abstracts from the particular content of the agent's reasons for so acting. The agent's interests, needs, and ends are not *in their particularity* normatively relevant factors. For this reason also, whether a party has appropriated or alienated property is not decided by or dependent upon whether such appropriation or alienation satisfies the particular interests, needs, or purposes that he or she may have at a given point in time. In this respect, the juridical analysis of the acts that transfer ownership contrasts with moral or ethical evaluation which makes an agent's particular purposes and incentives directly and even centrally relevant in assessing the goodness of his or her volition. Note that by abstracting from the particularity of purpose, interest, and so forth, the juridical analysis abstracts from just those factors that differentiate individuals. By implication, it views persons as identical.

Positively, the parties' acts of alienation or appropriation are viewed as fully integrated parts of an interaction between them, not as separate instances of individual conduct. This relational character also stamps the juridical analysis of the purposive quality of the parties' acts. Individuals are represented as having the kind of reasons, interests, or ends that are appropriate to them as participants in a *transfer* of ownership. The parties are represented as having reasons and interests that are intrinsically relational in the right way. It follows that such reasons and interests may not necessarily coincide with a party's reasons for transacting as viewed from his or her own standpoint. The latter perspective is not relevant since it is not the point of view of their relation. Once more, this analysis contrasts with ethical evaluation which certainly takes into account an agent's own understanding of his or her action. At the same time that they reflect the fact of relation, the reasons and interests that parties have as participants in a transfer of ownership must ultimately be the same for both. Unless this is the case, the parties cannot be identical in a way that abstracts from their particularities.

C. Is the Logic of Transfer Applicable to Contract?

If we must suppose that contract formation consists in a transfer of entitlement from one party to the other – as is necessary if the expectation principle is to function as a principle of compensation – the foregoing analysis of a transfer of ownership in the case of an executed conveyance of property should also apply to contract. Reflecting the logic of a transfer of ownership, it must be possible to understand contract as constituted by two mutually related acts of alienation and appropriation which are at once temporally successive and yet absolutely co-present. Nevertheless, there is, as was mentioned earlier, a basic difference between a present executed transfer of property and contract. In contract, the entitlement is transferred at the moment of agreement and therefore prior to and independent of actual physical delivery whereas in the case of a present transfer, there is no such temporal separation or explicit distinction between the moment when ownership is transferred and performance. The specifically contractual character of a right depends upon this separation. Moreover, in contrast to the so-called right *in rem* which is usually thought to result from a present transfer,[21] the right in contract is a right as against the other party only and to the other's performance – a right *in personam.* It is only with actual performance that this personal right against the other party becomes a real right against the world. Do these differences between a present transfer of property and contract preclude our understanding contract as a transfer of ownership between the parties?

The fact that a contractual transfer of right is accomplished prior to and independent of physical delivery presents a difficulty only if in principle there cannot be ownership or acquisition that is independent of physical detention. But in legal contemplation, this possibility is presupposed without question. The existence of a proprietary right does not, as such, depend upon an owner's having continuous physical possession of the object of the right. For example, this pen of mine remains my property even when I put it down and no longer have physical possession of it. Indeed, as Kant emphasized,[22] it is only if the pen can be viewed as juridically mine when I no longer physically hold it that I have a property right in it as distinct from a right of bodily integrity. If continuing physical possession were a prerequisite of having a right in the pen, that right could only be interfered with by touching me, and so it would become impossible to show that I have a property right in some *external* thing (the pen) in contrast with a right of personal or bodily integrity. But the law postulates just such property rights in external things. Consequently, owning something and having physical possession of it need not coincide. Ownership that is independent of physical detention must be thinkable from a juridical point of view.

21. I say "usually thought" because as I suggest in note 25 *infra,* this understanding of a present executed transfer may require revision.
22. *Supra* note 19 at pp. 401–403.

Nor does the fact that the right vests with physical delivery in a present transfer of property necessarily argue against the possibility of their separation, such as we find in contract. In a present transfer, it is not the physical delivery as such that confers ownership. Unless delivery expresses the requisite assents of the parties, no change in ownership takes place. Physical delivery is just the fulfilment of these assents and the mode of their existence. From a legal point of view, delivery is significant only if expressive of assent. The latter is therefore fully regulative with respect to the former. Contract makes this explicit by treating the parties' assents as the central – and indeed the whole – basis of the obligation. Unless expressions of assents require physical delivery in order to be ascertainable and effectual, the transition to contract is unexceptionable.

In this connection, it might be thought that the fact that the principle of first possession, which governs the appropriation of unowned things, requires some kind of initial, though not continuous, physical occupancy shows that physical detention of some sort is a general requirement for all acquisition, so that physical delivery may also be necessary for acquisition by contract. But this is not so. The requirement of occupancy for first possession is justified by the existence of conditions that are peculiar to it but that do not obtain in contract.

The principle of first possession governs the appropriation of something that is unowned and therefore formally available to anyone. The sort of things that can be so appropriated are individuated external (corporeal) objects that are independent of those who might appropriate them. And the right acquired by first possession is exclusive as against anyone else who comes afterward. Now, appropriation in general consists in the subordination of something to one's purposes to the exclusion of others. If we suppose that private law requires that acts of appropriation be publicly manifest to those who are excluded thereby, a prerequisite that there be some sort of initial physical occupation and some continuing sign of occupation seems justified in the above-stated circumstances of first possession. For it is only by physically bringing under one's control and power (that is, by occupying) an object of the kind contemplated under first possession that one can cancel its independence and thereby signal to others that one has subordinated it to one's purposes. Physical occupation of some sort is necessary to satisfy the publicity requirement.[23] By the principle of first possession, whoever occupies an unowned thing first becomes its owner relative to anyone else who comes after. And the juridically necessary act of occupation may be accomplished by a single individual alone, that is, by his or her unilateral act and choice.

By contrast, in contract the thing to be appropriated is *already* owned by (and subject to the purposes of) someone and it is therefore available to no one else. *Ex hypothesi,* it is already subordinated to its owner in a way that can be apparent to a second party. This thing can be acquired by the second party,

---

23. This rationale is suggested in such leading cases as *Pierson* v. *Post,* 3 Cai. R. 175 (N.Y. 1805).

not unilaterally as in first possession, but bilaterally, with and through the assent of the owner. The right acquired by the former is exclusive only as against the latter, not others. In these circumstances, the first party can transfer ownership in the thing to the second party without a change in physical possession. The second party need not occupy the thing in order to acquire it from the first. In contract, where acquisition is effected through the parties' interaction and the right acquired by one is exclusive only as against the other, acquisition must be public only as between these two parties. Thus, the publicity requirement is fully met so long as the two parties treat the thing as subject to their wills in a way that is mutually manifest as between them. More specifically, publicity is satisfied if the parties can make clear to each other their mutually related decisions to alienate and to appropriate in a way that recognizes the first party's initial ownership and the second party's acquisition. Now language is the most precise means by which the parties can signal mutual assent as between them. Accordingly, independent of any physical transfer, an agreement that enshrines the parties' assents in the appropriate way is in and of itself fully capable of effecting a transfer of ownership that satisfies publicity. In this respect, acquisition by first possession and contract are different.

Prima facie, then, the fact that contract, unlike a present transfer of property, separates the moment of assent from that of physical delivery need not disqualify it as a possible mode of transferring ownership. One may still ask, however, whether the fact that the right acquired at contract formation is a right *in personam* makes the logic of transfer inapplicable to contract? It might be assumed that, in contrast to a real right in a thing, a personal right is not a property right at all. This personal right is usually characterized as a right to the performance of a promise, not a right in a thing. Whereas it is readily apparent that one can transfer one's property in a thing, the same does not seem true of the performance of a promise: In what sense does a promisor own this performance and then transfer a right in it to the promisee?[24] We must therefore determine what exactly is the substance of the personal right to performance that is acquired in contract. The better view, I will now argue, is that while this right is indeed personal because it exists only as against a definite individual, it is nevertheless proprietary in character and therefore fully compatible with the idea of a transfer of ownership.

To begin, we should recall that from the point of view of contract law the wrong which a breach does to a promisee's right to performance consists in the promisee being deprived of the thing promised, including its value and use. This is made evident by the expectation remedy, whether expectation damages or specific performance, which aims to give the promisee physical possession of the

---

24. Stephen Smith raises and discusses this difficulty in S. Smith, "Towards a Theory of Contract," in J. Horder, ed., *Oxford Essays in Jurisprudence (Fourth Series)* (Oxford: Oxford University Press, 2000).

thing promised, including its value at the time performance is due. Money damages accomplish this purpose where the thing promised is not unique but is available to the promisee on a market: Damages represent both the value of the thing promised and the means of payment by which the promisee can obtain the thing, including its value, from the market. Specific performance, by contrast, is appropriate where the thing promised is for some reason unique so that it is only by giving or doing a specified thing that the promisee can be put into possession of the thing promised, including its value. The thing promised, it should be added, may be either an external object of some sort or a service. The aim of the law is put the plaintiff in the position he or she would have been in had he or she obtained physical possession of the thing promised in accordance with the terms of the contract. In legal contemplation, then, the right to performance consists just in a right to have exclusive physical possession of the thing promised in the manner stipulated by the contract. This right to physical possession vests at formation. It is either honoured by performance or injured by breach.

The right is proprietary in character. When performance is due, the promisee *already* has the right to possess the promised thing in accordance with the contractual terms and the promisor *already* has no such right. Now it is axiomatic that one who has the exclusive ownership of some thing has the right to possess it. The right to possess is an essential aspect of ownership. And unless one retains some right of physical possession, one ceases to be owner. The fact, therefore, that when performance is due the promisor already has no such right as against the promisee, and that the promisee alone does have such a right, means that the promisor has already ceased to be owner as against the promisee and that the promisee has already become one. This change in ownership takes place at formation. Delivery neither adds to nor affects in any way this juridical situation as between the parties. By putting the promisee into actual physical possession of the thing as promised, delivery merely respects the promisee's already existing right.

Moreover, because this right is against a definite individual – the promisor – and, more fundamentally, because the promisee acquires it through the promisor, it is a personal right. The fact that a right is personal does not entail that it is non-proprietary but simply goes to the mode of acquiring it. In contrast to a real right, which a person obtains by means of his or her act alone exercised upon some thing in accordance with the principle of first possession, a personal right supposes an acquisition that is accomplished through the combined acts of will of two parties – in particular, appropriation of some thing by means of another's alienation of it.[25]

25. To elaborate, the view that I am proposing is that, by first principles of juridical right, a real right is always and only a right in a thing that is acquired by first possession whereas a personal right is always and only a right in a thing that is acquired from another. Applied to contract, at formation the promisee acquires a personal right in a thing or service as against the promisor. Delivery does not alter in any way the relation of right as between the parties but only gives the promisee a real right, founded upon the principle of first possession, as against

The fact that the promisee may only take physical possession after formation and through delivery in accordance with the terms of the contract does not argue against formation's being the moment when ownership is transferred. Appropriation of any kind necessarily implies the possibility of taking physical possession and any act of taking physical possession necessarily occurs at a definite time and place and in a definite manner. This is as true of appropriation of an unowned thing by first possession as it is of contract. Any difference between them in this regard simply reflects the way in which they determine the modalities of taking possession. In the case of appropriation by first possession, the time, place, and manner of taking physical possession are decided by a single person alone and the act of taking possession coincides with, and indeed is a necessary condition of, appropriation. In the case of contract, on the other hand, the modalities of taking physical possession are fixed beforehand at the moment of formation by the promisor in agreement with the promisee: The time, place, and manner of taking physical possession simply reflect the particular way in which the promisor has alienated his or her property; the promisee cannot obtain physical possession in any other way without injuring the promisor's right of ownership. In contrast with acquisition by first possession, one can have in contract a *right* to physical possession before one actually takes physical possession, with the act of taking physical possession through delivery representing the exercise and fulfilment of this right. At the limit, the parties can agree that the promisee may exercise the right of taking physical possession instantly upon conclusion of contract formation. On this analysis, then, what a promisee acquires at formation by way of the transfer of ownership is either an external thing or a service, not the promised performance. Performance merely determines the way in which the promisee gains physical possession of the thing or service of which he or she already has rightful possession and specifies what the promisor must do or not do to avoid injuring the promisee's entitlement. The promisee's right to performance simply reflects the fact that the promisee is owner as against the promisor. [26]

all others. This analysis also applies to executed transfers of property. In the latter, as I have already noted, it is not the physical transfer of possession as such but the fact that the transfer embodies the parties' mutually related assents that allows us to infer a transfer of ownership. The cause of the transferee's proprietary interest in the thing transferred is the parties' assents. It is on this basis that the transferee has a right, as against the transferor, to retain the thing now in his or her physical possession and that the transferor can no longer assert his or her initial property in it. This right, founded upon the parties' wills, is, it must be emphasized, a right only as against the transferor. It diminishes or defeats only his or her claim to the thing. It is a right *in personam*. Although the transferee also has a proprietary interest in the thing transferred as against third parties – a right *in rem* – this is not founded on the transfer of ownership from the owner but on the fact that, relative to third parties, the transferee can reasonably claim first physical possession of it as something which they did not own. So, even a present transfer entails upon analysis the distinction between personal and real rights. Contract simply makes it explicit by separating them into the two distinct moments of agreement and performance.

26. In reaching this conclusion, I am departing from Kant's view. According to Kant, what the promisee acquires at formation is just the promise of performance. The promise is the substance of the promisee's personal right as against the promisor. See Kant, *supra* note 19 at

The promisee's so-called right to the promisor's performance reflects, then, a transfer of ownership at the moment of formation. It is a right that is at once personal and proprietary in character. Indeed, its specific proprietary nature is inseparable from its being a right *in personam.* Understood in this way, a right *in personam* is no less proprietary than a right *in rem.* The fact that contract formation gives the promisee a right to performance does not, I conclude, make the logic of transfer inapplicable to contract.

D. Conclusion

Let me briefly gather together the main points made thus far by referring them to the first fundamental question of modern contract theory, namely, the justification of the expectation remedy for breach of a wholly executory agreement. Taking Fuller's challenge to heart, we say that unless such an agreement can itself be a source of entitlements of the kind protected by expectation damages or specific performance, the expectation remedy cannot qualify as a principle of compensation – in contradiction with what is perhaps the most basic contention of contract law. We must therefore explore the possibility of conceiving contract, and more particularly the moment of agreement, as a mode of transferring ownership. In this Part, I have done this by starting with a familiar and relatively uncontested instance of acquisition by one person from another – a present, executed transfer of property – and by considering next the possibility of a purely contractual, non-physical transfer of ownership. Contract as transfer represents a conception of contract that seems to provide the beginnings of an answer to our first question, one that is responsive to Fuller's objection. Briefly stated, the logic of a transfer of ownership is an intelligible and juridically thinkable idea which, *prima facie,* seems applicable to contract no less than to a present transfer of property. If the law of contract can indeed be understood in terms of the logic of transfer, the expectation remedy is the natural and distinctively contractual principle of compensation.

The aim of Part III is to transform this "if" into a justified conclusion. It does so by trying to show how the main doctrines of contract law, both individually and in combination, embody the conception of contract as transfer. The latter functions as their organizing idea. But, it should be emphasized, this involves more than merely applying the logic of transfer as just presented. The organizing

pp. 424–425. On this point, my understanding of contract seems to fit better with Hegel's account. See Hegel, *supra* note 19 at para. 40 (Remark) and para.79. My view immediately raises a number of questions: Why, for example, is the risk of loss of the object during the interval between agreement and performance ordinarily borne by the promisor when, I have argued, it is the promisee who is owner vis-à-vis the promisor? Or why is it the case that ordinarily a promisee cannot recover profits gained by the promisor through breach of contract when there can be recovery of gains obtained through conversion of property? I cannot address these questions here. I think, however, that they can be readily answered from within the view that I have set out.

idea of contract as transfer is in fact worked out more fully and completely via the analysis of contract doctrines. For example, at this point, while we have identified the main conditions of contract as transfer, we do not yet understand how this conception can coherently combine the two seemingly contrary features of temporal sequence and simultaneous co-presence in the double consent needed to constitute a transfer. Nor have we explained how the parties can have individual exclusive rights yet have one identical thing at the same time, as is required by the principle of continuity. It will be through the analysis of contract doctrines in Part II that I hope to explain these features, in this way deepening our understanding of the organizing idea itself.

III. The Common Law Conception of Contract

My object in this part is to elucidate, through a detailed analysis of the doctrines of offer and acceptance, consideration, and unconscionability, the conception of contract that is implicit in the common law of contract. The analysis which follows orients itself by, and seeks to remain internal to, the legal point of view. It is guided by the idea of a public basis of justification. We begin with these doctrines of contract law, not because we assume that in their authoritative legal formulations they are fully true and reasonable nor because we view them as incontrovertible data which any theory must fit. Rather, we treat the doctrines just as provisionally fixed points for working out a conception of contract and we begin with them because no better or more natural starting point offers itself for the purposes of a public basis of justification. There is no guarantee in advance that the doctrines as ordinarily formulated and understood can be so justified. Moreover, as I emphasized in the Introduction, the reasonableness of a particular doctrine can be established only through its integration with the other doctrines in an intelligible and juridically meaningful whole. Finally, wherever possible, we begin with doctrines that are not only fundamental but settled and uncontested as well, at least from the legal point of view. Once again, we do this, not because it warrants their truth or reasonableness, but because it signifies that on these matters the authoritative public reason presents itself as of one mind and therefore provides us with doctrines and principles that can perhaps be worked up into a *public* conception of contract.

A. Offer and Acceptance

The first doctrine I examine is offer and acceptance. To begin, I present a brief summary of its main features. The description that follows will not, I believe, be controversial. Taking this set of features as a provisionally fixed starting point for further discussion, I then make more explicit the conception of contract which the doctrine seems to imply and I specify its role within this conception. Since, we shall see, promise is essential to offer and acceptance, the question naturally arises as to the significance of promise in the analysis of offer and acceptance. Does the presence of promise mean that contractual obligation is based upon the moral duty to keep one's word? After addressing this question, I end the discussion of offer and acceptance by explaining the limits of its role within the conception of contract and the need for other doctrines to supplement it.

1. THE MAIN FEATURES OF OFFER AND ACCEPTANCE AND ITS ROLE IN THE CONCEPTION OF CONTRACT. Along with the doctrine of consideration, the doctrine of offer and acceptance is traditionally thought to stipulate definite conditions that are essential to the formation of non-formal contracts at common law. This requirement is general. Put briefly, the doctrine of offer and acceptance holds that formation can only result from mutually related voluntary manifestations of assent by two parties to the same identical terms. The existence of these assents as well as the determination of their contents are decided in accordance with the so-called objective test. By this test, it is the *manifestation of assent as it reasonably appears to the other party* that is operative in bringing about formation. The relevant factor is not its author's state of mind; nor is the expression of assent treated as evidence of his or her mental attitude. Rather, the reasonably construed expression of assent in and of itself, not the thought process that produced it, is the operative factor in formation.[27]

The prevailing view[28] at common law is that there must be a first expression of assent, the offer, that is followed in time by a second, the acceptance. The offer must come before and must request the acceptance which, in turn, must be made after and in response to the offer. Now, it is widely supposed that, to constitute an offer, the first assent must include a promise. "An offer," Williston writes, "necessarily looks to the future [and] gives the person to whom it is addressed an assurance that, on some contingency at least, he shall have something."[29] To qualify as an offer, then, the first expression of assent must manifest a fully crystallized and fixed present decision to do or not do something in the future, thereby creating in the offeree the reasonable expectation that the offeror does not presently intend to change this decision before the time comes for performance. Further, the offer must say not only what the offeror promises to do but also what the offeree must do in return. The offer must contain all the terms of the contract to be made and must request an acceptance that assents to precisely the same terms.

---

27. On the definition and the role of the objective test, see S. Williston, "Mutual Assent in the Formation of Contracts" (1919) 14 Ill. L. Rev. 85 reprinted in *Selected Readings, supra* note 3, pp. 119–127 [hereinafter *Mutual Assent*]
28. Corbin thought differently. See Corbin, *supra* note 17 at Ch.1, s. 12 ("Simultaneous Expressions of Assent"). I note here that Kant takes the view that the empirical acts of assent must be temporally successive. Kant, *supra* note 19 at pp. 422–423.
29. S. Williston, "An Offer is a Promise" (1928) 23 Ill. L. R. 100 reprinted in *Selected Readings, supra* note 3, pp. 213–217.

In legal contemplation, such mutually related expressions of assent in their externality (that is, as they reasonably appear to the other party) are acts that alter the legal relations between the parties in the following ways. The immediate necessary legal consequence of an offer, standing alone, is that it gives the offeree a power – *not* a right – of acceptance. So long as an offer continues to stand (and this is decided in accordance with the objective test), the offeree may bring into existence a contractual relation, comprising contractual rights and corresponding duties, simply by accepting the proposed terms in the manner expressly or impliedly stipulated by the offer. It cannot be emphasized too much, however, that a contract results from two acts of will, not one, and therefore that unless and until there is acceptance, no contractual rights or duties whatsoever arise between the parties.[30] It follows from the fact that an offer confers merely a power but not a right of acceptance that prior to acceptance an offer may be revoked without infringing any contractual right in the offeree. In other words, there is in law a liberty to revoke an as yet unaccepted offer.

There is a final feature of offer and acceptance that must be noted. The doctrine of offer and acceptance, we have seen, requires that the offer precedes the acceptance in time. Absent temporal sequence, there is no contract formation. The assents must figure as separate acts which each originate with an individual party at a different moment in time. Temporally sequenced assents function, we may say, as the efficient cause of contract. This, however, is not the end of the matter. For the common law also holds that these same assents, still construed in accordance with the objective test and functioning as the efficient cause of contract, must be given at the same time: it must be possible to construe the assents in some sense as absolutely co-present and simultaneous, in addition to being temporally successive.[31] Unless they can be so conceived, there will not be contract formation. So viewed, the assents are treated under the rubric of the "union or meeting of the minds." The common law presents us, therefore, with the apparent paradox that the assents necessary for contract formation must be both separate in time and simultaneous.

---

30. It is worth noting here that the very first paragraph of Langdell's *Summary of the Law of Contracts* (Second Edition, 1880) states this basic requirement that a legally enforceable promise must be constituted by two acts of will, not one. Langdell's now generally derided method, often pejoratively referred to as " logical," "deductive," or "axiomatic," is nothing but an effort to understand, and to present the analysis of contract as rooted in and as implied by, this fundamental juridical thought. Its starting point is legal experience and it attempts to bring out the order which governs this experience. I would have thought that this makes his account, while not necessarily correct or satisfactory in all its details, at least systematic in the right way.

31. This feature is supposed in the case law. See, for example, *Dickinson* v. *Dodds,* (1874) 2 Ch. D. 463 at p. 472; *Household Insurance Co.* v. *Grant,* (1879) 4 Ex. Div. 216 at 220. A typical statement is found in J. P. Bishop's purely descriptive account of the positive law, *The Doctrines of the Law of Contracts in Their Principal Outlines, Stated, Illustrated, and Condensed* (St. Louis: F. H. Thomas and Company, 1878) at p. 62: "Each [party] must consent to exactly the same thing to which the other does, and at the same instant of time."

How, if at all, can these diverse features be held together? And what conception of contract do they imply? These are the main questions for discussion.

To begin, the expressions of assent that constitute offer and acceptance must be voluntary. Generally speaking, voluntariness goes to the existence, character, and conditions of the activity of choosing. Here, however, we seek a definition of the voluntary that belongs to the juridical and, in particular, to the law of contract. We need not assume that the voluntary in contract is identical with the voluntary in other domains of moral experience. Now, according to the traditional understanding of contract law, the voluntary plays a special role in contract in that it is the parties' wills, mutually related and objectively construed, that are in themselves the source of the parties' contractual rights and duties. I shall pursue this fundamental thesis and argue that each of the main doctrines of contract – more specifically, offer and acceptance, consideration, and unconscionability – contributes to the full and complete definition of the voluntary in contract. Through an ordered examination of these doctrines, we build up this definition step by step.

The first step in defining the voluntary in contract is provided by the doctrine of offer and acceptance. It is first because, we shall see, it sets out the elementary form of mutual assent that is obtained at contract formation. However, it should be kept in mind in the following discussion that it is *only* the first step and does not provide the complete elaboration of the definition of the voluntary. This it cannot do precisely because, as I will explain in more detail, it articulates *just* the form of mutual assent and does not specify the content which the assents must have if they are to give rise to contractual rights and duties. Besides stipulating formally that the parties must assent to the same terms, it does *not* determine *what* those terms must be for there to be a contract. This latter function, I shall argue, is performed by the doctrines of consideration and unconscionability.

The doctrine of offer and acceptance presents an extremely restricted criterion of voluntariness. It categorically excludes much that is relevant to the determination of the voluntary in other domains of law and morals, and perhaps this is the chief significance of its role. Under the doctrine of offer and acceptance, the voluntary is simply the quality of choice that is needed for expressions of assent to function as offer or acceptance. By this test, an expression of assent is voluntary if it is the product of a decision or choice in given circumstances. Here the voluntary equals purposiveness. Assent is purposive and hence voluntary so long as it need not be viewed as just the simple mechanical effect of some internal or external cause, whether human or natural. For example, my signature is not the outcome of choice and so not voluntary if it is produced by someone else forcibly moving my hand in the necessary way. But the fact that I sign in order to avoid an outcome which may be unwanted or even unjust does not preclude my signature from being something chosen in response to particular circumstances. It can still be a decision, and so be voluntary, whatever its motivation and however mistaken it may turn out to be.

The absence of the voluntary, so understood, entails the absence of one or both acts that are necessary for contract formation. At common law, it renders an agreement absolutely null and void *ab initio*. Where, however, the assents are the product of choice and thus purposive but are either mistaken or given to avoid an unwanted or even an unjust alternative, this does not vitiate their capacity to function as offer and acceptance. It does not make the agreement void *ab initio*. At law, it can result in the agreement being at most voidable at the election of the party who would not have transacted in the absence of the mistake or unwanted circumstances, where the mistake goes to the very foundation of the agreement or where the unwanted circumstances have been created by the other party's wrong. These considerations that render an agreement voidable do not come under the doctrine of offer and acceptance. To repeat, so far as offer and acceptance goes, the voluntary acts necessary for contract formation can exist even where an agreement is voidable. And that is precisely why, so long as there are offer and acceptance, the parties can decide to affirm their agreement even in the face of mistake or unwanted circumstances.[32]

In keeping with the objective test, the voluntary assent that is required by the doctrine of offer and acceptance does not, however, necessarily take into account or depend upon a party's actual particular reasons for giving assent. What a party must reasonably ascertain is just the existence, as an external fact, of the other party's assent to definite terms. It bears repetition that what counts is only what is made reasonably manifest to another and this need not coincide with a party's actual reasons or purposes. Further, while assent is voluntary only

---

32. To elaborate, if a party alleges that he or she has entered a contract on a mistaken assumption of fact, this does not prevent contract formation. There can still be offer and acceptance, even though the resulting obligation may be qualified by a tacit presupposition concerning the presumed existence of certain facts at the time of contract formation – facts about which one or both parties may have been mistaken. If the contract can be reasonably construed as implicitly founded upon such presupposition, it may be voidable at the election of the mistaken party. At the same time, the parties may choose to enforce the contract despite the mistake – something they cannot do if the agreement is void *ab initio*. Where assent has been given under the influence of another's unlawful conduct, the latter cannot enforce the agreement, not because there has been no consent, but rather because the agreement represents the materialization of his or her wrong. Enforcement of the contract is something of benefit to the wrongdoer – therefore something which the latter should not obtain when it results from his or her wrong. But here again the existence of duress does not prevent contract formation and the coerced party may elect to have the agreement enforced. As for the relation between the conception of voluntariness in offer and acceptance and norms of substantive fairness in contract, I discuss this in detail in the section on unconscionability, *infra* pp. 198ff. I simply note here that, like fundamental mistake or duress, unconscionability renders an agreement voidable, not void *ab initio*. For a helpful discussion of the distinction between void *ab initio* and voidable, see Corbin, *supra* note 17 at pp. 10–12. For a detailed and full treatment of the relation between consent (within offer and acceptance) and mistake, see G. E. Palmer, *Mistake and Unjust Enrichment* (Ohio: Ohio State University Press, 1962). The proposed analysis of the relation between consent and duress is an accord with writers of the natural law tradition such as Grotius as well as with contemporary scholars such as Dawson. See Grotius, *supra* note 17 at Bk. II, Chap. XI, v. and J. Dawson, "Economic Duress – An Essay in Perspective" (1947) 45 Mich. L. Rev. 253 at pp. 266–267.

insofar as it is purposive, the purpose or reason which makes it voluntary must, in accordance with the objective test, be intrinsically relational. To be intrinsically relational, a party's reason for making an offer must be the other's acceptance and vice versa. It is this – and *only* this – reason which is contractually relevant. But a party's particular reasons for transacting need not as such be relational in the required way. Therefore the fact that a party happens to have this or that reason for offering or accepting does not necessarily assure its relevance for the purposes of contract. Through the doctrine of offer and acceptance and in particular the objective test, contract law begins the procedure of specifying the sort of reason or purpose that *is* relevant to and necessary for contract formation by *not* according intrinsic juridical significance or weight to the particular reasons and purposes which the parties may happen to have.

The doctrine of offer and acceptance identifies voluntariness with a capacity to choose that is conceived in abstraction from the circumstances of choice. I have suggested further that the particular reason a party agrees to terms is not in and of itself a factor that is operative in bringing about formation. Consequently, the fact that a transaction does not fulfill a party's reason for entering it, or the fact that the party now views this reason as mistaken, does not, in itself, prevent or otherwise affect contract formation. Taking this analysis one step further, one can conclude that contract formation is, by its very nature, independent of whether transactions are to the overall advantage or benefit of one or even of both of the parties. The impact of performance on the well-being of the parties is, in itself, wholly irrelevant to the question of formation. This indifference to particular interest and advantage as such is reflected in the (contractually) unfettered liberty of a party to revoke an offer before it is accepted or to decline, for whatever reason, to make an offer in the first place, irrespective of the impact which such decisions may have on the other party's well-being. In and of itself, the fact that my interests or welfare will be adversely affected by your decision does not give me a claim – or even the beginning of a claim —in contract against you. The doctrine of offer and acceptance seems at its core to be indifferent to the very kinds of considerations that centrally concern distributive justice.

The doctrine of offer and acceptance implies, then, a very bare conception of the person. Parties are attributed a capacity for decision and purposive action that abstracts from the circumstances in which the capacity is exercised; that is, they are viewed as having a capacity for choice that is not determined by, but rather is independent of, all given factors both internal and external. In chains, we say, one can still be free. A party's particular intentions and motives, his or her personal features and moral qualities, and finally, his or her resources and interests, are all, as such, irrelevant to the analysis of offer and acceptance. This analysis does not directly take into consideration, then, the very things that distinguish one individual from another. Viewed in abstraction from them, individuals are necessarily identical. Hence, we may say, persons are conceived here as free just in virtue of their having a capacity for choice that is undetermined by the circumstances of choice and that they are equal just insofar as, being free, they are identical. Finally, because what matters for the analysis of offer and acceptance is simply whether one party has *acted* in a way that reasonably can be construed by the other as a voluntary expression of assent to certain definite terms, parties count just in virtue of their acts. The doctrine of offer and acceptance views them simply as free and equal agents who jointly bring about contract formation.[33]

In addition to being voluntary, the parties' assents, we have seen, must satisfy certain further requirements if they are to function as offer and acceptance: the assents must be mutually related in such way that they can be construed both as temporally successive and as simultaneous in accordance with the objective test. How are these aspects interconnected and what conception of contract do they suggest?

Consider, first, the requirement that the parties' assents must be temporally successive. To be a valid offer, the first assent must call for an acceptance; and reciprocally, to be a valid acceptance, the second assent must be given in response to the first and on the very same terms. The fact that the assents must be made in temporal sequence makes it possible for the parties themselves to bring about contract formation *in and through their interaction.* Because an offer must come first in time, it can address the other party who can then, in turn, respond to it. In this way, the offer can invite the participation of the offeree and

---

33. This conception of the person is essentially the same as the concept of personality that Hegel, for one, argues underlies abstract right. The difference between the two is just that the former belongs to a public basis of justification whereas the latter is part of a comprehensive philosophical account of right in which right expresses, and is constituted by, the freedom of the will as practical reason. In the public justification, the conception of the person is presented simply as implicit in the public legal culture – here, in the doctrines of contract law – and as fitting both with a certain idea of legal relation – here, a contractual relation in which parties are vested with correlative rights and duties at contract formation – as well as with the principles of contract law. The conception of the person is not presented as the ground or as constitutive of either this legal relation or these principles. In a public justification, no part is foundational relative to the others; rather, the distinct parts are presented as mutually supportive and intrinsically interconnected. In the philosophical accounts of Hegel or Kant, by contrast, personality, as freedom of the will and practical reason, is the conceptual basis and is itself constitutive of definite principles of right. According to Hegel, the claim that this is, and *must* be, the case can be vindicated only by viewing the account of right as one section or element in the whole chain of systematic philosophy set out in the *Encyclopaedia.* See, Hegel, *supra* note 19 at paras. 2 and 4. The truth and deepest significance of the account of right – and therefore of personality itself – can only be established as part of this totality. At the same time, Hegel himself suggests that the account of right can be detached from this comprehensive context and can be presented on its own in way that appeals to everyone's educated self-consciousness and moral experience. Ibid., para. 4. In this way, the elements in the philosophical account can be presented as parts of a public basis of justification. For a more detailed discussion of the role of the conception of the person in a public basis of justification of private law, see P. Benson, "Public Justification," *supra* note 12 at pp. 314–321. For a summary presentation of Hegel's conception of personality, see P. Benson, "Rawls, Hegel, and Personhood" (1994) 22 Political Theory 491.

be completed by it. The offer contemplates and creates the possibility of a relation between the two assents and this possibility is realized by the acceptance. No third party, such as a court, is needed to create a relation between the expressions of assent. The parties do so themselves. Since the objective test applies, the relevant point of view is always how what is said or done by one party reasonably appears to the other in the circumstances of their interaction. And this appearance the first party, as a reasonable person, is deemed to know. The cause of contract lies, then, entirely in the interaction between the parties.

Moreover, because each of the assents must state the terms of the whole transaction, each side necessarily incorporates on its face the whole relation between them. Mutual relatedness is intrinsic to each of the assents in their role as cause of contract. Thus the manner in which the parties' mutual assents bring about formation through interaction is itself relational through and through. The fundamental and irreducible unit of contract formation is not each of the assents taken separately and then summed together but rather these assents in their mutual relatedness. They have no standing or even existence, contractually speaking, outside of their relation. The basic form of contract is relation to another.

Unless an objective test is adopted, the expressions of assent cannot be temporally sequenced. On a subjective test, which holds that it is actual, inner assent to terms that is causally necessary for contract formation and that expressions of assent are merely evidence of such actual assent, the second party is not justified in treating even a clear expression of actual assent given by the first party at one moment as actual assent an instant later. For in the interval, however brief, the first party's mind may have changed. And, of course, a party is entitled to change his or her mind unless or until there is a valid acceptance. But there must be an interval between the offer and the acceptance, at least if the offeree is to ascertain the existence of the offer and to give the acceptance in response to it. So in this necessary interval, however small, between the offer and acceptance, the continued existence of assent must be confirmed by a fresh expression of actual assent given by the offeror. This, however, does not do away with the difficulty since, as long as we suppose that the offeree must respond to the this newest expression of assent, there must be a further interval and during this interval the offeror's intentions may have changed, requiring a new assent. And so on, *ad infinitum.* To avoid this consequence, the offer must be made at the very moment the offeree accepts. Accordingly, a subjective test requires that offer and acceptance be initiated at the same time. Whatever is said or done by the parties before or after that moment is irrelevant because it is assent that is either no longer or not yet in existence.

A subjective test rules out, therefore, a temporally sequenced offer and acceptance. Even if the simultaneous assents happen to state the identical terms, they do not do so *as mutually related.* They are just two expressions, having the same content, that exist side by side. In giving their assents, the parties do not themselves bring about any relation between them.

By contrast, on the objective test, the first party's expression of assent *continues* to exist as an external fact, prior to acceptance, unless or until it lapses by its own terms or is revoked by a further separate external expression of will by the first party. During the interval that necessarily separates the two assents, the offeror "must be considered in law as making during every instant . . . the same identical offer"[34] to the offeree. In virtue of its continuing existence, the first assent can be met by a second assent in response. There can be offer and acceptance on the basis of the parties' interaction alone.

Why, it may be asked, is it fair and reasonable for the law to impose an objective test on parties in a contractual setting? By way of an answer, a public justification of contract seeks a fit between this test and the essential character of the contractual relation as disclosed by the main doctrines of contract law. The doctrine of offer and acceptance teaches that contract is a certain union of assents. More particularly, it presents each side as contemplating the other as necessary to fulfill the very terms it proposes. Now, by making the participation of the other side a necessary condition of the fulfillment of its own terms, each side must reasonably acknowledge the pertinence of the standpoint of the other in construing what it has said or done to engage that participation. The other-directed orientation of the objective test mirrors the fact that each assent contemplates the existence and the participation of – and therefore a relationship with – the other as a condition of the fulfillment of its own terms. In addition, because the objective test abstracts from the parties' particular preferences, purposes, inward intentions and motives and makes salient just their mutually related acts, it refers solely to the external dimension in interaction and not at all to subjective moral factors that pertain to judgments of virtue and character. This is appropriate where the sole question is whether the parties are subject to coercible obligations *inter se*. The doctrine of offer and acceptance and the objective test are mutually supportive in conceiving contract under the idea of relation to another.[35]

On this basis, moreover, we can see why entitlements acquired at formation must be personal, that is, as between the contracting parties only. By the ob-

---

34. *Adams* v. *Lindsell,* (1818) 1 B & Ald. 681 at p. 683.
35. It should be noted that this explanation does not invoke the idea of estoppel. On an estoppel approach, if parties have actually assented to certain terms, they are bound because of their assent; if, however, one of them has *not* actually assented but nevertheless reasonably appears to the other to have done so, and the other party in accepting has reasonably relied on this appearance of assent, the first party is bound because estopped from denying the foreseeable consequences of such reliance. Now, in general, the kind of reliance which estoppel requires involves a change of position to one's detriment. And, in particular, to explain the enforceability of a wholly executory contract, estoppel must apply just to the fact that a party has accepted an apparent offer prior to and independent of any further action taken in reliance upon it. An obvious difficulty with this approach, as Williston correctly points out, is that the mere act of accepting an offer and the mere supposition that one has made a contract do not, in and of themselves, amount to such detrimental reliance. See Williston, "Mutual Assent," *supra* note 27 at p. 122.

jective test, the parties' assents are construed in accordance with their reasonable meanings *inter se*. The meaning is public only as between the parties. Taking publicity as a formal requirement of the assertion of rights, a party's contractual rights can be exclusive, therefore, only as against the other party, not as against a stranger to the contract. It is worth noting, finally, that we have reached the conclusion that contract rights can only be personal rights through a discussion of the doctrine of offer and acceptance alone, without as yet any reference to the doctrine of consideration.

Taking the requirement of temporal succession as given, how can the law also hold that the assents must in some sense be simultaneous? And precisely in what sense is this further requirement to be taken?

Viewed in light of the objective test, an unrevoked offer continues to be made up to and including the moment it is met by an acceptance. This is how the offer must be represented if there is to be contract formation. It is also necessary, we have seen, if contract formation is to result from the parties' interaction alone. Given this interpretation of the offer, it follows that when the offer is met by an acceptance there is a present expression of assent to definite terms (the offer) which is united with a second present expression of assent to the identical terms (the acceptance). In other words, to produce contract formation, there must be two absolutely *co-present and simultaneous* expressions of assent. The so-called meeting of minds, which is often stated to be an essential condition of contract formation, is just the parties' mutual assents viewed as simultaneous and co-present.

It is important to emphasize here that the so-called meeting of the minds is to be construed in accordance with the objective test and consists in this union of assents at the same instant. In legal contemplation, this union abstracts from the parties' inner mental dispositions and intentions, their personal features, needs, interests, and well-being. It is a relation between the two expressions of assent just in their externality. Like the analysis of the assents as temporally sequenced, their representations as simultaneous is framed in terms of the objective test. Unless the expressions of assent are appropriately detached from the parties' actual particular intentions and reasons, the entire doctrine of offer and acceptance must instantly collapse.

Viewed as simultaneous and co-present, offer and acceptance are formally identical and mutually related acts. Each is an assent to the very same terms – the whole transaction, whatever it may be. The fact that the assents are given by different persons is indeed a distinction; but, given the abstraction from temporal sequence as well as from particularities that differentiate one individual from another, it is a distinction that imports no difference. It is true that one party's right is the other's duty, and vice-versa. But we will see that the full definition of contract postulates a baseline in which the rights and duties of one party are identical in content to those of the other and in which parties have rights only insofar as they have duties.[36] here again, there is no difference. In short, the union of simultaneous assents that is necessary to bring about contract formation is a relation between two formally equal expressions of will.

The idea that contract formation depends upon and results from the offer and acceptance being simultaneous and co-present follows therefore from an analysis of contract formation that roots it in the parties' interaction alone in accordance with the objective test. Both representations of the assents – as separate in time and as simultaneous – belong to a single conception of contract formation. They are two aspects of one doctrine of offer and acceptance. Viewed in terms of *when* the parties *actually posit* or *originate* their acts of offer or acceptance, the assents must figure as temporally separate. When, however, these same assents are viewed at contract formation in light of the objective test, they are construed as co-present. But in so construing them, it cannot be the case that the common law is saying that the parties actually give their assents at the same time. This would directly contradict the requirement that they be made at different times. "Simultaneity" must therefore mean something other than "at the same moment in time." It cannot have a temporal significance. Perhaps it is on account of this contrast with the familiar and necessary fact that the assents must be given in time and indeed at different times that the notion of simultaneity – including the idea that an unrevoked offer is made at each instant up to and including the moment it is accepted – is commonly regarded as a legal fiction. I will return to this point later.

The foregoing analysis of mutual assent in the doctrine of offer and acceptance seems on its face to reflect certain central premises of the logic of a transfer of ownership. The doctrine requires that there be *two* mutually related assents that are initiated in *temporal sequence* yet that, when viewed objectively at contract formation, can be construed as absolutely *co-present*. The fact that there must be two assents is consistent with the fundamental idea that a transfer of right requires two parties and two acts of will: There must be alienation and appropriation. The requirement that the assents must be separate in time is compatible with their being viewed as acts of alienation and appropriation that are sequenced in accordance with the logic of a transfer of ownership: that the acceptance must come after the offer is consistent with the idea that appropriation by one from another must acknowledge and respect the other's initial right and must only take place with the other's consent. The fact that it is possible to view the parties' temporally sequenced assents as also simultaneous makes the requirement of offer and acceptance compatible with the idea of continuity as applied to the acts that constitute a transfer of ownership. Finally, the presentation of the parties in accordance with the objective test focuses just on their acts in abstraction from the their particular interests, needs, purposes and so forth –

---

36. See the analysis of equality in a contract of exchange under the doctrine of unconscionability, text at *infra* note 89 *et seq.*

in the very way that persons are viewed as participants in a transfer of owner-ship. In these respects at least, offer and acceptance construes the parties' in-teraction consistently with the logic of transfer.

2. THE SIGNIFICANCE OF PROMISE IN OFFER AND ACCEPTANCE. An of-fer, I have said, must contain a *promise* by at least the offeror. The admittedly essential presence of promise might seem to suggest that a more appropriate, or at least an intuitively more appealing, way to view the obligation in contract would be to understand it as rooted in the moral duty to keep one's promise. There is no need to invoke the more complicated idea of a transfer of owner-ship. This, however, would be mistaken. To see why, it is necessary to identify certain important differences between promise and contract, when the latter is conceived on the model of a transfer of right.[37] I should emphasize that in the following discussion I consider promissory duty and contractual obligation as they arise absent reliance.

In ordinary moral experience, one's duty to keep a promise – let us call it a duty of fidelity – arises just from the fact that one has made a promise: that is, from one's own undertaking in and of itself. Although the promise may be made to another, for another's benefit, or even with another's approval, the other's assent is not a causally operative element in bringing the duty of fidelity into existence. The promisor's act *alone* is sufficient to give rise to a duty of fidelity. By contrast, the obligation in contract arises only through the combined assents of two parties, not just one.

There is a second related difference between promise and contract. Given that the source of the duty of fidelity is in the promisor's will alone, the determina-tion of whether this duty exists, what it requires in particular circumstances, and whether it has been properly discharged must take into account the promisor's own conscientious evaluation of the pertinent considerations. (Recall here that what is under discussion is promissory duty that arises apart from reliance.) In contrast with contract, it would be unreasonable to use an objective test to determine whether someone has acted to bring him or herself under a duty of fidelity. Here in judging a promisor's conduct, a promisee should reasonably consider the subjective side; the promisor's actual intentions and motives as well as insight into the matter are morally relevant. In coming to a decision to promise or not in the first place, a promisor may, and morally speaking, should reasonably take into account such factors as the legitimate particular needs, in-terests, and responsibilities not only of him or herself and of the promisee but also of third parties. The promisor must ascertain whether promising someone

---

37. The following discussion draws on distinctions between contract and promise that are sug-gested by a number of writers including Grotius, Hobbes, and Hegel. See Grotius, *supra* note 17, Bk. II, Ch. XI, iv; T. Hobbes, *Leviathan,* ed. C. B. Macpherson (New York: Penguin Books, 1968), Part I, Ch. 14; and Hegel, *supra* note 19 at para. 79.

something in particular circumstances is good, all things considered. The relevant point of view must make reference to the promisor's own conception of the good. This standpoint governs right up to the moment of performance. The promisor must conscientiously determine that the relevant considerations, which existed at the time the promise was made, continue to exist when performance is expected. And these considerations, it bears repetition, make reference to particular needs, interests, purposes, and so forth. Whether a promisor has lived up to the requirements of fidelity is determined, at least in part, by the carefulness and conscientiousness of the promisor's assessment.

A third difference between promise and contract is that in making a promise, a promisor undertakes to do or give something in the *future:* consistent with the promisor's intention, the promisee does not acquire anything unless and until this undertaking is fulfilled.[38] From the standpoint of rights, everything depends upon whether this future performance takes place and whether the latter takes place permissibly depends in part upon the promisor's conscientious but subjective (that is, first-person) evaluation of what the duty of fidelity requires of him or her in the circumstances. In the case of contract, however, the parties' agreement exhaustively enshrines their full and complete present decisions to transfer ownership. At the moment of contract formation, the parties' assents have, then and there, *already* transferred entitlements: (at least) one party has *now* given up ownership and already recognizes it as vested in the other party who has *now* acquired it. As between the parties, the doing or giving is already and completely accomplished: From the juridical point of view, nothing remains to be done in the future except for the parties to act consistently with what they have already done.

That an offer must contain a promise in order to bring about contract formation may be explained in a way that is consistent with the foregoing differences between contract and promise. An offer must contain a promise, that is, a present and fully crystallized assurance, because otherwise there is no ascertainable juridical act or decision to which the law can attach legal consequences, such as the conferral of a power of acceptance on the offeree. The fact that the assurance must be future-oriented means that an offeree may, in accordance with the objective test, take the assent to continue for a definite duration after it has been initially given. In this way, an offer can anticipate and call forth a second assent which, in turn, can be given in response to it and on the very same terms. In other words, in virtue of the fact that an offer contains a promise, the parties can bring about contract formation through their interaction alone. In performing this role, the promise does not import any obligation, con-

---

38. This characteristic, which, in my account, belongs to promises only so far as they give rise to the moral duty of fidelity, Fuller attributes also to promises as they function contractually. In this context as in others, it is of the first importance to recognize and to keep clearly in mind the difference between the moral and the juridical. The basic flaw with Fuller's treatment of contract – as with Fried's – is that it fails to do so.

tractually speaking. It must be recalled here that the fact that an offer contains a promise goes hand in hand with the fundamental legal proposition that a not yet accepted offer, even if stated to be irrevocable, always remains revocable at will for whatever reason (provided the revocation is reasonably manifest). A promise confers only a power, not a right, upon the promisee. The fact that the offer contains a promise does not give rise to any obligation in law but simply determines the kind of existence which this inherently revocable assent has, objectively construed: It has a continuing existence for a certain duration.

What significance might the future-oriented form of promise have at the moment of contract formation, when the assets are viewed as simultaneous and co-present and when, *ex hypothesi,* entitlements are already transferred, leaving nothing more for the parties to accomplish in the future? The answer, in brief, is that the promissory element in the offer and, also, let us suppose, in the acceptance makes possible the essential contractual distinction between agreement and performance. For intrinsic to the form of every promise is the differentiation between the moment an assurance is given and the time for its fulfillment in action. In virtue of the promissory form of offer and acceptance, contract formation can be construed as a moment of non-physical appropriation that is separate and distinct from the time of physical delivery, as is required if the wholly executory contract is to be enforceable in accordance with the expectation principle understood as a principle of compensation. The fact that the promise is future-oriented does not imply that an actual transfer of rights has still to take place. From a legal point of view, the contractual relation and its immediate juridical consequence are fully realized, making the promisor's conscientious evaluation of the goodness of the promise or of the performance irrelevant. To repeat, the role of the promissory form at contract formation is that it allows the parties reasonably to view formation as consisting of acts of will that are distinct from and prior to actual performance. The difference between contract and promise is preserved.

3. MUST OFFER AND ACCEPTANCE BE SUPPLEMENTED BY OTHER DOCTRINES? The role of offer and acceptance within the common law conception of contract may be summarized as follows: it sets forth *the form of relation* which voluntary interaction between two parties must have if it is to give rise to contractual rights and duties. There must be two assents, not one, and these assents must be mutually related such that each can be conceived only in relation to the other. Each side postulates relation to the other as its defining feature. Moreover, in keeping with the objective test and the idea that contract arises through the parties' interaction alone, the assents must necessarily be conceived as empirically initiated in a temporal sequence and yet as co-present and simultaneous in some, as yet undefined, non-temporal sense. Construed as temporally successive, the assents are differentiated one from the other. Viewed as simultaneous, the assents can only be identical, since there is absolutely nothing that might distinguish them. The parties figure simply as identical, hence equal, participants in contract formation.

Nevertheless, precisely because the doctrine of offer and acceptance sets out *just* the form of relation that is distinctive of contract, it can be only the first step in articulating the conception of contract that takes the expectation principle as a principle of compensation. While offer and acceptance require that the parties must be *ad idem* with respect to the very same terms of the entire transaction, *what* those terms must consist in aside from holding that the offer must contain a promise remains unspecified. In other words, the doctrine does not identify a content that is suitable to the form of contractual relation which it sets out. Unless, however, such content is specified, the conception of contract remains incomplete. In addition, the worry that it is a legal fiction to interpret the parties' assents as simultaneous in addition to their being situated in time cannot be dispelled.

The need for a suitable content can be further explained as follows. Unless it is possible to represent the parties as having *some legally relevant reason or cause* for offering or accepting, their acts cannot count as voluntary and purposive. If no such reason or cause for transacting is apparent, how can one party reasonably conclude that the other *intends* to contract and if either party cannot so conclude how can he or she reasonably expect the other's performance? In accordance with the objective test, the doctrine of offer and acceptance holds, we have seen, that the parties' actual particular reasons for wishing to contract are in and of themselves irrelevant. However, it is not enough for the law to say in merely negative terms that a party's particular reasons are not relevant; it must also specify in positive terms what *does* qualify as a legally relevant reason. By requiring that there be two sides, each of which is given in relation to the other, the doctrine of offer and acceptance implies that each party acts in order to obtain the return act of the other. It implies, in other words, that the cause of or reason for each side is just the other side. This implication must be made explicit as a fully articulated doctrinal requirement of contract formation. It is by taking this further step that contract doctrine provides a suitable content for the form of contractual relation postulated by offer and acceptance.

More particularly, this further doctrinal requirement must represent each party as reasonably *wanting* the other's act. Unless the law makes reference to *some* conception of want, it cannot purport to be a doctrine of reasons for offering or accepting. It must therefore specify an object of want that can reasonably be attributed to an offeror or offeree as a participant in contract formation. However, this object of want – and therefore a party's legally relevant reason for acting – cannot be the other's act in a merely formal sense. One does not want another's act as such but rather the substance of that act: the thing promised or done by the other party. Moreover, in keeping with the standpoint of the objective test, this substance must be intrinsically relational in character. And the elucidation of the object of want must fit with the analysis of the parties' assents as both temporally successive and absolutely simultaneous. It must fully satisfy the principle of continuity and clarify both its essential character as well as its precise fit with the aspect of temporal succession. By showing that the interpretation of the parties' assents as simultaneous can be reflected in a content that is internal to their interaction and that makes reference to a conception of wants, contract doctrine can vouchsafe the reality of this interpretation from a legal point of view, thereby dispelling the suspicion that it might be a makeshift or mere fiction.

In short, contract doctrine must further specify a content that reflects the fact that there are two sides which, being both temporally successive and simultaneous, are at once *distinguished* from each other and *identical*. Only a content of this sort can reflect the analysis of mutual assent that is set out by the doctrine of offer and acceptance, in this way completing it as well as the conception of contract that underlies it. In the following two sections, I argue that the common law accomplishes this further doctrinal development in two steps, each of which is necessary and supportive of the other: the first is via the requirement of consideration; the second through the principle of unconscionability.

B. Consideration

No doctrine of the common law of contract is more distinctive of it or longer and more continuously established than the requirement of consideration. The following discussion examines the modern formulation of the doctrine that became settled by the beginning of the twentieth century in American and English decisions and scholarship – what might be called the classical doctrine of consideration. According to this formulation, consideration, no less than offer and acceptance, is a general requirement of contract formation, the absence of which renders an agreement void *ab initio*. Consideration is both central and necessary to contractual liability in the sense that the law postulates an intrinsic link between this requirement and the enforceability of the wholly executory contract according to the expectation principle. On this view, consideration, like the availability of expectation damages, is definitive and distinctive of contract. It is therefore striking, not to say unsettling, that over the last several decades scholars have repeatedly criticized the doctrine as artificial, unnecessary, internally inconsistent, or dysfunctional – in short, as an historical accident without rational foundation – to the point that some have reached the conclusion that contract law's rationality and moral acceptability would be enhanced by its abolition. The doctrine of offer and acceptance, by contrast, has not been similarly challenged. It is necessary, then, to investigate afresh the basis and the role of consideration.

This is the second main question of modern contract theory which, it may be recalled, asks whether there is an intrinsic connection between the requirement of consideration and the availability of the expectation remedy for breach of a wholly executory contract – and whether this connection makes contractual liability irreducible to promissory estoppel and to tort. By way of an answer, we must see what fit, if any, there is between the doctrine of consideration and the other main contract doctrines, when these are all viewed as aspects of a conception of contract that takes the expectation principle as a principle of compensation. Throughout, our inquiry is guided by the idea of a public basis of justification.

To this end, I first present the main features of the doctrine of consideration. Taking these features as provisionally fixed points for reflection, I then specify the rationale and role of consideration. I do so against the background of a critical discussion of Lon Fuller's well-known effort to link the rationale of consideration to legal formality and economic exchange. In contrast to Fuller's approach, which I find wanting from the standpoint of a public basis of justification, I propose a rationale that can account for the main features of the doctrine and that brings out the fit between consideration on the one hand and offer and acceptance on the other on the basis of a shared conception of contract. The two doctrines, I argue, stand together; they share the same plausibility and justification. The proposed rationale makes clear the fundamental difference between contract and promissory estoppel and shows how the doctrine of consideration reflects the logic of a transfer of ownership.

1. THE MAIN FEATURES OF CONSIDERATION. The doctrine of consideration holds that at common law a promise, standing alone, is insufficient to give rise to a contractual obligation, no matter how seriously and absolutely it may have been intended or how carefully and deliberately it may have been made. To be enforceable, the promise must be made for a legally valid consideration. Thus promise and consideration, like offer and acceptance, are both necessary for contract formation. Now consideration can be one of two things: either a present act or a promise. Moreover, the act or promise must be done or given in return for, and at the request of, the defendant-promisor's own promise. As authoritatively summarized by Patteson J. in *Thomas* v. *Thomas:* "Motive is not the same thing with consideration. Consideration means something which is of some value in the eye of the law, moving from the plaintiff: it may be some benefit to the defendant, or some detriment to the plaintiff; but at all events it must be moving from the plaintiff."[39] From a legal point of view, what conditions must be satisfied for an act or promise to qualify as a valuable consideration that moves from the promisee and that is irreducible to motive?

The *first* condition is that the act or promise must not be *already* owed by the promisee to the promisor and, correlatively, the promisor must not be *already* entitled to the act or promise as against the promisee. In particular, where

---

39. (1842) 2 Q. B. 851 at 859.

a promisee has already promised the promisor under a prior binding agreement between them the very thing which he or she now proposes again as a consideration for another promise by the same promisor, this further consideration, whether it be act or promise, does not move from the promisee and is without value in the eye of the law. It is no consideration at all and the new agreement is void for want of consideration. This first condition is stipulated by the "pre-existing duty" rule.[40]

Whereas the first condition is essentially negative, the *second* requires positively that consideration must move from the promisee. To move from the promisee, the consideration must be *independent* of the promise in the following sense.[41] It must be possible to view the consideration as something that genuinely originates with the promisee. Accordingly, it must be external to, and not merely the effect of, the promise. A consideration is therefore neither an aspect or condition of the promisor's promise nor just an effect which the promisor produces, as it were, in the promisee. We must therefore be able to construe the interaction as potentially initiated by the promisee. In effect, despite the fact that the promise comes first, it must be possible to view the substance of the consideration as something that is with the promisee and that the promisee might in principle have dealt with in some other way independently of and prior to that promise.

By way of an example of something that does *not* satisfy this requirement of independence, suppose that, in response to the promisor's promise to give the promisee a much wanted object, the promisee puts forward as consideration his or her feelings of satisfaction and gratitude or, alternatively, promises that he or she will respect the promisor's wishes by accepting the latter's promise. In legal contemplation, the promisee will be deemed to have provided nothing that moves from him or herself. Instead, the alleged consideration will be treated as

40. As settled in *Stilk* v. *Myrick* (1809) 2 Camp. 317. Note that this rule does not apply where the same consideration is given twice to two *different* persons, as held in *Scotson* v. *Pegg* (1861) 6 H. & N. 295. The pre-existing rule has been criticized by legal scholars. Recently, the English Court of Appeal has departed from the traditional formulation and application. See *Williams* v. *Roffey Bros. & Nicholls (Contractors)Ltd.*, [1991] 1 Q. B. 1 (C.A.). In this essay, I take the traditional formulation of the rule as a provisionally fixed aspect of the doctrine of consideration and determine what conception of contract it implies when it is taken in combination with the other features of the doctrine. Whether the approach taken in *Roffey* implies the same or some different conception of contract and whether it fits as well or at all with the other features of consideration are not questions that I explicitly address. However, my discussion of the traditional rule in section B.(3), *infra,* notes 76–77 and accompanying text, would suggest that the *Roffey* approach is incompatible with the common law conception of contract. For a good analysis of *Roffey* in light of the traditional requirements of consideration, see M. Chen-Wishart, "Consideration: Practical Benefit and the Emperor's New Clothes" in J. Beatson and D. Friedmann, eds., *Good Faith and Fault in Contract Law* (Oxford: Clarendon Press, 1995) 123.

41. As this paragraph makes clear, the requirement that the consideration must be independent of the promise does not preclude a relation between them. To the contrary, it establishes the possibility of a specific kind of relation between them: one where the promise and consideration can each induce and, in turn, be induced by the other.

moving from the promisor. The consideration would consist here simply in the promisee's evaluation of and reaction to the promise; it represents nothing more than the effect which the promise, with its anticipated benefit, has upon the promisee. It can *only* be viewed as coming after and as resulting from the promise. It is not possible to view the promisee as potentially initiating the interaction or as potentially choosing to use or dispose of the substance of the consideration in some other way.

Building upon the requirement that the consideration must move from the promisee, the *third* condition sets out the form of relation that must obtain between the promise and such a consideration: promise and consideration must be *mutually inducing*. The consideration must be requested by the promisor in return for the promise and must be given by the promisee in response to and in accordance with that request. More particularly, the promise must by its terms expressly or impliedly establish, first, that the promisee is to do or promise something in return for and because of the promise; and second, that the promise itself is given in return for and because of this act or promise. Thus the promise and consideration must each appear as inducements of the other; it must be possible reasonably to view each side not merely as the effect but also as the cause of the other. In Holmes's words, "it is not enough that the promise induces the detriment [i.e., the consideration] or that the detriment induces the promise if the other half is wanting."[42]

This requirement of mutual inducement is construed in accordance with the objective test. It is not, therefore, a question of the consideration being the promisor's actual sufficient reason for making the promise, or even just one of his or her actual reasons for doing so. The requirement of mutual inducement does not invite an inquiry into the actual or even the apparent particular motives of either party to the contract. Consideration is not the same thing as motive. To refer again to Holmes's statement of the requirement: "No matter what the actual motive may have been, by the express or implied terms of the supposed contract, the promise and the consideration must purport to be the motive each for the other, in whole or at least in part."[43] On this view, so long as it reasonably appears from the parties' interaction that the promise was made in return for and because of the promisee's act or promise and similarly the promisee's act or promise was given in return for and because of the promise, that is sufficient. More fundamentally, the reason for each side must be just the other side – the other's promise or consideration as the case may be – *in and of itself* and not the purpose which a party hopes to realize through receipt of the other side. While the law certainly does not deny the existence of such purposes and motives or their role in parties' deliberations, it treats them, in and of themselves, as juridically irrelevant, consistently with the objective test. Although the

---

42. *Wisconsin & Mich. Ry. Co.* v. *Powers* [hereinafter *Wisconsin*], (1903) 191 US 379 at 386.
43. Ibid.

doctrine of consideration, we shall shortly see, does relate consideration to a conception of the parties' wants, it does so in a way that does not equate consideration with motive.

It is important to emphasize that the requirement of mutual inducement presupposes the second condition that the consideration must move from the promisee and must therefore be independent in the sense indicated above. Indeed, unless the second condition is met, the promise and consideration cannot be thought of as mutually inducing. For the requirement of mutual inducement is met only if the consideration is not merely the effect of the promise but can also be its cause. And this is taken as possible only if the consideration is independent. Thus the fact that a promisor wants or even requests something in return for his or her promise will not as such necessarily satisfy the requirement of consideration. It must reasonably appear from the terms of the request that the thing is requested as something that is independent from the promise and that moves from the promisee in the required way.

Whereas the third condition of mutual inducement sets out the form of relation required by the doctrine of consideration, the *fourth* and final condition specifies the aspect of content. The consideration must have value in the eye of the law and it has value if it constitutes a legal benefit to the promisor or a legal detriment to the promisee. What then qualifies as a legal benefit or detriment?

Here we must keep in mind that the meanings of benefit and detriment are to be understood from a legal point of view.[44] Hence their characterization as *legal* benefit or detriment. Their meaning, we will see, need not coincide with benefit or detriment in fact, with economic gain or loss, or, finally, with sheer advantage or disadvantage. Moreover, the definitions of legal benefit and detriment at once presuppose and are framed by the preceding two conditions. However, while the requirement of legal benefit or detriment builds upon the previous conditions, it also adds something new. Thus legal detriment and benefit means something more than the mere fact that the promisee can owe the consideration to the promisor or that the promisor can be entitled to it as against the promisee because it was not already promised under a prior enforceable agreement, as required by the first condition. Similarly, detriment and benefit are not reducible to the fact that consideration may have moved from the promisee – and therefore was presumptively detrimental to him or her – as the second condition might seem to suggest or that it may have been requested – and thus was presumptively of benefit to the promisor – as the third condition seems to imply. The definition of detriment and benefit presupposes all this but includes something more as well.[45]

---

44. Williston properly emphasizes this point. See S. Williston, "The Effect of One Void Promise in a Bilateral Agreement" (1925) 25 Colum. L. R. 857 reprinted in *Selected Readings, supra* note 3, pp. 369–379 at pp. 374–375.
45. At certain points, Williston, incorrectly in my view, fails to recognize this. See his statement of the definitions of benefit and detriment in S. Williston, *A Treatise on the Law of Contracts*

The idea of a legal detriment or benefit goes to the *substance* of the consideration. The law looks at the *thing* done or promised by the promisee and asks whether, in the case of a return act, it is, or in the case of a return promise, it will, or apparently may be,[46] either a detriment to the promisee or a benefit to the promisor.[47] There is a legal benefit to the promisor if, but only if, it is reasonable to view the consideration, when executed, as something that could serve or benefit in some way the promisor's interests. To qualify as a legal benefit to the promisor, the consideration must not be already in the promisor's possession or under his or her exclusive rights as against the promisee and it must be something that can be wanted by the promisor quite apart from the fact that it may be in law a necessary condition of making an enforceable agreement. A consideration imposes a legal detriment upon the promisee if, but only if, it is physically possible for the promisee to refrain from giving up or doing what he or she proposes to give up or do by way of consideration[48] and the consideration can reasonably be viewed, when executed, as something that could be in some way prejudicial to or a limitation upon the promisee's interests. These interests can have *any* content whatsoever so long as they reasonably appear to be the interests *of* a given party, taken as an individual distinct from and independent of the other party. Thus interests may be "altruistic" as well as "self-regarding". Note also that a party's interests may be not only in things, services, and other persons but in his or her liberty of action as well.[49] Finally, while a

---

(3rd Ed.) (Mont Kisco: Baker, Voorhis & Co., Inc., 1957) [hereinafter "*Treatise*"] Vol. 1, s. 102A: "[Legal detriment] means giving up something which immediately prior thereto the promisee was privileged to retain. . . . Benefit correspondingly must mean the receiving . . . of some performance or forbearance which the promisor was not previously entitled to receive."

46. This is Williston's formulation to cover instances, such as conditional promises, where it turns out that a promised performance need not take place although at the time of formation the parties reasonably believe it can and may happen. See S. Williston, "Consideration in Bilateral Contracts" (1914) 27 Harv. L. Rev. 503 reprinted in *Selected Readings, supra* note 3, pp. 472–491 at pp. 489–490 [hereinafter "Consideration"].

47. I suppose as a methodological and substantive principle that there is at bottom one law of consideration for both unilateral and bilateral contracts. This principle is suggested early on by Lord Holt's statement that "where the doing a thing will be a good consideration, a promise to do that thing will be so too." *Thorpe* v. *Thorpe*, (1701) 13 Mod. 455. It finds support in accounts of the historical development of the doctrine of consideration. See D. Ibbetson, "Consideration and the Theory of Contract" in *Towards a General Law of Contract*, ed. J. Barton (Berlin: Duncker & Humblot, 1990) at pp. 85–88. And it is affirmed by eminent writers. See S. Leake, *An Elementary Digest of the Law of Contract* (London: Stevens and Sons, 1878), pp. 612–613 and S. Williston, "Consideration" *supra* note 46 at pp. 483–488.

48. This condition is clearly stated in Williston, *Treatise, supra* note 45, s. 102A at p. 384.

49. This paragraph interprets the influential definition of consideration stated in *Currie* v. *Missa* (1975) L. R. 10 Exch 153 at 162: "A valuable consideration in the sense of the law may consist either in some right, interest, profit, or benefit accruing to one party, or some forbearance, detriment, loss, or responsibility given, suffered, or undertaken by the other." Note that the text frames benefit and detriment with reference to distinct and separate interests of the parties. Williston emphasizes this feature: "That the promisor desired [the consideration] for his own advantage and had no previous right to it is enough to show that it was beneficial. If the promisor requested the act not for his own advantage, but from a charitable desire to benefit a

consideration ordinarily, and arguably always, will be simultaneously a benefit to the promisor and a detriment to the promisee, a widely expressed view is that it need not be both but can be just one or the other.[50]

Whether the consideration can be viewed as a legal benefit or detriment is to be inferred as a matter of fact from the particularities of the parties' interaction construed in accordance with the objective test. It should be emphasized that this specification of the parties' interests as part of the elucidation of benefit and detriment is worked out within a framework that is set by the objective test and that incorporates the previous conditions of a valid consideration enumerated above. The thing that is a benefit or detriment must be something that is initially independent of the promise and that *moves* from the promisee in response to the promisor's *request:* advantage or disadvantage is relevant only insofar as it satisfies these other conditions. Having found that the promisor has expressly or impliedly requested something that moves from the promisee, a court asks whether that thing may reasonably be viewed as something the receipt of which could be wanted by the promisor or the loss of which could be not wanted by the promisee in the circumstances of their interaction. If the promisor has requested something which reasonably may be viewed as something that *could* be wanted by a reasonable person in the promisor's particular circumstances, it qualifies as a legal benefit to the promisor that *is* wanted by him or her. And the same holds, *mutatis mutandis,* for the aspect of legal detriment, supposing that the consideration moves in the required way from the promisee.

third person, it may be doubted whether there is such a benefit as the law requires. . . . If, as consideration of his promise, A requests B to perform a legal duty which B owes to C, and B does so, it is insufficient consideration unless A requested the act for his own advantage, not C's." *Treatise, supra* note 45, s. 102A at pp. 382–383. My one difficulty with Williston's statement is that it seems to require the promisor's interest to be "selfish" or "self-interested," whereas, in my view, what is necessary is only that the interest be the promisor's own, whether it be "self-interested" or "altruistic."

50. A case of pure detriment would be presumably one where the promisee simply restricts his or her liberty of action in a way that does not at the same time give the promisor a service or object that serves the promisor's personal interests. This is how *Hamer* v. *Sidway* (1891) 27 N. E. 256 is often understood. While *Hamer* seems clearly to involve a detriment, is it so obvious that this detriment – the promisee's acts and omissions—could not be at the same time of some personal interest to the promisor who, as uncle of the promisee, would, after all, have an interest, both "selfish" and "altruistic," in his nephew's circumstances and development? An instance of pure benefit is even more questionable. Williston was of the view that cases such as *Scotson* v. *Pegg, supra* note 40, illustrate this possibility. See Williston, "Consideration" *supra* note 46 at pp. 486–487. In *Scotson,* the consideration promised the defendant had already been promised to another party. One judge, Martin, B., seems clearly to have viewed this as a situation of benefit to the defendant without any detriment to the plaintiffs. Ibid., at 300. However, it is less obvious that Wilde, B. shared this view. Ibid., at 301. ("Here the defendant, who was a stranger to the original contract, induced the plaintiffs to part with the cargo, which they might not otherwise have been willing to do, and the delivery of it to the defendant was a benefit to him.") In my opinion, even in this type of situation, there may be upon analysis a detriment to the promisee. In my discussion of the rationale of consideration, I suggest that simultaneous benefit and detriment would be more fully consistent with consideration's role within the common law conception of contract. See note 70, *infra,* and accompanying text.

In this way, the analysis of legal benefit and detriment specifies a conception of wants that is suitably detached from and independent of the parties' actual wants and motives. While the consideration must be something that could be wanted by the promisor in the circumstances, this does not necessarily ensure that it is actually wanted by him or her, let alone that it constitutes the promisor's actuating motive – or even a secondary motive – for making the promise. The question of whether the parties' actual particular interests, whether *ex ante* or *ex post,* are satisfied falls entirely outside the legal analysis of contract. At no point do we treat satisfaction, let alone a maximum satisfaction, of the parties' individual and joint interests as in and of itself a condition of the existence of a valid contract.

The foregoing presentation of the definitions of legal benefit and detriment does not equate benefit with actual *present* advantage to the promisor or detriment with actual *present* prejudice to the promisee. This would be inappropriate where the consideration is a counter-promise, as distinct from a return act. For such a promise-consideration can only be a present benefit or detriment if the promise is *already* binding. But it is only upon contract formation that the parties' promises can be legally binding. So the promise-consideration that is necessary for contract formation cannot consist in a present benefit or detriment. The same point holds for any attempt to equate legal benefit and detriment with, respectively, the legal entitlements and liabilities that accrue upon contract formation. Thus a legal benefit, say, cannot be the entitlement which the promisor will obtain from the promisee upon contract formation. Consideration is something that is necessary *to bring about* formation. The above definitions of legal benefit and detriment recognize this when they presuppose only that a promise-consideration *can* be binding – that is, that there is nothing in it which prevents it from being so[51] – and that it will or may, *if executed,* affect the interests of promisor or promisee in the required way. We thereby avoid a vicious circle.[52]

---

51. For example, in the case of mutual promises, the promise-consideration must not, legally speaking, be illusory. An illusory promise is one which, upon analysis, reserves to the one so "promising" an unconstrained power of unilateral cancellation or something similar. To carry a legal benefit or detriment, however, a promise must represent a completed act that objectively expresses an unambiguous and finalized commitment that does not leave the one promising any liberty to choose otherwise in this respect. The fact that a promise is illusory and so void as consideration from the legal point of view does not necessarily exclude that the promise might nevertheless impose some moral obligation on the one who made it or that it might be rationally wanted and so requested by the other party in lieu of receiving no promise at all. We see here the divergence between the legal point of view on the one hand and morals or economics on the other hand. In this connection, I note that a parallel requirement applies to unilateral contracts where the consideration is a present act. To qualify as a legal benefit or detriment, it must be both genuine and completed: it must be a party's *deed*, not merely his or her state of being; the party must have been in fact able to have done otherwise; and the deed must be completely performed. Otherwise it is no consideration at all.
52. Sir Frederick Pollock defined benefit and detriment in a way that, in the case of mutual promises, gives rise to a vicious circle. He thought that unless a promise given as consideration for

Now the common law definition of benefit or detriment has never required that the substance of the consideration have a certain particular content or value. In this respect, the requirement is strictly content-neutral. As early as 1587, it was held in *Sturlyn v. Albany* that "when a thing is done, be it never so small, this is sufficient consideration to ground an action."[53] By this principle, so long as there is just something of *some* legal benefit or detriment, this can qualify as valuable consideration. Indeed, the consideration need not have a determinate market value – it may be a peppercorn, for example – and yet it may still be something of legal benefit or detriment in the eye of the law. For this, it is simply necessary that the peppercorn, taken by itself and apart from the fact that it may as consideration have the legal effect of producing an enforceable agreement, be something that could be of use to the promisor or prejudicial to the promisee. As long as it can be so viewed and it reasonably appears from the parties' interaction that the peppercorn was requested in return for the promise, it can be a valuable consideration. The possibility of a nominal consideration is a necessary implication of the principle in *Sturlyn.*

In fact, so far as the doctrine of consideration is concerned, the question of the comparative values of the promise and consideration simply does not arise. Note that in the previous paragraph I said that the peppercorn must be "in return for" and not "the equivalent of" the promise. I want to emphasize this point that the relation between promise and consideration is, quite literally, *quid pro quo* – something for something – with no reference whatever to how much each of these somethings is in relation to the other.

To view the promise and consideration as either actually or presumptively equal in value would require the reduction of both to an identical qualitative dimension so that they could be compared in purely quantitative terms. However, the doctrine of consideration does not do this. On the contrary, it requires that the thing promised or done in return for and at the request of the other party's promise be *qualitatively different* from the promise.[54] The express and implied

another promise is itself already legally binding and therefore already imposes a legal obligation or gives a legal right, it cannot be, respectively, either a legal detriment or a legal benefit. But, at the same time, one cannot assume that the first promise is already legally binding without also supposing that it does not itself need consideration to be enforceable – which it does. The vicious circle, in short, is that there cannot be detriment without legal obligation but equally there cannot be legal obligation without detriment. "What logical justification is there for holding mutual promises good consideration for each other?" Pollock asked. "None, it is submitted," was his reply. 28 L. Q. R. 101. A number of writers, including Anson, Ames, and Williston, criticized the circularity of Pollock's definition of legal benefit and detriment. They proposed an alternative definition which, broadly stated, characterizes benefit and detriment in terms of the thing promised – not the promise as such nor the obligation which might attach to it – and they held that there is a legal benefit or detriment where a consideration, if executed, will or may confer a benefit upon the promisor or cause a detriment to the promisee. The text concurs with their definition and their line of reasoning.

53. (1588), Cro. Eliza. 67.
54. The requirement that promise and consideration must be qualitatively distinct is reflected in cases from very early on. See, for example, Ibbetson, *supra* note 47 at p. 73.

terms of the transaction, reasonably construed, must present the promise and the consideration as two qualitatively different things. They are two different things that are related. Thus a consideration that is identical with the promise or that differs from it only in degree or quantity and not in kind cannot constitute a benefit or detriment, even if it is requested by the promisor. It is not a valid consideration at all.

Consideration has to do, then, *just* with the fact that there is something that can reasonably be viewed as either positively or negatively related to the apparent wants of the promisor and the promisee respectively. It has to do, therefore, with the qualitative specific usability of a concrete object or service, not its comparative value relative to other things. Consequently, if one wishes to characterize the doctrine of consideration as a "bargain theory"[55] on account of its requirement that the promise and consideration must be mutually induced, one should guard against assuming the further conclusion which the idea of bargain might be taken to imply, namely, that the doctrine of consideration postulates the promise and consideration as equal in value or the promisor as wanting the consideration as the equivalent of his or her promise. This it does not do.

The above four conditions define a valuable consideration that moves from the promisee. If the parties' assents are to bring about contract formation they must have a form and content that satisfy these conditions. These four conditions – and, importantly, whatever these conditions imply – specify the kind of assents that can function as the efficient cause of contract formation. In legal contemplation, assents that satisfy these conditions are mutually related as follows. On the one hand, the promise and consideration must be initiated in temporal sequence. Ordinarily, consideration must be given in response to and after the promise – and in any event after the request.[56] On the other hand, the law views the promise and consideration as absolutely simultaneous and co-present. Indeed, it holds that unless it is possible to conceive them as being at one and the same instant, the consideration is no consideration at all and the promise is a *nudum pactum*.[57] Not less than the relation of temporal sequence, the requirement of simultaneity belongs to the account of contract formation and is an

---

55. As do the *Restatement (Second) of Contracts* (St. Paul, MN: American Law Institute Publishers, 1981) at s. 71 and many, if not most writers. Williston is typical when he defines consideration as "the exchange or price requested and received by the promisor for the promise." *Treatise, supra* note 45, s. 100 at p. 370. It is worth noting that Salmond explicitly rejects this characterization. *Supra,* note 5 at p. 195.

56. In the so-called past consideration cases where the consideration is in fact given *before* the promise, an early and continuously followed line of decisions in English law holds that the promise is enforceable so long as the consideration is induced by a prior request on the part of the promisor and the later promise may reasonably be viewed as in fulfillment of that request. In these circumstances, the law views the later promise as joining with the earlier request and as together constituting one thing made for the sake of the consideration. The seminal case is *Lampleigh* v. *Braithwait* (1615) Hobart 105.

57. By way of example, see *Nichols* v. *Raynbred* (1615) Hobart 88 where it is stated that "the promises must be at one instant, for else they will be both nuda pacta."

essential characteristic of the assents that bring a contractual relation into existence. How the doctrine of consideration is able to construe the promise and consideration as both temporally sequenced and simultaneous is a central question that I will address shortly.[58]

Taking these as the main features of the doctrine of consideration, I now turn to the question of the rational basis and the role of consideration in the theory of contract. By way of background and in order to set the stage for my own explanation, I shall first discuss what is surely the most influential defense of the doctrine of consideration in the twentieth century, namely, Fuller's essay "Consideration and Form."[59] Finding his approach wanting from the standpoint of a public basis of justification, I then propose an understanding of consideration that accounts for its main features and that brings out the intrinsic fit between it and offer and acceptance, showing both to be mutually supportive and necessary aspects of contract as a transfer of right.

2. FULLER'S RATIONALE FOR CONSIDERATION: THE CENTRALITY OF LEGAL FORMALITY AND ECONOMIC EXCHANGE.

Simply stated, Fuller's thesis is that only those promises that meet certain formal and substantive policy concerns should be enforced and that by and large the doctrine of consideration correctly identifies those non-formal transactions that satisfy this condition. The argument is premised upon the idea that contractual liability, in contrast with liability in tort or in unjust enrichment, is distinctively founded upon what Fuller calls "the principle of private autonomy." By this "most pervasive and indispensable"[60] of the basic conceptions of contract, the law treats parties as having a legal power to change, within limits, their voluntary legal relations *inter se*. On this view, contracts are voluntary transactions which enshrine a rights-altering function. And while Fuller presents reliance and unjust enrichment as two other substantive bases of contractual liability, he also emphasizes that there is no intrinsic connection between the latter and either the conception of contract as a voluntary transaction or such central features of contract as the objective test for formation and the availability of expectation damages as the normal remedy for breach.

According to Fuller, once contracts are viewed as voluntary transactions through which individuals can arrange and direct their legal relations, legal form becomes crucial because it is desirable that persons should exercise this power under conditions that guarantee the desiderata which underlie the use of such formalities. These desiderata are reflected in the following three functions of form. First, the existence of a legal formality provides *evidence* that a transaction has taken place; second, it serves as a check or *caution* against inconsiderate or impulsive action; and third, by marking off legally enforceable transactions from those which are not, it offers individuals legally effective means of

---

58. At pp. 172ff.   59. (1941) 41 Colum. L.R. 799.   60. Ibid., p. 806.

channeling their intentions and thereby of accomplishing their objectives. Where a class of voluntary transactions is not invested with a suitable legal formality, the policies underlying form may nevertheless be satisfied informally and naturally by the forces native to the situation in which the transactions arise. In such circumstances, the guarantees that would otherwise be provided by a legal formality are rendered superfluous.

The fact that a given class of voluntary transactions may be invested with a legal formality, or though informal, may naturally satisfy the desiderata of form is, however, only a necessary and not a sufficient condition of enforceability. There are, Fuller points out, significant costs associated with the enforcement of transactions, not the least of which is that this reduces the area of an economically and socially valuable field of voluntary social intercourse in which statements of intention and even assurances may be given, altered, or withdrawn with relative facility and without incurring legal liability. Given such costs, Fuller asks what sorts of voluntary transactions are of sufficient substantive importance from a social and economic point of view to justify enforcement. In a society whose social and economic ordering is significantly accomplished through a private property regime and market transactions, the principle of private autonomy furthers important social and economic goals when it is applied to voluntary transactions that directly involve or are ancillary to exchanges of economic value. In contrast to the purely gratuitous and wholly unrelied-upon promise, transactions of this kind are conducive to the production of wealth, the division of labour, and so forth. According to Fuller, then, economic exchange is the principal type of voluntary transaction which the law should enforce – so long, of course, as the desiderata of form are satisfied as well.

Fuller's thesis is that the doctrine of consideration is justified just to the extent that it properly singles out those non-formal voluntary transactions that satisfy the formal and substantive criteria already discussed. He concludes that the doctrine can largely be defended on these grounds, especially where the transaction is a half-completed exchange – that is, a contract where, in return for the other party's promise, the promisee confers a tangible executed benefit on the promisor.

In the half-completed exchange, the element of exchange, which in itself satisfies the substantive criterion of economic and social importance and to a lesser degree the desiderata of form, is reinforced by the factor of unjust enrichment and by the natural formality that is involved in the surrender and the acceptance of a tangible benefit. On this basis, Fuller contends that the half-completed exchange presents the strongest case for legal enforcement and he therefore designates it the contractual archetype against which all other transactions are to be compared and evaluated. In particular, Fuller holds that the wholly executory bilateral contract, which consists just of mutual promises, should not be put on a complete parity with the half-completed exchange. He explicitly rejects the well-settled principle that "where the doing of a thing will be a good consideration, a promise to do that thing will be so too."[61] The very factors which, according to Fuller, make the half-completed exchange paradigmatic do not apply at all, or only apply to a much lesser degree, to the wholly executory contract. While Fuller's defense of consideration is based upon the principle of private autonomy and not reliance, it challenges the centrality of the wholly executory contract no less than his reliance-based explanation of expectation damages brings into question the centrality of the expectation principle.

From the legal point of view, however, a half-completed exchange is simply one possible instance of a unilateral contract where the consideration is not a return promise but a return act. The fact that this return act confers a tangible benefit having economic value – let alone one that is regarded by the parties as equivalent in value to the thing promised – is in no way necessary to its being a valid consideration. While by definition a unilateral contract must be a partly executed transaction, it certainly need not be a partly executed exchange.[62] The definition of unilateral contract does not single out or privilege transactions that satisfy Fuller's main substantive criterion. More generally, while a transaction involving the exchange of economic values may certainly satisfy the requirement of consideration for both unilateral and bilateral contracts, the doctrine of consideration – far from requiring that it be an exchange – is entirely indifferent as to its being such. Conversely, the fact that parties view their interaction as involving a mutually advantageous exchange will not necessarily give it validity from a legal point of view. The latter need not coincide with or answer to the perspective of "commercial reality". Thus an illusory promise or an act that has already been promised under a prior enforceable agreement between the parties will not be a sufficient consideration, despite the fact that the promisor may have requested it and viewed it as a valuable benefit in the circumstances of the parties' interaction. For the purposes of defining, interpreting, and applying the requirement of consideration, the factor of economically valuable exchange contributes nothing in its own right.

What about Fuller's view of the connection between form and consideration? This is a more difficult question and it requires a more nuanced treatment. To begin, it is worth noting, as Fuller does,[63] that in the historical development of the doctrine of consideration certain judges held that the role of consideration is best understood by analogy to the seal or to some other legal formality. For them, the legal requirement of consideration could be met, for instance, by an agreement being reduced to writing or, for example, by a "moral" consideration, that is, where, on independent legal or moral grounds, the promisee ought to have done in any case what he or she promised as a consideration. Such extensions or revisions of the doctrine would be reasonable enough on the premise

---

61. Ibid., p. 816. The words quoted are those of Lord Holt from *Thorpe* v. *Thorpe, supra,* note 47.
62. Salmond, for one, emphasizes this point. *Supra,* note 5 at p. 195.
63. Ibid., p. 799, notes 1 and 2.

that the role of consideration is akin to that of a legal formality. The fact, however, that they were decisively and explicitly rejected and did not become part of the classical doctrine suggests that the analogy to form may not capture the essential role of consideration.[64] Why might this be so?

The analogy to legal formalities seems to imply the following view of consideration. Consideration is taken to be a legally instituted device that enables parties to accomplish their aims by making otherwise unenforceable gratuitous promises binding. First and foremost, it serves this channeling function. As applied to consideration, the channeling function must presupposes that parties wish to create legally binding relations and that they request or give consideration *for the purpose of* producing this consequence. Moreover, for the desiderata underlying the cautionary function to be met, the requesting or giving of consideration has to be the focus of the parties' attention in such a way that it would ordinarily and naturally impress upon them the legal import of their acts, thereby discouraging hasty or inconsiderate decisions on their part. And finally, the evidentiary function can be meaningfully satisfied only on this same supposition that consideration is requested or given in order to achieve this legal consequence. Evidence of a transaction that does not meet this condition must be irrelevant so far as the principle of private autonomy is concerned.

But to so view the role of consideration is to emphasize what is merely contingent and incidental in its operation and to miss what is necessary. While it is certainly true that in given circumstances a consideration may satisfy more or less effectively the desiderata of form, there is nothing in the definition, interpretation, or application of the requirement which is fundamentally oriented toward its doing so. The fact that consideration performs the functions of a legal formality in certain instances plays no essential role in its definition, interpretation, or application. This is true even in the one clear instance where parties ordinarily request and give consideration for the very purpose of making an enforceable promise – where the consideration is purely nominal. Let me elaborate.

The law does not suppose that parties who request or give consideration actually intend, or even generally would intend, this as a way of giving legal effect to their wishes. This would make directly salient the parties' particular purposes and subjective intentions. But like offer and acceptance, the requirement of consideration is defined, interpreted, and applied in accordance with the objective test and by this test whether something qualifies, for example, as a request for consideration is independent of the particular purpose or intention that a party has in making it. Whereas consideration, viewed on the model of a legal formality, requires that each party understand and appreciate *from his or her own standpoint* the legal significance of consideration and request or give it on this basis, the objective test finds a request when a party's words or deeds appear to

---

64. It is worth noting here that the *Second Restatement of Contracts* rejects form as a satisfactory rationale for the requirement of consideration. *Supra,* note 55 at s. 72, Comment.

suggest one from the point of view of the *other* party and on this basis attaches legal consequences to them. So long as a request reasonably may be found in the terms of the promise interpreted in light of its surrounding circumstances, this is sufficient. Thus a request may be merely *implied* by law – not something intrinsically suited to channel intention or to focus the mind.

The same point holds for the substance of the consideration itself. A valid consideration, we have seen, can be ever so small and economically insignificant and, given the objective test, it need not be the principal, or even an incidental, object of the promisor's actual desires or motives. If this is so, the minds and intentions of both parties may in fact be focussed on everything but the consideration. A valid consideration of this kind need not represent for either party a means of channeling his or her intentions. Nor need it put them on notice of the legal consequences that will flow from the promise if enforced, as is necessary if it is to satisfy the cautionary function. Whether a given consideration fulfills the functions of a legal formality is a matter of contingency so far as the definition, interpretation, and application of the requirement is concerned.[65]

If the fundamental role of consideration is that it fulfills the functions of form, the fact that parties *expressly* treat something as a consideration for the shared reason of giving legal effect to their intentions should be sufficient or at least relevant. It is neither. Indeed, unless something can count as a legal benefit to the promisor or a detriment to the promisee *apart from* the fact that they view it as a means of creating legal relations it will not constitute a valuable consideration at all.

It is true that where consideration is purely nominal, there can be a valid consideration which the parties may in fact have treated as a legal formality. This *seems,* then, to be an instance where one might plausibly infer that it is precisely because the parties so view the consideration that the law upholds it as valid. Indeed this is the reason Fuller himself offers for the legitimacy of a purely nominal consideration: "the parties have taken the trouble to cast their transaction in the form of an exchange."[66] But even here the fact that the parties may have regarded the consideration as a legal formality is, as such, irrelevant. As discussed above, the legal possibility of a nominal consideration follows simply from the well-settled principle enunciated in *Sturlyn* that so long as there is something of some benefit or detriment there can be valuable consideration, however small or indeterminate its value may be. It must reasonably appear, however, from the parties' interaction that the nominal consideration has been requested in return for the promise and that it is something that the promisor could possibly want or the promisee not want apart from the fact that the parties may view it as a way of making the promise legally enforceable. If these conditions

---

65. Andrew Kull reaches a similar conclusion on this point. See A. Kull, "Reconsidering Gratuitous Promises" (1992) 21 J. of Leg. Studies 39, pp. 52–55.
66. *Supra,* note 59 at p. 820.

are not met, the fact that the parties regard the consideration as a formal requirement necessary for the creation of legal relations between them cannot save it. The analysis of nominal consideration is no different than that of any valid consideration.

The difficulty with Fuller's invocation of form runs deeper. On the one hand, the doctrine of consideration carefully articulates a number of requirements which, in legal contemplation, specify a kind of relation between the promise and consideration which make the promise qualitatively irreducible to a gratuitous promise. From a legal point of view, a promise for consideration is a promise that is *different in kind* from a purely gratuitous promise. For example, the former promise must be one that requests the consideration and therefore that presents itself as just one side of a relation which is completed by the consideration, whereas a purely gratuitous promise is complete standing on its own. Yet, on Fuller's approach, this distinction is not preserved. The gratuitous promise that is put under seal and the promise that has a consideration count as the same kind of promise. Viewed as a legal formality, consideration is something that is added to a gratuitous promise. Like a seal, consideration represents a mechanism by which a gratuitous promise can be made enforceable. The fact that Fuller's defense of consideration is fully compatible with and indeed suggests the elision of the qualitative difference between gratuitous promises and promises for consideration means that it does not explain what is most central to and distinctive of the doctrine.

The upshot of the preceding discussion is that neither the substantive idea of economic exchange nor the role of legal formalities can rationalize the main features of the doctrine of consideration. Each ground has essential implications that are out of sync with the legal point of view. This disqualifies Fuller's explanation as a public basis of justification.

Indeed both grounds are unsatisfactory even when viewed against Fuller's own objective of understanding contract law as an expression of the principle of private autonomy. An exchange for economic value is but one instance of a voluntary transaction. That it may have particular social or economic significance contributes nothing to its being a voluntary transaction or to its being founded upon private autonomy. The principle of private autonomy provides no basis for singling out the economic exchange for special recognition. Moreover, Fuller's invocation of form does not illuminate what he deems to be the defining feature of any voluntary transaction – namely, that it can be a *rights-altering* legal relation. His invocation of form does not so much explain as presuppose the possibility of a rights-altering transaction; it argues in favour of giving legal effect to this possibility in circumstances where the desiderata of form (as well as the concerns of substance) are satisfied. What we need, however, is to know how in the first place this rights-altering function is conceivable and hence possible. We must be able to understand it in terms of the kind(s) of acts that can accomplish it. In and of itself, a gratuitous promise does not – and in legal contemplation it inherently cannot – give rise to an obligation and a corresponding right. Unless, therefore, we show how a promise and consideration, unlike a gratuitous promise, can create entitlements and duties at contract formation, we cannot explain the rights-altering function of voluntary transactions. We need to explain how promise and consideration can function as the content of acts that create contractual rights and duties. The analysis of consideration as legal formality does not do this.

I will now suggest an alternative justification for the doctrine of consideration that is intended to fulfil this task. In keeping with the idea of a public basis of justification, this account should preserve and explain the doctrine's main features in one unified account. This account should also fit with the analysis of offer and acceptance presented earlier. We are looking for an integrated understanding of both doctrines that makes clear and explicit the conception of contract that underlies them. On the view that I shall suggest, the requirement of consideration, like that of offer and acceptance, is a general requirement that specifies the sort of voluntary interaction that is necessary to constitute a transfer of right between the parties. It is essential to a conception of contract in which the expectation principle can function as a principle of compensation. This view gives no special place to economic exchanges in general or to the half-completed exchange in particular. For it regards both as just possible instances of a transfer of right. Nor does it rest content with showing that consideration may, certain contingent circumstances obtaining, fulfill the functions of legal formality to a greater or lesser extent. While the proposed rationale does not deny that consideration may perform this function of form, it does not deem this factor essential or even pertinent to understanding the requirement in the first instance as a necessary and general condition of contract formation. Consideration is not an extrinsic feature that is merely added to a gratuitous promise, whose presence ensures that the promise, which may be morally though not legally binding, also satisfies the desiderata of form. Instead, it specifies those aspects of the parties' acts as well as the relation between their acts that allow their interaction reasonably to be construed as a transfer of rights at contract formation.[67] Contract is a rights-altering transaction because it transfers rights. Thus, in contrast to Fuller's own explanation, the conception of contract as transfer vindicates his central claim that contractual liability is founded upon the principle of private autonomy. That at least is what I hope now to show.

---

67. On the view that I am proposing, the difference between consideration and the seal is this: The former specifies a definite kind of interaction between the parties on the basis of which it may reasonably be inferred against both parties that they have transferred rights *inter se;* the latter, by contrast, is simply a mechanism created by the positive law that produces the legal consequence of a transfer. In the philosophical accounts of contract of Kant and Hegel, the seal, like all legal formalities, presupposes civil society and the administration of justice whereas such doctrines as offer and acceptance or consideration belong to "private right" (in Kant) or to "abstract right" (in Hegel). Hegel is particularly clear and instructive on this distinction. See Hegel, *supra* note 19 at paras. 213 and 217.

3. AN ALTERNATIVE JUSTIFICATION: CONSIDERATION AS ESSENTIAL TO A TRANSFER OF RIGHT

(i) The Negative Role of Consideration: Not a Gratuitous Promise. For the purpose of elaborating a rationale for consideration that satisfies the idea of a public basis of justification, no starting point is more natural or appropriate than the elementary distinction drawn by the common law between the purely gratuitous promise, the *nudum pactum* which cannot give rise to contractual liability, and a promise given for a valuable consideration, which can. This contrast is conceptual and definitive of the doctrine of consideration. The contrast is meaningful and illuminating because, as I have already said, a promise that is supported by a valuable consideration and one that is gratuitous are not identical promises distinguished just by the fact that a consideration is added to the one but not to the other. On the contrary, they are intrinsically different kinds of promises. Each has a categorically distinctive form or structure that of necessity produces fundamentally different juridical effects.

More specifically, the law, we may say, characterizes a gratuitous promise in terms of the following three features the first two of which pertain to its essential structure while the third goes to its necessary juridical effect.

First, the operative act that constitutes a gratuitous promise and that gives rise, we shall suppose, to a moral duty to keep it, is *the promisor's undertaking alone.* While the promise may be made to, for, or with the assent and approval of the promisee, it is the promisor alone who makes it. In contrast to a contract, a gratuitous promise consists in one act of will, not two. *Second,* although a gratuitous promise may be made in response to or may itself induce a promise or act on the part of the promisee, the two expressions of will do not in legal contemplation form a whole. In other words, *it is not possible to represent the two as mutually inducing.* One act can *only* be represented as coming either before or after the other in time; the act that comes first is viewed exclusively as the cause, and not also the effect, of the second act. The parties' interaction, then, is not represented in law as mutually related sides of a single transaction. *Third,* a gratuitous promise does not in and of itself give the promisee any right as against the promisor. The parties' entitlements relative to each other remain after the promise exactly as they were before. A gratuitous promise *does not transfer any right to the promisee.* In the absence of detrimental reliance by the promisee, breach of such promise is not actionable on any principle of compensation known to the common law.

The first step in elaborating a public justification for consideration consists in seeing whether the main features of the doctrine in fact ensure that a promise for consideration is irreducible in concept and structure to a gratuitous promise. Ensuring this difference would be the essential function and purpose of the doctrine, stated negatively.

In contrast to the first feature of the gratuitous promise – namely, that it is rooted in the promisor's act alone – the doctrine of consideration requires that the parties' interaction unambiguously manifest a two-sided character. More specifically, the promise and consideration must be mutually distinct and irreducible one to the other; and further, each of the two sides, by its very terms, must posit the other as essential to its own completion, so that in keeping with the parties' intentions objectively construed, neither side standing alone is sufficient to form a contractual relation.

First, the requirement that consideration must be independent of the promise in the sense explained above[68] ensures that the consideration functions *as a second content* that moves from the promisee and that is not merely an aspect or part of the promise. Moreover, by the terms of the agreement, the promise and consideration must, on analysis, figure as qualitatively different from each other. Where, to the contrary, there is merely a quantitative difference between them, the law construes the smaller as part of and as included in the larger. In such circumstances, it subtracts the former from the latter and leaves standing only the one-sided remainder. In other words, it holds that the two sides are in reality a one-sided gratuitous promise.

The requirement that a consideration must be a legal benefit to the promisor or a legal detriment to the promisee supports and fills out the analysis of the parties' interaction as two-sided. A promise, we may presume, is a benefit to and therefore something wanted by the promisee. If the promisee is to respond with more than a mere expression of satisfaction in the promise – which can only be viewed in legal contemplation as coming from the promisor rather than from the promisee – the promisee's response must consist in something that is a detriment to, and so *not* wanted by, him or her. This is precisely what a consideration must be. The fact that the consideration must be a detriment to the promisee fits with the requirement that it must also be independent. At the same time, whereas the promise represents a detriment for the promisor, the consideration for which the promise is given must be a benefit – the exact contrary. The requirement of benefit and detriment ensures that from the standpoints of both promisor and promisee, the promise and consideration are two qualitatively distinct sides.

The fact that a primary function of consideration is to set up a second side in addition to the promise justifies the rule that a sufficient consideration need only consist in some legal benefit or detriment, irrespective of what or how much it is. All that is necessary and sufficient to establish a second side is the existence of *some* benefit or detriment. For this purpose, reference to the particular quantitative and qualitative features of the consideration is superfluous. The rule is thus neither incoherent nor unreasonable, as certain writers have suggested.[69]

In addition to being a second side that is distinct from the promise and that moves from the promisee, consideration, I have said, completes the promise –

68. See note 41 *supra,* and accompanying text.
69. For example, see Fried, *supra,* note 7 at p. 29.

and vice versa. Promise and consideration are intended as two *mutually related* sides. The promise is a discrete and crystallized decision that, by its manifest intention, is given to combine with the consideration. This is what the promise must reasonably contemplate by its very terms, as reflected in the crucial requirement that it must *request* the consideration as *quid pro quo*. The request thereby posits the promise as just one part of a whole that is formed by the combined promise and consideration. The promise is given only as a part of this whole. And since, in turn, the consideration must be provided in response to and on the very terms of this request, it is also given on the very same premise. The requirement of benefit and detriment fits with and fills out this schema. In law, no one is presumed to intend to give up a benefit or to take on a detriment for nothing in return. Viewing the promisor's request for consideration as being for something that is in return for promise is in keeping with this presumption. For since the promise and consideration represent, respectively, a detriment and benefit to the promisor, we view the promisor as taking on a detriment for something and not nothing when we construe the consideration as *quid pro quo*. And the same point applies *mutatis mutandis* to the promisee.

Indeed, insofar as a consideration can be viewed as *both* a benefit to the promisor *and* a detriment to the promisee, it reflects even more fully the idea of mutual relation. As a detriment, the consideration refers to the promisee who provides it as a second content in return for the promise; as a benefit, the consideration points to the promisor who requests it in return for the promise. A consideration that is at once benefit and detriment thus directly embodies the form of two-sided relation. And the same is true of the promise itself if we suppose it to be a detriment to the promisor and a benefit to the promisee. Viewed in this light, each side of the relation is itself relational in character.[70]

This brings me to the second way in which the doctrine of consideration ensures that a promise for consideration is irreducible to a gratuitous promise. A

---

70. At note 50, *supra,* I indicated that it is very difficult to find – and implausible to expect – instances of consideration that are not in fact both benefit and detriment. I am now suggesting that there is a rational basis for favouring an interpretation of the doctrine that requires both aspects. At the very least, this point challenges any attempt to reduce the requirement to just one of the two aspects, as does, for example, Salmond, *supra* note 5 at pp. 195–196, who contends that the requirement can and should be formulated in terms of detriment alone. I should add that the fact that courts generally look for either a benefit or a detriment and are satisfied when they find just one of them is not necessarily inconsistent with the view that I am now proposing. This judicial practice is not premised upon a supposed impossibility or even difficulty of finding both benefit and detriment; nor is it based upon any clear or authoritative articulation of why it might be unnecessary or unimportant to be able to do so. To the contrary, it is perfectly possible to view the insistence that there be either benefit or detriment as consistent with the assumption that having found one, the other may be supposed or identified as a matter of course. This question is to be settled in light of the most reasonable account of consideration within the common law conception of contract. I wish to thank Daniel Batista for pointing out to me the fit between a consideration requirement of both benefit and detriment and the two-sided character of contract.

gratuitous promise, I have said, can *only* be viewed in legal contemplation as coming before and as the cause of the promisee's response: The parties' interaction cannot be represented as mutually related sides of a single transaction. By contrast, the doctrine of consideration construes the promise and consideration as *both* temporally successive and absolutely co-present.

The first point is that unless a consideration is given in response to and after the promisor's request, the two sides cannot be linked through the parties' interaction alone. But secondly, this does not preclude the promise and consideration from being construed as simultaneous. To the contrary, because the requested consideration must be independent of the promise, there can be nothing in it that *necessitates* its only going after the promise. Nor is the consideration necessarily reducible to being just the effect of the promise. Being something that the promisee might have used or otherwise disposed of irrespective of and prior to the promisor's request, the consideration can stand on its own and move from the promisee to meet the promise. Nothing prevents the consideration from functioning as cause of the promise. The requirement that promise and consideration be mutually induced fulfills this possibility. For by this requirement, promise and consideration are each made in return for and because of the other. Each is at once cause and effect of the other. Now insofar as each is both cause and effect of the other, the relation between them necessarily *abstracts from temporal sequence;* otherwise, each, as both cause and effect of the other, would have to be at once before and after the other, which is impossible. As mutually induced, both sides must be simultaneously postulated or neither can be. The promise exists in legal contemplation only insofar as the consideration also exists, and vice-versa.

The doctrine of consideration and in particular its requirement of mutual inducement confirm what we had to suppose in connection with offer and acceptance, namely, that "simultaneity" means not that the promise and consideration must happen at the same instant in time – which would directly contradict the requirement of sequence – but rather that they are construed as co-present *in abstraction from time.*[71] The previous analysis entails no fiction. By requiring the temporally successive promise and consideration each to be the inducement of the other, the doctrine of consideration stipulates that they must have a character which makes inconsequential the distinction in time. Temporal sequence turns out simply to be the mode in which indifference to the temporal is embodied.

Moreover, nothing less than a supposition of mutual inducement in some form or another will allow the two sides that form a contractual relation to be

---

71. Kant was the first thinker to identify and to elucidate this feature in relation to both private law in general and contract in particular. See Kant, *supra,* note 19 at pp. 401–408 and 422–423. I discuss this aspect of Kant's analysis in P. Benson, "External Freedom According to Kant" (1987) 87 Colum. L. Rev. 559, pp. 565–567.

conceived as simultaneous and co-present at formation. It is minimally necessary if the sides are to be linked in more than just a one-way temporal or causal
sequence. This is a general and conceptual point. And if by a "bargain" theory
of consideration is meant any view which makes central this requirement of mutual inducement, then a doctrine of consideration must take this form if it is to
make possible this conceptualization of the parties' acts at formation.

Here is the appropriate place to discuss the important question of the relation between contract and so-called detrimental reliance. Is detrimental reliance
simply an alternative basis upon which to found *contractual* obligation and liability? As I will now explain, the requirement that promise and consideration
must be mutually induced with the consequence that they can be construed as
simultaneous as well as temporally successive sets up a fundamental structural
contrast between contract and reliance-based promissory liability. The one
cannot be reduced to the other.

Reliance-based promissory liability presupposes the following sort of relation between the parties.[72] First, there must be a promise or some other representation by one party upon which the other may reasonably rely. An essential
condition of such reasonableness is that the second party must reasonably be
able to construe the first party's intention as inviting reliance upon the promise
or representation. Reasonable reliance must be invited or induced. This establishes a relation of justified dependency of the second party upon the first. And
whether or not there has been such inducement is decided in accordance with
an objective standard that views the first party's words and deeds, appropriately
situated, from the standpoint of the second, taken as a reasonable person. Second, there must be actual reliance by the second party in the sense that, in reliance upon the promise or representation, he or she must change position to
his or her potential detriment: the second party must forego some opportunity
or incur some cost in reliance upon the promise or representation. Such change
in position must create the potential for a loss of something of value – for example, the lost value of the opportunity foregone or of the expense if wasted.
Third, the first party, as a reasonable person, must be able to foresee the risk of
such loss if due care is not taken. While fulfillment of the promise or representation will always constitute reasonable care, something less or other than this
may also suffice, depending upon circumstances.

It follows that the relation between promise and consideration on the one
hand and that between promise (or representation) and reliance on the other

---

72. On the view proposed here, reliance-based liability encompasses, among other things, liabil-
    ity in tort for negligent mistatement or performance arising out of a voluntary assumption of
    responsibility, liability under s. 90 of the *Restatement of the Law of Contracts (Second),* and
    promissory estoppel. I discuss the reliance principle in more detail in P. Benson, "The Basis
    for Excluding Liability for Pure Economic Loss in Tort Law" in D. Owen, ed., *The Philosophi-
    cal Foundations of Tort Law: A Collection of Essays* (New York: Oxford University Press, 1995)
    [hereinafter *Excluding Liability*].

differ in the following respect. Whereas the promise must request the consideration as *quid pro quo*, this is not true of reliance-based liability. Reliance must only be reasonable and this requires that it be induced or invited in the way just discussed. Such inducement is not the same thing as requesting something in return as *quid pro quo*. This is reflected in the fact that, in given circumstances, reliance that is just reasonably foreseeable may be enough to imply the required inducement to rely. More particularly, in contrast to the relation between promise and consideration established by the request, inducement implies a link between promise and reliance that is necessarily and exclusively sequential: The reliance must, and can *only,* be conceived as coming after the promise. Otherwise, the relation between the one who induces and the other who relies cannot be construed as a relation of dependency of the latter upon the former. Similarly, the idea of inducement sets up a causal relation between promise and reliance that is one-way, not mutual. In short, the inducement that links the promise and reliance does not imply their representation as simultaneous and co-present.

The fact that in reliance-based liability the inducement and reliance must be temporally successive but cannot also be simultaneous means that such liability is incompatible with an essential premise of the logic of a transfer of ownership. It cannot possibly satisfy the requirement of continuity. Accordingly, it is impossible to conceive the one who *relies as acquiring an entitlement to the thing promised or represented.* The representation or promise cannot, as such, confer upon the plaintiff anything that he or she did not already have – or could have had – before the parties' interaction. Reliance-based analysis cannot view the promise or representation as one side of a transfer of rights between the parties. Thus, there can be no intrinsic connection between reliance-based liability and the expectation principle, taken as a principle of compensation.

And this is how a claim in detrimental reliance is widely understood. The promisor is duty bound to use reasonable care so that the second party's reliance does not result in his or her being made worse off as compared to the position he or she occupied before the decision to rely. As Seavey explains, "the wrong is not primarily in depriving the plaintiff of the promised reward but in causing the plaintiff to change position to his detriment."[73] Reliance-based liability does not view the promisee as having a legally protected interest in the performance of the promise or in the fulfillment of the representation as such. Rather, the protected interest is only in the position that he or she occupied prior to relying and therefore prior to the parties' interaction. As a matter of fairness and reasonableness between the parties, the defendant must act consistently with the plaintiff having a protected interest in the value of this pre-reliance position: but for the defendant's inducement, the plaintiff would not have changed position – that is, foregone an opportunity, incurred a cost, and so forth – and so would have

---

73. W.A. Seavey, "Reliance Upon Gratuitous Promises or Other Conduct"(1951) 64 Harv. L. Rev. 913 at p. 925.

possessed a value which has now been diminished or lost as a result of the defendant's lack of due care. This pre-reliance position provides the conceptual baseline against which injury and compensation are determined.

Detrimental reliance does not make a promise binding as such. In relation to contractual rights, the claim here must be viewed as a shield, not a sword. So long as the promisor takes reasonable steps, for example, to enable the promisee to regain his or her pre-reliance position, the promisor is at liberty to withdraw the promise or representation after he or she has made it and even after the promisee has relied upon it. Although the appropriate measure of recovery for loss caused by reliance may in given circumstances equal the value of the promise or representation, this is pure happenstance from a conceptual point of view. It does not reflect an identity in the bases of liability that lead to this result.

What is often referred to as "promissory estoppel" has all the markings of the principle of detrimental reliance applied in a contractual setting. A typical situation in which promissory estoppel applies is where the parties are contractually subject to certain terms and where one party, whether by promise or by representation express or implied, leads the second party reasonably to conclude that he or she may depart from those terms but then, inconsistently, requires strict compliance to the latter's prejudice. If, in reasonable reliance upon the first party's promise or representation, the second changes position to his or her detriment, the first party may be estopped from asserting his or her rights under the contract to the extent that justice requires. Here the detriment may consist in the fact that by not complying with the contractual terms, the second party would ordinarily disqualify him or herself from receiving certain benefits under the contract which the first party is bound to provide only upon such performance. For estoppel to apply, we must suppose that, but for his or her reliance upon the first party's promise or representation, the second party would in fact have fulfilled the contract terms, thereby qualifying for the benefits. Receipt of the benefits constitutes the second party's protected interest and provides the baseline against which liability and compensation are determined. It represents the position which the second party must give up, that is, alter, in reliance upon the first.

The core idea of promissory estoppel is that in the above circumstances the first party is precluded from asserting the contractual terms as if he or she has made no promise or representation and as if the second party's change of position is just his or her own decision or at his or her own risk, where this assertion would put the second in the wrong or cause him or her a prejudice. Precisely because the change in position has been made at the first party's inducement and invitation, the law will not allow this party to say to the one who reasonably relied: "This is *your* act and you are damnified by *your own* doing."[74]

---

74. This formulation is taken from Cardozo's illuminating application of estoppel in *Imperator Realty Co., Inc.* v. *Tull* (1920) 127 N. E. 263.

Rather, as a matter of reasonablenss and fairness as between the parties, the first party cannot disown responsibility for the consequences of the other's detrimental reliance, more specifically, for foreseeable injury to his or her protected interest resulting from such reliance. While the first party may have the liberty to reassert the strict contractual terms unqualified by his or her promise or representation even after the other has changed position – in other words, while the first party is not contractually bound by the promise but may revoke it – he or she must do so in a way that enables the second to regain this initial position and comply with the contractual terms without loss. Where the first party unreasonably fails to do this, he or she violates a duty of care owed the second in these circumstances. On this analysis, the existence of a contractual relation between the parties merely provides the occasion or circumstance for the operation of reliance-based liability. Promissory estoppel is not a species of contractual liability. This is the meaning of the statement that it can be used as a shield, not a sword.

Reliance-based liability, including promissory estoppel, is best understood as a species of tort, not contractual, liability.[75] Whereas tort in general presupposes that a plaintiff has a protected interest that originates prior to and independent of the parties' interaction, contract supposes an interest that arises soley through their interaction. The role of promise in tort is categorically different from its function in contract. In tort, a promise makes pertinent as a matter of fairness the promisee's position prior to the parties' interaction but does not as such give the promisee a protected interest. There is no intrinsic connection between tort-based promissory liability and the expectation principle. From the point of view of contract, a promise that merely induces but does not request reliance is in form and effect simply a gratuitous promise.

I now turn to the third and last contrast between the gratuitous promise and a promise for consideration, namely, that the latter, unlike the former, can transfer rights to the promisee. I have already said that whereas a gratuitous promise is something that can be viewed as *only* before *or* after the promisee's own act and so cannot possibly fit with a basic condition of a transfer of right, the requirement of mutual inducement means that the promise and consideration *can* be construed as "at the same time" in the sense of being represented in abstraction from temporal conditions, thereby making for an inherent connection between the requirement of consideration and the expectation principle. As I will now explain, this connection is also implied or at least suggested by another part of the doctrine – the pre-existing duty rule discussed earlier.

The pre-existing duty rule requires that an act or promise given by a promisee as consideration must not have been already provided as consideration in a prior binding agreement between the parties. In the eye of the law, a consideration

---

75. This is the view taken by Seavey, among others. *Supra* note 73. I also argue for this characterization in *Excluding Liability, supra* note 73.

that does not meet this requirement cannot be a legal benefit or detriment and cannot move from the promisee. According to the most influential statement of this rule,[76] it is justified, not on grounds of public policy, but simply as a direct implication of the doctrine of consideration. It applies quite apart from whether the promisee has subjected the promisor to undue pressure or duress which might in law render their new agreement voidable. A consideration that runs afoul the pre-existing duty rule is no consideration at all and, absent fresh consideration, the new agreement is void *ab initio*. The fact that the consideration already promised is requested by the promisor or that, as a matter of commercial reality, it may be of practical benefit to the promisor to receive it rather than nothing at all is irrelevant.

Against this view, Ames has objected[77] that if the new promise can reasonably be understood as a fresh act of will which the promisee was not obliged to provide and if the promisor thinks it sufficient to his or her interest to give a counter-promise in return for this new act of will, why shouldn't such mutual promises be valid considerations each for the other, particularly since any disparity in comparative value between them is not a bar?

In my view, there is only one answer to Ames that is available to the law consistently with its own premises. Unless we are to say that what makes a return promise valuable consideration in legal contemplation is the fact that it consists either in the mere mouthing of words or in the mere form of an assurance divorced from the substance of the performance undertaken – something that Ames does not want to say – there can be no stopping short of the conclusion that a promise-consideration is valuable only if it conveys the assurance of a performance that substantively can be a legal benefit to the promisor or a legal detriment to the promisee. Now if, as the pre-existing duty rule holds, a promise already made under a prior binding agreement between the parties cannot be given again as a valuable consideration despite the fact that we must suppose that this promise states on its face a valid benefit or detriment – for otherwise it could not constitute valuable consideration in the prior binding agreement – it must be because the repeated promise cannot again convey the required substantive assurance. And this, in turn, must be because the substance of the promise-consideration has already been given and so *already belongs* to the promisor by virtue of the prior enforceable promise and so can no longer move from the promisee. As a matter of rights, the promisee, having already given the substance of the consideration to the promisor, is no longer in a position to give again what is no longer with him

---

76. *Stilk* v. *Myrick, supra* note 40.
77. J. B. Ames "Two Theories of Consideration" (1899) 12 Harv. L. Rev. 515 and (1899) 13 Harv. L. Rev. 29 reprinted in *Selected Readings, supra* note 3, pp. 320–343 at pp. 339–342. In my view, Ames's objection is the most interesting and subtle challenge to the pre-existing duty rule. This is because it takes seriously the purported connection between this rule and the requirement of consideration and it challenges the law's understanding of that connection on its own grounds.

or her but is now with the promisor. While, as Ames contends, a promisee may, in promising again, be doing a fresh act which he or she is under no obligation to do, the act of so promising can be no better than the mere mouthing of words, being in legal contemplation wholly devoid of the substance that makes it valuable.

The pre-existing duty rule is thus defensible precisely on the premise that upon formation and prior to performance, the substance of consideration – the thing promised – already belongs to the promisor as by exclusive right against the promisee. The rule reflects a conception of contract as a transfer of right. It must be supposed if the third difference between a gratuitous promise and a promise for consideration – namely, the fact that the latter but not the former is inherently linked with the expectation principle – is to be sustained.

The doctrine of consideration, I conclude, does carve out a promise that differs in kind from the gratuitous promise in the three principal ways discussed above. In doing so, it fulfils its negative role within the conception of contract. This negative function in turn allows consideration to perform the positive role of establishing the form of a two-sided relation in the medium of the parties' legally relevant wants. As I will now explain, the doctrine thereby provides a content for the purely formal analysis of mutual assent that is set out by offer and acceptance.[78]

(ii) The Positive Role of Consideration. By ensuring that the promise and consideration constitute two distinct but mutually related sides – in fundamental contrast with the gratuitous promise – the doctrine of consideration clearly fits with and preserves the form of two-sided relation that is required by offer and acceptance. However, it goes further and fills out an aspect which, although necessary to offer and acceptance, remains undeveloped and merely implicit in it. In this consists the doctrine of consideration's central and distinctive contribution to the common law conception of contract. Let me elaborate.

While the doctrine of offer and acceptance implies, via the objective test, that each side of the contractual relation must be the reason for or cause of the other side, it does not make this explicit through a legal requirement. Rather, it only rules out the parties' actual particular interests and motives as legally irrelevant reasons. Unless, however, contract doctrine contains a positive analysis of what constitute legally relevant reasons for offering and accepting – reasons that reflect the strictly relational standpoint of the objective test – it cannot fully elucidate these acts as voluntary and so cannot provide a satisfactory account of contract as voluntary transaction.

To fill this gap, there must be a doctrinal requirement of contract formation that makes reference to *some* conception of the parties' wants. Promises (or acts)

---

78. The doctrine of offer and acceptance is formal, it may be recalled, because it stipulates that there must be two sides, that each must contain the whole transaction, that they must be mutually related in definite ways, and so forth, without specifying what the two sides must be. The doctrine simply does not address the question of content.

are given – and so can come into existence – because parties envisage some good which they wish to realize thereby. This also bears on the elucidation of voluntariness in contract. For voluntary conduct is purposive and therefore is directed toward some good. Accordingly, the full definition of voluntariness in contract must include the idea that contracting embodies some notion of individual benefit. Only in this way are we able to view the parties as *choosing* to transact. Unless, therefore, a promisee may reasonably infer from all appearances that the promisor has some reason for promising and that this reason includes some expectation of benefit, the promisor is not entitled to regard the promise as a voluntary expression of will.

The contribution of the doctrine of consideration is in two steps. First, via the requirement of mutual inducement, it establishes that each side is, and must be, the reason for or cause of the other. At this first step, the analysis remains purely formal, and in this respect it does not advance beyond the similarly formal analysis in offer and acceptance. But it takes a second step which is the doctrine's central and distinctive contribution. With the substantive requirement of legal benefit and detriment, it specifies the *content* that a side must have to function as the reason for and cause of the other side. Viewed in terms of benefit and detriment, a consideration relates to the separate interests of a given party, but in a way that detaches from the party's actual particular motives for transacting. Benefit and detriment entail a conception of wants that is specified in accordance with the objective test. Moreover, benefit and detriment import a definite relation between the parties: *Qua* detriment to the promisee, the consideration gives content to the fact that the consideration moves from the promisee and is independent of the promise, with the consequence that, in contrast to an expression of mere satisfaction, gratitude or respect, it need not be viewed as the promise's effect only but can also be its cause and reason; *qua* benefit to the promisor, the consideration gives content to the fact that it moves to the promisor and at his or her request, thereby showing the promise to be a voluntary act. Consideration is thus something that can be given and wanted by parties just in their role as joint participants in a two-sided relation. Here, then, is a positive analysis that specifies a contractually relevant conception of wants that shows how each side may objectively be construed as the reason for and cause of the other, thereby fulfilling what is required by, but remains merely implicit in, the doctrine of offer and acceptance.

While at first glance the requirements of the doctrine of consideration might appear excessively conceptual or abstract, it is precisely in virtue of this abstractness that the doctrine can fulfill its role in a way that is at once natural and comprehensive in scope.

To elaborate, a contractual relation, as distinguished from an executed present transfer of property, presupposes that at least one side of the relation is constituted by a promise. This is a necessary condition of there being a contractual obligation upon at least one of the parties. For the purposes of the analysis of contract, juridical acts may be divided naturally and exhaustively into the two sub-categories of present act and promise. Now if contract, as the doctrine of offer and acceptance supposes, is to consist in a two-sided relation that is formed by two acts of will, it follows that at least one side must be a promise, with the other being either an act or a promise. And if, as offer and acceptance also postulates, the two sides are to be mutually related in and through the parties' interaction alone, they must, as so related, have contents that unambiguously assure that they count as two, not one, and that each is the reason for or cause of the other. But the requirements introduced by the doctrine of consideration, that the second side must have a content that moves from the promisee, that is requested by the promisor and given in response to that request, that induces the first side just as it is induced by it, that is qualitatively different from the first side, and, finally, that is something of benefit to the promisor and of detriment to the promisee, together articulate in the most elementary and encompassing terms the necessary conditions of just such a relation. And because the doctrine is expressed at a high level of abstraction, it provides a framework that can apply to *any* voluntary interaction between individuals. Far from being an historical anachronism, a peculiarity of the common law, or even a technicality of the positive law, the doctrine of consideration seems to be an utterly fundamental and necessary feature in any conception of contract which takes it to entail a relation of the kind required by offer and acceptance.[79]

It should be emphasized, finally, that these requirements of consideration, as well as those of offer and acceptance, together articulate a conception of relation that is *normative* through and through. It is not as if it is only the duty of fidelity that is distinctively normative. The contractual relation is not this moral duty enforceable with a sanction. Rather, it represents *a different kind of normative phenomenon.* It belongs to the *juridical,* that is, to a normative category that pertains solely and strictly to a relation between two persons consisting in correlative rights and duties enforceable by coercion. The obligation in contract comes under the right, not the good.

How might we state the distinctive normativity of contract in intuitive terms? Very briefly, we begin with an idea of interaction in which each party manifests assent in such a way that the equal participation of the other is enlisted as necessary to complete it. Each side reasonably intends his or her assent to function

---

79. Charles Fried accepts the legal requirement of offer and acceptance at the same time that he rejects the doctrine of consideration. *Supra* note 7 at pp. 28–43. My account of the fit between the two doctrines suggests that the endorsement of the first doctrine coupled with the rejection of the second is without basis. Moreover, if, as Fried contends, the normative ground of contractual obligation is the moral duty to fulfil one's word such that there is nothing in principle that precludes a gratuitous promise from giving rise to an enforceable contractual obligation, offer and acceptance no less than consideration ceases to be a necessary condition of contract formation.

only as part of the parties' combined assents. Now by enlisting the participation of the other and by taking part in this interaction, each party brings him or herself under the principles of right that reasonably apply to the interaction. The central claim of this essay is that contract may reasonably be viewed as entailing a transfer of right or ownership. So far, I have suggested that the requirements of offer and acceptance and of consideration specify a form of interaction that satisfies certain basic premises of a transfer of ownership. Moreover, in Part II, I argued that the logic of a transfer of ownership is no less applicable in principle to contract than it is to a present transfer of property. Where parties have interacted in a way that may be reasonably construed as a present transfer of property, we do not think, so far as their relation *inter se* goes, that they can reasonably refuse the legal effects of their acts. They may be reasonably held to have transferred ownership. The same is true of interaction satisfying the requirements of offer and acceptance and of consideration, supposing, of course, that such interaction reflects the logic of a transfer of ownership. Certainly, imputing this legal effect to the parties' acts must be consistent with the respect their freedom and equality. Unless this is the case, the parties would have reasonable grounds for complaint. But as I will explain in Section III, the principles of contract formation together with the principle of unconscionability articulate a reasonable conception of the parties' freedom and equality.

(iii) The Limits of the Doctrine of Consideration's Contribution to the Conception of Contract. In light of the foregoing analysis of the positive role of consideration, the question naturally arises: Is the content specified by the doctrine of consideration all that is necessary to complete offer and acceptance, such that the two doctrines can fully articulate a conception of contract that enshrines the expectation principle as a principle of compensation? Or is there a need for a third doctrine to fulfill the very conception of contract which these principles of formation presuppose? The short answer is that while the interconnected requirements of mutual inducement and of benefit and detriment articulate, respectively, the form and content of a doctrine of contractually relevant reasons for transacting, they do so incompletely when viewed in light of the analysis of the contractual relation in offer and acceptance as well as the logic of a transfer of right. Therefore, in addition to offer and acceptance and consideration, a third doctrine is needed.

To elaborate, the doctrine of offer and acceptance postulates mutually related assents that are not only temporally successive but simultaneous and identical as well. In keeping with the objective test, the reason for and cause of each side must be the other. Insofar as the sides are construed as identical, each must have the same reason as the other. In addition, the logic of transfer includes as part of its requirement of continuity not only that the acts of alienation and appropriation be simultaneous but also that it be possible to view the object or objects transferred as one and the same thing belonging to the parties at the same time. Now while the doctrine of consideration, via its requirement of mutual inducement, views the promise and consideration *in formal terms* that are compatible with the above features of simultaneity and identity, the same is *not* true of its analysis of their necessary *content*. The central characteristics of this content are qualitative difference and temporal sequence, not identity and simultaneity. These features make for a content that is consistent with the representation of offer and acceptance as two distinct and temporally successive sides which, as distinct, function each as the reason for or cause of the other. But this content cannot reflect the equally necessary representation of the assents as co-present and identical or show how each side, viewed as identical to the other, can be the other's reason and cause.

Everything follows from the fact that in the doctrine of consideration the promise and consideration count – and *only* count – as two qualitatively different things. There is simply no basis for construing the parties as having the same thing. Since the thing promised and the consideration must be qualitatively different, the parties can only have different things, not one and the same thing, at the same time. Put in other words, the parties can only have the same thing at different times. Moreover, supposing that promise and consideration are mutually induced and that they are therefore each the reason for the other, the fact that they must be different means that each side's reason and cause must also be different, not the same. This standpoint of difference and temporal sequence is also reflected in the requirement of legal benefit and detriment. The consideration that counts as a benefit to the promisor cannot be the same for the promisee. Rather, it must be the contrary – a detriment. Moreover, the very categories of benefit and detriment are individual-specific and therefore single out parties as distinct and different: "benefit," for example, does not connote "benefit to people in general" but benefit to a reasonable person in the particular circumstances of a specific party, the promisor. While a consideration that is both a benefit to the promisor and a detriment to the promisee refers simultaneously to both parties and is therefore relational to this extent, benefit and detriment, being individual-specific, are not intrinsically relational. But, in keeping with the objective test, the doctrine of offer and acceptance requires that the promise and consideration be precisely such.

That the doctrine of consideration through its substantive requirement of legal benefit and detriment construes the promise and consideration as two distinct though mutually related sides is the essential first step toward fulfilling the bilateral character of offer and acceptance. Contract is a relation between two wills. However, it is *only* the first step. The analysis of the promise and consideration must reflect the fact that in the doctrine of offer and acceptance the parties' assents are not just different and temporally successive but identical and simultaneous as well. It must be possible to show that the promise and consideration count as two identical sides. It is necessary, then, to take a further step beyond the doctrine of consideration. There must be a contract doctrine that reduces the qualitatively different contents of the promise and consideration to one and the same thing. It must do this as a fundamental and general requirement of contract formation and in a manner that, far from contradicting or even standing in tension with the doctrine of consideration, preserves and builds upon it. Moreover, the identical content in both sides must be intrinsically relational, in this way establishing that each side has the sort of identical reason for transacting that fully reflects the character of relation postulated by offer and acceptance. And finally, if it is true that the expectation principle can function as a principle of compensation only if contract is explicable as a transfer of right, this further step must also fully satisfy the principle of continuity. It is via the doctrine of unconscionability, I shall now argue, that the common law takes this step.

C. Unconscionability

In this section, I address the last of the three questions of modern contract theory which I identified in the Introduction. At stake here is the relation between contractual liberty on the one hand and contractual fairness on the other. In particular, we ask whether there is a reasonable notion of contractual fairness that fits with offer and acceptance and consideration as well as with the conception of contract that informs them.

To answer this question, I first identify a set of legal principles that articulates a conception of fairness in contractual transactions. We are looking for a doctrine which, like offer and acceptance or consideration, specifies a *general* requirement for all non-formal contracts at common law, not one that holds merely for certain categories of contracts that are distinguished by their particular subject matter, the special circumstances in which they are entered, or, finally, the sorts of parties who make them. Interpreted appropriately, unconscionability is this general principle that states a necessary condition of an enforceable contractual obligation as such. The next step is to explore the fit between unconscionability on the one hand and the principles of contract formation on the other. Because the principles of contract formation are on their face indifferent to distributive concerns, this fit is possible only if the proposed conception of contractual fairness is also non-distributive in character. This, I argue, is in fact the case. Indeed, as I explain, unconscionability not only fits with but also definitively completes these principles by specifying a content that fully realizes the form of contract set out in offer and acceptance and partially fulfilled by consideration. With unconscionability, the form and content of the contractual relation are fully and completely articulated. There is no need for a further basic doctrine. I then try to show that none of the other main competing approaches to unconscionability is satisfactory. The alternative approaches can neither fit with nor complete the principles of contract formation or the conception of contract that they presuppose. Finally, I present the notion of contractual liberty which is implied by the principles of contract formation and I explain why there is no tension between it and the non-distributive conception of contractual fairness that is embodied in the doctrine of unconscionability. In the common law conception of contract, liberty and equality are reconciled.

1. The Main Features and the Role of Unconscionability

While it is now widely accepted that the law of contract does, and must, incorporate a doctrine of unconscionability that articulates a norm of contractual fairness, different interpretations of the doctrine are to be found in judicial decisions and in legal scholarship.[80] In contrast to the settled doctrines of contract formation, there is at present no single formulation of unconscionability that has received general acceptance across all common law jurisdictions. Rather than begin, however, by detailing and discussing the different alternatives, I will instead present straightaway the formulation that I shall argue is, and must be, intrinsic to contract as such. This formulation is clearly articulated in certain leading English and Commonwealth decisions.[81] Moreover, it arguably informs, even if only implicitly, the major civil law systems.[82] And it is explored in a philosophical tradition stretching from Thomas Aquinas and Duns Scotus through Grotius to Hegel. I hope to show that it, and no other interpretation of unconscionability, is intrinsic to contract. It alone fits with the doctrines of contract formation because it alone can complete them consistently with their underlying conception of contract.

According to this formulation, the doctrine of unconscionability holds that a contract which otherwise satisfies the requirements of formation may be set aside if, but only if, the following two conditions are met.

First, there must be a gross discrepancy between the comparative values of the consideration and the promise in circumstances where, *prima facie,* it appears that the parties intended an arm's length exchange transaction. Where, as will ordinarily be the case, the subject matter of the promise and consideration consists of commodities that have an exchange value on a competitive market, the measure of the comparative values will be the relevant competitive market prices of these commodities at the time of contract formation.

Second, in the face of a gross disparity in comparative values, a court must ascertain the reason for the disparity. A gross disparity in values calls for an

---

80. For an instructive recent survey and discussion of the different conceptions of unconscionability, see S. M. Waddams, "Unconscionable Contracts: Competing Perspectives" (1999) 62 Sask. L. Rev. 1.
81. The single most influential and illuminating judicial statement is still the concurring opinion of Lord Denning M.R. in *Lloyd's Bank* v. *Bundy* (1974) 3 All E. R. 757 at pp. 763–766. For a good recent judicial discussion of the principle, see *Norberg* v. *Wynrib* (1992) 92 DLR (4th) 449 (SCC) at pp. 477–480 (per Sopinka J.).
82. On this point see James Gordley's seminal essay "Equality in Exchange" (1981) 69 Cal. L. Rev. 1587.

explanation. It may or may not have resulted from the impoverished party's taking on the risk of the loss or intending to enrich the other party by this amount at his or her own expense. If it did so result, the contract will be upheld, despite the gross discrepancy. On the other hand, if there was no such donative intention or assumption of risk, the contract is subject to being set aside as unconscionable, all other things being equal. The law, it must be emphasized, does not presume that the disparity was the result of an assumption of risk or donative intention. It must reasonably appear from the particular facts of the parties' interaction as interpreted in light of the surrounding circumstances that this was indeed the case.[83] Now ordinarily, unless the impoverished party *expressly* assumed the risk of loss or manifested donative intent, the existence of "impaired bargaining power" on the part of that party will justify the inference that the reason for the disparity was *not* donative intention or assumption of risk, leading to a finding of unconscionability. For the purposes of unconscionability, there is "impaired bargaining power" if the party either did not know the going market price or knew it but reasonably could not obtain it. Note that the party's ignorance or necessity must be with reference to the going market price. Even then, impaired bargaining power in the form of ignorance or necessity is not legally significant in and of itself. It does not as such represent an injustice, let alone an evil, to be avoided. The ultimate question is whether or not in given circumstances a gross disparity in values resulted from donative intent or assumption of risk (express or implied). The legal significance of a finding of impaired bargaining power is just that it can be relevant to, and sometimes dispositive of, this question of fact.

It should be emphasized that a finding of unconscionability does not depend upon whether or not the enriched party has practised undue influence, duress,

---

83. Grotius' statement of the principle is instructive: "And there is no reason why one should say that whatever either party has promised in excess should be considered a donation. Such is not ordinarily the intention of persons making contracts of this kind [involving consideration] and such an intention ought not to be assumed unless apparent.Whatever, in fact, the parties promise or give, they should be believed to promise or give as on an equality with the thing which is about to be received, and due by reason of that equality." *Supra,* note 30, Bk. II, Ch. XII, at p. 344. I should emphasize here that both in Grotius and in the accompanying text, the discussion of presumed intention is from the standpoint of first principles of juridical right. In practice, perhaps because unconscionability is generally raised as a defence to a contract claim and perhaps also because it is often reasonable to assume, at least *prima facie,* that there is a going market price generally known and accessible to the parties, the one who pleads unconscionability may have to establish the existence of impaired bargaining power if a court is not to conclude that the reason for the discrepancy was an assumption of risk. This may mislead one into thinking that the law presumes as a matter of basic principle that parties intend as equivalents whatever terms they agree to (however grossly inadequate the consideration may be) and that when the law nevertheless sets contracts aside as unconscionable this must be because it views impaired bargaining power as in and of itself an evil to be redressed. I discuss this view at text accompanying footnote 93, *infra.* where I argue that it is incompatible with the common law conception of contract. My formulation of the significance of donative intent and impaired bargaining power for unconscionability has benefited from discussion with Sophia Reibetanz.

fraud, or misrepresentation upon the one impoverished. It is not at all necessary that the latter's ignorance or necessity be caused by the other party. There need not be a fiduciary relationship between them. Nor is it necessary that one party overbears the will of the other or that the enriched party commit, legally speaking, a wrong against the other. The sole jointly necessary and sufficient conditions are simply that, first, there is a gross inequality in the comparative values of the promise and consideration and that, second, this discrepancy does not result from an assumption of risk or donative intention. Finally, a finding of unconscionability does not result in an agreement's being void *ab initio,* as does the absence of either offer and acceptance or consideration. Rather, it renders an agreement voidable at the sole discretion of the impoverished party. Conversely, despite a gross lack of equivalence, an impoverished party may still affirm the agreement with these disadvantageous terms and have it enforced against the other party – something neither party may do if the principles of contract formation have not been met.

If the doctrine of unconscionability is to be consistent with the view that a contract is formed by the parties' voluntary interaction alone, it must be possible to articulate this doctrine in terms of the parties' presumed intentions. On this formulation, the doctrine would presume that parties to a contract intend to transfer what is theirs on terms that are equivalent or, at least, not grossly lacking in equivalence. This would be just the other side of the legal presumption *nemo praesumitur donare.* Moreover, in the ordinary circumstance where the things transferred are commodities, the law would impute to the parties an intention to obtain equal value as measured by market prices. This presumption, however, would *not* suppose that the parties are *obliged* to transact on such terms but merely that they are enabled to do so, if they choose. Thus, the presumed intention can be displaced by persuasive evidence, satisfying the objective test, that, in effect, a party has waived the possibility of equivalence, whether by assuming the risk of impoverishment or by intending it.

The question is: On what basis might the law reasonably impute to individuals an intention to transact for equal value just in virtue of their role as contracting parties and make this an essential condition of enforceability? My answer is in two steps. First, I explain why contracting parties may reasonably be presumed to intend a transaction for equal value. Second, I argue that market price is for juridical purposes a reasonable measure of equal value where the things exchanged are commodities.

In a public justification of contract, it is essential that any imputation of presumed intention to the parties fits with the main contract doctrines and therefore draws from the same underlying conception of contract.[84] Here the presumed intention at issue is not imputed to parties on the basis of what they may say or

---

84. See my previous remarks on the conception of the person in a public basis of justification, note 33, *supra.*

do on the occasion of a given interaction. Rather, it is to be imputed to them as participants in a transfer of entitlements prior to any inquiry into these factors. At the same time, it is crucial that the presumed intention reflects the voluntary character of contract. It must express the juridical significance of the parties' wills – and *only* this. Presumed intention is not to be viewed as an invitation to import into the legal analysis of contract values and considerations which, however valid they may be from some other standpoint, do not belong to the elucidation of the relation of will to will which the doctrines of contract formation suppose.

What, then, can be the basis of a presumed intention to transact for equal value? If the intention is to be imputed reasonably to the parties as participants in a contractual relation independent of any consideration of their particular interaction, it must pertain to some aspect of their wills that is necessary to transfer rights from one to the other at contract formation. This aspect is conceptually prior to the particulars of their interaction since, whatever the parties may say or do, unless their interaction embodies the logic of a transfer of right, it is irrelevant from the standpoint of a conception of contract that enshrines the expectation principle. Now the one aspect of this logic that is not reflected in the doctrine of consideration is the requirement that the parties be represented as having one and the same thing at the same time. As applied to the common law, this requirement entails *that the promise and consideration be reducible to some single dimension or substance – to one and the same thing – notwithstanding their diversity.* The common law conception of contract must therefore postulate a presumed intention on the part of parties to transact on terms that allow for such a representation. This presumed intention, when further specified, is an intention *to give and receive equal value,* as I will now explain.

The explication of this presumed intention must start with and build upon the doctrine of consideration. The latter postulates, as we have seen, two qualitatively distinct contents for the promise and consideration: something for something else. Under this aspect, the promise and consideration count as concretely different useful things: things that in virtue of their distinct attributes can possibly satisfy diverse needs and purposes. This is essential to the very possibility of the promise and consideration being construed as legal benefit or detriment. The positing of qualitative difference is the essential contribution and the defining character of the requirement of consideration. Consequently, if, as continuity requires, there is to be one identical thing that is owned by both parties, it must be something which can be found *in a relation between two different useful things.*

Value is just this. Something can have value only if it is of some possible use to another. Moreover, the value of something is expressed, not in relation to itself, but in relation to another thing that is qualitatively different from itself. Value is, and can *only* be, embodied in a two-sided relation. When things are so related, they are viewed in purely quantitative terms: so much of one thing equals some much of something else. Value must suppose, then, that the different useful things can be reduced to one substance or dimension that is characterized in purely quantitative terms. Value is the purely quantitative that at once presupposes and abstracts from qualitative difference.[85]

When, by the terms of their transaction, parties give and receive things that are of *equal* value, they have at the beginning and at the end of the transaction something that is the same. It is true that each side gives and receives things that are different when these are viewed under the aspect of benefit and detriment. But regarded in terms of value, there is absolutely no difference between them. As embodiments of equal value, the promise is the same thing as the consideration; one thing can be substituted for the other. There is a complete abstraction from their particularities. Moreover, as owners of things having equal value, the parties count in this respect as identical, notwithstanding their different interests, purposes, needs, and so forth. They figure as equal owners in abstraction from all particularities of persons and things.

Given a two-sided relation that is formed by a promise and a qualitatively distinct consideration, the only way in which the parties can be represented as having one thing at the same time is if the requested consideration figures as equal in value to the promise. The law must therefore reasonably presume on the part of the promisor the intention to receive such a consideration in return for his or her promise. This is what a promisor must be presumed to want as a participant in a contractual relation. If this were impossible, the parties' interaction would not satisfy continuity and so could not possibly be analysed as a transfer of right, with the consequence that the expectation principle could not be vindicated as a principle of compensation.

But what about market price as the *measure* of equal value where the objects exchanged are commodities? Is there a juridical as distinct from an economic basis for making this measure part of the parties' presumed intentions?

Courts apply a going competitive market price where the subject matter of a contract consists of commodities as distinguished from unique goods.[86] From the standpoint of economic analysis, an essential condition of something qualifying as a competitive market price is that, while it may result from and be realized in innumerable particular transactions, it cannot be affected by any one of these transactions or by the particular needs, purposes, and interests of those who transact. All must take as given the same identical price, irrespective of

---

85. "In property, the quantitative character which emerges from the qualitative is value." Hegel, *supra* note 19 at para. 63 (Addition).

86. Where a unique good is given in return for another, the value of each is necessarily and directly expressed in relation to the other. The doctrine of unconscionability provides no basis for setting aside the agreement because the requirement of equivalence is necessarily satisfied. Of course, the agreement may be voidable for duress, misrepresentation, undue pressure, and so forth, but these grounds are different and distinct from unconscionability as understood here.

their differences and particularities. The competitive market price presupposes, then, that economic agents have different preferences, interests, and purposes, but, at the same time, it abstracts from these. Now while a competitive market price may serve such economic functions as efficient resource allocation, we are looking for something else – its possible *juridical* significance. And this lies precisely in the market price's indifference toward the particularities and individual purposes of transacting agents. It is in virtue of this feature that value can fulfill the requirement of continuity. Market price is suited by its very indifference to particularity to function as the measure of equal value. *Homo Oeconomicus* and *Homo Juridicus* share the very same abstractness from particularity. Far from being the imposition of an extrinsic or collective perspective on the parties' interaction, the competitive market price is a measure of value which the law may reasonably impute to parties as part of their presumed intentions.[87] It is a measure of value that perfectly fulfills the *contractual* function of value as the aspect under which the parties can have the same thing at the same time.

The fact that the common law makes unconscionability depend upon *gross* inadequacy of consideration (or gross lack of equivalence) rather than upon just any degree of inadequacy however small may be explained along the following lines. A competitive market price is an ideal notion which obtains at long-term equilibrium. It is only approached, and never fully realized, by actually existing market systems, even on the supposition that these are competitive. Thus for any given commodity, supposing that we have identified the relevant market, there will be in reality an always changing range of going market prices rather than one unique, stable price. In addition to this dynamic aspect, the definition of what constitutes the relevant market will itself be ordinarily indeterminate, at least to some extent. It is reasonable to assume that parties take the risk of contracting on terms that fall somewhere within this range of prices: it is always possible that an item I purchased at a given store might be bought for less (or more) at another store that belongs to the same, more or less extensively defined, market. Stating the criterion in terms of gross or manifest lack of equivalence ensures, practically speaking, that a price which is deemed unconscionable falls outside this range and therefore that the one who receives it cannot necessarily be assumed to have taken the risk of receiving less or paying more than the market price.

This presumption of an intention to transact for equal value is supremely regulative: everyone, just in virtue of his or her role as contracting party, is presumed as a reasonable person to have this intention. At the same time, it is

---

87. As an historical matter, it is worth noting that from the start – beginning, say, with Thomas Aquinas – when writers formulated a conception of equality in exchange, they regularly viewed market price as the appropriate measure of equality. For a full and detailed account, see Gordley, *supra* note 82 at pp. 1604–1617.

important to emphasize, no one is legally obliged to transact for equal value. At common law, a contract is not voidable for unconscionability if the gross lack of equivalence has objectively been willed by a party, whether in the form of an assumption of risk or by a donative intent. A party can waive the receipt of equal value. This reflects the general principle that one is at liberty to abandon or to give to another one's own thing, so long as it is something alienable. But it is only the owner who can decide to give his or her own away. Thus the power to abandon the receipt of equal value presupposes that the equivalent is something that belongs to the party. A party who has waived the receipt of an equivalent in a particular instance is still represented as having a general capacity to receive and have equal value. The presumed intention to transact for equal value is still regulative. It functions as the normative baseline against which the parties' interaction is construed. To qualify as a contract, a transaction must honour each party's capacity to receive equal value.

Given a presumed intention to receive equal value that requires a court to ascertain whether a party has in fact reasonably waived its receipt in particular circumstances, two fundamental categories of contractual relation fall out. Either the terms of a contract entail an exchange of equivalents as measured by the relevant market price, or they do not. In the former case, the transaction is enforceable as a *contract of exchange*. In the latter case, it is not to be presumed that the parties view the unequal sides as equivalents or that the disadvantaged party intends to give a gift. To the contrary, unconscionability shows itself to be a regulative principle by holding that the terms are enforceable if, but only if, it reasonably appears that at the moment of contract formation the disadvantaged party *does* in fact intend the lack of equivalence: he or she must take on the risk of this loss or willingly sustain it in order to confer a benefit on the other party. If this can be shown, the agreement is enforceable as a *contract of gift*. Otherwise, it is voidable.[88]

This division of contracts into gift and exchange (including some genuine combination thereof) is comprehensive and exhaustive. Moreover, it seems to fit with the model of contract as a transfer of right. So far as the logic of a transfer of right goes, there can be only two basic categories of transfer: a gift, where

---

88. Note that by this definition a contract of gift is *not* a gratuitous promise but a two-sided relation in which one party has accepted less than equal value. Why, it may be asked, does unconscionability render an agreement merely voidable and not void *ab initio*, as does the absence of consideration or mutual assent? By way of an answer, so long as there exists a two-sided relation, the parties are free to decide the comparative values of what they give and receive. A party is at liberty to accept less than equal value. The party may do so either at formation – in which case there is an enforceable contract of gift – or when performance is due – in which case the party affirms an agreement which was not originally intended as a gift contract and so would not be enforceable against him or her, absent subsequent affirmation. However, if the agreement does not evidence the kind of two-sided relation required by the doctrines of offer and acceptance and consideration, it cannot possibly qualify as a transfer of right. It is merely a gratuitous promise which, even if repeatedly affirmed by a party, can produce no contractual effects.

one party alienates and the other appropriates, and an exchange, where each party both alienates and appropriates. The doctrine of unconscionability ensures, then, that every enforceable contract comes under one of the possible categories of a transfer of ownership.

So understood, the doctrine of unconscionability is, however, non-distributive in character. Indifferent to the parties' particular purposes, needs, or advantage, the requirement of equivalence ensures merely that parties have the capacity to receive the same value which they give. It does not assure an initial or continuing fair distribution of resources. Rather, it just enables parties to have at the end of transactions whatever value they happen to possess at the start. This does nothing to mitigate differences in starting points or to even out inequalities in the distribution of holdings. Indeed, as Marx emphasized, equality in exchanges between capital and labour is fully consistent with capitalist accumulation and the creation of surplus value to the relative disadvantage of labour. Not only does the requirement of equal value not mitigate inequalities in distribution; it is perfectly compatible with social and economic processes whose tendency is away from equality in holdings. The principles of contract formation and the doctrine of unconscionability share the same non-distributive point of view.

Stated in positive terms, what the doctrine of unconscionability does is to ensure that parties can acquire rights against each other only in a way that respects the other throughout as an equal owner with a capacity for rights. This is an essential condition of it being reasonable to construe the parties' voluntary interaction as a transfer of right. Indeed, the doctrine of unconscionability implies a conception of the person that makes salient only a party's capacity for ownership and for voluntary action. As owners of the same value without reference to any particular features that might differentiate them, the parties count simply as formally equal participants in a voluntary transaction. This is the equality of corrective, not distributive, justice.[89] It represents the idea of fairness that is intrinsic to contract.

The doctrine of unconscionability, via the regulative principle of equal value, construes the relation between promise and consideration in a way that makes the parties' interaction fully consonant with the logic of a transfer of ownership. Promise and consideration count as one and the same thing, and this identical thing – value – is something that is strictly and intrinsically relational. At any and every point in the legal analysis of the contractual transaction, hence in abstraction from temporal conditions in the sense of being indifferent to temporal positions, the parties each have the same thing. Here then is a content that fully satisfies the principle of continuity. The common law, it turns out, contains the

---

89. I discuss the defining features of corrective and distributive justice in more detail in "The Basis of Corrective Justice and Its Relation to Distributive Justice" (1992) 77 Iowa L. Rev. 515, at pp. 529–549.

very sort of principle that the logic of a transfer of ownership suggests it must have if contract is to be intelligible as a transfer of right. Moreover, we saw that in light of its principle of equal value, the common law must divide contracts into two basic types, contracts of exchange and contracts of gift, and this is in conformity with what the logic of transfer implies. There is a final point of congruence. Equal value is a content which, according to the doctrine of unconscionability, the parties may reasonably be presumed to want. By this presumption, the law represents the parties simply as identical agents who exercise their rights and powers of ownership by giving and receiving equal value. But this is nothing other than the conception of the person which is supposed by a transfer of ownership. With unconscionability, the fundamental conditions and features of a transfer of ownership are satisfied. As I will now explain, this principle is also compatible with the doctrines of contract formation and completes them.

First, the doctrine of unconscionability supplements consideration in a way that builds upon and preserves it. It specifies a content that is fully relational by viewing the distinct substances of the promise and consideration under an aspect – value – that is intrinsically relational. The fact that promise and consideration must be qualitatively distinct is taken up by the doctrine of unconscionability as its first indispensable step toward construing them as expressions of value. For it is only if the substance of the promise and the consideration can be seen as useful to the parties that they can possibly be construed as values. In addition, only a promise and consideration that are qualitatively distinct can possibly be conceived as equal in value: equivalence states, and can only be understood as, a relationship between two qualitatively distinct things. The fact that something which differs from a promise in merely quantitative terms cannot be a valid consideration for that promise ensures, then, that this necessary condition is satisfied. Moreover, the fact that the parties have equal value at any and every point in the contractual analysis and therefore have the same thing in abstraction from temporal differences fits with and completes the doctrine of consideration's merely formal representation of the parties' assents as simultaneously related in a non-temporal sense, through its requirement of mutual inducement.

So long as the role of the doctrine of consideration is limited just to specifying a content that consists of two qualitatively distinct sides in complete indifference toward the question of their comparative values, there can be no conflict with unconscionability. Whereas the doctrine of consideration, by being indifferent to comparative value and in particular by recognizing a purely nominal consideration, makes it *possible* for contracts to be two-sided relations that are gift or exchange contracts, the doctrine of unconscionability ensures the *actuality* of these categories of contract by requiring that contracts be either genuine exchanges for equal value or genuine gift transactions that result from donative intention or assumption of risk. On this understanding, then, there is a division of labour between these doctrines within the conception of contract. Unconscionability fills the space that is unoccupied by consideration.[90]

It also completes the doctrine of offer and acceptance. Offer and acceptance, we saw, postulate a two-sided relation of which each side is intrinsically related to the other and the two are not only temporally successive and distinct but also simultaneous and identical. In keeping with the objective test, each side must function as the cause of and reason for the other. Accordingly, offer and acceptance holds that the account of contractually relevant reasons must reflect two aspects: the reason for or cause of a given side must be the other side viewed as both different from and the same as it. Now unconscionability construes the promise and consideration in a way that fully embodies the form of contractual relation implied by offer and acceptance. As givers and receivers of equal values, the parties are utterly indistinguishable and have identical rights and duties. Whereas the doctrine of consideration requires that each side be qualitatively different and that, as such, it function as the reason for or cause of the other, unconscionability shows each side to be identical to the other and, as identical, to be the other's cause and reason. Unconscionability makes explicit and fulfils a conception of wants that is detached from the parties' actual particular interests, motives, and needs, thereby completing an account of contractually relevant reasons that reflects the standpoint of the objective test. And because the content which unconscionability specifies abstracts completely from particularity, it embodies *just* the form of abstract equality that offer and acceptance requires. Here content is form and form is content. There is a complete identity of one with the other.

With the doctrine of unconscionability, we are now able to see how the common law conception of contract integrates what are necessary yet seemingly contradictory or at least mutually exclusive propositions, namely, that, given the objective test, the parties' assents must be conceived as both temporally successive and simultaneous. In offer and acceptance, the parties' assents are represented in purely formal terms *both* as initiated at different times – otherwise they cannot bring about contract formation through their interaction alone – *and* as

---

90. The impulse to extend the reach of consideration beyond its proper limit and to use it to fill the space that should rightly be filled by unconscionability has sometimes proved irresistible. It is reflected in the view that defines consideration as the price or equivalent, as distinct from the *quid pro quo,* of the promise. It is also reflected in a now rejected and historically suspect understanding of the principle in *Sturlyn, supra* note 53, which took the latter as holding that the doctrine of consideration bars, and is not merely indifferent toward, inquiry into the adequacy of consideration. The historical perspective is discussed in Gordley, *supra* note 82 at pp. 1594–1598. This impulse to extend the import of consideration is understandable. The possibility of construing the promise and consideration as equivalents is a necessary feature of a conception of contract that is coherent with the expectation principle. Since the consideration requirement is an essential condition of contract formation and has to do with a suitable content for the parties' mutual assents, it is perhaps natural, though still mistaken, to think that it also deals with the aspect of equal value. This is the case with Langdell's view which I have excerpted at note 92, *infra.*

"at the same time," understood in a non-temporal sense. This formal analysis must be supplemented by a content in which it is reflected. Through the requirement of benefit and detriment, the doctrine of consideration specifies a content that sets out two mutually related sides – promise and consideration – that are qualitatively distinct and temporally successive, thereby embodying the first aspect of the analysis of mutual assent in offer and acceptance. Next, through the principle of equal value, the doctrine of unconscionability construes the promise and consideration in a way that shows them to be absolutely identical and simultaneous, thereby incorporating the second aspect. Indeed, because value can be expressed only as between two qualitatively different things and can be realized only insofar as ownership of these things changes hands, it is a content that preserves difference and temporal sequence while sublating them. Value is the unity of temporal succession and simultaneity.

2. Alternative Approaches to Contractual Fairness

Having argued for the fit between unconscionability and the doctrines of contract formation as well as having explained its essential role in the conception of contract as a transfer of right, I wish now briefly to consider the main alternative approaches to contractual fairness. My contention is that they are incompatible with the common law conception of contract and are therefore unsatisfactory from the standpoint of a public basis of justification.

The principal alternative approaches may be divided into two groups. At one end is the view[91] that the common law should not recognize as part of the law of contract proper any general principle that would set aside agreements on other than purely procedural grounds such as fraud, misrepresentation, duress, undue influence, and so forth. None of these grounds justifies non-enforcement on the basis of a criterion that makes directly relevant the comparative values of the two sides of an agreement. They do not investigate, let alone require, adequacy of consideration. On this view, there should simply be no inquiry into substantive unfairness and therefore no doctrine of unconscionability as formulated above. By way of justification, it is contended that there can be no meaningful idea of equal value because "value" is nothing other than the subjective and particular valuation a given individual places on an object in light of his or her actual particular needs, interests, and purposes. Specifically, unless I value your object more than my own and similarly unless you value my object more than your own, we will not exchange them. Exchange, it is therefore argued, postulates, not equality, but inequality and difference. If, nevertheless, it is supposed that contract requires some notion of equivalence, then this

---

91. Randy Barnett takes this view. See R. Barnett, "A Consent Theory of Contract," (1986) 86 Colum. L. Rev. 269 at p. 284. As does Nozick. See R. Nozick, *Anarchy, State and Utopia* (New York: Basic Books, 1974) at pp. 64–65, note 13.

approach contends that, in the absence of misrepresentation, fraud, or duress, parties should reasonably be taken to have exchanged equivalents simply in virtue of the fact that they have decided to agree to these terms rather than to no transaction at all.[92]

At the opposite end is the view[93] that the aim of contractual fairness should be to redress the inferior quality of contracts that are obtainable by those who are relatively less advantaged in terms of resources, social class, opportunities, power, and so forth. By way of illustration, consider an agreement of loan to a poor person. Suppose that the poor person's uncertain and vulnerable financial state poses a credit risk to the lender who therefore insists on the inclusion of terms that protect against that risk. In comparison with the terms obtainable by a rich person, this agreement gives less to and places a greater burden upon the poor person. The view that we are now considering would hold that this difference between the two agreements is a sufficient basis for finding the loan to the poor person unconscionable. Differences in bargaining power are to be corrected or evened out insofar as they lead to inequalities in individuals' opportunities to contract as well as in the outcomes of their transactions. Inequality of bargaining power becomes the central concern.

Neither of these two approaches is compatible with the conception of contract that underlies the principles of formation. And this for the same reason: They give priority of place to factors that make it impossible to bring the promise and consideration under one substantive aspect or to represent the contracting parties as formally identical in the way that the doctrine of offer and acceptance implies and as must be supposed if contract is to consist in a transfer of right from one party to another.

More particularly, the first approach rules out inquiry into the adequacy of consideration on the ground that equal value, as measured by the market price, has no place in the analysis of contractual obligation. The principle of equal value is not regulative. Accordingly, no distinction between contracts of exchange and contracts of gift is possible on this approach. The basis of its refusal is the supposition that contract is, and can only be, understood with reference to the parties' particular purposes, preferences, and interests. This, however, is

---

92. "[T]he law has never abandoned the principle that a consideration must be commensurate with the obligation which is given in exchange for it; that, though the smallest consideration will in most cases support the largest promise, this is only because the law shuts its eyes to the inequality between them . . . [V]alue . . . is a thing which the law cannot measure; it is not merely a matter of fact, but a matter of opinion. If, therefore, the promisor . . . is willing to give the promise for the sake of getting the consideration, the consideration will be equal to the promise in value for all the purposes of the contract. From this it is but an easy step to the conclusion that, whatever a promisor chooses to accept as the consideration of his promise, the law will regard as equal to the promise in value, provided that the law can see that it has any value," Langdell, *supra* note 30 at pp. 70–71.

93. This view is found in R. Hale, "Bargaining, Duress and Economic Liberty" (1943) Colum. L. Rev. 603 and in Kronman, *supra* note 10.

incompatible with the relational point of view taken by the objective test. It does not fit with the analysis of the parties' interaction as entailed by the doctrine of offer and acceptance. It makes central a set of considerations that in and of themselves are irrelevant. And it means that the notion that the parties can have one and the same thing is unintelligible. So it is incompatible with the conception of contract as a transfer of right and cannot cohere with the expectation principle being taken as a principle of compensation. Nor will this difficulty be rectified by holding that, in the absence of misrepresentation, fraud, or duress, the parties may be *taken* to have treated the objects exchanged as equivalents simply in virtue of their decision to transact. Given its interpretation of value in terms of the parties' different particular preferences and interests, this view of equivalence can at most be a purely formal stipulation that in no way entails the idea of equal value. It does not specify a content that is intrinsically relational and identical in the required way. The fact that parties have transacted may be enough in the case of an exchange of unique goods where equivalence is necessarily found in the actual terms of the agreement. Where, however, the transaction is an exchange of commodities, this fact is no longer determinative. Here, market price must be taken as the baseline in construing the parties' reasonable intentions. Given the objective test, there is no other stable or fully satisfactory criterion.

The second alternative approach to contractual fairness is also incompatible with the common law conception of contract. On this approach, an agreement may be unenforceable simply because it is not as good a contract as one obtainable by another who is more advantaged in resources, social position, opportunities, and so forth. But this comparison ignores the question of whether the terms of exchange in the less desirable transaction are, nevertheless, for equal value. To return to the example of the loan to the poor person, the less favourable terms obtained by the borrower may reflect the fact that he or she poses a credit risk to the lender. Unless we are to require individuals altruistically to assume the risk of uncompensated losses which they have not caused, the lender cannot reasonably be expected to shoulder a credit risk posed by the poor person without obtaining something of equal value in return. *Nemo praesumitur donare.* On the other hand, where a wealthy borrower does not pose this risk, the lender cannot claim this return. Thus the fact that the terms of the agreements with the poor and rich borrowers may be substantively different may be not only compatible with but also required by the principle of equal value. Despite the more desirable terms obtainable by the rich borrower, the agreement with the poor borrower may be an exchange for equal value. By holding the loan to the poor person unenforceable unless the value given him or her is the same as that obtained by a rich borrower – notwithstanding the financial risk posed by the former alone – this version of unconscionability makes *in*equality in exchange a condition of enforceability. It therefore also makes it impossible to represent the parties as having one thing at the same time. And, like the first approach, it does this on the basis of factors, such as the parties' particular needs, purposes, resources, and well-being, that are in themselves irrelevant from the relational point of view of the objective test and of the principles of contract formation.[94]

3. The Relation between Liberty and Fairness in Contract

We are now in a position to discuss the relation between liberty and fairness in contract, which is the focus of the last of the three questions of modern contract theory. To begin, I briefly present a view of contractual liberty which is in tension with any conception of unconscionability as a distinct principle of contract. Explaining why this view is untenable clears the way for an understanding of contractual liberty that is fully compatible with the notion of contractual fairness that is embodied in the non-distributive conception of unconscionability outlined above.

According to a view which was widely accepted in the nineteenth century by writers and judges in both common law and civil law jurisdictions, the law of contract should recognize not only that parties have a liberty to promise or not as they wish – that is, freedom *to* contract – but also that they can choose the content of their self-imposed obligations as they desire – freedom *of* contract.[95] At the same time, these freedoms entail concomitant responsibilities: having decided to promise and on what terms, parties are responsible for their decisions and should rightly be held to them as a matter of law. On this view, the law should not inquire into the substantive fairness of the terms of a promise freely made. There is no room for a doctrine of unconscionability as a distinct principle of contract. A concern for fairness in contract must be extrinsic to, and potentially in tension with, this view of freedom of contract. The question is whether contractual liberty, so conceived, is implied by the common law of contract and in particular by its doctrines of contract formation.[96]

Certainly, the liberty to promise or not is presupposed by the doctrine of offer and acceptance. No one is under an antecedent duty to another to make him or her an offer. Parties are free to decline to transact with others and this liberty is complete irrespective of the reasons they may have for so deciding. Similarly, no one is obliged to promise or to assent to any particular terms. Others have no right against me that I propose or agree to anything in particular. Understood in

---

94. For additional and related criticisms of the second approach, see Waddams, *supra,* note 80 at pp. 13–16.
95. I have taken the terms "freedom to contract" and "freedom of contract" from Unger, *supra* note 11 at pp. 619 and 625.
96. Charles Fried's account of contractual obligation on the basis of the "promise principle" is the most carefully argued contemporary example of this view. *Supra,* note 7. I have discussed Fried's theory in greater detail in "Abstract Right," *supra* note 15 at pp. 1095–1117 and in "Public Justification," *supra* note 12 at pp. 288–294.

this way, freedom to and freedom of contract are fundamental to the common law conception of contract. Here, there is a true liberty of action against which others cannot assert any claims of right. Notice, however, that this freedom is strictly negative: Persons are not under any obligation to make promises or to enter transactions nor are they duty-bound to promise or to agree to particular terms.

The view that we are now considering does not, however, give this merely negative import to contractual liberty. It also asserts that, in the absence of factors vitiating voluntariness, such as duress, fraud, or misrepresentation, parties ought to be held to their decisions to promise on whatever terms they may have chosen simply because they have so promised. Here it is no longer a question, negatively, of not being under an antecedent obligation to promise or propose particular terms, but rather, positively, of being under a legal duty to fulfill whatever one has promised. It is this positive consequence that is problematic once freedom of contract is conceived in this way. For the notion of obligation upon which this conception of contractual freedom rests is the moral duty to keep a gratuitous promise. Let me elaborate.

According to this view, it is just the fact that one has voluntarily promised something on certain terms that justifies the law in holding that one is legally obliged to perform. One need not have so promised in the first place. But, this view contends, once having done so (free from duress, fraud, misrepresentation, and so forth) one cannot reasonably expect the law of contract to permit one to escape from the promise, whatever its terms: If it were to do so, the law would fail to take seriously one's moral power to assume self-imposed obligations; it would dishonour one's capacity for autonomy and treat one as an infant.[97] This view presupposes that one can bring oneself under a contractual, that is, a juridical, obligation through one's own act alone. So long as this act is voluntary, it is, in and of itself, sufficient to give rise to an obligation in contract. On this view, the will that is foundational to contractual obligation is the single will of an individual taken by itself.

On its face, this conception of contractual liberty certainly conflicts with any principle that would set aside an agreement on grounds of substantive unfairness. But more than this, it is out of sync with the fundamental character of contractual obligation as reflected in the doctrines of contract formation and, more generally, with the pervasive understanding of obligation in private law.

If I have tried to show one thing in my discussion of both the doctrines of offer and acceptance and of consideration it is that these doctrines postulate a relation between wills, and not the single will of the promisor, as the fundamental and the irreducible unit in the understanding of contract. By definition, contractual liberty ends where obligation begins. The source of obligation in

---

97. This is how Fried explains the moral necessity of holding persons to their promises. *Supra* note 7 at pp. 20–21.

contract is this relation of will to will. One cannot bring oneself under a contractual obligation by one's act alone. Moreover, unless this relation between wills is intelligible as a transfer of right, one cannot explain why breach of this obligation entitles the promisee to the expectation remedy as due compensation. Accordingly, the meaning of contractual freedom or, in other words, of voluntariness in contract must be understood in relation to a transfer of right, not a gratuitous promise. It is therefore the liberty to choose terms that can constitute a two-sided relation which can transfer entitlements from one party to another at contract formation and independent of any detrimental reliance. It is only an exercise of *this* liberty by both parties that can bring either of them under a contractual obligation.

More generally from the standpoint of private law, as distinct, say, from that of moral virtue, it is *not* true that a promisor is infantilized unless he or she is held liable for breach of a promise that is not part of a transfer of right. To the contrary, because the breach of a purely gratuitous promise does not injure the rights of the promisee, it simply represents an exercise of liberty on the part of one who, in Kant's characterization, is his or her own master (*sui iuris*) and beyond reproach (*iusti*).[98] In private law, it must be emphasized, the parameters of obligation are defined by a prohibition against conduct (whether act or omission) that injures or otherwise interferes with whatever belongs to others as under their exclusive rights. A juridical obligation is, and can only be, owed to another; it proscribes injuring, not failing to confer benefits; and the interference must be with what comes under the other's exclusive right as against the injurer. In private law, there can only be liability for misfeasance. But breach of a gratuitous promise, that is, of a promise that does not and cannot transfer rights, injures no contractual rights and so is nonfeasance.

Once freedom of contract is understood as the liberty to enter (or not) a relation with another that transfers rights, it does not stand in tension with the doctrine of unconscionability, as I have presented it. To the contrary, both freedom of contract and contractual fairness turn out to be distinct but mutually supportive aspects of the complete analysis of the same underlying conception of contract.

On the one hand, individuals are permitted but not obliged to offer and accept, to promise and give consideration, to exchange for equal value or voluntarily to enrich the other party. As I have emphasized, the requirement of equal value is facilitative in that a party may certainly choose to accept unequal value. With respect to the decision to transact or not, the common law conception of contract gives individuals an unfettered liberty to do as they please. The parameters of liberty are the rights of others and unless or until a party has done something in combination with another that transfers rights to him or her, there can be, contractually speaking, no obligations or corresponding rights as between them but just liberty.

---

98. Kant, *supra* note 19 at p. 394.

On the other hand, only certain kinds of acts and only a certain kind of relation between these acts bring a contractual relation with contractual rights and duties into existence. Parties must do something that may reasonably be interpreted as offer and acceptance as well as promise and consideration and the two sides must be mutually related in the requisite manner. Absent the use of a recognized legal formality, parties cannot choose some other way to bring about contract formation. There can be no legally significant intention to create legal relations except as expressed through acts that satisfy the principles of contract formation. It is uncontroversial that that common law recognizes no liberty in this respect. The same idea holds for unconscionability. Just as there is no liberty to create a contractual obligation via a route other than offer and acceptance and promise and consideration, so there is no liberty to do so except by an exchange contract or a gift contract. For as I have tried to show, it is only on this condition that the parties' assents may reasonably be construed as part of an interaction by which one acquires an exclusive right from and against the other. No less than the principles of contract formation, unconscionability is an essential step in defining the voluntary for the purposes of contract law. Both are fundamental and intrinsic to the complete elaboration of the conception of will that underlies contractual obligation.

IV. Conclusion

In this essay, I have tried to work out in some detail a conception of contract that answers the three main questions of modern contract theory. This conception is developed on a public basis of justification. Thus, it presents the conception as implicit in the main doctrines of contract law. This conception, in turn, makes explicit the unity of the doctrines in one intelligible idea. We bring out this conception by explaining how the doctrines fit with each other. Each doctrine is conceptually necessary to the other. The way we verify the role of any one doctrine is by showing that it is animated by the very same conception that informs the other doctrines. At the same time, each of the doctrines contributes in a distinct way to the full elaboration of the conception.

Moreover, while the doctrines are, upon analysis, fully consistent with each other and mutually supportive, it is not just a matter of their being consistent in a purely formal way. Rather, they together form an integrated whole that is intelligible and reasonable from a juridical point of view. We know this in virtue of the logic of a transfer of ownership. For this logic articulates the necessary conceptual premises of a relatively self-contained form of juridical relation which, in the case of a present executed transfer of property, we think of as effective and determinative of rights and duties between persons. We do not doubt that individuals can transfer property to others by way of executed gift or exchange or that such transfers can give rise to new rights and duties between them. My basic thesis is that the logic of a transfer of ownership that animates present transfers of property is also instantiated in contracts and, more specifically, in the main doctrines of the common law of contract. Indeed, it is their organizing idea. Thus these doctrines articulate a kind of relation between persons which we can also recognize as juridical: that is, as determining correlative rights and duties between contracting parties. Contract, no less than a present transfer of property, is intelligible and plausible from this normative point of view.

In virtue of this same logic we can say not only that the different contract doctrines supplement each other but that, in addition, there is a certain order and sequence whereby, cumulatively, one doctrine builds upon another until together they form a complete whole. Beginning with a conception of contract that takes the expectation principle as a principle of compensation, we start with the doctrine, namely, offer and acceptance, that represents the most formal elucidation of the kind of relation which this principle supposes – a two-sided relation that can transfer rights – and move to the doctrines, namely, consideration and unconscionability, that progressively specify a content suitable for this form. With the elaboration of the doctrine of unconscionablity, the fit between form and content is achieved and all the logical premises of a transfer of ownership are satisfied. In this way, we can know that the public basis of justification is complete, at least insofar as the basic structure of the conception of contract has now fully been made explicit in the doctrines of the law. These doctrines – the expectation principle, offer and acceptance, consideration, and unconscionability – constitute the four pillars of the common law conception of contract.

To conclude this essay, I wish to note three limits of the public justification as I have presented it here. These limits naturally suggest work that remains to be done.

To begin, while I have tried to set out the basic structure of the common law conception of contract, I have not discussed a number of important aspects of contract law which, although they do not specify its basic structure, nevertheless fill it in or follow from it. For example, there are the many rules relating to implied terms and conditions – the law of mistake and non-disclosure, frustration, conditions antecedent and subsequent, fundamental breach, anticipatory repudiation, and, more generally, interpretation. There is the more controversial question of the rights of third party beneficiaries as well as a range of more specific issues having to do with remedies for breach of contract, contractual fairness, and the relation between contract and tort. A public basis of justification aims to be complete in the sense that, through the conception of contract, it ideally is able to answer all or most of the questions that arise in relation to contract formation and breach. The contention is that the conception of contract has the necessary resources to do so. Of course, to answer these questions, it may be necessary to supplement the basic structure of this conception with various presumptions and propositions of law. However, it is important to note that, on the approach I am taking, the latter are not to be introduced *ab extra* and should not take us outside the conception of contract. Rather they are to be understood as implications of that conception when it is suitably specified to address these other questions. Essential to this approach is the idea that a contract does not admit of any gaps once it is understood in terms of the conception of contract. The demonstration that this is indeed the case cannot, however, be undertaken in the present essay.[99] This is the first limit.

Among the sorts of questions which a public conception of contract should also address are those that concern the constraints which may appropriately be placed on the operation of contract principles in light of social and economic values: issues of policy. To address these kinds of questions, a public justification must supplement the conception of contract, which makes explicit the pure juridical relation that is latent in contract doctrines, with an account of *the role of an actual regime of contract in civil society*. Whereas the conception of contract elucidates contract doctrines in terms of an idea of obligation that consists *just* in a negative prohibition against injuring what belongs to another by exclusive right and refers to notions of freedom and equality that abstract altogether from the parties' actual intentions, particular purposes, needs, and well-being, a justification of the existence of contract in civil society brings into play the latter considerations. Contract is now viewed as a common good that goes some way toward serving human needs and interests, both moral and material. The actual existence of an effectively functioning contractual regime becomes a matter of normative significance, for otherwise these needs and interests cannot be met. For the same reason, it becomes important that the methods of contracting be certain and publicly knowable in advance to enable individuals to use contract to achieve their ends. Hence the importance of legal formalities and certain legal presumptions that may not reflect the fundamental character of the contractual relation.[100] Similarly, it now becomes important that all individuals, as participants in civil society, have access to the contract regime and so, as a matter of public policy, the operation of the principles of contract formation may be constrained to ensure that the opportunity to transact is free from discrimination.[101]

The fact that the public justification as presented in this essay does not supplement the conception of contract with an integrated account of the role of contract in civil society is this essay's second limit. At the same time, I wish to

---

99. In "Public Justification," *supra,* note 12 at pp. 321–334, I sketch an argument as to why the conception of contract need not admit of gaps and how it provides a framework for analysing non-disclosure, mistake, and frustration.

100. This is the place for Fuller's rationale for consideration on the basis of the functions of legal formality and the social significance of exchange.

101. Hegel's account of the role of contract in civil society is particularly instructive. It is found in *The Philosophy of Right, supra,* note 19 at paras. 189–195, 208–210, and 213–217. Note that this discussion builds upon but is framed in different terms than his prior analysis of contract in Abstract Right, Ibid., at paragraphs 71–81. The conception of contract which I have presented in this essay corresponds to the latter only.

emphasize that these two parts of a public justification of contract represent distinct, though inter-connected, points of view with differing sets of values and that, in analysing a given issue of contract, one must guard against introducing considerations that are irrelevant or inappropriate to the standpoint one has taken up. Thus with respect to the elucidation of the conception of contract, the central question is how a breach of promise can be understood as a wrong, juridically speaking: that is, as an injury to something which comes under another's exclusive right. Whether the duty to perform can reasonably be understood as a coercible obligation not to injure another's right is the fundamental problem raised by Fuller and others and it is at the heart of the three questions of modern contract theory. I have argued that it can be so conceived on the supposition that contract is a transfer of right. In contrast to an account of the role of an actual regime of contract in civil society, the proposed analysis does not ascribe any value as such to the fact that people transact – it only prescribes the terms which must be observed *if* they choose to do so – and it is indifferent as to whether their actual individual needs and interests are served by the principles governing formation and breach. The task of settling the question of the juridical character of breach is nonetheless preliminary to an inquiry into the role of an actual regime of contract in civil society.

Whereas the first and second limits apply solely *within* the public basis of justification, the third concerns the relation between this form of justification and more comprehensive theoretical treatments of contract – in particular, a philosophical account. In the Introduction, I noted that the conception of contract developed here on a public basis of justification is at most the *first* (and necessarily provisional) step in theorizing the law of contract. This point merits emphasis. As part of a public justification of contract, this conception is just one step removed from the actual doctrines and principles of the law. It rests on and is framed in terms of a number of premises which it takes as presuppositions. Therefore, it does not, and cannot, purport to be the most complete, that is, the most integrated, systematic, and comprehensive theoretical account of contract, let alone a philosophy of contract.

The question is what might be the next step in moving toward a more comprehensive account? One might think that the most natural way would be to move directly from something like the conception of contract presented here, whether by itself or supplemented by an account of the role of contract in civil society, to a "theoretical approach," whether economic, utilitarian, or Kantian, which elucidates contract from a more comprehensive standpoint. My own view is different. It seems to me that, continuing with the idea of a public basis of justification, we should next seek an understanding of the main areas of private law that makes explicit their unity in terms of a single conception of obligation, perhaps through a comprehensive notion of property and a corresponding conception of the person. This would elucidate the obligation in contract at an even higher level of abstraction. Beyond this, and still working within the framework of a public basis of justification, it would be but a natural step to determine whether we can unite private law, now understood as a whole, and public law, with its own distinctive characteristic relations of right, values, and conception of the person. This integration of the juridical and the political at an even higher level of abstraction would nevertheless preserve the distinctiveness of each. The conception of contract that would find its place within this more comprehensive public justification would represent the most satisfactory point that could be reached by a public justification of contract. It would only be then that our understanding of contract would be complete for such purposes. The business of a philosophy of contract, as distinguished from a public basis of justification, would be to comprehend the truth of this understanding.[102]

102. I wish to thank Jeremy Fraiberg, Malcolm Thorburn, and Ernest Weinrib for their helpful comments on the first draft of this article. I am much indebted to Daniel Batista for his close editing of all the drafts and for his valuable substantive suggestions; and to Gregory Bordan for his important clarifications concerning fundamental aspects of the argument as a whole.

5

The Theory of Contracts

MELVIN A. EISENBERG

I. Introduction

The purpose of this paper is to develop a theory of contracts. The enterprise involved in developing such a theory needs explication, because legal theory has many branches. One branch of legal theory concerns fundamental jurisprudential issues, such as what constitutes law. Another branch concerns institutional issues, such as the nature of adjudication. However, when we talk about the theory of a specific area of law, like contracts, we mean a theory about the substantive content of the rules in that area. In this paper, I will use the terms *theory of substantive law* and *theory of contracts* in that sense.

Even with this restriction, there are different conceptions of the tasks that a theory of contracts may perform. For example, the theory of contracts could be a theory of what the content of contract law is, or a theory of what the content of contract law should be. In this paper, I take the position that the primary task that a theory of contracts should perform is to provide a principle for establishing the best content of contract law, that is, a principle for establishing what the content of contract law should be.

Theories of substantive law can themselves be categorized in various ways. For purposes of this paper, I distinguish between metric and generative theories of substantive law. *Metric* theories identify one or two variables that when properly applied result in determinate legal outcomes (or, under some theories, explain legal outcomes), in a manner somewhat analogous to scientific principles that predict determinate outcomes.

In contrast, *generative* theories focus on the methodology that should be employed to produce the best rules of law. Unlike metric theories, which, at least in principle, result in or explain determinate outcomes by drastically restricting the number of relevant variables, generative theories can accommodate a large number of variables. Indeed, it is partly the multivalue nature of such theories that renders them generative rather than metric. Just as metric theories are somewhat analogous to scientific principles that predict determinate outcomes, so generative theories are analogous to theories of science itself, which do not predict specific outcomes, but instead instruct us how to do science. In this paper, I will develop a generative theory of contracts.

Legal theories of all kinds are marked to a significant extent by the way in which they relate doctrinal propositions to social propositions. By *doctrinal propositions,* I mean propositions of legal doctrine. By *social propositions,* I mean all propositions other than doctrinal propositions. The types of social propositions most salient to modern Western law are moral norms, policies, and empirical propositions (propositions that describe the way in which the world works, such as statements concerning individual behavior and institutional design, that describe aspects of the present world, such as statements concerning the existence of a trade usage, or that describe historical events, such as statements concerning how a trade usage developed). For ease of exposition, in the balance of this paper when I refer to social propositions I mean social propositions that are relevant and meritorious and that can properly be taken into account by a lawmaker.[1]

Under some conceptions of legal theory, often described as "formal," social propositions are irrelevant. Under *axiomatic* legal theories, for example, fundamental doctrinal propositions are established on the ground that they are self-evident. The task of such theories consists of determining and explicating these propositions. Similarly, under *deductive* legal theories many or most doctrinal propositions are established solely by deduction from other, more fundamental doctrinal propositions. The task of such theories consists of drawing these deductions.

Under other conceptions of legal theory, moral norms and policies play an important or decisive rule. For example, *interpretive* legal theories proceed by determining the social propositions that are to be found in the most fundamental doctrines, or that meet some standard of fit with and best justify or rationalize doctrine as a whole or significant areas of doctrine. These social propositions are then used to explain the law, or to reinterpret, reformulate, criticize, or reject doctrines that the social propositions do not justify or rationalize. The task of such theories consists of determining the relevant social propositions, and using them to explain, reinterpret, reformulate, criticize, or reject portions of doctrine. Interpretive theories have important normative elements, but they are not full-blooded normative theories, because the choice of moral norms and policies that they can employ is restricted by the body of existing institutional decisions. Under *normative theories,* in contrast, doctrinal propositions are generated by moral norms and policies that are utilized because they are meritorious, independent of their relation to existing institutional decisions. The task

---

1. The analysis in Part I draws upon, but modifies and extends, portions of my book, *The Nature of the Common Law* (1988). Chapters 1–4 of that book contain a fuller exposition of some elements of the analysis in Part I.

of such theories consists of determining the social propositions that are appropriate to the formulation of doctrinal propositions, and establishing the doctrinal propositions that the social propositions generate.

In Part II, I examine these four kinds of theories. I will show that axiomatic
and deductive theories of law cannot be sustained; that interpretive theories can
perform important tasks, especially in the area of judicial lawmaking, but are not
adequate for the task of establishing the best rules of contract law; and that this
task can be performed only by normative theories.

In Part III, I examine two leading kinds of normative theories of contract law,
each of which turns on a single value – respectively, the moral value of autonomy
and the welfare value of giving effect to revealed preferences.

Finally, in Part IV, I develop a generative, multivalue theory of contract law.

II. Four Conceptions of a Theory of Contracts

A. Axiomatic Theories

Axiomatic theories of the content of law take as a premise that fundamental doctrinal propositions can be established on the ground that they are self-evident.
As Holmes said, disparagingly,

> I sometimes tell students that the law schools pursue an inspirational combined with a
> logical method, that is, the postulates are taken for granted upon authority without in-
> quiry into their worth, and then logic is used as the only tool to develop the results.[2]

As suggested by Holmes's observation, axiomatic theories may easily be
coupled with deductive theories. The school of thought now known as classical
contract law, which held sway from the mid-nineteenth century through the
first part of the twentieth century, was based on just such a coupling. Among
the axioms of this school were that only bargain promises have consideration,
that bargains are formed by offer and acceptance, that the measure of damages
for breach of contract is expectation damages, and that contracts must be interpreted objectively.

In the strictest version of axiomatic theories, like the school of classical contract law, no room is allowed for justifying doctrinal propositions on the basis
of moral and policy propositions. So, for example, Langdell, speaking to the
question whether an acceptance by mail was effective on dispatch, said:

> The acceptance . . . must be communicated to the original offerer, and until such com-
> munication the contract is not made. It has been claimed that the purposes of substan-
> tial justice, and the interests of contracting parties as understood by themselves, will be
> best served by holding that the contract is complete the moment the letter of acceptance

---

2. O. W. Holmes, "Law in Science and Science in Law" in *Collected Legal Papers* (New York: Harcourt, Brace & Howe, 1920) 210 at 238.

is mailed; and cases have been put to show that the contrary view would produce not only unjust but absurd results. The true answer to this argument is that it is irrelevant. . . .[3]

Axiomatic theories of law cannot be sustained. No significant doctrinal proposition can ultimately be justified either on the ground that it is self-evident or on the basis of another doctrinal proposition. Doctrinal propositions can ultimately be justified only by social propositions.[4]

For example, although an actor can justify an action on the ground that the action is required by statute, the legislature itself cannot normally justify a statute on that basis. Except in very rare and almost hypothetical cases (such as those in which statute is constitutionally required), the legislature can justify a statute only on social grounds.

Similarly, although a court many, under some conceptions of the theory of adjudication, justify a result solely on the ground that it is applying a rule laid down by an earlier case, we can always trace the origins of a common law rule back to a point where that justification is unavailable, and only social grounds will do.

Furthermore, in a modern Western society, doctrinal propositions can ultimately be justified only by certain kinds of social grounds: namely, policies and moral norms mediated into doctrine through empirical propositions.

So, for example, in a modern Western society doctrinal propositions cannot be justified by historical propositions. That expectation damages have been granted for breach of contract in the past is not alone justification for continuing to grant expectation damages. That specific performance has been withheld in certain kinds of cases in the past is not alone justification for continuing to withhold specific performance in those kinds of cases. Of course, the continu-

---

3. See C. C. Langdell, *Summary of the Law of Contracts,* 2nd ed. (1880) at 15, 20–21.
4. It might be argued against this position that some doctrinal propositions that have the form and substance of a definition are self-evident. Perhaps so, doctrinal propositions that would qualify are hard to find. Many doctrines that have the form of a definition are really substantive rules, for example, the provision of the Uniform Commercial Code that an "agreement" is "the bargain of the parties in fact . . . including course of dealing or usage of trade."

   Other doctrinal definitions are simply fragments of substantive rules. This is typically the case, for example, of defined terms in a statute whose function is to allow the legislative draftsman to substitute a short definition for a long term.

   Even doctrinal propositions that have both the form and substance of definitions typically need justification. If a doctrinal definition corresponds to the ordinary-language definition of the defined term, the definition is not a doctrine, but simply part of the language. Many legal definitions do differ from the ordinary-language meaning of the same term. So, for example, *Restatement (Second) of Contracts* §2 defines a promise as "a manifestation of intention to act or refrain from acting in a specified way, so made as to justify a promisee in understanding that a promise has been made." In contrast, the dictionary defines a promise as simply a declaration assuring that one will or will not do something. See *The American Dictionary of the English Language* (New College ed., 1981) at 1047 [hereinafter *The American Dictionary*]. Similarly, *Restatement (Second)* §24 defines an offer as "the manifestation of willingness to enter into a bargain, so made as to justify another person in understanding that his assent to that bargain is invited and will conclude it." In contrast, the dictionary defines an offer simply as the act of presenting for acceptance or rejection. See *The American Dictionary,* ibid. at 912. In such cases the legal definitions are not self-evident and need justification.

ation of an established doctrine may be justified by considerations like the protection of reliance, the desirability of stable systems, and the possibility of unintended consequences when changes are made. However, considerations like these are moral and policy considerations, not historical considerations, and in any event they will only infrequently justify doctrines that lack independent moral and policy support. Similarly, a doctrine may be established by a historical event, like a judicial decision or a legislative act, but in a modern Western society such events will confer doctrinal status on a proposition only because there are social reasons for recognizing at law doctrines established by such events.

In short, a distinction must be drawn between the justification of a doctrine and the justification for following a doctrine. Once a doctrine has been adopted it may be justifiably *followed,* either in the interest of stability, reliance, and the like, or because of social reasons for following rules that have been adopted in a certain way. However, those elements only justify following the doctrine, not the doctrine itself.

In the balance of this paper, I will refer to doctrines that are justified by applicable moral norms and policies, mediated through empirical propositions, as *normatively justified,* and to doctrines that are not so justified as *normatively unjustified.*

B. Deductive Theories

Deductive theories take as a premise that many or most doctrinal propositions can be established solely by deduction from other, more fundamental doctrinal propositions. In the modern period, the explicit use of deductive theory is infrequent. However, deductive theory was an integral part of the school of classical contract law, whose teachings have a continuing impact on contract law. That school conceived of contract law as a set of fundamental legal principles that were justified on the ground that they were self-evident, and a second set of rules that were justified on the ground that they could be deduced from the fundamental principles.

For example, it was an axiom of classical contract law that in principle only a bargain promise had consideration – that is, was enforceable – although exceptions were recognized for certain kinds of promises that were enforceable on purely precedential grounds. The issue then arose whether a firm offer – an unbargained-for promise to hold an offer open – was legally enforceable. The conclusion of classical contract law was, no.[5] This conclusion was justified by deduction alone. The major premise was that only bargains had consideration. The minor premise was that in the case of a firm offer, the promise to hold the offer open is not bargained for. The conclusion was that a firm offer was not enforceable.

5. See, for example, *Dickinson* v. *Dodds* (1876) 2 Ch. 463.

Another axiom of classical contract law was that bargains were formed by offer and acceptance. The issue then arose whether an offer for a unilateral contract – an offer to be accepted by the performance of an act – was revocable before performance had been completed even if the offeree had begun to perform. The conclusion of classical contract law was, yes.[6] This conclusion too was justified by deduction alone. The major premise was that an offeror could revoke an offer at any time prior to acceptance unless he had made a bargained-for promise to hold the offer open. The minor premise was that an offer for a unilateral contract was not bargained for and was not accepted until performance of the act had occurred. The conclusion was that an offer for a unilateral contract was revocable even after the offeree had begun to perform.

Langdell's view that an acceptance can be effective only on receipt was also based on deductive reasoning: By axiom, a bargain can be formed only by offer and acceptance. By axiom, an expression cannot be an acceptance unless it is communicated to the addressee. By deduction, an acceptance can be effective only on receipt.

Although classical contract law coupled axiomatic and deductive theories, a deductive theory may be utilized even when its doctrinal starting-points are established by normative justifications, rather than on the ground that they are self-evident. Regardless of the way in which doctrinal starting-points are determined, however, deductive theories are no more sustainable than axiomatic theories. A doctrine, even if normatively justified, may serve as a prime facie premise in legal reasoning, but cannot serve as a conclusive premise of legal reasoning, because all doctrines are always subject to as-yet-unarticulated exceptions based on social propositions. Such an exception may be made because the social propositions that support the doctrine do not extend to a new fact-pattern that is within the doctrine's stated scope. Alternatively, such an exception may be made because a new fact-pattern that is within the doctrine's stated scope brings into play other social propositions that require the formulation of a special rule for the fact-pattern.

For example, suppose there is a justified doctrinal rule that bargain promises are enforceable. A case now arises, for the first time, in which a party to a bargain with a minor seeks to enforce the contract against the minor. If the applicability of a legal rule to a new fact-pattern that is within the stated scope of the rule could be justified by deductive logic alone, the minor would be liable. The major premise would be that bargains are enforceable. The minor premise would be that the minor made a bargain. The conclusion would be that the minor is liable. But this conclusion should not be drawn, because the social propositions that support the bargain rule do not support the application of the rule to bargains with minors. One reason for the rule that bargain promises are enforceable is that actors are normally good judges of their own interests. This

---

6. See, for example, *Petterson* v. *Pattberg,* 248 N.Y. 86, 161 N.E. 428 (1928).

reason for the rule does not extend to minors. Therefore, the rule should be made subject to an exception for minors.

Similarly, suppose there is a justified doctrinal rule that donative promises are unenforceable. A case now arises in which a donative promise was reasonably relied upon to the promisee's cost. If the applicability of a doctrinal rule to a new fact-pattern that is within the stated scope of the rule could be justified by deductive logic alone, the promisor would not be liable. The major premise would be that donative promises are unenforceable. The minor premise would be that the promise was donative. The conclusion would be that the promise is unenforceable. But this conclusion should not be drawn, because a social proposition other than those that support the donative-promise principle applies to the case: When one person, *A,* uses words or actions that he knows or should know would induce another, *B,* to reasonably believe that *A* is committed to take a certain course of action, and *A* knows or should know that *B* will incur costs if *A* does not take the action, *A* should take steps to ensure that if he does not take the action *B* will not suffer a loss.[7] This proposition is weightier, in the donative-promise context, than the propositions that support the donative-promise rule in the absence of reliance. Therefore, an exception should be made to the donative-promise rule when the promisee has reasonably relied upon the promise.

Here is another, more complex example: Often an issue arises as to whether an expression in response to an offer constitutes an acceptance. Suppose there is a justified doctrinal rule that an expression by an offeree constitutes an acceptance if a reasonable person in the offeror's position would interpret the expression as an acceptance, even if the offeree does not subjectively intend his expression to be an acceptance. This rule is justified because in the typical case a person who intends something other than the reasonable meaning of his expression has used language carelessly, so that the offeree is at fault for creating a reasonable expectation in the offeror that the offer has been accepted.

The following case now arises: *A* makes an offer to *B,* and *B* responds with an expression that he does not subjectively intend to be an acceptance. A reasonable person would interpret *B*'s response as an acceptance, but *A* does not so interpret it. *B* does not perform. *A* sues *B* for breach of contract, falsely claiming that he interpreted *B*'s response as an acceptance. If the applicability of a doctrinal rule to a new fact-pattern that is within the stated scope of the rule could be justified by deductive logic alone, *B* would be liable. The major premise would be that whether an expression constitutes an acceptance depends upon the reasonable meaning of the expression. The minor premise would be that the reasonable meaning of *B*'s expression is that *B* has accepted *A's* offer. The conclusion would be that *B* is liable. But *B* should not be liable (and will not

---

7. See T. M. Scanlon, "Promises and Practices" (1990) 19 Phil. & Pub. Aff. 199.

be under American law[8]), because an exception for shared subjective understanding should be hived off from the existing rule. The existing rule is supported by norms concerning fault. However, when there is a shared subjective understanding, *B* may have been at fault, but his fault caused no injury to *A*. Furthermore, *A* himself is at fault, for falsely claiming that he interpreted *B*'s response as an acceptance.

These cases illustrate why a legal doctrine can never be justified solely on the ground that it can be logically deduced from another legal doctrine, even if the other doctrine is normatively justified. Even a normatively justified doctrine can and should be made subject to exceptions when the social propositions that support the doctrine do not extend to the subject-matter of a proposed exception, or other social propositions justify making an exception for that subject-matter.[9] Accordingly, the applicability of a doctrine to a fact-pattern that falls within the doctrine's stated scope is always dependent on a conclusion that social propositions do not justify creating an exception for the fact-pattern. Correspondingly, even when an application of a doctrine seems straightforward and easy, it is straightforward and easy not as a matter of deductive logic alone, but because social propositions do not justify the creation of an exception to cover the case at hand.

C. Interpretive Theories.

When we think of a work of contracts scholarship as a work of contracts theory, what we usually mean is that the author's enterprise is to get at the root of some area of contracts. Often, the methodology that implicitly underlies such work can be described as interpretive, in the sense of that term developed by Dworkin. That is, the work often proceeds by describing some area of contract law and then determining the social propositions that are to be found in the most fundamental doctrines in the area, or that meet some standard of fit with and best justify or rationalize doctrine in that area as a whole. These social propositions are then used to explain the law governing that area, or to reinterpret, reformulate, criticize, or reject doctrines in the area that the social propositions do not justify or rationalize.

A major problem presented by work that takes this form is that the author must have a theory of substantive law to fashion the very legal materials he is interpreting. That is, the substantive content of an area of law, *A,* that is examined with the objective of fashioning a theory of *A* can only be described by

---

8. See *Restatement (Second) of Contracts* §201(1); cf. *Emor, Inc.* v. *Cyprus Mines Corp.,* 467 F.2d 770 (3rd Cir. 1972); *Perry and Wallis, Inc.* v. *United States,* 427 F.2d 722 (1970); *Cresswell* v. *United States,* 173 F. Supp. 805 at 811, 146 Ct. Cl. 119 at 127 (1959); *Della Ratta, Inc.* v. *American Better Community Developer, Inc.,* 38 Md. App. 119, 380 A.2d 627 (1977).
9. See Section II.C, *infra.*

having a theory of law. This problem is especially evident in areas of law, like contracts, that are largely products of the common law. One reason why it is impossible even to describe the content of the law of contracts without a theory of law has already been discussed: Existing doctrine is always subject to as-yet-unarticulated exceptions. A statement of existing doctrine in categorical terms, without taking account of such exceptions, would be inaccurate. Since these potential exceptions cannot be determined from doctrine itself, they can only be determined on the basis of a theory of law that allows such exceptions to be established even though they have not yet been officially made.

Another reason why the content of a common law subject, like contracts, cannot be described without a theory of substantive law stems from the fact that the relevant body of precedents in a given area will almost necessarily display some degree of inconsistency. I need to define here what I mean by consistency in the law. If consistency in the law meant only that when all the facts of two cases are the same the result should be the same, then every precedent would necessarily be consistent with every other precedent, because the facts of every precedent are different. Under such a view, the concept of consistency would have little or no meaning in legal reasoning. But consistency does have meaning in legal reasoning, and that meaning turns on social propositions.

Thus, for purposes of legal reasoning two *precedents* are consistent if they reach the same result on the same relevant facts, and inconsistent if they reach different results on the same relevant facts. What facts are relevant, for these purposes, turns entirely on social propositions. For example, as a matter of social propositions – and only as a matter of social propositions – it is often relevant to liability for an accident that a party was intoxicated, but seldom if ever relevant that a party was wearing a red hat. We could think of societies in which it would be relevant that a party to an accident was wearing a red hat. For example, it might conceivably matter in the Vatican. But under the social propositions of our society, it would not be relevant.

Whether a *rule* and its exceptions, or two different rules, are consistent as a matter of legal reasoning also turns entirely on social propositions. This meaning of consistency is most easily illustrated in the context of a rule and an exception to the rule. A rule and an exception are consistent if, and only if, one of the following conditions holds:

1. The social proposition, *SP1,* that supports the rule does not extend to the cases covered by the exceptions; or
2. The exception is justified by a different social proposition, *SP2,* and there is good social reason, in the class of cases at hand, to allow *SP2* to either trump *SP1* or to figure, along with *SP1,* in the creation of an exception that is a vector of both social propositions.

Take the bargain rule and the exception for minors. The rule and the exception are consistent because, and only because, the social propositions that support the rule depend in part on the respect due to a promisor's consent, and that respect is not due where consent is given by a minor.

In contrast, suppose a court were to hold that a bargain made by a clergyman is not enforceable against the clergyman, even if the bargain is not religious in nature (that is, even if it does not concern issues of dogma, or the allocation of authority within a church, or the like). Such an exception would be inconsistent with the bargain rule, because the social propositions that support that rule extend to clergymen as well as laymen, and no other social proposition supports a special status for clergymen in this regard. It is easy to imagine social propositions that would support a special clergyman status for other purposes, or in another society or time. In the middle ages, for example, there was a clergyman exception under the criminal law: Clergymen could be prosecuted for felony only in ecclesiastical courts, and therefore were not subject to capital punishment.[10] Even today, religious bargains made by clergymen might well be unenforceable. But social propositions in contemporary society would not support a clergyman exception for secular bargains. That is the reason, and the only reason, why a clergyman exception would be inconsistent with the bargain rule.

A similar analysis applies to the consistency of two rules, as opposed to a rule and an exception. Two rules will be consistent if, and only if, one of the following conditions holds:

1. The two rules are supported by the same social propositions;
2. Each rule is supported by different social propositions and the social propositions are not in conflict in the case at hand, because either the social propositions that support one rule have no bearing on the other, or, because they do have a bearing but would not lead to a different rule; or
3. The two rules are supported by different social propositions that are in conflict in certain cases, in the sense that taken alone the different social propositions would lead to different rules to govern those cases. However, each social proposition has a range of applicability in which it does not conflict with the other, and there is good reason why, in those cases, either one social proposition should be subordinated to the other, or one or both rules should reflect the conflicting social propositions in different ways.

Given this meaning of consistency, although the common law will always be moving toward internal consistency based on congruence with social propositions, some transient inconsistency in the body of the common law at any single moment is inevitable. To put this differently, at any one time there is always a preliminary, partially inconsistent, version of the common law that is moving toward a wholly consistent version of the common law. In some cases, common law doctrines will have been formulated at a time when the social propositions

10. See F. Pollock and F. W. Maitland, *The History of English Law,* vol. 1, 2nd ed. (London: Cambridge University Press, 1898) at 441–457.

that were then relevant differ from the social propositions that are now relevant, and the courts will not have had the occasion to move the law forward. In other cases, courts will believe that some doctrines were normatively unjustified to begin with, and will riddle the doctrines with inconsistent distinctions, that is, with exceptions that are supported by social propositions that undermine the basic rule, as a way station toward full overruling.

For example, under the legal-duty rule a modification of a bargain is unenforceable if one party's performance consists only of an act he had already contracted to perform.[11] This rule is not normatively justified:[12] Call a party who proposes to modify a contract so that he will receive a greater price but will not render a greater performance, A, and call a party who agrees to such a modification, B. Many modifications of this kind are agreed to by B on the basis of a belief, shared by A and B, that as a result of some initial misapprehension or later changed circumstance, fair dealing requires a readjustment of the contract to reflect either the original purpose of the contractual enterprise, or the equities as they stand in light of the parties' original tacit assumptions. Other modifications are agreed to by B as reciprocity for past modifications that A has agreed to in B's favor, or because B expects that if he agrees to the present modification A will reciprocate by agreeing to future modifications. Thus the legal-duty rule, under which such modifications are unenforceable, conflicts with the virtues of accommodation, ongoing cooperation, and fair dealing between contracting parties.

Accordingly, the courts have made a number of inconsistent exceptions to the legal-duty rule. Under one exception, the rule is inapplicable where A's contractual duty is owed to a party other than B.[13] This exception is inconsistent with the rule, because the exception can be supported only on the reasoning that the grounds for enforcing bargains are applicable even when one party only promises to do what he is already contractually obliged to do. Under that reasoning, however, the basic rule is unjustified. (If the legal-duty rule was justified on the ground that a threat to withhold performance of a contract puts the other party under duress, then it might matter that the duty was owed to a third person rather than to B. Classically, however, the application of the rule did not turn on whether the promisor was under duress.)

Under another exception, the legal-duty rule is inapplicable if the duty is to pay a debt whose total amount is disputed, even though the performance consists of paying the part that is admittedly due.[14] This exception is inconsistent with the rule for the same reason that the third-party exception is inconsistent. Still other courts have held the rule inapplicable by concluding that in the cases before them, the parties had "rescinded" their prior contract and then made a

11. *Restatement (Second) of Contracts* §73 (1979).
12. See, for example, M. A. Eisenberg, "Probability and Chance in Contract Law" (1998) 45 U.C.L.A. L. Rev. 1006 at 1034–1048.
13. *Restatement (Second) of Contracts* §73 comment d.
14. Ibid. at §§73 comment f, 74.

"new" one[15] – a conclusion that can be drawn, if a court so desires, in any case that falls within the rule. And under modern law, a modification is enforceable if it is fair and equitable in view of circumstances not anticipated when the original contract was made[16] – an exception that is not only inconsistent with the doctrine that performance of a legal duty is not consideration, but that probably covers the great majority of the cases to which that doctrine purports to apply. (The legislatures have also intervened. Many statutes provide that promises within the rule are enforceable if in writing,[17] and under the Uniform Commercial Code a promise modifying a contract for the sale of goods is binding despite the rule.[18])

Good reasons justify the practice of inconsistent distinguishing. It may sometimes be best for courts to move to the best rule in steps, even at the price of inconsistency during the transition. A court may properly decide that if it is uncertain how given conduct should be treated, it may give effect to its uncertainty by carving out only a portion of the conduct for special treatment, on a provisional basis, provided the line it carves is rationally related to the court's purpose. For example, a court may believe that a doctrine is not normatively justified and yet may not be confident that its belief is correct. The court may then properly draw an inconsistent distinction as a provisional step toward full overruling. Alternatively, a court may properly formulate an exception at a level of generality below that necessary for the exception to be fully principled, as a provisional step toward full generality. For example, a court faced with a relied-upon donative bailment promise in the early twentieth century might have made an exception to the rule that donative promises were unenforceable, but limited the exception to bailment promises because it was not yet sufficiently confident to formulate a general reliance exception.

Inconsistent distinguishing may also be used as a technique for dealing with the problem of reliance on precedents. Inconsistent distinguishing allows the courts to protect at least those who relied on the core of a doctrine, that is, that part of a doctrine that cannot be even plausibly distinguished, while signaling to the profession that the underlying doctrine has been advanced to candidacy for overruling. Thus by using the technique of inconsistent distinguishing, a court may simultaneously move the law toward normative justifiability, protect past justified reliance on the core of a doctrine, diminish the likelihood of future justified reliance, and prepare the way for an overruling that might not have otherwise been proper.

The common law may also be inconsistent at any given moment because it may include deeply seated organizing concepts that lead to inconsistent treatment

15. See *Schwartzreich v. Bauman-Basch, Inc.,* 231 N.Y. 196, 131 N.E. 887 (1921).
16. *Restatement (Second) of Contracts* §89 (1979).
17. See Cal. Civ. Code §§1524, 1697; Mich. Comp. Laws Ann. §566.1; N.Y. Gen. Oblig. Law §5–1103.
18. U.C.C. §2–209.

of like transactions over long periods of time. For example, the distinction between the organizing concepts of property and contract led for a long time to special rules for leases that were inconsistent with the general rules of contract law. Even when this kind of inconsistency begins to break down, there will be a transitional period in which the status of inconsistent doctrines that have not yet been swept up in the reformation is uncertain.

Given the high likelihood of inconsistency in the common law at any given moment, a commentator who wants to describe the law must pick and choose between precedents, suppressing or even rejecting some while accepting and sometimes emphasizing others. The body of precedents will not itself instruct a commentator which precedents to reject or suppress and which to accept or emphasize. Accordingly, the commentator must employ a theory of substantive law, implicit or explicit, to choose which precedents will count, and of those, which will count for a little and which will count for a lot.

A final reason why the common law cannot be described without a theory of substantive law is that often it will often not be entirely clear just what rule a precedent establishes. Under accepted principles of the common law, the rule of a precedent can be deemed to be either the doctrinal proposition the court explicitly states to be the rule it adopts, or a rule that is consistent with the result of the precedent and with those of its facts that are relevant under applicable social propositions. Often, a number of different rules are consistent with the result and the socially relevant facts of a precedent. Accordingly, in describing the law in common law areas, the very data that is described – that is, the precedents – must inevitably be in part a product of a theory of how to describe the data.

This is well illustrated by Julius Stone's critique[19] of Arthur Goodhart's theory[20] that the rule of a precedent is the result reached on those facts of the precedent that the precedent court considered material. Stone demonstrated that it was virtually impossible to apply Goodhart's theory, because the material facts in a case can often be stated at different levels of generality, and each level of generality will tend to yield a different rule.

Stone used for his demonstration a famous British case, *Donoghue* v. *Stevenson*.[21] A friend had purchased a bottle of ginger beer for the plaintiff in a café. The bottle was opaque. After the plaintiff drank part of the ginger beer she discovered a decomposed snail in the bottle. Plaintiff suffered shock and severe gastroenteritis, sued the manufacturer of the ginger beer, and won.

Before *Donoghue,* a manufacturer who negligently produced a defective product was ordinarily liable only to its immediate buyer. It was clear that

---

19. J. Stone, *The Ratio of the Ratio Decidendi* (1959) 22 Mod. L. Rev. 597. See also A. Simpson, *The Ratio Decidendi of a Case* (1957) 20 Mod. L. Rev. 413 (1958) 21 Mod. L. Rev. 155 (1959) 22 Mod. L. Rev. 453.
20. A. Goodhart, *Determining the Ratio Decidendi of a Case* (1930) 40 Yale Law J. 161. See also, A. Goodhart, *The Ratio Decidendi of a Case* (1959) 22 Mod. L. Rev. 117.
21. *McAlister (or Donoghue)* v. *Stevenson* [1932] L. R. App. Cas. 562 (H.L.).

Donoghue abandoned this rule, because it held the manufacturer liable although the plaintiff was not its immediate buyer. As Stone pointed out, however, under Goodhart's theory it would be far from clear what rule the *Donoghue* court adopted, because the various material facts in the case could be characterized at vastly different levels of generality. For example, the vehicle of harm in *Donoghue* could be characterized as an opaque bottle of beverage, a bottle of beverage, a container of chattels for human consumption, a chattel, or a thing. The defendant could be characterized as a manufacturer of nationally distributed goods, a manufacturer, a person working on goods for profit, or a person working on goods. The injury could be characterized as a physical personal injury, a physical personal or emotional injury, or simply as an injury. Under the Goodhart theory, therefore, *Donoghue* could stand for a number of rules, constructed from permutations of the material facts at various levels of generality – for example, for the rule that if a manufacturer of nationally distributed goods that are intended for human consumption produces the goods in a negligent manner, it is liable for resulting physical personal or emotional injury; or for the rule that if a person working on goods for profit is negligent, he is liable for resulting physical personal injury if he packaged the goods in such a way that the defect was concealed.

Judge Cardozo's famous opinion in *MacPherson* v. *Buick Motor Co.*[22] provides a classic illustration of the way in which a precedent not only can be described to stand for more than one rule, but can be completely transformed to stand for a rule different than the rule the precedent stated. *MacPherson* grew out of injuries suffered by the plaintiff as a result of the sudden collapse of a new Buick the plaintiff had purchased from a dealer. One of the car's wheels had been made of defective wood, and the car had collapsed because the spokes of the wheel had crumbled into fragments. MacPherson sued Buick. Buick had not made the wheel, but instead had purchased it from another manufacturer. There was evidence, however, that reasonable inspection by Buick could have discovered the defects in the wheel. MacPherson won a jury verdict against Buick, and Buick appealed.

Prior to *MacPherson*, the rule stated by the New York cases was that a manufacturer who negligently produced a defective product was liable only to its immediate buyer, unless the product was of a *kind* that is "imminently" or "inherently" dangerous, like poison. In *MacPherson*, Cardozo effectively adopted a straightforward negligence rule, under which the negligent manufacturer of any defective product is liable to any person who would foreseeably be injured as a result of the manufacturer's negligence, whether or not that person was the manufacturer's immediate buyer. However, Cardozo did not formally overrule the precedents. Instead, he transformed the old rule by a new construction of the facts and results of the precedents, or more accurately of the facts and

---

22. *MacPherson* v. *Buick Motor Co.*, 217 N.Y. 382, 111 N.E. 1050 (1916).

results he chose to emphasize. By using this method, Cardozo was able to construct a rule, based on the precedents, that was contrary to the rule that the precedents stated. The transformation of precedents by utilizing their results and facts rather than by applying the rule they stated, is accepted by the legal system as an entirely legitimate technique and is by no means limited to *MacPherson*.

Accordingly, a commentator who seeks to describe the content of an area of common law must first determine which precedents will stand for the rules they state, and which precedents stand for a rule based on the results and the facts of the precedent. In the former case, he will then have to make the further choice which statements in the precedent to emphasize and which to suppress or ignore. In the latter case, he will have to make the further choice which facts to select and how to characterize the results. These determinations and choices can not be made without a theory of substantive law, because seldom will the precedents themselves dictate the way the determinations and choices should be made.

What is true of common law areas is by and large true of statutory areas. Statutory doctrines, like common law doctrines, will often be subject to unstated exceptions. (The most famous example is the slayer rule, under which a murderer is not allowed to inherit from his victim even though the relevant statute requires such inheritance.[23]) Furthermore, statutes are no more self-interpreting than decisions. Notwithstanding the posture of strict textualists, statutory language always needs to be interpreted in light of its context, so that we can only know what a statute means if we have a theory of statutory interpretation.

In short, one who seeks even to describe the law must have a theory of substantive law by which to choose what as-yet-unarticulated exceptions should be recognized, to chose between inconsistent authorities, and to choose what rule any given authority establishes. I have already shown why such a theory can be neither axiomatic nor deductive. What alternatives are left? One possibility would be a theory that used some kind of mechanical algorithm to make the necessary choices. That possibility is a mirage. Another possibility would be to describe law on the basis of what can be predicted that judges would do. That alternative, however, would in turn require a theory of how to make such predictions.[24]

---

23. See, for example, *Riggs* v. *Palmer,* 115 N.Y. 506, 22 N.E. 189 (1889).
24. A powerful but different kind of objection, famously made by H. L. A. Hart, is that the predictive account fails to come to grips with the internal aspect of law:

   [I]f we look closely at the activity of the judge or official who punishes deviation from legal rules (or those private persons who reprove or criticize deviations from non-legal rules), we see that rules are involved in this activity in a way which this predictive account leaves quite unexplained. For the judge, in punishing, takes the rule as his *guide* and the breach of the rule as his *reason* and *justification* for punishing the offender. He does not look upon the rule as a statement that he and others are likely to punish deviations, though a spectator might look upon the

Realistically, therefore, the choices involved in describing legal doctrine, at least in common law areas like contracts, must be guided at least in part by elements other than doctrine; in particular, by normative elements. The critical question then arises, must these normative elements be linked to existing institutional decisions, and if so, what should be the nature of that link?

One possible theory is that the normative elements employed in describing law should be those that are explicitly or implicitly found in doctrine. Peter Benson has developed just such a theory.[25] However, just as contrasting doctrinal rules can be found in the body of doctrine, so too can contrasting normative ideas. For example, one of the basic normative ideas that Benson identifies in contract doctrine is that contract law is strictly objective and therefore rejects a purely subjective test of interpretation. In fact, however, American contract law includes purely subjective tests of interpretation. For example, under American contract law if the parties subjectively attach the same meaning to an expression, that meaning prevails even though it is unreasonable.[26] Objective interpretation comes into play only if the parties do not share the same subjective interpretation – and even then, in certain kinds of cases one party's subjective interpretation may trump the other party's objectively more reasonable interpretation.[27] Another basic normative idea that Benson finds in contract doctrine is that when a contract is formed, each party has a legal right to possession of the performance promised by the other.[28] If that were the case, however, a party

rule in just this way. The predictive aspect of the rule (though real enough) is irrelevant to his purposes, whereas its status as a guide and justification is essential. The same is true of informal reproofs administered for the breach of non-legal rules. These too are not merely predictable reactions to deviations, but something which existence of the rule guides and is held to justify. So we say that we reprove or punish a man *because* he has broken the rule: and not merely that is was probable that we would reprove or punish him.

H. L. A. Hart, *The Concept of Law* 10–11. For an expanded statement of the internal perspective, see ibid. at 8–91 (2nd ed. 1994).

25. P. Benson, "The Idea of a Public Basis of Justification for Contract" (1995) 33 Osgoode Hall L. J. 273 [hereinafter "Public Basis"].
26. Thus *Restatement (Second) Contracts* §201(1) provides that "[w]here the parties have attached the same meaning to a promise or agreement or a term thereof, it is interpreted in accordance with that meaning."
27. Thus under *Restatement (Second) Contracts* §201(2), if *A* and *B* attach different subjective meanings, M and N, to an expression, and *A* knows that *B* attaches meaning N while *B* does not know that *A* attaches meaning M, *B*'s subjective meaning will prevail over *A*'s even though *A*'s meaning is more reasonable than *B*'s.
28. "Public Basis," *supra* note 25, at 317, 319, 320–24. Still a third basic normative idea that Benson finds in existing contract doctrine is that there can be no liability for nonfeasance. In fact, however, contract law provides various examples of a duty to bestir oneself. For example, if *A* stands by while *B* renders valuable services for *A*'s benefit, and *A* knows or should know that *B* expects payment, *A* must bestir himself or pay for the value of the services, at least if bestirring himself imposes no great burden. See *Day* v. *Caton,* 119 Mass. 513 (1876); *Restatement (Second) of Contracts* §69(a) and Comment *b*. Similarly, if *A* makes an offer to *B* that has no fixed duration, *B* has no right to accept the offer after a reasonable time has elapsed. Nevertheless, if *B* accepts the offer after a reasonable time has elapsed but within a time that *B* may plausibly have believed to be reasonable, *A* must bestir himself to inform *B* that his

to a contract would be entitled not merely to damages on breach, but to specific performance – just as if A withholds possession of property that B has a right to possess, B is entitled to an order of replevin, not merely damages. In contrast, under the common law specific performance will not ordinarily be granted for breach of contract.

In short, contrasting normative ideas can be found in contract law, depending on how doctrine is described, what features are emphasized and what features are subordinated, and how different features are ranked in importance. Contract-law doctrine will not tell us how to make these choices. Interpretive theories therefore need to employ normative criteria outside doctrinal materials, both to determine the basic normative ideas of a doctrinal area and to rank those ideas.

A second type of interpretive theory, famously developed by Dworkin deals with this problem. Dworkin's theory is complex and has changed somewhat over time, but it has always involved interpretations that satisfy some designated standard of fit with prior institutional decisions and that best justify those decisions as a coherent whole in terms of political morality.

Insofar as Dworkin's theory seeks a best justification in terms of political morality, it has a very strong normative component. Even Dworkin's theory, however, is not a theory of the best content of law. Rather, it is a theory of adjudication, or perhaps more accurately, a theory for determining what the law is from a judge's perspective. Although normative considerations play a critical role in Dworkin's theory, they are limited to those considerations that will fairly fit prior institutional decisions. This constraint is inappropriate in a theory of the best content of the law, because such a theory should reflect all moral norms and policies that are relevant and meritorious.[29]

D. Normative Theories

Accordingly, interpretive theories are no more adequate as theories of the best content of law than are axiomatic or deductive theories. Legal rules can ultimately be justified only by social propositions, and a satisfactory theory of the best content of law, or of any given area of law, like contracts, must be based on all policies, moral norms, and empirical propositions that are relevant and meritorious, not just moral values that are connected in some way to prior in-

---

acceptance arrived too late, or else will be contractually bound. See *Phillips* v. *Moor,* 71 Me. 78 (18970); *Restatement (Second) of Contracts* §70.

29. It is true that the mass of available institutional decisions might often allow a court to plausibly adduce different norms to explain past decisions, and thereby gives the courts running room in the selection of norms. However, if the process of adjudication is to have integrity under Dworkin's theory, a court cannot be free to begin with the universe of norms that are meritorious and then look around for institutional decisions that support those norms. Rather, a court with integrity is required to sincerely apply some designated standard of fit even if, as a result, the court must exclude some meritorious norms in establishing the law.

stitutional decisions, I will call theories of the best content of law that are based on all relevant and meritorious social propositions *normative theories*. The balance of this paper will concern such theories.

Much of the recent work on normative theories of contract has involved metrical theories based on a single social value – in particular, either the moral value of autonomy or the welfare value of enforcing revealed preferences. The former type of metrical theory is deontological; the latter, consequentialist, These theories are normative rather than interpetive because the metrics on which the theories turn are employed on the basis of their merit, not on the basis of their connection with prior institutional decisions, although commentators utilizing these theories often seek some legitimation in the theories' explanatory power.

In Part III, I consider autonomy and revealed-preference theories and show that they are inadequate to the task of producing the best content of contract law, in large part because as a result of their metrical nature they exclude a rich range of relevant and important values. In Part IV, I develop a generative theory of contracts, which recognizes a wide range of values in determining the best content of contract law.

III. Two Types of Single-Value Normative Theories

A. Autonomy Theories

Autonomy theories of contract are based on the concept that allowing an individual to freely own and dispose of property and freely exercise his will to make choices concerning his person, labor, and property is a value that is paramount in the moral enterprise generally, paramount in the moral obligation to keep a promise in particular, and, therefore, paramount in contract law. As stated by Charles Fried in his book *Contract As Promise*,[30]

. . . [T]he law of torts and the law of property recognize our rights as individuals in our person, in our labor, and in some definite portion of the external world, while the law of contracts facilitates our disposing of these rights on terms that seem best to us. . . . And the will theory of contract, which sees contractual obligations as essentially self-imposed, is a fair implication of liberal individualism. . . .

* * *

. . . [M]orality requires that we respect the person and property of others, leaving them free to make their lives as we are left free to make ours. This is the liberal ideal. This is the ideal that distinguishes between the good, which is the domain of aspiration, and the right, which sets the terms and limits according to which we strive. . . .

---

30. C. Fried, *Contract as Promise: A Theory of Contractual Obligation* (Cambridge, MA: Harvard University Press, 1981).

Everything must be available to us, for who can deny the human will the title to expand even into the remotest corner of the universe.[31]

Autonomy theories of contract, with their virtually sole focus on individual freedom, the protection of property rights, and the will, are not coextensive with more general moral theories of autonomy that stress the concern and respect due to others as valued human beings, as opposed to only the respect due to others' free exercise of their wills. Essentially, autonomy theories of contract tend to be strong theories of individual liberalism, will theories of contract, or both.[32] As used in these theories, therefore, autonomy is essentially a synonym for individual freedom and will, and in the balance of this paper I will use the terms *autonomy* and *autonomy theories of contract* in that way.

Fried's book is the leading exemplar of an autonomy theory of contracts, and an examination of Fried's argument provides a useful way to consider autonomy theories of contract in general. Fried begins with an inquiry into why there is a moral obligation to keep a promise. He argues that this obligation cannot be founded in act-utilitarianism, rule-utilitarianism, or the institution of promising, but instead must be deontologically based. The deontological basis on which Fried centers his theory is the moral value of the respect that is due to a promisor's autonomy:

. . . [R]espect for others as free and rational requires taking seriously their capacity to determine their own values. . . . Others must respect our capacity as free and rational persons to choose our own good, and that respect means allowing persons to take responsibility for the good they choose. And, of course, that choosing self is not an instantaneous self but one extended in time, so that to respect those determinations of the self is to respect their persistence over time. If we decline to take seriously the assumption of an obligation because we do not take seriously the promisor's prior conception of the good that led him to assume it, to that extent we do not take him seriously as a person. We infantilize him . . . .[33]

Fried then argues that autonomy theory shows that contract law is promise-based, morality-based, and autonomy-based. "[S]ince a contract is first of all a promise, a contract must be kept because a promise must be kept."[34] "Since contracts invoke and are invoked by promises, it is not surprising that the law came to impose on the promises it recognized the same incidents as morality demands."[35] "The law of contracts . . . is a ramifying system of moral judgments working out the entailments of a few primitive principles – primitive principles

31. Ibid. at 2, 7–8.
32. As stated by James Gordley in *Contract Law in the Aristotelian Tradition,* at p. 278 in this book: "Most contemporary contracts theorists who write in the Kantian tradition. . . . do not try to show that a free and rational being would regard certain rules as binding without regard to any purpose that such a being wants to pursue. They are Kantians only in the sense that they place freedom or reason at the apex of their theories."
33. Fried, *supra* note 30 at 20–21.
34. Ibid. at 17.   35. Ibid. at 21.

that determine the terms on which free men and women may stand apart from or combine with each other. These are indeed the laws of freedom."[36]

One of Fried's central claims is that the autonomy theory of contract explains the remedy of expectation damages, which Fried sees as a crucial element that distinguishes contract law from other branches of law, such as torts. Under autonomy theory, he says, promises should be enforced "as such" – that is, simply because the promise was made, not because enforcement of promises will enhance social welfare. In contrast, the "reliance view" of contract, which Fried views as a tort-based competitor of the autonomy theory of contract, does not focus on the promisor's autonomy. Rather, the reliance view focuses on an injury suffered by the promisee, "and asks if the [promisor] is sufficiently responsible for that injury that he should be made to pay compensation,"[37] which may be less than the promisee's expectation. If, however, "a person is bound by his promise and not by the harm the promisee may have suffered in reliance on it, then what he is bound to do is just its performance."[38]

Fried's description of contract law as promise-based is important, but not new.[39] By the nature of the subject, with few exceptions contract law cannot get off the ground unless a promise has been made.[40] If Fried claimed that every element of contract law is promise-based, that would be new. However, Fried does not make such a claim. On the contrary, a large part of his book concerns issues of contract law that even in Fried's view cannot be determined simply by the parties' promises, such as mistake or changed circumstances. The importance of Fried's argument, therefore, lies not in his claim that contract law is promise-based, but in his theory that contract law is based on, and in significant part only on, the moral value of autonomy, which, when applicable, trumps all other moral values.

This theory, and all autonomy theories of contract, suffers from four basic overlapping defects: (1) An autonomy theory of contract is not a necessary predicate of a promise-based contract law. (2) Autonomy theories of contract cannot alone generate complete and desirable rule of contract law. (3) Although respect for autonomy in its individual-freedom sense is an important moral value, that value is too narrow to provide an exclusive basis for the morality of promising and contract law. (4) Autonomy theories of contract are inconsistent

---

36. Ibid. at 132.   37. Ibid. at 4.   38. Ibid. at 19.

39. See, for example, M. A. Eisenberg, "Donative Promises" (1979) 47 U. Chic. L. Rev. 1 ("The law of contract is for the most part the law of promises.") [hereinafter "Donative Promises"].

40. Authors of some theories of contract law, such as relational theory, sometimes say that contract law is not or should not be promise-based. Often these statements mean only that important parts of contractual relationships and contract law are or should be based on elements other than the parties' promises – not that contract law is applicable even to parties who have not initially established a relationship based on explicit or implicit promises. When these statements mean more than that, they are wrong. Relationships and obligations may be based on elements other than promises, like custom and status, but the law dealing with relationships and obligations of that kind is and should be developed separately from the law dealing with promise-based relationships.

with basic principles of contract interpretation and cannot alone support the enforceability of promises.

I will address these issues in turn.

1. An autonomy theory of contract is not a necessary predicate of a promise-based contract law. Autonomy theories of contract argue that the law of contracts can be promise-based and morality-based only if it is grounded in a moral obligation that arises as a result of the promisor's exercise of his will. But it can be argued just as persuasively that the moral obligation to keep a promise is based not on the promisor's will, but on the legitimate expectation that the objective meaning of the promisor's expression arouses in the promisee. Accordingly, a promise-based and morality-based contract law need not be grounded in respecting the promisor's will, but can instead be grounded in respecting the promisee's expectation.[41]

There are at least two reasons why a lawmaker could adopt a rule that promises are legally enforceable on moral grounds even if the lawmaker was unconvinced by the autonomy argument. To begin with, there are varying critical accounts of the moral obligation to keep a promise, many or most of which claim that all competing accounts are unsatisfactory. A lawmaker who agreed with all those claims might nevertheless want to impose a legal obligation to keep promises, or at least certain kinds of promises even though he has not been convinced by any of the competing accounts. For example, such a lawmaker might want to impose a legal obligation to keep promises, or at least certain kinds of promises, because such an obligation will promote the general welfare. Indeed, Fried concedes that although rule-utilitarianism may not support the moral obligation to keep a promise, it can morally justify legislation to make promises enforceable:

41. Consider, in this connection, the following comment by George Fletcher on Kant's view of the law and morality of contract:

No particular individual has a right that I act out of duty. Of course, one might speak loosely of the right of humanity that I act morally. But rights characteristically have a differentiating function. The holder of the right distinguishes himself from those who do not have the performance coming to them. Rights in this sense do not exist in Kant's moral theory.

It is tempting to take [the] moral duty [to keep one's promises] as the foundation of the legal institution of contracting. After all, what is a contract but two reciprocal promises? Kant attributes this view to Mendelssohn and squarely rejects it. His reasoning is important. In a contractual relationship, each side acquires control over the choices . . . of the other. Each suffers a restraint on his freedom by placing his capacity to act in the power of the other. Each vests the other with a right to compel his performance. . . .

In the analysis of promising, the relevant perspective is the internal consistency of the promisor's willing; in contracting under law, the focus shifts to the right of the obligee to control the choices of the obligor. The different outcomes under the moral and legal theory highlight divergent concerns: the former with the promisor's internal struggle and the latter with the program of power and control between two distinct individuals.

G. Fletcher, "Law and Morality: A Kantian Perspective" (1987) 87 Colum. L. Rev. 533 at 545, 547.

There is . . . a version of rule utilitarianism that makes a great deal of sense. In this version the utilitarian does not instruct us what our individual moral obligations are but rather instructs legislators what the best rules are. If legislation is our focus, then the contradictions of rule-utilitarianism do not arise, since we are instructing those whose decisions can *only* take the form of issuing rules. From that perspective there is obvious utility to rules establishing and enforcing promissory obligations.[42]

Fried explains this concession on the ground that "Since I am concerned [in this part of my argument] with the question of individual obligation, that is, moral obligation, this legislative perspective on the argument is not available to me." That explanation, however, loses its force the moment Fried turns to contract *law,* which does involve a legislative perspective.

Alternatively, a lawmaker who is unconvinced by any of the critical accounts of the moral obligation to keep a promise might nevertheless conclude that promises should be enforced as a matter of social morality, and that in the area of contracts, as a matter of critical morality, the law should follow social morality so as to protect reasonable expectations. For either of these reasons, a lawmaker could adopt a promise-based contract law on principled grounds without subscribing to an autonomy theory of contract.

2. Autonomy theories of contract cannot alone generate complete and desirable rules of contract law. The legal rules in many areas of contract law can be superseded by agreement. For example, contracting parties can, within certain limits, change the remedies for breach of their contract and define the kinds of changed circumstances that will constitute an excuse for nonperformance. To the extent that contracting parties can supersede contract-law rules, contract law does indeed respect party autonomy. However, autonomy theories of contract cannot determine the content of the rules in these areas, because those rules must be based on something more than the parties' actual choices.[43] Of course, a lawmaker who makes a default rule may be deemed to be attentive to party choice in the sense that he seeks to make the rule that the parties would have agreed to if they had addressed the issue. Nevertheless, the rule will typically be one that is not actually chosen by the parties (except in the case, probably atypical, in which both parties know the default rule, both agree to it, and both agree to make no provision in the contract on the issue the rule covers).

In other areas of contract law, contract disputes arise only because the promise has run out – because, for example, the parties have left a gap, or made their contract under a mistake, or did not foresee a certain kind of event that eventually occurred and drastically affected the contract. Here again, and for the same

---

42. Fried, *supra* note 30 at 16. Ibid. at 46.
43. R. Craswell, "Contract Law, Default Rules, and The Philosophy of Promising" (1989) 88 Mich. L. Rev. 489.

reason, autonomy theory, taken alone, will often leave us in the dark. (Fried does not dispute this point. Indeed, he explicitly adopts it, and more than half his book is concerned with areas of contract law that fall into this category.)

Even in those areas in which autonomy theories could determine the content of contract-law rules, such theories are too impoverished to alone generate desirable rules of contract law.

To begin with, autonomy theories improperly exclude, as the basis of contract law, all values except moral values. So, for example, Fried claims that "[t]he law of contracts . . . is a ramifying system of moral judgments."[44] However, law generally, and contract law in particular, should be based not only on moral norms, but on considerations of policy, that is, considerations of public welfare.

That policies, like moral norms, should figure in contract-law rules is not surprising. If lawmakers are to establish rules to govern social conduct, it is desirable for them to consider whether those rules will be conducive to the general social welfare. Moreover, the relationship between morality and policy is itself disputed. Many believe that rightness reasons ultimately depend on general-welfare considerations. Even those who deny that dependence would usually agree that in judging whether conduct is right or wrong, it is relevant whether the conduct is conducive to the general social welfare.

The limits of a theory that refuses to take policies into account are well illustrated by simple donative promise – that is, donative promises unaccompanied by some special element like reliance. Under an autonomy theory that is wholly based on the exercise of will in making a promise, all promises, including simple donative promises, should be enforceable. Fried takes this position, as he must: There are no grounds, he says, for not enforcing such promises.[45]

In fact, simple donative promises are generally unenforceable under Western law. That Western law takes this position does not in itself show that autonomy theory is wrong. What is important is that there are a number of good reasons for this position. One of these reasons is that simple donative promises raise serious evidentiary problems, because given the spontaneity with which such promises are often made, a perjurious claim that such a promise was made may be found credible by a jury despite the absence of corroborating evidence. As a result, in this area the moral norm of keeping promises collides with the policy value of preventing fraud. Enforcing simple affective donative promises would also conflict with the policy of generally leaving affective issues within the private domain.

Contract remedies also illustrate why contract law must take policy propositions into account. Fried claims that the autonomy theory of contracts explains contract remedies. He correctly points out that the basic remedy for breach of contract is expectation damages. This remedy is explained by autonomy theory,

44. Fried, *supra* note 30 at 132.
45. Fried, *supra* note 30 at 37.

he says, because under autonomy theory a promise must be enforced "as such." But Fried has the matter upside down. Enforcing a promise "as such" would require that the promisor be ordered to perform, not that he be ordered to pay monetary compensation. As Scanlon points out:

If one fails to fulfill a promise, one should compensate the promisee if one can, but the obligation one undertakes when one makes a promise is an obligation to do the thing promised, not simply to do it or compensate the promisee accordingly. . . . The central concern of the morality of promises is therefore with the obligation to perform; the idea of compensation is of at most secondary interest.[46]

In contrast, the basic rule of the common law is that compensation is the ordinary remedy for breach of contract, and the courts will order performance only in exceptional cases. The reason why contract remedies do not reflect autonomy theory is that autonomy theory takes no account of policy values, and a rule requiring specific performance of all promises, or even of all enforceable promises, would conflict with important policy values, such as the policy in favor of mitigation of damages. Therefore, far from supporting autonomy theory, as Fried claims, the law of contract remedies further illustrates the impoverished nature of that theory.

3. Although respect for autonomy in its individual-freedom sense is an important moral value, that value is too narrow to provide an exclusive basis for the morality of promising and contract law. Autonomy theories are also too *morally* impoverished to alone generate desirable rules of contract law. For autonomy theorists like Fried, autonomy in the sense of individual freedom is a trumping moral value. When the freedom card is played, no room is left for other values, because "respect [for] the persons and property of others. . . . is the ideal that distinguishes between the good, which is the domain of aspiration, and the right. . . ."[47] But this is too narrow a view of the morality of promising and contract. The moral obligations owed to others, and contract law, both should and do include due concern and respect for interests other than property and the physical person. Many examples could be adduced. I will give just two. One involves moral reasons why simple donative promises should not be enforceable; the other concerns promises that morally should not have been sought.

(a) *The morality of virtue; donative promises.* Under the limited morality of autonomy theories of contract, simple donative promises should be enforceable. In fact, the almost universal rule in Western law is that they are unenforceable. This rule is supported not only by reasons of policy but also by reasons of morality.

One of these reasons concerns the impact that enforceability would have on the moral values of gifting. The world of contract is a market world, largely

---

46. Scanlon, Promises and Contracts, this book, at p. 92.
47. Fried, *supra* note 30 at 7–8.

driven by relatively impersonal considerations, and focused on commodities and prices. In contrast, much of the world of gift is driven by affective considerations like love, affection, friendship, gratitude, and comradeship. That world would be morally impoverished if it were to be collapsed into the world of contract. Making simple affective donative promises enforceable would have the effect of commodifying the gift relationship. Legal enforcement of such promises would move the gifted commodity, rather than the affective relationship, to the forefront and would submerge the affective relationship that a gift is intended to totemize. Simple donative promises would be degraded into bills of exchange, and the gifts made to perform such promises would be degraded into redemptions of the bills. It would never be clear to the promisee, or even the promisor, whether a donative promise that was made in an affective spirit of love, friendship, affection, gratitude, or comradeship, was also performed for those reasons, or instead was performed to discharge a legal obligation or avoid a lawsuit. Affective moral values are too important to be trumped by the value of autonomy, and would be undermined if the enforcement of simple affective donative promises was mandated by law.

There is another moral reason for not enforcing simple donative promises. The argument for making who simple donative promises enforceable usually focuses only on the moral obligations of the promisor. However, just as a donative promisor has moral obligations, so too may a donative promisee. Suppose, for example, that A, who has made an affective donative promise to B upon which B has not yet relied, does not want to perform. Perhaps A has a reason that is important to him but does not constitute an objectively satisfactory excuse. Perhaps A has simply changed his mind. It may be morally wrong for A to break his promise, but also morally wrong for B to insist on performance, because where a simple donative promise is made for affective reasons, virtue requires the promisee to generously release a repenting promisor.

An article by Andrew Kull, *Reconsidering Gratuitous Promises*,[48] is instructive in this regard. Kull argues that simple donative promises should be enforceable, but also concludes that if, say, Uncle has made a donative promise to Nephew and later changes his mind, it might well be "unthinkable" for Nephew to sue Uncle.[49] But if suit to enforce a donative promise made for affective reasons is unthinkable, how can the enforceability of such promises be desirable? The unenforceability rule prevents the unthinkable from occurring, by capturing, as the value of autonomy does not, the promisee's obligation to release a repenting promisor from a simple affective donative promise.

(b) *The morality of what we owe others; promises that morally should not have been sought.*[50] Another important type of case in which moral values play a crucial role in determining the enforceability of promises involves bargains be-

---

48. A. Kull, "Reconsidering Donative Promises" (1992) 21 J. Leg. Stud. 39.
49. Ibid. at 63.
50. Portions of the analysis in this section draw heavily on Michael J. Trebilcock's brilliant book, *The Limits of Freedom of Contract* (Cambridge, MA: Harvard University Press, 1993) at 78–91.

tween two actors, *A* and *B*, in which it was morally improper for *B* to have sought the promise that *A* made, although the bargain is not illegal and *A* is better off, by his own assessment of his welfare, than he would have been if he had not encountered *B*.

Take the following example:

The Desperate Traveler. A, a symphony musician, has been driving through the Arizona desert on a recreational trip, when he suddenly hits a rock jutting out from the sand. *A's* vehicle is disabled and his ankle is fractured. He has no radio and little water, and will die if he is not soon rescued. The next day, *B*, a university geologist who is inspecting desert rock formations, adventitiously passes within sight of the accident and drives over to investigate. *A* explains the situation and asks *B* to take him back to Tucson, which is sixty miles away. *B* replies that he will help only if *A* promises to pay him two-thirds of his wealth or $500,000, whichever is more. *A* agrees, but after they return to Tucson he refuses to keep his promise, and *B* brings an action to enforce it.

Autonomy theories of contract have only limited tools at their disposal to deal with such cases. Sometimes they try to deal with such cases through the concepts of duress or coercion. These are concepts with which autonomy theories are comfortable, because a promise that is coerced or made under duress is not a result of an autonomous choice. However, these concepts both turn on whether the promisee has made wrongful threats or exerted wrongful pressure. Determining whether a threat or pressure is wrongful requires some moral scale other than autonomy in the sense of individual freedom; otherwise, the concepts of coercion and duress would add nothing to the concept of autonomy. In a case like *The Desperate Traveler,* however, if *B* acted wrongfully in seeking *A*'s promise, that is not because *B*'s offer interfered with *A*'s autonomy, or because *A* had no effective choice, but because the terms of the bargain violated the moral norm that one person should not exploit the life-threatening situation of another by exacting undue compensation for rescue. If *B* had set a fair price – for example, a price related to his time, trouble, and expenses for losing a day in the field and making a 120-mile round-trip to Tucson and back – *B* should recover even though *A* had no effective choice whether to accept it.[51]

The relevance of moral norms concerning what we owe others is not confined to cases of life and death. Take, for example, the following cases, set out by Michael Trebilcock:

... The chairman of a university department offers a permanent academic position to a mediocre young female research assistant on condition that she sleep with him. An employer offers a job to a destitute woman on condition that she sleep with him . . . .[52]

---

51. This is the position taken by admiralty law. Under that body of law a contact to salvage a vessel in distress is enforceable, but only to the extent that the price is fair.
52. Trebilcock, *supra* note 50, at 90.

In these cases too the women's promises – the promises of sex – should be un-enforceable; not, or not only, because the research assistant or the destitute woman lacked autonomy or were put under duress, but because by seeking the promises of sex the employers treated the women as means to the end of sex-ual gratification, rather than as ends in themselves, and thereby improperly vi-olated the women's dignity and self-respect.[53]

Moral norms that concern dignity and self-respect have a wide-ranging ap-plication in law. For example, they help account, at least in part, for the legal rules that prohibit selling children, sex, or body parts. Admittedly these prohibitions, and others like them, are contestable, in part just because they limit autonomy and in part because some believe that the social institutions to which these pro-hibitions lead may have less desirable welfare implications than the institutions that would be created in the absence of the prohibitions. The issue here, how-ever, is not whether any given prohibition of this kind is, in the end, desirable or undesirable. Rather, the issue is that in considering whether a bargain should be enforceable, it morally counts against enforceability, in a way freedom val-ues cannot explain, that the bargain would violate the moral obligation to have concern and respect for the dignity and self-respect of others.

Fried distinguishes, in this regard, between what he calls the good and the right. The good, he says, is merely aspirational. The right, which is a moral duty, consists of leaving others "free to make their lives as we are left free to make ours."[54] This conception of moral duties is too narrow, because the interests of others may make legitimate moral claims. On the assumption that the women in both cases would not otherwise have been offered jobs by the employers, in some sense the employers left the women free to make their lives; indeed, in some sense they added one more choice to the women's lives. But offers that add choices like those the employers gave the women violate the good, and prom-ises made in response to such offers that violate the good in this way should not be enforceable.

4. *Autonomy theories of contract are inconsistent with basic principles of contract interpretation, and cannot alone support the enforceability of prom-ises.* I have shown that an autonomy theory of contract is not a necessary predi-cate of a promise-based contract law; that autonomy theories of contract cannot alone generate complete and desirable rules of contract law; and that respect for autonomy in its individual-freedom sense is too narrow to provide an exclusive basis for the morality of promising and contract law. In addition, autonomy the-ories of contract are inconsistent with basic principles of contract interpreta-tion, and cannot alone support the enforceability of promises.

---

53. See ibid. at 91. Here again, there may be a divergence here between autonomy theories of contract and Kantian or post-Kantian autonomy theories of morality. The analysis in the text takes issue with the former kind of theories but not necessarily the latter.
54. Fried, *supra* note 30, at 7.

(a) *Autonomy theories of contract are inconsistent with the basic principles of interpretation.* A basic and normatively justified principle of contract law is that if two parties subjectively attach different subjective meanings to an expression, one meaning is more reasonable than the other, and neither party knows the meaning attached by the other, the more reasonable meaning prevails.[55] Under this principle, an actor may be liable for breach of contract even though he did not choose – did not exercise his will – to make a promise. Specifically, an actor will be liable if he used an expression that he subjectively believed was not a promise but that the addressee reasonably understood to be a promise. The basic principles of interpretation therefore present a fundamental dilemma for an autonomy theory that is wholly based upon the subjective exercise of the will in making a promise. The proponent of such a theory must either (i) stick with the theory, and conclude that the basic principles of interpretation are wrong and that subjective interpretation should always prevail – an unappetizing choice as a matter of either morals or policy; or (ii) give up the theory.

Fried never really confronts this dilemma. One autonomy theorist, Randy Barnett, has sought to avoid the dilemma by simultaneously arguing for objective interpretation and what he calls a consent theory of contracts.[56] Barnett's usage, however, varies from the normal meaning of consent. Consent is a subjective, not an objective, concept. When we say that a person has consented to something, we do not mean that he gave the appearance of consenting; we mean he actually consented. Barnett's theory therefore does not resolve the dilemma any more than does Fried's, because his "consent" theory does not require actual consent, or more accurately, requires no consent al all.

(b) *Autonomy theories of contract cannot support the enforceability of promises.* Autonomy theories of contract are built on respect for choice. In contrast, contract law coerces actors who choose not to perform. It is true that contract law only coerces an actor to hold to a choice that he did make at one time; but this is a choice the actor no longer stands by. If he did, there would be no need to invoke the machinery of the state. There may be good reasons why the state should coerce a party to hold to his earlier choice despite the fact that he now autonomously rejects that choice, but those reasons cannot be found in the idea of respect for autonomy. Nothing in autonomy theory compels favoring earlier choices over later choices, and coercing a contracting party to take an action he now autonomously declines to take.[57] In short, the autonomy theory of contract does not support the legal enforcement of promises against the promisor's will.

55. See text at note 7–8, *supra.*
56. R. Barnett, "A Consent Theory of Contracts" (1986) 86 Colum. L. Rev. 269.
57. See P. Benson, "Abstract Right and the Possibility of a Nondistributive Conception of Contract: Hegel and Contemporary Contract Theory" (1989) 10 Cardozo L. Rev. 1077 at 1115 [hereinafter "Abstract Right"].

Perhaps for this reason, Fried adds a second string to his bow. Promises should be enforceable, he says, not only out of respect for the promisor's autonomy, but also out of respect for the promisee's trust in the promise:

The obligation to keep a promise is grounded not in arguments of utility but in respect for individual autonomy *and in trust.* . . .[58]

[A] promise-breaker [uses] another person. In . . . promising there is an invitation to the other to trust, to make himself vulnerable; . . . the promise-breaker then *abuse[s] that trust.*[59]

But this promisee- and trust-based explanation of the moral obligation to keep a promise makes Fried's promisor- and autonomy-based explanation unnecessary. Furthermore, once the spotlight is shifted to protection of the promisee, the inquiry should not be confined to respect for the promisee's *trust.* Rather, the issue should be what respect does a promisor owe to a promisee *generally,* and how should that respect be shown. There is no reason to conclude that the only moral way in which a promisor can show respect for a promisee is by performing his promise. Indeed, Fried himself strenuously asserts that a promisor is *not* morally obliged to perform the promise; that payment of cash compensation suffices.

Furthermore, as Benson points out, a promisor may show his respect for the promisee in other ways than either performing or paying compensation:

[T]he conclusion that a given breach constitutes an abuse of trust will [often] be far from evident. We will want to consider a number of diverse and potentially conflicting factors, such as the promisor's motives for breaching, whether in reaching the decision to breach, the promisor gave appropriate weight to the promisee's interests, whether the promisor tried his or her best to perform in the circumstances, whether the promisor was willing to compensate the promisee for reasonable reliance losses, whether the promisor apologized for the breach or sought to justify it in some way, and so on.[60]

Recall the case of the donative promise. Suppose that Uncle A has promised to make a gift of money to Nephew B at a certain time in the future. A now approaches B and explains that his life circumstances have changed – perhaps he has unexpectedly married late in life – and he believes that the performance of his promise would no longer be appropriate. A asks B's forgiveness and offers to compensate B for any injury B has suffered in reliance on the promise. Has not A treated B with due respect?

Moreover, respect is a two-way, not a one-way, street. For example, suppose that in the last hypothetical, B, although he does not especially need the money, rejects A's overtures and insists on payment. Who is treating whom with a lack of due respect? Or suppose that a singer who has contracted to sing a tiny role

58. Fried, *supra* note 30, at 17. (Emphasis added.)
59. Ibid. at 16. (Emphasis added.)
60. See "Public Basis," *supra* note 25 at 291–292.

in a regional opera is offered an unparalleled opportunity to sing a lead at the Met on a conflicting date. The singer explains his thrilling good fortune to the regional opera, offers to pay its expenses in finding a replacement, sincerely apologizes for any inconvenience that will be caused, and asks for a release. Has not the singer treated the regional opera company with due respect? Would the opera company treat the singer with due respect if it declined to release him?

Similar cases can arise in pure commercial contexts, as where C makes a commercial contract with D, suffers reverses that would make performance exceptionally burdensome, and tells D, with sincere apologies, that performance is no longer economically viable for him but that he will reimburse D for any out-of-pocket or opportunity costs that D may have suffered in reliance on the contract.

However cases like these should be morally resolved, they cannot be morally resolved simply in terms of respect for the promisor's free will or abuse of the promisee's trust. In the context of promising, mutual respect transcends both autonomy in the sense of individual freedom and an exclusive focus on the promisee's trust.

B. Revealed-Preference Theories

Autonomy theories of contract are based on the moral value of respect for choice. Another class of single-value theories of contract is also based on respect for individual choices as expressed in promises. Under this class of theories, however, choice is respected not for moral reasons, but because it will lead to Pareto or Kaldor-Hicks efficiency by giving effect to private preferences. (A transaction or an institutional decision is Pareto efficient if it makes someone better off while making no one worse off. An institutional decision is Kaldor-Hicks efficient if the gains to those who win as a result of the decision are sufficient so that if the winners chose to pay the losers enough to make the losers indifferent to the decision, the winners would still have gains left over.) I will refer to such theories as *revealed-preference theories*.[61] Just as autonomy theories of contract eschew welfare values, so revealed-preference theories of contract eschew moral values. Unlike autonomy theories of contract, which have been explicitly worked out by commentators like Fried and Barnett, revealed-preference theories of contract tend to be implicit as theories of contract

---

61. I use this terminology because it is conventional, but it is somewhat misleading. The term "revealed preferences" implies that the preferences that an actor objectively expresses – "reveals" – are his actual preferences. In fact, however, an actor's objectively expressed preferences may differ from his actual preferences. For one thing, the objective meaning of an actor's expressions may not correspond to the subjective meaning he attaches to those expressions. More fundamentally, as Robert Cooter has pointed out, "the inference from choices to preferences . . . seems [both] inevitable and imperfect. The preferences of others are neither opaque nor transparent to us. Rather, choices reveal preferences imperfectly. . . ." R. Cooter, *Do Good Laws Make Good Citizens? An Economic Analysis of Internalizing Legal Values*, U.C. Berkeley Law Economics Working Paper 2000-8 at 23 (2000).

law generally, although they are often relatively explicit in the analysis of individual contract issues.

Revealed-preference theories are essentially applications of normative or welfare economics to contract law. The role of welfare economics in a theory of contracts must be distinguished from the role of positive economic analysis. Positive economic analysis does not, in principle, take a normative position. Rather, it instructs us about some likely consequences of adopting a given rule in terms of the incentives and disincentives the rule will provide, and the probable effects of these incentives and disincentives. Positive economic analysis is therefore consistent with, and indeed an important tool for, any theory of contracts that allows empirical propositions to mediate from policies and moral norms to doctrines.

In contrast, welfare economics does take a normative position, as follows: Respect for the preferences expressed in private decisionmaking will have the effect of making people better off, under their own view of better off, and will therefore lead to Pareto efficiency, Kaldor-Hicks efficiency, or both. In contrast, collective decisionmaking, expressed in the decisions of public institutions, is unlikely to have that effect, at least in the absence of significant market failures.

In its strongest formulation, welfare economics is viewed as a demand of justice. So, for example, Alan Schwartz has written that one aspect of justice "basically holds that just outcomes arise when people are permitted to do the best they can, under the circumstances. This is because, the theory goes, people are the best judges of what maximizes their own utility; hence, allowing them to make unrestrained choices is most likely to maximize utility for the individual and society as a whole."[62]

Welfare economics leads naturally to the following theory of contracts: In the absence of a defect in consent, contracts are Pareto efficient, because if both parties did not believe the contract made them better off they would not have made it. The role of contract law, therefore, should be to facilitate making contracts and, in the absence of defects in consent, to enforce contracts as made.

Autonomy theories are deontological theories based on the moral value of respect for choice. Revealed-preference theories are consequentialist theories based on the social-welfare value of respect for choice. The differences in the grounding of these two kinds of theories should not conceal that both theories are single-value theories based on respect for choice. For that reason, the objections to autonomy theories of contract are largely applicable to revealed-preference theories of contract as well. Since I have already discussed those

---

62. A. Schwartz, "Justice and the Law of Contracts: A Case for the Traditional Approach" (1986) 9 Harv. J. L. & Pub. Pol. 107 at 107. A second aspect of justice that Schwartz identifies is justice as fair distribution. "This principle holds that the state has an obligation to insure that the circumstances in which people are trying to do the best they can are not terribly unfair to them." Ibid. at 107.

objections in the former context, I will generally limit the discussion in this section to some nuances those objections take on when applied in the latter context.

1. Revealed-preference theories cannot alone generate complete rules of contract law. Revealed-preference theories, like autonomy theories, cannot alone generate complete rules of contract law. Take, for example, those rules of contract law that can be superseded by agreement. Rules that can be superseded by agreement are often referred to as default rules, on analogy to standard settings of computer programs that can be altered by a user to fit his individual needs, like margin settings and line spacings. This terminology is inapt. Unlike standard margins and line spacings, legal rules guide behavior, create rights, and may result in substantial liability, even if they can be superseded by agreement. Furthermore, rules that can be superseded by agreement in theory are often not easy to supersede in practice. For one thing, superseding them often involves significant costs. For another, most people probably do not know contract law and therefore will end up bound by rules that can be superseded simply because they do not know that it is in their interest to supersede the rules.[63] Analogizing legal rules that can be superseded to margin settings and line spacings therefore conceals more than it reveals. Legal rules that can be superseded by agreement might better be characterized as defeasible, in the sense that they regulate the rights of the contracting parties unless and until they are validly superseded.

To the extent that contract-law rules are defeasible, contract law reflects the value of private choice, and therefore the welfare principle reflected in actual-preference theories. But revealed-preference theories do not tell us much about the content that defeasible rules – default rules – should have. Many commentators have advanced, as an algorithm for establishing the content of default rules, that such rules should have the content that the parties would have agreed upon if they had addressed the relevant issue. Some of these commentators attempt to shoehorn default rules established under this algorithm into revealed preference theories by arguing that default rules involve hypothetical consent, are contractual, or both. This argument is specious. "Hypothetical consent" is an oxymoron like "hypothetical pleasûre." If an actor actually consents, there is consent. If an actor does not actually consent, there is no consent.

Nor are default rules contractual, in the sense that they are rules made by contracting parties or based on the actual revealed preferences of parties to a contract that is to be enforced. Instead they are rules that are applied only in the *absence* of a contractual provision, and they may or may not be the rules that the parties to a given contract would have agreed to if they had addressed the relevant issue. No one can know what rule the parties to an actual contract, with individual differences in bargaining power, information, risk-aversion, and the like, would have agreed to. Furthermore, different legislators and judges will often have different views on what most parties would have agreed to if they had

---

63. See Section IV. B.2.a, below.

addressed a certain kind of issue. Thus even under the what-the-parties-would-have-agreed-to algorithm, the content of default rules is established not by consent, and not by party agreement, but by collective action – by government decision. (This is even more obviously true of default rules established by other algorithms, like rules that are designed to force the sharing of information.[64]) In this regard, it is an open question, little attended to by default-rule theory, what percentage of all relevant parties must be expected would agree to a proposed rule under the what-the-parties-would-have-agreed-to algorithm. Must the lawmaker be confident that 100 percent of all relevant parties would have agreed to a proposed default rule if they had considered the issue? If so, few default rules would be adopted. If less than 100 percent suffices, some parties will necessarily be subject to a default although they would not have agreed to it if they had addressed the issue. Assuming that result is acceptable, how low can the percentage get? Does 75% suffice? Does 51% suffice? And how is it to be determined what percentage suffices? Whatever the answer to these questions, it is clear that we have moved away, and perhaps vanishingly far away, from enforcing the revealed preferences of the actual contracting parties.

2. *Although respect for revealed preferences is an important policy value, that value is inadequate to provide an exclusive basis for contract law.* Respect for revealed preferences is an important policy value, but there are strong reasons why that value, taken alone, is inadequate to generate the best content of contract law.

First, revealed-preference theories are impoverished even on the level of social welfare, because they exclude other important policy values, such as the value of keeping intimate and other affective relationships free from the intrusion of state power.

Second, revealed-preference theories improperly exclude moral norms, other than the value of respect for revealed preferences, as elements in establishing the best rules of contract law.[65] However, significant areas of contract law do and should turn in part on moral norms – for example, what constitutes unfairness in the bargaining process or improper advantage-taking, and what kinds of promises may be properly sought in bargained-for exchanges. Furthermore, contract law is to a significant extent about the protection of reasonable expectations, and moral norms are a good indicator of what reasonable expectations are likely to arise out of contracting behavior.[66] The exclusion of moral norms from the determination of the best rules of contract law can therefore frustrate the protection of reasonable expectations.

---

64. See I. Ayres and R. Gertner, "Filling Gaps in Incomplete Contracts: An Economic Theory of Default Rules" (1989) 99 Yale Law J. 87.
65. There is often a moral subtext of libertarianism to actual-preference theories, but the subtext is just that, and in any event it does no different work in such theories than does the concept of respecting revealed preferences.
66. Cf. M. Friedman, "The Social Responsibility of Business is to Increase its Profits," *N.Y. Times,*

Third, revealed-preference theories depend on the universal applicability of a rational-actor model of human psychology. This model, however, has been shown to be unrealistic and unpredicative over a significant range of behaviors.[67]

3. Revealed-preference theories cannot alone support the enforceability of contracts. Revealed-preference theories, like autonomy theories, are unable to alone support the enforceability of promises, and for much the same reason. The expressed preference of a promisor when he makes the contract is to keep his promise. The expressed preference of the promisor when the contract is sought to be enforced is to not keep his promise; otherwise, there would be no reason for the promisee to seek legal enforcement. Nothing in revealed-preference theory alone can tell us which of these two preferences the law should respect. As Benson states in his essay-review of Trebilcock's *The Limits of Freedom of Contract:*

> ... A theory that purports to be a theory of *contract* must, at a minimum, be able to explain why ... priority should be given, at least in certain circumstances, to the initial set of preferences. ... Moreover, given that the object of such a theory is the *law* of contract, a further essential requirement is that the theory explain how it can be legitimate to exercise coercion against a party who fails to comply with the contract terms even though these no longer represent his preferences. ...
>
> Why the first set of preferences should ever be given priority is by no means obvious. Viewed simply as expressions of preferences, there is no qualitative difference between the decision to contract and [the decision to not perform]. There is nothing in their origin, formation, or felt significance which distinguishes them. Each is shaped by a similar range of factors and each represents what a party wants at any given point in time. The *only* difference between them is that one happens to come before the other. Given this temporal sequence, the challenge to finding a basis for ascribing priority to the first set of preferences is this: if the aim is just to ascertain preferences to and to ensure their satisfaction (as with efficiency theories), the second set of preferences and not the first should have precedence because it represents, so far as one can tell, a party's actual preferences – what he actually wants. The first set has been superseded and replaced by the second.[68]

And as Trebilcock shows, because of the problem of inconsistent preferences over time, priority cannot be ascribed to the original preference (that is, the promise) on Pareto-efficiency grounds.

> ... [E]x ante and *ex post* Paretian perspectives are likely to lead to very different welfare inferences. From an ex ante perspective, if both parties to a contract at the time of entering into the agreement feel that it will make them better off, then the fact that one

---

Sept. 13, 1970, 6 (magazine) at 32: "[A corporate executive's] responsibility is to conduct the business in accordance with [the shareholders'] desires, which generally will be to make as much money as possible while conforming to the basic rules of the society, both those embodied in law and those embodied in ethical custom."

67. See Section IV.B.2.b, *infra.*

68. "Public Basis," *supra* note 25 at 285, 286–287.

or both of them are subsequently disappointed following the revelation of new information about the contract subject matter should be irrelevant. However, from an *ex post* perspective, if one or both parties, subsequent to entering into a contract, find that the contract has made them worse off relative to their pre-interaction status, we would end up excusing most contract breaches.[69]

Trebilcock calls this problem the Paretian dilemma. Because of this dilemma, he points out, the enforcement of contracts on efficiency grounds, as opposed to moral grounds, can be supported, if at all, only under a Kaldor-Hicks efficiency framework. But Kaldor-Hicks efficiency entails just the kind of collective decisions that revealed-preference theories purport to eschew:

> If one moves from a Paretian efficiency framework to a Kaldor-Hicks efficiency framework . . . to better address these dilemmas raised by the Paretian framework, a new set of difficulties has to be confronted. In designing a set of legal rules to structure and constrain the contracting process in order to promote Kaldor-Hicks efficiency . . . the strong welfare claim made on behalf of the private ordering process has been largely abandoned. That is, the argument that we can more confidently infer positive welfare effects from voluntary and informed transactions or exchanges between individuals than from collective resource allocation decisions or regimes to which all affected parties have not unanimously consented is not central to Kaldor-Hicks efficiency. . . .[70]

In short, insofar as the enforceability of a given class of promises, such as bargain or commercial promises, is supported by a welfare reason, the reason can only be a collective decision that the general social good is furthered by making the class of promise enforceable. That collective decision is not based solely on deference to revealed preferences, although the fact that enforceability is tied to preferences that a promisor once expressed is relevant in determining the general social good.

IV. A Multivalue Theory of Contracts

In Part III, I analyzed the two most prominent metric, single-value theories of contract and showed that those theories cannot alone generate complete and desirable rules of contract law. It is a reasonable conjecture that any metric, single-value theory would suffer from the same problems. The attractions of single-value theories are obvious. Because they are metric theories, they appear capable of producing determinate results, and because they are single-value theories, they appear to avoid the dissonance caused by conflicting values and the difficulties produced if conflicting values need to be accommodated. These advantages, however, are apparent, not real. Part of the human moral condition is that we hold many proper values, some of which will conflict in given cases, and part of the human social condition is that many values are relevant to the

---

69. Trebilcock, *supra* note 50, at 244.
70. Ibid. at 245.

creation of a good world, some of which will conflict in given cases. Contract law cannot escape these moral and social conditions. In contract law, as in life, all meritorious values must be taken into account, even if those values may sometimes conflict, and even at the expense of determinacy. Single-value, metric theories of the best content of law must inevitably fail precisely because they deny the complexity of life.

Accordingly, the theory of contracts – the principle that tells us how to make the best possible rules of contract law – must accommodate multiple values, and therefore must be a generative rather than a metric theory. In this Part, I develop such a theory, which I call *the basic contracts principle*. The basic contracts principle has two branches. The first branch describes the content that contract law should have, while the second describes the manner in which that content should be determined. The two branches are related, because what the content of a rule should be depends in part on how that content should be determined. The principle is as follows:

1. If but only if appropriate conditions are satisfied, and subject to appropriate constraints, the law should effectuate the objectives of parties to a promissory transaction.
2. The rules that determine the conditions to and the constraints on the legal effectuation of the objectives of parties to promissory transactions, and the way in which those objectives are ascertained, should consist of those rules that would be made by a non-self-seeking and fully informed legislator who seeks to make the best possible rules of contract law by taking into account all relevant moral, policy, and empirical propositions (the *Legislator*). When more than one such proposition is relevant, the Legislator should exercise good judgment to give each moral, policy, and empirical proposition proper weight, and to either subordinate some propositions to others, or craft a rule that is the best vector of the propositions, considering their relative weights and the extent to which an accommodation can be fashioned that reflects those relative weights to the fullest practicable extent.

The Legislator, rather than the judge, plays the central role in the basic contracts principle because a legislator, unlike a judge, is free from an obligation to following existing doctrine. Because the Legislator is not bound by existing doctrinal propositions, but instead is an author of such propositions and can re-author them at any time, his only concern is that doctrinal propositions properly reflect social propositions. Of course, the Legislator will want doctrinal propositions to be internally consistent, but for reasons explored in Part II that result will follow if the Legislator establishes doctrinal rules that properly reflect social propositions – that is, if the Legislator applies the basic contracts principle.

That the basic contracts principle depends on the rules the Legislator would make does not mean that contract law should be made by the legislature. The theory of contracts must be distinguished from institutional theory, which addresses such issues as what are the best institutions to make different kinds of legal rules, how should those institutions be structured to that end, to what constraints should those institutions be subject, and so forth. Because of institutional constraints, any given body of law at any given moment of time may not have the best content it should have over the long run. For example, one of the constraints on courts is that they must attend to the interest of doctrinal stability, especially, although not only, because they act retrospectively. As a result of this constraint, the courts may for periods of time follow rules that are not the rules that would be best if the interest in doctrinal stability were put to one side. Similarly, and to the same effect, courts are not institutionally free to consider all relevant and meritorious social propositions, but instead are normally confined to those social propositions that have substantial social support.

It is for just these reasons that the central figure in the basic contracts principle is the Legislator, not the courts. But in the actual world a legislature is also subject to institutional constraints that may lead it to adopt rules that are not the best rules, even if the legislature is disinterested and fully informed. For example, although the legislature normally acts prospectively, and can ameliorate the problems raised by transition costs in various ways, there are nevertheless good institutional reasons why a legislature would take transition costs into account, More fundamentally, there are good institutional reasons, which need not be rehearsed here, why a legislature would allow the courts to develop certain bodies of law, including the body of contract law.

Accordingly, the central role played by the Legislator in the basic contracts principle does not require that the legislature instantly adopt the best rules of contract law, or even that contract law should be made by the legislature. That does not mean that the central role played by the Legislator in the basic contracts principle serves no function. Because the Legislator, unlike a legislature, is free of institutional constraints in determining the best content of contract law, giving pride of place to the Legislator instructs all members of the profession how to generate that content. Over the short run, that instruction is more likely to be carried out by academic members of the profession than by legislators or courts, but this does not limit the power of the instruction over the long run.

To put this differently, the theory of contracts is the theory of the best content of contract law over the long run, not the theory of what contract law should be at any moment of time when institutional constraints are taken into account.

———————

There has been a basic tension in contract theory between those who argue that promise is almost everything and those who argue that promise is almost nothing. Those who argue that promise is almost everything claim that the conditions to and the constraints on the enforceability of promises can be derived from the promise, or at least from the will or revealed preference of the promisor. Those who argue that promise is almost nothing claim that the artillery of contract law can be wheeled up even without a promise. The basic contracts principle takes a path between these views. Under the first branch of the principle, contract law normally doesn't get off the ground unless a party has made a statement that is or can fairly be interpreted to be a promise, or at least is set in a promissory matrix. Under the second branch of the principle, the conditions to and constraints on the enforceability of a promise, and the manner in which a promise is to be interpreted, do not depend solely on the promise or the will or revealed preference of the promisor, but instead also depend on all relevant policy, moral, and empirical propositions.

So, for example, the fairness of the basic social structure may be a condition to the enforcement of contracts, but that condition cannot be derived from the parties' promises, wills, or revealed preferences. Similarly, it is impossible to derive the rule that simple unrelied-upon donative promises are unenforceable, or the rules concerning mistake, or the rules concerning promises that should not have been sought, simply from the promises, wills, or revealed preferences of contracting parties. The same is true of constraints that should be placed upon the effectuation of the objectives of contracting parties even when the conditions to enforceability are satisfied. For example, the limits on the remedy of specific performance, the limits on the enforceability of liquidated-damages and form-contract provisions, and the obligation to mitigate damages, cannot be derived from the promises, wills, or revealed preferences of contracting parties.

In the balance of Part IV, I will further elaborate the basic contracts principle by considering the problems that arise under that principle when relevant social propositions conflict; the kinds of values and empirical propositions that should be taken into account under that principle; the role of distributive justice under that principle; and whether and to what extent promises should be legally enforceable under that principle.

A. Conflicting Social Propositions and Good Judgment

An objection that might be made to the basic contracts principle is that the body of contract law generated under that principle will be internally inconsistent because social propositions will often conflict. Of course, in many applications all relevant social propositions will point in the same direction. For example, all social propositions that are relevant and meritorious point toward the rules that fraud should be a defense and that offers lapse after a reasonable time unless otherwise provided. However, even where social propositions do conflict in given applications, they are not for that reason inconsistent. If each of two conflicting moral norms has established its credentials in independent territories, we do not want to walk away from either norm just because there are territories where they conflict. For example, the moral norm "don't lie" is not inconsistent with the moral norm "venerate human life," even though under certain circumstances venerating human life might require lying – as in lying to an assassin about his victim's whereabouts. It does not lessen our commitment to truth-telling that we believe it is sometimes morally permissible not to tell the truth. Goals too are not inconsistent just because they conflict in certain applications. For example, the goal of developing a fruitful and rewarding career is not inconsistent with the goal of being a nurturing parent, although pressures of time may lead to a conflict between the two goals in some cases.

Correspondingly, the body of contract law generated by the basic contracts principle will not be internally inconsistent just because the social values that the lawmaker draws upon and the goals the lawmaker tries to accomplish conflict in certain cases, as long as each value and goal is meritorious and has a range of applications in which it does not conflict with the others. Where conflicts do occur, the lawmaker must make a legal rule that gives a proper weight and role to each of the conflicting values or goals in the context at hand. The lawmaker may accomplish this end either by concluding that in the context at hand one value or goal trumps all others, or by crafting a rule that is a vector of all relevant values and goals.[71]

A related objection that might be made to the basic contracts principle is that it provides no metric for giving a proper weight and role to conflicting social propositions. The premise of that objection is accurate. The principle does not provide such a metric. Instead, under that principle, when social propositions conflict the Legislator must exercise good judgment concerning the weight and role to be given to each proposition in the issue at hand – just as when values or goals conflict in life, decisions must be made by exercising good judgment concerning the weight and role to be given to each value or goal. However, the requirement of good judgment does not confer unrestricted discretion. When conflicting social propositions are relevant to establishing a given rule, only that rule should be adopted that properly takes each proposition into account. To this end, the lawmaker must determine such issues as the relative weight and degree of relevance of the conflicting propositions and whether and to what extent the propositions can be mutually accommodated.

B. The Kinds of Values And Empirical Propositions That Should Be Taken into Account under the Basic Contracts Principle

Many kinds of choices need to be made by the Legislator under the basic contracts principle. I will focus in this section on three of these choices: whether, when moral norms are relevant, the Legislator should choose norms on the

---

71. *Cf.* K. Kress, "Legal Indeterminacy" (1989) 77 Cal. L. Rev. 283 at 305–230, 331–336; K. Kress, "Coherence and Formalism" (1993) 16 Harv. J. L. & Pub. Pol. 639 at 650–667.

basis of critical or social morality; whether the Legislator should assume that actors know the rules of contract law; and whether the Legislator should base contract-law rules purely on rational-actor psychology.

  1. Critical Morality or Social Morality. When moral values are relevant under the basic contracts principle, should the relevant values be those of critical
morality or social morality? (By *critical morality* I mean moral standards whose
truth does not depend on community beliefs and attitudes, except insofar as
such beliefs and attitudes are relevant to the application of the moral standards.
By *social morality* I mean moral standards that claim to be rooted in aspirations
that apply to all members of the community and, on the basis of an appropriate
methodology, can fairly be said to have substantial support in the community,
can be derived from norms that have such support, or fairly appear as if they would
have such support.)

  In establishing *common law* rules, as a matter of critical morality courts should
normally be limited to the use of social morality. A basic function of courts is to
conclusively resolve disputes deriving from a claim of right that is based on the
application, meaning, and implications of the society's existing standards. If
courts were not required to employ social morality when moral norms are relevant in establishing the law, there would be no place to which a member of the
society could go to vindicate a claim based on the society's existing standards.
Furthermore, given the removal of the courts from ordinary political processes,
the legitimacy of judicial lawmaking depends in large part on the employment of
a process of reasoning that begins with the society's standards, rather than with
those standards a judge personally thinks best as a matter of critical morality. Requiring courts to employ the society's standards also alleviates the retroactivity
of judicial lawmaking by ensuring that decisions are rooted in standards that the
disputants either knew or had reason to know at the time of their transaction, albeit standards that had perhaps not been officially translated into legal rules. And
because the society's standards are based on observable criteria, a process of judicial lawmaking that requires the courts to draw on those standards is replicable
by the profession and thereby facilitates planning and dispute-settlement.

  These constraints do not apply to *legislatures,* which draw their legitimacy
from democratic election, which normally act only prospectively, and whose
functions include the establishment of new standards, rather than the resolution
of disputes based on the meaning, implications, and application of the society's
existing standards. Accordingly, where morality is relevant to the establishment
of contract-law rules, a body of contract law established under the basic contracts principle should be based on critical morality. However, there are several
reasons why as a matter of critical morality a lawmaker may or should take social morality into account under the basic contracts principle.

  To begin with, critical and social morality probably do not differ much in the
area of contract law. To put this differently, in this area it is not easy to identify

values that are part of social morality but are rejected by critical morality, or that are established by critical morality but have not made their way into social morality. At the same time, social morality in this area is usually both better developed and more accessible than critical morality. Settled philosophical analyses of the moral issues raised in contract law are not thick on the ground. Indeed, even the most basic moral issue in this area – the reason why there is a moral obligation to keep a promise – is still under active philosophical debate. Therefore, one reason for using social morality when moral values are relevant under the basic contracts principle is that in this area social morality is more accessible than, and can serve as a presumptive surrogate for, critical morality.

Furthermore, contract law is to a significant extent about the protection of reasonable expectations. One kind of expectation that surrounds a contract is that contracting partners will conform to the basic moral norms of the society that apply to contracting behavior. Social morality may therefore be relevant to determining reasonable expectations. Versions of this point are captured in the economists' disfavor of "opportunistic" behavior by contracting parties (that is, self-seeking with guile); in the merchant's obligation under the Uniform Commercial Code to observe reasonable commercial standards of fair dealing; and in the principle against unfair surprise.[72]

In short, when moral norms are relevant, in theory under the basic contracts principle the Legislator should be guided by critical morality. At least in the area of contracts, however, social morality is a presumptive surrogate for critical morality. Furthermore, given the importance of reasonable expectations in contract law, the Legislator may properly believe that as a matter of critical morality contract law should reflect, or at least be highly attentive to, the morality of the society.

The constraint on the social propositions that a court can properly employ means that the best body of the *common law* of contracts may diverge from the best content of the contract law as generated by the basic contracts principle, even without regard to the constraints on the courts that follow from the interest in doctrinal stability. The extent of this divergence will principally be a function of the extent to which social morality differs from critical morality. Because in the area of contract law that difference is likely to be relatively slight, over the long run the best content of the common law of contracts is unlikely to diverge significantly from the best content of contract law under the basic contracts principle.

2. Fundamental choices between conflicting empirical propositions. Just as the application of the basic contracts principle may require recurring fundamental choices between critical and social morality, so too it may require recurring fundamental choices between certain kinds of conflicting empirical propositions. In fact, these choices are even more important than the choice between

---

72. See UCC §§1–203, 2–103(1)(b), 2–302, Comment 1.

critical and social morality. That choice is more theoretical than real, because in the subject-matter of contract law the two kinds of morality seldom differ. In the case of empirical propositions, however, there are two areas in which starkly different alternatives are often presented.

(a) *Knowledge of the law.* The first of these areas concerns the extent to which actors know the rules of contract law. If actors know the rules of contract law, then those rules can serve as incentives and disincentives to various kinds of conduct and may properly be established in significant part with that end in mind. If, however, actors do not know the rules of contract law, then the role that contract-law rules can serve in providing incentives and disincentives will be limited, and contract law should not be established in significant part with that end in mind. Furthermore, if actors know the rules of contract law, reasonable expectations can be defined in terms of the law, while if actors do not know the rules of contract law, the law should be established on the basis of reasonable social expectations.

This problem is pervasive in contract law, although seldom brought to the surface. I will give three examples, drawn from the areas of consideration, damages, and offer and acceptance.

(i) *Consideration – the principle of reliance.* It is sometimes said that the principle that justified reliance can make a promise legally enforceable is circular, because reliance is justified only if the promisee believes that reliance will make the promise legally enforceable. Thus Randy Barnett states:

. . . A prediction that a promise can reasonably be expected to induce reliance by a promisee or third party will unavoidably depend upon whether the promisee or third party believes that reliance will be legally protected. The legal rule itself cannot be formulated based on such a prediction, however, without introducing a practical circularity into the analysis. . . .

* * *

. . . [W]hen we seek to discern "reasonable" (or prudent) reliance on a promise, a conclusion cannot be reached that is independent of the perceived enforceability of the promise, which brings us full circle to the question of enforceability with which we started. A theory based only on reliance cannot, therefore, answer this question.[73]

This analysis holds, however, only if we believe that actors normally know the law of consideration. If actors normally do not know that law, then the question we want to ask is not whether reliance on a promise is justified under law, but whether reliance on a promise would be justified under social propositions. The answer is that reliance on a promise would be so justified. The *Restatement of Contracts* defines a promise as "a manifestation of intention made in such a

---

73. Barnett, *supra* note 56 at 275, 315.

way as to justify the [addressee] in understanding that a commitment has been made."[74] Since a promisee understands that a commitment has been made, and since in the normal case a promisor is morally bound to keep that commitment, a promisee is reasonable in relying upon a promise even if he does not know that a relied-upon promise is legally enforceable. Accordingly, the rule that reliance makes a promise enforceable reflects relevant social propositions under the basic contracts principle, and is not circular.

(ii) *Damages – the principle of Hadley v. Baxendale*. The principle of *Hadley v. Baxendale*, which cuts off full expectation damages against a breaching party – normally, a seller – provides another example of the centrality of the question whether actors know the law. That principle has been rationalized in different ways at different times, but the modern rationale is that the principle forces buyers to reveal to sellers information concerning the damages they will incur on breach, thereby allowing sellers to stratify prices and precautions so that low-damages buyers do not inappropriately subsidize high-damages buyers. However, this rationale works only if buyers generally know the principle. If buyers generally do not know the principle, they are likely to justifiably believe that unless the contract otherwise provides, sellers will stand behind their promises and pay full compensation for all losses proximately caused by breach. Thus the modern rationale of the principle of *Hadley v. Baxendale* does not support the principle unless actors know the law.

(iii) *Offer and acceptance – overtaking repudiations*. Suppose that an offeree mails an acceptance, but then changes his mind and repudiates the acceptance by a faster means of communication. The repudiation reaches the offeror before the acceptance does, so that when the offeror receives the offeree's mailed acceptance he knows that the offeree does not in fact intend to accept. The Comment to *Restatement of Contracts* § 63 takes the position that the mailbox rule, under which an acceptance is effective on dispatch, is applicable in such cases, so that the offeree is bound unless the offeror relies upon the repudiation. The rationale for this position is that otherwise an opportunistic offeree could speculate at the offeror's expense during the time required for the acceptance to arrive. However, opportunism would be possible only if the offeree either knows or would reasonably expect the mailbox rule. If an offeree would reasonably expect that an acceptance is effective only on receipt, he would not be acting opportunistically in posting and then repudiating an acceptance, because he would have nothing to gain by using a slow mode of transit for the acceptance. On the contrary, he would be taking the risk (as he saw the matter) that the offeror would revoke by a fast mode before the acceptance arrived.

These examples are suggestive, not exhaustive. They illustrate two general points: First, reasonable expectations do not depend on the law unless actors

---

74. *Restatement (Second) Contracts* §2.

know the law. Second, a rule of contract law should not be established on the basis of the incentives and disincentives that the rule would provide unless it is likely that actors will know the rule. Whether it is likely that actors will know a given rule of contract law must be determined on a rule-by-rule basis. Our experience as lawyers is that most actors do not know contract law. Indeed, if most actors know contract law, why do we bother to teach contracts in law schools?

It might be thought that actors who regularly contract will learn the contract-law rules that pertain to their contracting. Even if this proposition were true, its application would be limited to contract-law rules that apply only to actors who contract regularly, and there are few such rules. In any event, it is unlikely that the proposition is true. Even actors who contract regularly are likely to know the relevant rules of contract law only if they are tutored by lawyers on those rules, get into court on a repeated basis, or are normally counseled when they make contracts. In most cases, none of these conditions will prevail. For example, even lawyers who regularly draft contracts for a certain client are unlikely to tutor the client on contract law except to the extent that a given contract raises minefield issues. This is especially true where the client is an organization and decisionmaking power over contracts is dispersed over a large number of different persons in the organization.

There are some areas where it *is* likely that actors will either know the law in advance or will be counseled on the law when they make a contract. In those areas, contract-law rules can sensibly be made on the basis of the incentives and disincentives they will provide. In general, however, the prospect that actors will know the rules of contract law seems low, and a contract-law rule should not be based on the incentives or disincentives that the rule will provide unless the Legislator has good reason to believe that the rule is likely to be known – or, perhaps, unless all other competing considerations are in balance.

(b) *Rational-actor psychology or limited-cognition psychology.* A second type of recurring fundamental empirical choice that must be made under the basic contracts principle is between rational-actor psychology and limited-cognition psychology. Rational-actor psychology posits that an actor who must make a choice in the face of uncertainty will rationally select the option that maximizes his subjective expected utility. Rationality requires, among other things, that the likelihood of uncertain consequences be evaluated by actors without violating the basic rules of probability theory.[75] Acceptance of rational-actor psychology tends to lead to enforcing every contract, and every provision of every contract, as written (unless there is fraud, incapacity, duress, or the like) on the ground that rational actors are the best judges of their own utility and express that utility in making their contracts.

Although rational-actor psychology is the foundation of the standard economic *model* of choice, the empirical evidence shows that this model often

---

75. See R. M. Dawes, *Rational Choice in an Uncertain World* (Fort Worth, TX: Harcourt Brace College Pub., 1988) at 14, 146–163.

diverges from the *actual psychology* of choice, due to limits of cognition. As Tversky and Kahneman point out, expected-utility (rational-actor) theory "emerged from a logical analysis of games of chance rather than from a psychological analysis of risk and value. The theory was conceived as a normative model of an idealized decision maker, not as a description of the behavior of real people."[76] In contrast to rational-actor psychology, limited-cognition psychology tends to lead to heightened scrutiny of certain classes of contracts or certain classes of provisions in which the shortfalls in the rational-actor model are especially significant.

For purposes of contract law, three kinds of limits of cognition are especially salient: bounded rationality, irrational disposition, and defective capability.

(i) *Bounded rationality.* If the costs of searching for and processing (evaluating and deliberating on) information were zero and human information-processing capabilities were perfect, an actor contemplating a decision would make a comprehensive search for relevant information, would process perfectly all the information he acquired, and would then make the best possible substantive decision – the decision that, as of the time made, was better than all the alternative decisions the actor might have made if he had complete knowledge and perfect processing abilities, and that would therefore maximize the actor's subjective expected utility. I will call such a decision an optimal substantive decision.

In reality, of course, searching for and processing information involves costs, in the form of time, energy, and perhaps money. Therefore, the search will normally be limited. Furthermore, the ability to process information that is obtained by search and to solve problems is constrained by limitations on computational ability and on the ability to calculate consequences, understand implications, make comparative judgments on complex alternatives, organize and utilize memory, and the like.[77] Hence, actors will often process imperfectly even the information they do acquire, and such imperfections in human processing ability increase as decisions become more complex and involve more permutations.[78] Accordingly, rationality is normally bounded both by limited information and limited information-processing ability and capacity,[79] so that even if the actor's search is rational[80] the actor's substantive decision may not be optimal.

(ii) *Irrational disposition.* Bounded rationality is not necessarily irrational, although it may lead to suboptimal substantive decisions. However, two bodies

76. A. Tversky and D. Kahneman, "Rational Choice and the Framing of Decisions" (1986) 59 J. Bus. (Supp.) S251 at S251.
77. See J. G. March, "Bounded Rationality, Ambiguity, and the Engineering of Choice" (1978) 9 Bell J. Econ. 587 at 590; H. A. Simon, "Rational Decision-making in Business Organizations" (1979) 69 Am. Econ. Rev. 193 at 502–503.
78. See James J. Marsh and Herbert A. Simon, *Organizations* 171 (1st ed. 1958).
79. See H. A. Simon, *Administrative Behavior,* 3rd ed. (New York: Free Press, 1976) at 79–109.
80. See G. J. Stigler, *The Economics of Information* (1961) 69 Pol. Sci. 213.

of empirical evidence show that actors are often systematically irrational in certain ways – that is, often fail to make rational decisions even within the bounds of the information they have acquired.

The first body of empirical evidence concerns actors' dispositions. This evidence shows that actors tend to be systematically overoptimistic. (Lawyers do not realize this because they are trained to be systematically pessimistic.) The dispositional characteristic of undue optimism is strikingly illustrated in a study by Baker and Emery, appropriately titled *When Every Relationship Is Above Average*.[81] Baker and Emery asked people who were about to get married to report on their own divorce-related prospects, as compared to the divorce-related prospects of the general population. The disparities between perceptions as to the general population and expectations as to self were enormous and were almost invariably in the direction of optimism. For example, the respondents correctly estimated that 50 percent of American couples will eventually divorce. In contrast, the respondents estimated that their own chance of divorce was zero.[82] Similarly, the median estimate of the female respondents was that courts award alimony to 40 percent of women who divorce. In contrast, 81 percent of the female respondents expected that a court would award them alimony if they requested it.[83] Similarly, the respondents' median estimate of how often spouses pay court-ordered alimony was that 40 percent paid. In contrast, 100 percent of the respondents predicted that their own spouse would pay all court-ordered alimony.[84]

(iii) *Defective capability.* Just as certain defects in disposition systematically tilt actors' judgments toward undue optimism, so certain defects in capability systematically distort the way actors search for, process, and weigh information and potential future scenarios. Within the last thirty years, cognitive psychology has established that people use certain decisionmaking rules (heuristics) that yield systematic errors, and that other aspects of actors' cognitive capabilities are also systematically defective. "[T]he deviations of actual behavior from the normative model are too widespread to be ignored, too systematic to be dismissed as random error, and too fundamental to be accommodated by relaxing the normative system."[85] Among the systematic defects in capability that are particularly salient to contract law are defects associated with the availability and representativeness heuristics, defective telescopic faculties, and defective risk-assessment faculties.

(A) *Availability.* Because human information-processing ability is limited, actors who have acquired information that is relevant to a decision, whether through a present search or past learning, must employ heuristics to process the

---

81. Lynn A. Baker and Robert C. Emery, *When Every Relationship Is Above Average: Perceptions and Expectations of Divorce at The Time of Marriage* (1993).
82. Ibid. at 443.   83. Ibid.   84. Ibid.
85. Tversky and Kahneman, *supra* note 76 at S252.

information efficiently. One of these heuristics is known as *availability*. When an actor must make a decision that requires a judgment about the probability of an event, he commonly judges the probability on the basis of data and scenarios that are readily available to his memory or imagination. This heuristic leads to systematic biases because the salience of data and scenarios, and therefore the ease with which an actor imagines a scenario or retrieves data from memory, is affected by factors other than objective frequency and probability.[86]

For example, recent occurrences are usually easier to retrieve from memory than earlier occurrences. As Tversky and Kahneman point out, "It is a common experience that the subjective probability of traffic accidents rises temporarily when one sees a car overturned by the side of the road."[87] Similarly, data and scenarios that are instantiated, vivid, and concrete will normally be more salient than data and scenarios that are general, pallid, and abstract, such as statistical findings and generalized probabilities.[88] For example, Lichtenstein et al. asked a large number of respondents to estimate the frequency of forty-one causes of death in the United States. The respondents overestimated the frequency of memorable and dramatic killers, like homicide, accidents, and natural disasters, and underestimated the frequency of quiet killers, like asthma, emphysema, and diabetes.[89] In another experiment, researchers recited lists of well-known personalities to groups of subjects. All the lists contained names of both men and women, but in some lists the men were more famous than the women while in others the women were more famous than the men. When asked to determine whether men or women were more numerous in a list, the subjects erroneously concluded that whichever gender was represented by a greater number of famous – and therefore more salient – persons was more numerous.[90] In general, "[v]ibrant examples simply outweigh more reliable, but abstract base rate information."[91]

(B) *Representativeness.* The availability heuristic concerns the manner in which actors bring acquired data to mind and imagine future scenarios. Another heuristic, *representativeness,* concerns the manner of making judgments about the adequacy of search. As the concept of bounded rationality implies, actors seldom collect all relevant data before making decisions. Rather, they usually

86. See Dawes, *supra* note 75 at 92–94; A. Tversky and D. Kahneman, "Availability: A Heuristic for Judging Frequency and Probability," in D. Kahneman, P. Slovic and A. Tversky, eds., *Judgment Under Uncertainty: Heuristics and Biases* (Cambridge: Cambridge University Press, 1982) at 16, 166, 174–75 [hereinafter "Availability"]; A. Tversky and D. Kahneman, "Judgment Under Uncertainty: Heuristics and Biases" in Kahneman, Slovic, and Tversky, *ibid.* at 3, 11 [hereinafter "Judgment"].
87. Ibid. at 11, 27.
88. See R. Nisbet and L. Ross, "Human Inference: Strategies and Shortcomings of Social Judgment," 43–62 (1980); cf. Tversky and Kahneman, "Availability," *supra* note 86, at 176.
89. See S. Lichtenstein et al., "Judged Frequency of Lethal Events" (1978) 4 J. Experimental Psychology: Hum. Learning & Memory 551.
90. See "Judgment," *supra* note 86.
91. S. T. Fiske and S. E. Taylor, *Social Cognition* (Reading, MA: Addison-Wesley Pub. Co., 1984) at 252.

make decisions on the basis of some subset of the data, which they judge to be representative.[92] In making that judgment, however, actors systematically and erroneously view unduly small samples as representative. In particular, actors systematically and erroneously take the small sample of present events as representative, and therefore predictive, of future events.[93] In this way, as Arrow has observed, "[t]he individual judges the likelihood of a future event by the similarity of the present evidence to it," while ignoring other evidence, such as prior occurrences and the quality of the sample.[94]

(C) *Faulty telescopic faculties.* Another type of defect in cognition concerns the ability of actors to make rational comparisons between present and future states: Actors systematically give too little weight to future benefits and costs as compared to present benefits and costs.[95] Thus Martin Feldstein concludes that "some or all individuals have, in Pigou's . . . words, a 'faulty telescopic faculty' that causes them to give too little weight to the utility of future consumption."[96]

(D) *Faulty risk-estimation faculties.* A defect of capability related to faulty telescopic faculties is the systematic underestimation of risks.[97] Based on the work of cognitive psychologists, Arrow observes that "It is a plausible hypothesis that individuals are unable to recognize that there will be many surprises in the future; in short, as much other evidence tends to confirm, there is a tendency to underestimate uncertainties."[98] In fact, empirical evidence shows that people often not only underestimate but ignore low-probability risks.

The choice between rational-actor and cognitive psychology, like the choice between the proposition that actors know contract law and the proposition that they do not, must be made on a rule-by-rule basis. The limits of cognition normally have little bearing on rules concerning the price provisions of bargained-out contracts. However, the limits of cognition have great bearing on some classes of contracts and some classes of contractual provisions, and the legal rules governing these classes should reflect those limits.

One such class consists of liquidated damages provisions. Bounded rationality and rational ignorance have special bearing on such provisions. At the time a contract is made, it is often impracticable, if not impossible, to imagine all the scenarios of breach to which such a provision may apply. Similarly, the inherent complexity of figuring out the application of a liquidated-damages

---

92. See A. Tversky and D. Kahneman, "Belief in The Law of Small Numbers" in Kahneman, Slovic & Tversky, *supra* note 86 at 23, 24–25.
93. See K. J. Arrow, "Risk Perception in Psychology and Economics" (1982) 20 Econ. Inquiry 1 at 5.
94. Ibid.
95. See M. Feldstein, "The Optimal Level of Social Security Benefits" (1985) 100 Q. J. Econ 303 at 307.
96. Ibid.
97. See T. H. Jackson, *The Logic and Limits of Bankruptcy Law* (Cambridge, MA: Harvard University Press, 1986) at 237–240.
98. Arrow, *supra* note 93, at 5.

provision to every possible scenario of breach is often likely to exceed actors' calculative and deliberative capabilities.

Furthermore, even on the doubtful assumption that a party could imagine all scenarios of breach, and has the capacity to calculate and deliberate upon the application of a liquidated-damages provision to each scenario, the benefits of the search and information-processing required will often to be very low as compared to the costs. For example, suppose that contracts are performed at least 95 percent of the time – which, observation suggests, is likely – and that a contracting party attempted to process the application of a liquidated-damages provision to every scenario of breach. Then all the costs of searching for and processing the more remote applications of a liquidated-damages provision would have to be taken into account, but the benefits of such processing would have to be discounted by 95 percent. As a result, search and deliberation efforts can be expected to be very limited.

The problem of disposition also bears significantly on liquidated-damages provisions. Because actors tend to be unduly optimistic, a contracting party will probably believe that his performance is more likely, and his breach less likely, than is actually the case. Accordingly, undue optimism will reduce even further the amount of deliberation that actors give to liquidated-damages provisions.

Finally, defective capabilities have particular relevance to liquidated-damages provisions. The availability heuristic may lead a contracting party to give undue weight to his intention to perform, which is vivid and concrete, as compared with the abstract possibility that future circumstances may compel him to breach. Similarly, because a contracting party is likely to take the sample of present evidence as representative of the future, he is apt to overestimate the extent to which his present intention to perform is a reliable predictor of his future intentions. Furthermore, because actors have faulty telescopic faculties, a contracting party is likely to overvalue the benefit of performance, which will normally begin in the short term, as against the cost of breach, which will typically occur, if at all, only well down the road. And because actors tend to underestimate risks, a contracting party is likely to underestimate the risk that a liquidated-damages provision will take effect.

As a result of all these factors, liquidated-damages provisions should be subjected to special scrutiny to determine whether the parties had a well-thought-through intention that the provision would apply in a scenario of breach like the one that actually occurred.

Another class of provisions on which the limits of cognition have special bearing consists of preprinted terms in form contracts. Most preprinted terms are nonperformance terms that relate to the future and concern low-probability risks. Accordingly, the cognitive problems associated with liquidated-damages provisions, including bounded rationality, undue optimism, systematic underestimation of risk, and undue weight on present as opposed to future costs and benefits, apply as well to most preprinted terms.

Of these problems, bounded rationality plays a particularly powerful role. Call a party who prepares a form contract a form-giver, and a party who is presented with a form contract a form-taker. A form-giver typically offers a package, consisting of a physical commodity coupled with a form contract that states the terms on which the physical commodity is sold. The two parts of the package, in turn, consist of a number of subparts. The physical commodity has physical attributes, such as size, shape, and color. The form contract has both business and legal attributes, such as price, quantity, and limitations on remedies.

To make an optimum substantive decision, the form-taker would, at a minimum, carefully search through and deliberate on all the legal attributes of all the form contracts that are coupled with all the physical commodities he is considering. Analyzing legal attributes in this manner, however, will almost invariably be unduly costly. First, a form contract often contains a very large number of legal terms. Form insurance contracts, for example, typically include thirty, forty, or even more such terms. Moreover, the meaning and effect of the preprinted terms will very often be relatively inaccessible to nonlawyers and even to many lawyers. During the oral argument of *Gerhardt* v. *Continental Insurance Cos.*[99] before the great New Jersey Supreme Court of the time, Chief Justice Weintraub looked at the insurance policy at issue and said, "I don't know what it means. I am stumped. They say one thing in big type and in small type they take it away." Justice Haneman added, "I can't understand half of my insurance policies." Justice Francis said, "I get the impression that insurance companies keep the language of their policies deliberately obscure."[100]

The bottom line is that the low probability that preprinted terms will come into play drastically reduces the benefits of search and deliberation, while the verbal and legal obscurity of such terms renders the cost of search and deliberation very high. Furthermore, the length and complexity of form contracts are often uncorrelated to the dollar value of the transaction. Where form contracts involve a low dollar value, the cost of search through and deliberation on preprinted terms – let alone the cost of legal advice about the meaning and effect of the terms – will be prohibitive in relation to the benefits. Faced with preprinted terms whose effect the form-taker knows he will find difficult or impossible to fully understand, which involve risks that probably will never mature, which are unlikely to be worth the cost of search and processing, and which probably are not subject to revision in any event, a rational form-taker will typically decide to remain ignorant of the preprinted terms. Form-givers understand and exploit this phenomenon. Accordingly, a preprinted term should be unenforceable if the form-giver had reason to know that the form-taker would not have expected the term because it undercuts the expectations the

---

99. 48 N.J. 291, 225 A.2d 328 (1966).
100. "New Jersey court Overrules Small Print in Policy", *Jury Verdicts Wkly. News* (Supp. to *Jury Verdicts Wkly.*) (13 January 1969) 3.

form-taker will have on the basis of the negotiated provisions and purpose of the transaction.

C. The Role of Distributive Justice[101]

An important question for the theory of contracts is whether the criteria of distributive justice should figure among the social propositions that generate contract law under the basic contracts principle. The concept of distributive justice is expansive, but at its core it concerns the criteria for the proper distribution of wealth and other resources among members of the community.[102] The central issue for moral philosophers who consider distributive justice is to establish such criteria. Appropriate legal institutions must then determine whether the distribution in a given society is just in light of the proper criteria, and if not, what kinds of legal rules should be utilized to promote a redistribution. I will first develop the thesis that the goal of promoting redistribution normally should not figure in generating contract-law rules under the basic contracts principle, and then briefly discuss several qualifications of that thesis.

1. The basic issue. Anthony Kronman, for one, has argued that "considerations of distributive justice . . . *must* be taken into account [in designing rules for exchange] if the law of contracts is to have even minimum moral acceptability."[103] Kronman supports this normative argument with the positive claim that various contract-law rules *do* serve redistributive ends. Among his examples are laws prohibiting racial discrimination in employment and the sale of real property, and the rule prohibiting a waiver of the warranty of habitability in residential-housing leases. Kronman argues that these and other rules serve redistributive ends because they have as an objective a redistribution of wealth in favor of traditionally disadvantaged groups.

Some of the rules to which Kronman points are not really rules of contract law. Take, for example, rules prohibiting racial discrimination in employment and the sale of real property. When a lawmaker wants to prohibit a certain sort of conduct, it may choose to include, within the prohibition, conduct of the relevant sort that finds expression in contracts. However, we usually do not think of such prohibitions as rules of contract law even when the conduct to be prohibited can find expression only in bargains, so that the prohibition concerns only bargaining behavior. So, for example, we do not consider the rule that prohibits bargains to commit a crime to be a rule of contract law. Similarly, we do not consider laws that prohibit dealing in drugs to be contract-law rules, even though for the most part the only way to deal in drugs is to make

---

101. On the issues discussed in this section, see, generally Benson, "Abstract Right" *supra* note 57, and P. Benson, "The Basis of Corrective Justice and Its Relation to Distributive Justice" (1992) 77 Iowa L. Rev. 515.
102. See for example, ibid. at 535–36.
103. A. Kronman, "Contract Law and Distributive Justice" (1980) 89 Yale Law J. 472 at 474.

bargains for their purchase and sale. The rules that prohibit racial discrimination in contracting are no more contract-law rules than are the rules that prohibit bargains to commit a crime or to deal in drugs.

On the other hand, some of the rules to which Kronman points *can* be characterized as contract-law rules. This is true, for example, of the rule that prohibits waiver of the warranty of habitability in residential leases, the *habitability rule*, because this rule regulates specific provisions in otherwise-proper contracts, rather than generally prohibiting a given sort of conduct. However, although the habitability rule may indeed have been motivated in part by distributional considerations, it is better justified by considerations of cognition and externalities.

There is, to begin with, a problem of bounded rationality. Residential leases are almost invariably form contracts, and the courts may believe that form waivers of the warranty of habitability so far undercut a residential tenant's reasonable expectations, and are so unlikely to be brought home to and be understood by the tenant, that they should be unenforceable for that reason alone. Even where such a waiver is brought home and understood it entails a cognitional problem. Residential tenants may fail to make rational decisions concerning such a waiver because if residential housing is in decent condition when the tenant moves in, the present condition of the housing will be highly salient, while the effect of the waiver is highly abstract and the risk involved in the waiver may seem extremely low. Waivers of the warranty of habitability also involve significant externalities, because residential tenants often have families, including minor children, who will be impacted by dangerous conditions without their knowing consent. Although cases might be found in which a residential tenant read the lease, understood the meaning of the waiver, made a rational decision to agree to it, and had no minor children, the law may properly take the position that the likelihood of such cases is so small that it can be ignored in the interest of administrability.

Thus the empirical basis of Kronman's positive claim that contract law presently includes rules that serve redistributive ends is inconclusive. However, even if the positive claim were conclusively demonstrated, it would not establish the normative claim that contract law must serve redistributive ends. I therefore return to that claim.

One way in which redistributional goals might be served in the context of contract law would be through a rule that any suit based on breach of contract is a proper occasion for judicial redistribution whenever a redistribution is appropriate under the standards that should govern redistribution, wholly apart from the contract and the breach at issue. Such a rule would be exceptionally unappealing. Its operation would be completely haphazard. It would warrant redistribution even from an innocent party to a breaching party. If known, it would considerably dampen contracting activity.

An alternative approach would be to take redistributional goals into account in shaping rules of contract law that affected classes of contract in which one generic party is wealthier on average than the other. This classes-of-contracts approach would, for example, be applicable to contracts between landlords and tenants, or between merchants and consumers, but not to contracts between merchants. This approach would be much more limited than one that allowed any suit on a contract to be an occasion for redistribution. Nevertheless, even this approach would license the creation of special rules of contract law for all provisions of all relevant classes of contracts. For example, if the habitability rule is indeed justified on redistributive grounds, then so too might be any other special rule governing landlord-tenant or merchant-consumer contracts, such as a rule that when a landlord or merchant has breached a contract, a tenant or consumer has no obligation to mitigate damages.

Kronman might answer that it would indeed count in favor of such a rule, or any given rule that affects a relevant class of contracts, that the rule serves a redistributive goal, but that this is not decisive; whether any such rule should be adopted would depend on whether the redistributive goal is overridden by other values. However, if it is proper to take the promotion of redistributive goals into account in designing all contract-law rules governing the relevant classes of contracts, it is plausible to conclude that the redistributive goal would be sufficiently weighty to carry the day in respect of a number of those rules. Accordingly, the classes-of-contracts approach, whatever its precise scope, would cause redistributions in a variety of ways between parties to contracts that fell within the relevant classes. This gives rise to the following problem: If general – that is, noncontract – law adequately required redistribution between the kinds of parties involved, then there would be no need to employ contract law as an instrument to effect redistribution. Accordingly, the predicate of a classes-of-contracts-approach must be that general law would not require a redistribution between the parties if they had not entered into a contract. It is not easy to see, however, why the fact that parties have entered into a contract requires or even licenses the law to redistribute wealth from one to the other when the law would not require such a redistribution if they had not entered into a contract.

Finally, it is incorrect to say, as Kronman does, that the law of contracts cannot have moral acceptability unless considerations of distributive justice are taken into account. To have minimum moral acceptability the law of contracts need not have a redistributive aspect; instead, it need only reflect relevant moral norms, such as norms against unfair advantage-taking.

2. *Contract-law rules should not require the courts to order unfair redistributions.* The thesis of Section 1 is that contract law should generally not be used as an instrument to promote redistribution. That does not mean that there are no connections between contract law and justice. One connection is that contract law should not *require* the courts to order unfair redistributions. In particular, although contract-law rules that reflect moral norms generally will not produce a redistribution between the parties, they will often prevent the courts from ordering an unfair redistribution. For example, a rule that a desperate

traveler will not be required to pay more than a fair price for an adventitious rescue will not ordinarily effect a redistribution of resources from rescuers to travelers. Instead, such a rule will prevent the state from making an enforced and unfair redistribution from travelers to adventitious rescuers. The same is true of rules concerning procedural unconscionability, and rules against unfair advantage-taking. The effect of such rules is normally not to shift wealth to the wronged party, but to prevent the state from shifting wealth to the party who is in the wrong. More generally, as James Gordley in particular has argued, the justice of contracts is corrective rather than distributional justice.

3. Reallocational rules on collapse. It is also important to distinguish between contract-law rules that would serve a redistributional end and contract-law rules that allow a court to reallocate losses where a contract has collapsed because of a mistake or changed circumstance that excuses full performance. In such cases, it often happens that by the time the excusing event becomes known or occurs, one or both parties have incurred costs in performing or preparing to perform the contract, and the salvageable value of those costs is less than their amount. The issue then arises whether the courts should let such costs rest where they happen to fall, or should reallocate them between the parties; and if the latter, on what basis.

At least in some instances, the best rule is to allow the court to reallocate these costs, so that the losses of the parties are not determined purely by the accident of who first performed or prepared. Reallocation-on-collapse rules might appear to be rules that serve as instruments of redistribution. That appearance, however, is deceiving. The justification of reallocation-on-collapse rules is not to achieve a proper distribution of wealth in society. Rather, it is that contracting parties themselves would want such rules, because the transaction costs of planning for the allocation of losses upon every possible scenario of collapse are too great. Correspondingly, a reallocation under such a rule would not be based on the criteria for the proper distribution of wealth in a society, but on the nature and purpose of the contractual enterprise in which the parties engaged. Under reallocation-on-collapse rules, therefore, losses can, for example, be reallocated from more wealthy parties to less wealthy parties.

4. The basic structure. One further qualification needs to be made to the thesis developed in Section 1. Contract law as an institution is acceptable only if the basic structure of the society is fair. If the basic social structure is unfair, rules designed in part to accomplish corrective justice within that structure, including the rules of contract law, may not be justifiable.

D. *Whether and to What Extent Promises Should be Legally Enforceable*

As shown in Part III, autonomy and revealed-preference theories do not, taken alone, support the legal enforcement of promises, because nothing in either type of theory shows why the law should respect a promisor's earlier decision and expressed preference to promise and perform, rather than his later decision and expressed preference not to perform. The basic contracts principle is not embarrassed by difficulty. It is enough under this principle if morality, policy, and experience lead to a rule that promises, or certain types of promises, should be enforceable.

In this Section I will discuss whether, and to what extent, promises should be legally enforceable under the basic contracts principle. Because of limits of space, and because I have addressed many of these issues in detail elsewhere,[104] the discussion in this section will be suggestive rather than comprehensive.

It is a premise of this discussion that there is a moral obligation to keep a promise. Certainly that is so as a matter of social morality, and contributions by various philosophers, including importantly Thomas Scanlon, go toward showing that it is so as a matter of critical morality.[105] Given that premise, the issue is whether there should also be a *legal* obligation to keep a promise, and if so, what the remedies should be for breach of that obligation. I will discuss those issues in turn.

1. Enforceability. Under the basic contracts principle, the moral obligation to keep a promise is a strong but not sufficient starting-point for concluding that there should be a legal obligation to keep a promise. It is a strong starting-point, because under the basic contracts principle the Legislator should take moral norms into account in making contract law. It is not a sufficient starting-point, because under the basic contracts principle the Legislator must also consider policy and empirical propositions. More generally, the conclusion that private conduct violates a moral norm does not alone justify the use of collective resources to sanction the conduct. For example, in some cases, like cutting in line, the injury caused by the violation of a moral norm is not significant enough to justify a legal sanction. In other cases, like the failure to support aged parents who cannot support themselves, the legal enforceability of a moral norm would intrude too far, without sufficient justification, into intimate areas better governed by social norms. In still other cases, like unrelied-upon, informal, affective donative promises, the legal enforceability of a moral norm would raise difficult problems of administrability. As stated by Scanlon, "The fact that some action is morally required is not, in general, a sufficient justification for legal intervention to force people to do it; and the rationale for the law of contracts does not seem to be . . . an instance of the legal enforcement of morality."[106]

---

104. See R. Cooter and M. A. Eisenberg, "Damages for Breach of Contract" (1985) 73 Cal. L. Rev. 1432; M. A. Eisenberg, "The World of Contract and The World of Gift" (1997) 85 Cal. L. Rev. 821; M. A. Eisenberg, "The Principle of *Hadley* v. *Baxendale*" (1992) 80 Cal. L. Rev. 563; M. A. Eisenberg, "The Principles of Consideration" (1982) 67 Cornell L. Rev. 640; M. A. Eisenberg, "The Bargain Principle and its Limits" (1982) 95 Harv. L. Rev. 741; "Donative Promises," *supra* note 39.
105. See Scanlon, *supra* note 7.
106. Scanlon, Promises and Contracts, *supra* this book, at pp. 99–100.

Accordingly, under the basic contracts principle the law should not simply require that all promises be performed. Instead, the law should effectuate the objectives of parties to a promissory transaction if, but only if, appropriate conditions are satisfied, and subject to appropriate constraints. The issue then is, what additional moral or policy elements, beyond the moral obligation to keep a promise, should make a given type of promise enforceable, assuming that all other appropriate conditions (such as capacity) are satisfied and that no special constraints apply. I will briefly describe three such considerations.[107]

To begin with, the law should enforce types of promises whose enforcement will enhance social welfare. The major type of promise that should be enforceable on social-welfare grounds consists of bargain promises, including promises that are in aid of or ancillary to bargains. Bargains serve social welfare, both because they increase wealth by trade and because they facilitate private economic planning by allowing actors to allocate risks and to coordinate economic activity through the acquisition of control over inputs and outputs. Enforcing bargain promises furthers the welfare purposes that such promises serve.

Next, the law should enforce types of promises whose breach tends to cause significant harm to the promisee – in particular, promises that have been relied upon, so that the promisee is worse off than he would have been if the promise had not been made. The principle here is one of liability for significant harm caused by an actor's fault. The promisor is at fault for having made a promise and then breaking it, and that fault caused a loss to the promisee, because the promise induced the promisee to incur costs that he would not otherwise have incurred, on the reasonable assumption that the promise would be kept.

The law should also enforce promises that are made to compensate a promisee, *B,* who has previously conferred a benefit for which the promisor, *A,* is morally but not legally obliged to compensate *B,* as where *B* has rescued *A* from danger at some cost to himself. Presumably, in such cases *A* is not legally obliged to compensate *B* only because it is deemed desirable to protect actors against liability for benefits that they might have declined to accept and pay for if they had been given the choice, and because of the severe difficulty in many such cases of measuring the value of the benefit to *A.* A later promise to make compensation invariably removes the first obstacle and normally removes the second. Such a promise should therefore be enforceable.

These three considerations – social welfare, significant harm, and a moral obligation to make compensation – are not exhaustive. The point here is not to catalog the considerations that, when added to the moral obligation to keep a promise, should make a type of promise legally enforceable. Rather, the point is simply to illustrate the way in which the moral obligation to keep a promise may be combined with other moral or policy considerations to justify legal enforceability.

---

107. I use the word *consideration* here in its ordinary sense, not in its legal sense. However, when the legal term is properly construed the two meanings converge.

2. *Remedy.* Even if a given type of promise should be enforceable, under the basic contract principle the *extent* of enforceability is subject to appropriate constraints. Some of these constraints concern remedy. Just as promises should not be legally enforceable simply because they are morally binding, neither should promises be enforced to their full extent simply because they are legally enforceable. The issue of remedy is complex, in part because the relevant economic analysis is both difficult and unsettled. As a general principle, however, the remedy for the breach of an enforceable promise should be based on the reason why the promise should be legally enforceable, subject to constraints based on morality, policy (principally, efficiency), and experience.

Accordingly, if a type of promise should be legally enforceable because, and only because, breach of that type of promise tends to cause significant harm to the promisee, the remedy should normally be measured by the promisee's harm. In particular, if a promise is enforceable because, and only because, the promisee has been harmed by relying upon it, damages should normally be measured by the amount reasonably required to put the promisee in the position he would have been in if the promise had not been made ("reliance damages").

Similarly, if a type of promise should be legally enforceable because, and only because, the promisor was under a prior moral obligation to compensate the promisee for a benefit conferred, damages should normally be measured by the amount of compensation that was morally required prior to the promise, but no more than the amount promised.

If a type of promise should be legally enforceable for a welfare or policy reason, the remedy should normally be based on what is necessary to effectuate the policy. In the case of bargain promises, which should be enforced because of the desirability of increasing wealth by trade and facilitating private economic planning, the remedy should be based on what will best effectuate those objectives, subject to constraints of morality, policy, and experience. Normally, an expectation-based remedy – either specific performance or expectation damages (that is, the amount required to put the promisee in the position he would have been in if the promise had been kept) – should be the starting-point for effectuating the welfare reasons for enforcing bargain promises. Expectation-based remedies give promisees assurance that exchanges over time will be completed, and more generally provide correct incentives for the performance of bargain promises by either making the promisor perform or placing on the promisor the promisee's loss of his share of the bargain's value in the event of breach. This, in turn, causes the promisor to sweep that loss into his calculus of self-interest, initially in deciding the level of precaution he should take to ensure that he will be able to perform, and later in deciding whether to perform or breach. In contrast, if the promisor is liable only for reliance damages – the principal competitive measure – when deciding whether to perform or breach he will not internalize the full value of performance to the promisee.

Furthermore, by directly affecting the probability that a bargain promisor will perform, expectation damages and specific performance have an indirect effect upon the promisee's behavior, which can be stated in terms of planning. A bargain promisee who knows that the remedy for breach will give the promisor a strong incentive to perform can plan effectively, because he can order his affairs with confidence that he will realize the value of his planning, either through the promisor's voluntary or compelled performance or through an expectation-based remedy. In contrast, under a regime of reliance damages a promisee could plan only on the basis that if breach occurs the law will put him back to where he was when he started. Since planning is by nature forward-looking, the backward-looking nature of reliance damages would be a shaky foundation for ordering complex affairs. Moreover, it is in the promisor's interest that the promisee be able to plan reliably, because the ability to do so will make the promisee willing pay a higher price for the promise.

The position that expectation-based remedies should be the starting-point for breach of a bargain promise has been contested on the ground that the prospect of expectation damages will lead contracting parties to "overrely," that is, to incur more costs in reliance on their contract than is justified given the statistical probability of breach. In many or most cases, however, overreliance is not possible because expectation damages are invariant to reliance. (This is true, for example, when expectation damages are measured by the difference between the contract price and the market or cover price.) Of course, in some cases damages are measured by the amount of the promisee's lost profits, and profits may depend in part on the extent of the promisee's reliance. Even in these cases, however, overreliance normally will not be a problem, partly because it is economically imprudent for a promisee to count on being compensated for overreliance through litigation, partly because overreliance will normally have only a trivial effect even if engaged in, and partly because the problem of overreliance can be dealt with by calculating lost profits on the basis of reasonable rather than actual reliance.[108]

Other concerns may also be raised by expectation-based remedies. In general, however, the defects of expectation-based remedies are slight, and no convincing and easily administrable alternative remedy has been shown to better promote the welfare objectives that bargains serve, although policy and experience do suggest various constraints on expectation-based remedies, such as limitations on the availability of specific performance, limits on expectation damages based on reasonable foreseeability, and a requirement of mitigation.

---

108. There are other concerns that may be raised by the remedy of expectation damages. My claim is that, whatever the defects of the expectation measure may be, in general it promotes the welfare goals that bargains serve better than any other easily administrable remedy.

6

Contract Law in the Aristotelian Tradition

JAMES GORDLEY

I. Introduction

Aristotle's works on ethics, politics, physics, and metaphysics were rediscovered in the West toward the end of the twelfth century. For a long time thereafter, many regarded him, in Dante's words, as "the master of those who know."[1] In the seventeenth century, Hobbes could still complain that his ideas dominated the "the Philosophy-schooles, through all the universities of Christendome."[2]

During these centuries, as I have described elsewhere,[3] philosophers and jurists built the first systematic theory of contract law. It was a synthesis of Aristotelian philosophy and Roman law. Roman law had been studied in Western universities since its rediscovery about 1100. For all their subtlety, however, the Roman jurists were not theorists. A first step toward a theory was taken by Thomas Aquinas who developed a systematic moral philosophy based on Aristotle, which incorporated Roman legal concepts and rules. Gradually, jurists borrowed ideas from Aristotle and Thomas and read them into Roman texts. Then, in the sixteenth and early seventeenth centuries, a group centered in Spain and known to historians as the "late scholastics" tried to explain as much of Roman law as possible on Aristotelian and Thomistic principles. Among the leaders of this group were Domingo de Soto (1494–1560), Luis de Molina (1535–1600), and Leonard Lessius (1554–1623). They gave Roman law a theory and a systematic doctrinal organization for the first time.

In the seventeenth century, the founders of modern critical philosophy broke with the Aristotelian tradition. Paradoxically, during the same century, many of the conclusions of the late scholastics were borrowed and disseminated

---

1. Dante Alighieri, *La Divinia Commedia: Inferno IV,* 130–32, ed. by C. H. Grandgent and C. S. Singleton (Cambridge, MA: Harvard University Press, 1972).
2. T. Hobbes, *Leviathan or the Matter, Forme and Power of a Commonwealth,* ed. by A. R. Waller (Cambridge: Cambridge University Press, 1935) at I.i.2.
3. See J. Gordley, *Philosophical Origins of Modern Contract Doctrine* (Oxford: Clarendon Press, 1991) at 69–111 [hereinafter *Philosophical Origins*].

throughout Europe by the founders of the northern natural law school, Hugo Grotius (1583–1645) and Samuel Pufendorf (1632–94).[4] In its broad outlines, the Aristotelian approach to contract law was still recognizable in the work of eighteenth century natural lawyers[5] and in the drafting of the French Civil Code,[6] although its Aristotelian foundations were forgotten. Jurists did not break sharply with the past until the rise of "will theories" in the nineteenth century.

The novel feature of the will theories was not the idea that the parties bound themselves to a contract by expressing the will to do so. Writers in the Aristotelian tradition had said the same. The break was to jettison other concepts that had been part of the Aristotelian explanation. This essay will make the strong claim that we need these other concepts to understand contract law.[7] Contemporary theorists run into difficulties because, like the will theorists, they try to do without them. We will consider three fundamental problems: why contracts should be enforced; what determines the content of a contractual obligation; and what the consequences of breach should be. We will describe what writers in the Aristotelian tradition said about these problems. We will frequently go beyond what they said and explore the implications of their approach.

As has often been pointed out, in the *Nicomachean Ethics* Aristotle wrote about virtue rather than law. Nevertheless, the writers he influenced approached these problems by discussing Aristotelian virtues. One was the virtue of promise-keeping. These writers described a promise in much the same way as the nineteenth-century will theorists: A person who makes a promise expresses his will to be obligated. The will theorists, however, thought it axiomatic that the will of the parties should be respected. They failed to explain why it should be. Consequently, they did not adequately address the first problem we will consider: why contracts should be enforced. In contrast, in the Aristotelian tradition, promising was regarded as a means to an end. When the promise concerns goods and services, the end is to enable people to get what they need to live a good life. For this end to be served, people have to make the right decisions about what contributes to such a life. In doing so, they exercise the virtue of prudence. They also need purchasing power. When the society sees that purchasing power is fairly distributed, it exercises the virtue of distributive justice. In the first part of this essay, we will see that to understand the purpose of contract law, we need to return to these ideas. Contract law can do its job to the

---

4. I will be citing Grotius, Pufendorf, and other members of the northern natural law school along with earlier writers who were self-consciously writing in the Aristotelian tradition. I do not mean to imply that they were self-consciously in this tradition themselves. Pufendorf was not. Grotius was, I believe, although other scholars disagree. See ibid. at 121–125.
5. Ibid. at 69–111.
6. J. Gordley, "Myths of the French Civil Code" (1994) 42 Am. J. Comp. L. 459 at 460–483.
7. In doing so, it will belatedly address some questions I was asked by Dennis Patterson years ago in an open letter. D. M. Patterson, "An Open Letter to Professor James Gordley" [1991] Wis. L. Rev. 1432.

extent that the decisions of the contracting parties are prudent and the distribution of wealth in a society is just.

For the will theorists, moreover, the parties' promises or expressions of will are the source of their obligations. In principle, the parties are obligated only to what they promised, and they may promise anything that is not illegal. Consequently, the will theorists could not resolve the second problem we will consider: what determines the content of the parties' obligations. Sometimes the law holds the parties to terms on which they never expressly agreed, and sometimes it disregards terms on which they did agree. In contrast, in the Aristotelian tradition, the parties' obligations depend, not only on their express will, but on the type of arrangement they enter into when they promise. There are two basic types of arrangements that the law should respect: exchange and gift. They correspond to the Aristotelian virtues of commutative justice and liberality. While distributive justice secures a fair share of wealth for each person, commutative justice preserves the share that belongs to each. In voluntary transactions, when people exchange, commutative justice requires that the resources exchanged be equivalent in value so that neither party's share is diminished. Liberality means, not merely that a party gives away resources, but that he gives them away sensibly, as Aristotle said, giving "to the right people the right amounts and at the right time."[8] Writers in the Aristotelian tradition thought that the rules that govern the parties' obligations should depend, not simply on their will, but on which type of arrangement they had made. The rules should ensure, so far as practicable, in the case of an exchange, that each party receives an equivalent, and in the case of a gratituous contract, that the donor behaves sensibly. We will consider these ideas in the second part of this essay.

Moreover, for the will theorists, the reason the promisor is bound is simply that he willed to be bound. They were therefore unable to explain what the consequences should be when a contract is breached. As Lon Fuller and William Perdue pointed out in a famous article, the fact that a person has promised to do something does not explain what should happen if he fails to do it.[9] It is not obvious whether he should be liable for the full value of his performance or only for any harm the promisee has suffered. As we shall see in the third part of this essay, in the Aristotelian tradition, that question was answered by saying that a promise may confer a right on the promisee to demand performance. If so, for the promisor to infringe this right would be a violation of commutative justice.

The Aristotelian tradition was different in other ways as well. For example, although writers in this tradition thought that parties enter into contracts by

---

8. Aristotle, *Nicomachean Ethics,* trans. W. D. Ross, in R. McKeon, ed., *The Basic Works of Aristotle* (New York: Random House, 1941) 935 at IV.i 1119^b.–1120^a.

9. L. L. Fuller and W. R. Perdue, "The Reliance Interest in Contract Damages" (1936) 46 Yale L. J. 52, at 58, 58 n. 9 (criticizing "will theory" and mentioning the German will theorist Bernhard Windscheid).

expressing the will to do so, their concept of will was based on Aristotelian ideas about human choice, and that concept influenced their doctrines of fraud, mistake, and duress.[10] This essay will concentrate on features of the Aristotelian tradition that are in the most striking contrast to modern theories because they concern, not choice itself, but what people should choose to do.

We will not linger over the shortcomings of the will theories. They are out of favor today largely because they cannot resolve the problems just described. We will try to show, however, that the contemporary theories of contract have not escaped these shortcomings because of a characteristic that they share with the will theories. The most widely held modern theories, like the will theories, are voluntaristic. They place a value on choice that is independent of the value of what the parties have chosen. It is true that contracts are voluntary. But contract law is not merely concerned with whether an agreement was made voluntarily. It is concerned with how, through voluntary agreements, people are able to get things that help them live a better life while being fair to others. Consequently, it is concerned with the value of what is chosen.

II. The Reasons for Enforcing Promises

Contract has often been described as a system of private allocation of resources. Under what conditions, then, can we say that there has been a normative improvement, a change for the better, in how resources are allocated? A straightforward answer is that the conditions are two: that people use their purchasing power to acquire the resources they should, and that each person has the purchasing power he should have to acquire resources. In Aristotelian terminology, contract improves the allocation of resources to the extent people exercise the virtues of prudence and distributive justice. We will consider these virtues in turn.

A. Choice and the Virtue of Prudence

In the Aristotelian tradition, choices matter because of the contribution they make to a good life, a life that realizes, so far as possible, one's potential as a human being. Leading such a life constitutes human happiness. It is the ultimate end to which all actions are a means either instrumentally or as constituent parts of such a life. In the *Politics,* Aristotle explained that "[t]he form of government is best in which every man, whoever he is, can act best and live happily."[11] In the *Ethics,* he described the different virtues as different acquired capacities to live this distinctively human life.[12] Material things are worth acquiring only because they contribute to it.

10. See *Philosophical Origins, supra* note 3 at 85–93.
11. Aristotle, *Politics,* trans. B. Jowett in R. McKeon, *supra* note 8 1127 at VII.i 1324ᵃ.
12. *Nicomachean Ethics, supra* note 8 at V.vii.

To choose rightly is to choose what contributes to such a life. To speak of right and wrong choices does not imply that the same choices are right for everyone. People are different and so are their circumstances. It does mean that whenever anyone chooses rightly, his choice contributes to his life for reasons other than the fact that it is chosen. Moreover, to speak of right and wrong choices does not mean that there is always only one right choice or best choice a person should make. Freedom of the will, according to Thomas Aquinas, means not merely that one could choose to do wrong but that there are often different ways to choose rightly, no one of which is best.[13] Even so, the choice one makes may matter very much. It matters which of many possible beautiful buildings an architect chooses to build even though one cannot rank order their beauty. For Thomas, it mattered that God created this particular universe, but he discussed God's freedom in the same way as that of human beings: There is no best of all possible worlds that God had to create.[14]

In the Aristotelian tradition, a virtue is an acquired capacity to choose rightly. The virtue of prudence enables a person to judge what will contribute to such a life.[15] When he acquires goods and services, he uses a type of prudence usually translated as "economic prudence" or "household management."[16] To choose rightly, he may need the virtues of temperance and courage as well. Temperance and courage, respectively, are the capacities to choose without being deflected by pleasure or fear.[17] An addict would need these virtues to abstain despite the pleasure he craves or the pain of self-denial.

In the Aristotelian tradition, then, choice matters. The defining characteristic of a human being is that he moves toward his end by reason and will. If the right choices were always made for him by someone else, he would not be living the life appropriate for a human being. As we have seen, choice matters even when there are several right choices one could make. Nevertheless, choice is not all that matters. It matters that a person chooses rightly.

Modern theories, in contrast, tend to be voluntaristic in the sense that they place a value on choice that is independent of the value of what is chosen. They do so in different ways. The nineteenth-century will theorists simply assumed that choice matters without explaining why. They defined contract in terms of the will of the parties but they had no theory about why the will should be respected. As Valérie Ranouil said of the French will theorists, "[t]he contract is obligatory simply because it is the contract."[18]

13. Thomas Aquinas, *Summa theologiae* (Madrid: La Editorial Catolica, 1961) at I-II, Q. 10, a. 2; Q. 13, a. 6.
14. Ibid. at I, Q. 19, aa. 3, 10.
15. Ibid. at II–II, Q. 47, a. 2; *Nicomachean Ethics, supra* note 8 at VI. v.
16. Ibid. at II–II Q. 50, a. 3; *Politics, supra* note 11 at I. viii.
17. Ibid. at II–II Q. 123 a. 3; Q. 141 a. 3; *Nicomachean Ethics, supra* note 8 at III. ix 1117ª 30–34; III. x 1117ª 24–25.
18. V. Ranouil, *L'Autonomie de la volonté: naissance et évolution d'un concept* (Paris: Presses universitaires de France, 1980) at 72, quoting E. Gounot, *Le principe de l'autonomie de la volonté*

Some modern theorists have tried to explain why choice matters. This essay will discuss two types of theories. According to one type, which goes back to the utilitarians, the law enforces contracts so that people's preferences can be satisfied to the greatest extent possible. The choices of the contracting parties are respected because they reveal the parties' preferences. In another type of theory, which goes back to Kant and Hegel, choices matter because they are an expression of freedom or autonomy. Contracts are binding because that is a necessary consequence of freedom.

Both types of theory emerged from the crisis through which philosophy passed in the seventeenth and eighteenth centuries. Descartes founded modern critical philosophy on a new method in which the only permissible starting points were matters that could not be doubted and the only legitimate conclusions were those reached by deductive logic. Reason was equated with deductive logic.

This method broke with the Aristotelian tradition. Writers in that tradition had not tried to show by deductive logic that there are better and worse ways to live one's life. They had thought that first principles could only be established dialectically, that is, by showing that if one denied the principle, one would reach absurd conclusions or no conclusions at all. If one denied that the objects of choice can be better or worse, human choice would no longer be meaningful. Nor did they think that choices are to be made by deductive logic. They are made by prudence. Prudence is a reason applied to choice-making. Unlike an animal, which acts out of appetite, a human being can choose a course of action because he understands that it is good. To understand it is good, he uses a type of prudence (*nous* for Aristotle, *intellectus* for Thomas Aquinas) which has been translated as "understanding" or "intuition."[19] To say there is such an ability is simply to say that somehow we are able to see that some choices are better and worse. If we could not, we would never be able to act rightly. To call this ability "prudence" does not explain how it works. In any case, this ability is not deductive logic. Prudent people understand things that they cannot demonstrate.

Applying the new method, philosophers soon discovered that there was no way to prove deductively that some objects of choice were normatively better or worse. John Locke and David Hume concluded that one could only say that the person choosing felt a desire or inclination for something, an inclination that could not be based on reason. According to Locke, "the philosophers of old did in vain inquire whether the *summum bonum* consisted in riches, or bodily delights, or virtue or contemplation; they might have as reasonably disputed, whether the best relish were to be found in apples, plums or nuts."[20] According

en droit privé: Contribution a l'étude critique de l'individualisme juridique (Thesis, Paris 1912) at 129.

19. *Nicomachean Ethics, supra* note 8 at IV. xi; *Summa theologia, supra* note 13 at II–II, Q. 49, c. 2.
20. J. Locke, *Essay on Human Understanding* in *The Works of John Locke* Vol. 1 (London: T. Tegg, W. Sharpe and Son [etc.], 1823) 273 at II.xxi.55.

to Hume, "'Tis not contrary to reason to prefer the destruction of the whole world to the scratching of my finger."[21]

Hume concluded that normative statements are merely statements about one's inclinations. One cannot say that these inclinations are better or worse. The new method of doubting whatever cannot be proved deductively had led exactly where an Aristotelian would have expected: to scepticism that human choice has normative value. For an Aristotelian, however, the very fact that the method led to that conclusion would show that the method is wrong.

After Hume, it might have seemed that philosophers must either reject modern critical philosophy or stop theorizing about ethics. Instead, some of them tried to construct an ethical theory while agreeing with Hume that one cannot say that some objects of choice are normatively better than others. There were two ways to try to do so. One was to claim that choosing in accord with one's inclinations or desires is normatively good whatever the objects of one's choice. The other was to claim it is not, and then find some normative foundation for making a choice other than desire or inclination. Utilitarians such as Jeremy Bentham went the first way. They claimed that what matters normatively is to maximize satisfaction or pleasure, which can, in principle, be measured in units of pleasure and pain called utility. Kant and Hegel went the second way. They claimed that what matters normatively is that a choice be made freely or autonomously. They defined freedom as choice without regard to the choice-maker's inclinations or purposes.

Two hundred years later, when we theorize about contract law, we still find ourselves at the same crossroads, looking in the same two directions. Nevertheless, today, few of the intellectual heirs of Bentham, Kant, and Hegel believe in the concepts that these philosophers regarded as critical to the success of their enterprise. Few believe in utility as a quantity of pleasure or satisfaction, or in freedom as a capacity to choose without regard to one's own inclination or purposes. Modern theorists are right to reject these concepts. They fail to realize, however, that these concepts are central to the philosophical traditions they claim to represent. One cannot make sense of these traditions without these concepts.

We will examine these contemporary theories by considering, first, why the law usually respects the choices of contracting parties, and then, why it sometimes does not. We will see that these are questions that a voluntaristic theory cannot answer. We will then examine some contemporary theories that are not voluntaristic in the sense just described. We will see that they break with the modern philosophical tradition and lead in a direction one can only call Aristotelian.

---

21. D. Hume, *A Treatise of Human Nature*, ed. by L. A. Selby-Bigge (Oxford: Clarendon Press 1888) at 416.

1. WHY THE LAW USUALLY RESPECTS THE PARTIES' CHOICES. We will consider theories based on preference satisfaction and then those based on autonomy.

a. Theories based on preference satisfaction. According to Bentham, what matters is satisfaction or pleasure. It can, in principle, be measured in units of pleasure and pain called "utility."[22] More pleasure is better than less. Bentham claimed that, in general, utility is maximized by allowing people to choose for themselves since "no man can be so good a judge as the man himself, what gives him pleasure or displeasure."[23] Contracts increase utility since each party, in his own judgment, is made better off.

One notorious problem with the theory is that to turn pleasure or satisfaction into a normative principle seems to violate our deepest feelings about morality. It is true that pleasure or satisfaction, for Bentham, is not the same as physical gratification. A dedicated scholar or a martyr for a noble cause supposedly finds study or martyrdom more satisfying than their other alternatives or they would do something else instead. Nevertheless, it is strange to think that what ultimately matters is satisfaction, whatever its source, whether it comes from study or serving a noble cause or idleness or drinking or drugs. No one would think the horror of a rape accompanied by torture is lessened to the extent the perpetrator enjoyed himself. Anyone would be appalled to find his child took pleasure in tearing the wings off flies.

John Stuart Mill tried to escape by claiming that pleasures differed not only in quantity but in quality. "Human beings have faculties more elevated than the animal appetites." One could "assign to the pleasures of the intellect, of the feelings and imagination, and of the moral sentiments a much higher value as pleasures than to those of mere sensation."[24] Critics have pointed out that this answer hardly solves the problem. If the activities of higher value are preferable simply because they are more pleasurable, then pleasure still determines the value of an activity. If they are preferable because they are higher, and higher because they engage our more elevated and distinctively human faculties, then we are back in an Aristotelian world in which some ways of living are more worthwhile than others whether or not they happen to be more pleasurable.

Moreover, for Bentham's utilitarianism to work, "pleasure" or "satisfaction" must be something that accompanies all choices and for the sake of which all choices are made. But why should one think so? It is true that if one person drinks beer on a hot day, another studies, and a third suffers martyrdom because his convictions require it, all three did what they preferred to do under the circumstances. But why should one think that these choices are made to obtain

---

22. J. Bentham, *An Introduction to the Principles of Morals and Legislation,* ed. by J. H. Burns and H. L. A. Hart (London: Athlone Publishers, 1970) at I.i–iv, 11–12; IV.i–vi, 38–40 [hereinafter *Principles of Morals*].

23. Ibid. at XIII.iv, 159.

24. J. S. Mill, *Utilitarianism,* ed. by O. Priest (Indianapolis: The Bobbs-Merril Co., 1957) at 11.

some single thing called "pleasure" or "satisfaction" that accompanies every choice? It is like saying that because people regard what they choose as choice-worthy, their choices are accompanied by "choice-worthiness," and they choose in order to get as much of it as they can.

Fifty years ago, Paul Samuelson noted that many economists "have ceased to believe in the existence of any introspective magnitude or quantity of a cardinal, numerical kind."[25] They had also discovered that they did not need to be utilitarians to build their descriptive models. To draw supply and demand curves, they merely needed to assume that people do prefer some courses of action to others. One could speak of preferences and preference satisfaction without imagining there is some quantity that they are maximizing when they choose what they prefer.

J. R. Hicks claimed that this approach had liberated economists from philosophical commitments. They no longer needed to be utilitarians.[26] That is true. Economists themselves sometimes fail to realize how completely the new approach has emancipated them. Some of them seem to think that when people make choices, they must be maximizing something, even if it is not utility.[27] Under the new approach, however, people need not be maximizing anything at all. Suppose that this morning, in order of preference, I would like to wear my blue, my brown, and my green sports jacket. Suppose that this afternoon, I will go to a committee meeting, because it needs to be done; if there were no meeting, I would shop for groceries, because that needs to be done, too; and if neither needed to be done, I would read a book. The new approach, in effect, assigns numbers to each of these possible choices which indicate the order in which I prefer them. Assigning the numbers says nothing about how or why I make these choices. The new approach assumes no more than that people have preferences, which, by the new approach, is merely to assume that people make choices.

To make normative claims, however, one cannot get by saying so little. Those who make such claims have attached normative value to "efficiency" or "wealth maximization" which they define in terms of preference satisfaction. For Pareto, "efficiency" is improved if one can increase one person's ability to satisfy his preferences without decreasing that of others. To make normative claims for efficiency, one must assume that it is good for people to satisfy more of their preferences. Why should that be?

One possible answer is that satisfaction is good, whatever a person happens to find satisfying. But that answer is really a return to the utilitarian assumptions

25. P. A. Samuelson, *Foundations of Economic Analysis* (Cambridge, MA: Harvard University Press, 1976) at 91.

26. J. R. Hicks, *Value and Capital: An Inquiry into Some Fundamental Principles of Economic Theory* (Oxford: Clarendon Press, 1939).

27. See, for example, M. Trebilcock, *The Limits of Freedom of Contract* (Cambridge, MA: Harvard University Press, 1993) at 2–3 ("[E]conomics assumes that individuals . . . attempt to maximize their desired ends (which may be of infinite variety).").

that economists have rejected. It treats "satisfaction" as something that accompanies every choice and for the sake of which every choice is made.

Another possible answer is that it is good for people to get what they prefer as long as what they prefer is good. To say so is to go in the same direction as John Stuart Mill. As before, we must then assume that some choices are better and worse, and that people have some capacity to choose for the better. We will have returned to something like the Aristotelian idea of a normatively good life and capacities or virtues that enable one to live it.

A third possible answer is to claim that it is good for people to satisfy more of their preferences without regard to whether they thereby live a normatively better life or a more pleasurable or satisfying one. Preference satisfaction means that one gets what one chooses, and a person who does is *ipso facto* better off.

Sometimes economists seem to give that answer. They define a "preference" as that which a person actually chooses. "Thus," Samuelson observed, "the consumer's market behavior is explained in terms of preferences, which are in turn defined only by behavior. The result can very easily be circular. . . ."[28] Circular or not, this procedure is unacceptable for one who claims that preference satisfaction is normatively good. The idea that preference satisfaction is good in itself is hardly a self-evident premise.

Indeed, it contradicts common sense. I have put a hypothetical case to five well-known economists and members of the law and economics movement, one of whom won the Nobel prize. A man whose yacht was sinking radioed his position to the Coast Guard and was told that, for whatever reason, it could not reach him for six days. He got into a lifeboat with a six-pack of beer, which is all that he had on the yacht to drink. He knew (never mind how) that if he drank one can each day, he would survive. Instead, he drank four cans the first day, two the second, and was found dead on the sixth. Is this efficient? Four economists said yes. The fifth (as it happens, the Nobel prize winner), said that it couldn't happen.

Economists who take this position are making a much more radical claim than Aristotle. He merely said that sometimes we choose rightly. They are saying that *ipso facto* all choices are right.

We should not conclude that economics is a false science or that its conclusions do not have normative value. We should conclude that efficiency or wealth maximization are of normative value precisely to the extent that people practice Aristotelian virtues of prudence, courage, and temperance that the economists never mention.

b. Theories based on autonomy. The other approach, which traces back to Kant and Hegel, values choice because it values autonomy or freedom. In one

---

28. *Foundations of Economic Analysis, supra* note 25 at 91. Similarly, Arthur Allen Leff objects that it is "definitionally circular" to say "what people do is good, and its goodness can be determined by what they do." A. A. Leff, "Economic Analysis of Law: Some Realism about Nominalism" (1974) 60 Va. L. Rev. 451 at 458.

respect, the starting point was like that of Bentham. Kant and Hegel described one's choices as based on desire or inclination. According to Kant, to pursue happiness *(Glückseligkeit)* or act on the principle of self-love *(Selbstliebe)* means to seek pleasure *(Lust)* and avoid displeasure *(Unlust)*.[29] As with Bentham, the terms "pleasure" and "pain" are not used to describe physical sensations. Supposedly, a person can perform even the most altruistic acts out of desire or inclination. According to Kant, some people are so constituted that "without any other motive of vanity or self-interest, they find a pleasure in spreading joy around them, and can take delight in the satisfaction of others. . . ."[30] They are nevertheless acting out of a desire to get what they happen to want.

In contrast to Bentham, however, Kant and Hegel denied that choices prompted by desire or inclination were morally significant. A person who follows his desires or inclinations is not acting morally. Indeed, he is not acting freely because his choice depends on something he does not choose: namely, what his desires and inclinations happen to be.[31] They embarked on what an Aristotelian would regard as a doomed enterprise: to explain how a choice can be free and morally significant without regard to the value of what one seeks to have or to do by choosing.

This enterprise required them to define "freedom" in an odd way. To be free, to most people, means to decide for oneself such matters as whom to vote for, whether to marry, whether to buy a new car, or whether to study law rather than medicine. For Kant and Hegel, these choices are not free if they are made in order to have a new president, a spouse, a car, or a career in law or medicine. Although people do make such choices to have something they want, freedom means that a person acts, not because he wants something, but because he is a free and rational being. To be free, an action must have its source in one's self rather than one's inclinations.[32]

The question thus becomes: What would a free and rational being choose, not because it is good for himself or others, but simply because he is free and rational? Our concern here is whether, by asking this question, Kant and Hegel could answer the one we are addressing: Why are promises or contracts binding?

Kant said that a rational being would choose according to the ultimate principle of rationality: the law of noncontradiction. Such a choice is free because it has its source in one's rational nature and not in one's inclinations. Since the law of noncontradiction means that contradictory propositions cannot both be true, Kant concluded that a rational being would act according to a maxim that at the same time he could will to be universal law.[33] Otherwise, he would be willing a contradiction.

---

29. I. Kant, *Kritik der praktischen Vernunft*, in *Werke in Zwolf Bänden*, Vol. 4, ed. by W. Weischedel (Weisbaden: Suhrkamp Verlag, 1956) 107 at 129.
30. I. Kant, *Grundlegung zur Metaphysik der Sitten*, in Vol. 4 ibid., 7 at 24.
31. Ibid. at 79–80.   32. Ibid.   33. Ibid. at 51.

Few people today, even those who are influenced by the Kantian tradition, really think it is possible to get from the law of noncontradiction to rules of conduct. We can see why if we consider Kant's explanation of why promises are binding. A person in hard circumstances might be tempted to borrow money and promise to repay it without intending to keep his promise. But he cannot will universally that people do so. If they did, Kant said, "the promise itself would become impossible, as well as the end that one might have in view in it, since no one would consider that anything was promised to him, but would ridicule all such statements as vain pretences."[34]

As Roger Sullivan noted, one can understand that argument in three different ways.[35] While Sullivan thought any of them would work, in fact, none of them does. First, the contradiction might be "pragmatic": If the person under hard circumstances willed that everyone could break promises, he would be willing a world in which no one would lend money to him on the strength of his own promise.[36] His own end would be thwarted if everyone played by the same rules. But surely, he could imagine rules by which he could achieve his end even if everyone played by them. He might will universally that astute people break promises, or people in sufficiently hard circumstances, or people who confront such circumstances for some particular reason, such as having loved not wisely but too well.

Second, the contradiction might be "conceptual": Promises by their very definition are binding, and so one cannot will universally that they are not.[37] It is true, of course, to will that promises never bind would be a logical contradiction, like willing that brakes never stop cars or circulatory systems never circulate blood. But that does not explain why the brakes or circulatory systems or promises should exist at all.[38] With brakes or blood vessels, the answer is

---

34. Ibid. at 53.
35. R. J. Sullivan, *Immanuel Kant's Moral Theory* (New York: Cambridge University Press, 1989) at 169–170, taking these distinctions from C. M. Korsgaard, "Kant's Formula of Universal Law," (1985) 6 Pac. Phil. Q. 24.
36. Harrison interprets Kant that way, and so finds his argument unsatisfactory. J. Harrison, "Kant's Examples of the First Formulation of the Categorical Imperative," in R. P. Wolff, ed., *Kant: A Collection of Critical Essays* (Garden City, NY: Anchor Books, 1967) 228 at 235–236.
37. Kemp approves of Kant's argument because he interprets him in this way, but his reason is merely that this interpretation is not subject to the objections one can make to the pragmatic contradiction. J. Kemp, "Kant's Examples of the Categorical Imperative," 252–253 in Wolff, ibid., 246 at 252–253. Korsgaard agrees with Kant because she confuses the conceptual with the pragmatic contradiction. She thinks the conceptual contradiction is that if we conceive of a world where promises are not kept "the practice of offering and accepting promises would have died out under stress of too many violations." See Korsgaard, *supra* note 35 at 28. But that is the pragmatic contradiction: If no one keeps promises, the deceitful promisor will find no one to believe him.
38. Thus Murphy objects that "the concept of making a promise presupposes some empirical social institutions." He regards the categorical imperative as a "metaethics" which only identifies the conditions under which a code of conduct would be rational. J. G. Murphy, *Kant: The Philosophy of Right* (London: Macmillan, 1970) at 42, 46. Similarly, John Searle revived the conceptual argument by showing that the very definition of a promise allowed one to infer, from

functional: Drivers need to stop, and animal cells need nourishment. Is the answer functional in the case of promising?

If so, then the contradiction is "teleological": Promise breaking is inconsistent with the purpose of promising. But then the question is, whose purposes? Kant did not want to say that promises must be binding for people to achieve their own purposes. Pursuit of those purposes is not morally significant. Moreover, in that event, whether and when a promise is binding would depend on how these purposes might best be accomplished, just as the structure of a brake depends on when and at what speed a driver needs to stop. Instead, in some passages, Kant suggested that "nature" has a purpose in giving us our faculties, and that is why we must cultivate them.[39] The purpose of speech, he said, is to communicate our thoughts. It would be inconsistent with it to lie or break promises.[40] Kant's most sympathetic followers have thought this argument is inconsistent with his claim that a choice is free and rational when it is not made for any further purpose.[41] Moreover, in Kant's world, is hard to see how "nature" could have ends or why people should respect them.

Hegel realized that some other way had to be found to get from the concept of a free and rational being to institutions such as promise or contract. To do so, he invented a strange method which was neither deductive logic nor a functional analysis but seems to have the properties of both. According to Hegel, the free will, in order to be self determining, must embody itself in something that is other than the will itself and nevertheless is not determined by inclination; therefore, a person must have the capacity to own "things," "things" being whatever is not free.[42] But the will does not achieve its full determination merely by owning things since it is then related merely to that which is other than itself. It becomes fully actualized only through relation to another will, and does so through contract where the will of one party, with respect to something owned, becomes identical to the will of the other, so that ownership is transferred.[43]

---

the fact that a promise had been made, that it ought to be kept. J. Searle, "How to Derive 'Ought' from 'Is'" (1964) 73 Phil. Rev. 43. But he later explained that the "ought" in question was one internal to the practice of promising. One could still reject the practice entirely or argue that some promises do not need to be kept, which is the point I am making here. J. Searle, *Speech Acts* (London: Cambridge University Press, 1969) at 188–189. See R. Craswell, "Contract Law, Default Rules, and the Philosophy of Promising" (1989) 88 Mich. L. Rev. 489 at 495–496 [hereinafter "Philosophy of Promising"].

39. *Grundlegung der Metaphysik der Sitten, supra* note 30 at 54, 57. Similarly, nature's purpose in giving us reason is not so that we can be happy but so that we act morally, since if nature had merely intended us to be happy, it could have done so more effectively by some other means. Ibid. at 20.

40. I. Kant, *Die Metaphysik der Sitten,* in *Werke,* vol. 4, *supra* note 29, 303 at 563.

41. Sullivan, *supra* note 35 at 190–91; J. R. Silber, "The Highest Good in Kant's Ethics," (1963) 73 Ethics 179 at 187–188, 190; M. Gregor, *Laws of Freedom* (London: Blackwell, 1963) at 134–135.

42. G. W. F. Hegel, *Grundlinien der Philosophie des Rechts,* ed. by G. Lasson (1911) at §§41–46.

43. Ibid. at §§71–75.

My problem is that I don't see why this explanation counts as an explanation. Like deductive logic, this method tries to show there is a necessary relationship among concepts: The will is free, an external thing is not free and therefore other than the will. But it is not deductive logic of the sort a mathematician uses. Like a functional analysis, it concerns how a free being would solve some sort of a problem: Such a being needs to be actualized or determined or embodied. But it is not a functional analysis. Nothing is said about why a free being encounters such a problem or the constraints under which he must solve it. If the explanation is neither logical nor functional, it is hard to see what it explains.

Few contracts theorists today are Hegelians. Peter Benson and Alan Brudner are notable exceptions.[44] It is to their credit that they see clearly what Hegel saw: that if one wishes to get from the idea of a free and rational being to the institution of contract, one cannot do so as Kant did, by way of the categorical imperative. One cannot do so at all unless Hegel's method is valid. If it is not, then the entire Kantian-Hegelian enterprise was impossible from the start.

Most contemporary contracts theorists who write in the Kantian tradition are no longer engaged in this enterprise. They do not try to show that a free and rational being would regard certain rules as binding without regard to any purpose that such a being wants to pursue. They are Kantians only in the sense that they place freedom or reason at the apex of their theories. Contract law exists for the sake of freedom or rationality. But then, how is one to get from such empty concepts to any definite conclusions about contract law? The difficulties are illustrated by the work of Charles Fried and Ernest Weinrib.

Fried places freedom at the apex. The purpose of the institution of promising is to be as free as possible. "In order that I be as free as possible, that my will have the greatest possible range consistent with the similar will of others, it is necessary that there be a way in which I can commit myself."[45] But as Benson notes, to speak of the largest possible range of choice is to imagine that quantities of freedom that can be larger or smaller.[46] But what would make one range of choices larger or smaller than another?[47] It cannot be the number of alternatives among which a person might choose, whether he wants them or not.[48] It

---

44. P. Benson, "Abstract Right and the Possibility of a Nondistributive Conception of Contract: Hegel and Contemporary Contract Theory" (1989) 10 Cardozo L. Rev. 1077 [hereinafter "Abstract Right"]; A. Brudner, "Reconstructing Contracts" (1993) 43 U. T. L. J. 1.

45. C. Fried, *Contract as Promise: A Theory of Contractual Obligation* (Cambridge, MA: Harvard University Press, 1981) at 13. As Benson notes, in doing so, he breaks with Kant. Kant wanted to conceive of duty, not in terms of purpose, but "in complete abstraction from our wants and needs." "Abstract Right," *supra* note 44 at 1109.

46. "Abstract Right," *supra* note 44 at 1109.

47. As Johnson notes in his criticism of Fried, "individual autonomy can be maximized and distributed in many different ways. . . ." C. D. Johnson, "The Idea of Autonomy and the Foundations of Contractual Liberty," (1983) 2 L. and Phil. 271 at 283.

48. As noted by F. H. Buckley, "Paradox Lost"(1988) 72 Minn. L. Rev. 775 at 816, 824; Trebilcock, *supra* note 27 at 165.

cannot be the extent to which a person can choose what he wants since then the scope of each person's freedom would depend on the extent of his desires.

Moreover, if the institution of promising is explained as a means of increasing our freedom, the rules that govern that institution should be those that serve this purpose. Fried seems to be afraid of that possibility. He asks why a person should keep a promise, if, in a particular case, to break it would extend his own range of freedom, and the promisee has not changed his position in reliance. He answers that even though, by hypothesis, the promisee has not relied on the promise, nevertheless, the promisor has inspired his "trust" and led him to become "vulnerable."[49] Therefore, to break the promise would be contrary to "Kantian principles of trust and respect."[50] Presumably, however, the promisee has been treated with disrespect only if the promisor has violated the rules that govern the institution of promising. As Fried's critics have noted, nothing in his theory tells us what those rules are.[51] Yet his answer assumes that breaking a promise is always a violation of them. But why should that be, if, under the circumstances, keeping the promise does not serve the purpose for which this institution is established?

In contrast, although Weinrib speaks of freedom, he places rationality or coherence at the apex of his theory. He tries to show that there is a rational structure immanent in contract law as we know it. This structure, he believes, is captured by the Aristotelian concept of commutative (or corrective) justice: A contract of exchange is a single transaction in which each party transfers something equivalent in value to what he receives.[52]

While his conclusion sounds Aristotelian, Weinrib claims that his approach is Kantian because it values rationality without regard to the purposes of the parties or society. The rational structure of contract law does not depend upon the purposes of the parties since the definition of commutative justice abstracts from the particular performances they wish to give and receive. This structure does not depend upon social purposes which are external to the transaction because, were the rules of contract law shaped by any such purpose, they would have to favor one party over the other and so violate commutative justice. Moreover, they would necessarily extend beyond the interaction of the two parties to the exchange which is all that matters from the standpoint of commutative justice.[53]

49. Fried, *supra* note 45 at 16.
50. Ibid. at 17.
51. Trebilcock, *supra* note 27 at 165; P. Benson, "Contract" in D. Patterson, ed., *A Companion to Philosophy of Law and Legal Theory* 24 at 39 (London: Blackwell, 1996) 24 at 39 [hereinafter "Contract"]; A. T. Kronman, "A New Champion for the Will Theory" (1981) 91 Yale Law. J. 404 at 409; "Philosophy of Promising", *supra* note 38 at 490; M. A. Eisenberg, "The Theory of Contracts," this volume, pp. 223ff [hereinafter "Theory of Contracts"].
52. E. J. Weinrib, *The Idea of Private Law* (Cambridge, MA: Harvard University Press, 1995) at 73, 83 [hereinafter *Private Law*].
53. Ibid. at 212–213.

He links his position to Kant's by pointing out that for Kant, a free choice is one made with regard to its rational form but not with regard to any particular purpose.[54] Nevertheless, his real reason for wanting to abstract from purpose seems to be that otherwise, contract law as we know it would not be coherent. That is what his arguments against a purposive account are designed to prove. Unlike Kant, he does not try to show that any free and rational being must respect the rules of commutative justice.[55]

Consequently, the question that Ken Kress and others have asked Weinrib is: why, then, does coherence matter?[56] His answer to Kress was that any justification of anything must be coherent.[57] That is true, but one cannot ask people to obey rules or a society to enforce them merely because they are coherent. Even if one could, Weinrib doesn't claim the rules of contract law as we know it are the only coherent ones possible.

The problem here is like the one encountered by contemporary theories of preference satisfaction. Once one rejects the original utilitarian claim that choices are made for the sake of pleasure or satisfaction, "preference satisfaction" means little more than "choosing." Similarly, once one rejects the Kantian and Hegelian claim that a free and rational being would be bound by certain rules without regard to his purposes, "freedom" and "rationality" mean little more than "choosing" and "thinking coherently." While those ideas might figure in a theory of contract, one cannot build a theory on them alone.

2. WHY THE LAW SOMETIMES DOES NOT RESPECT THE PARTIES' CHOICES. Thus far we have seen that if all that matters is preference satisfaction or autonomy, we cannot even explain why the law usually honors the choices that the contracting parties make. We now turn to the question of why the law sometimes does not do so. Sometimes, it does not allow people to contract even when the rights of third parties are not affected. For example, it prohibits prostitution, the sale of addictive drugs or dangerous products, and contracts to work under unsafe conditions or to sell oneself into slavery.

From an Aristotelian standpoint, choices are right or wrong depending on whether they contribute or detract from the sort of life a human being ought to live. Consequently, we can see why sometimes an individual's decisions can be trumped. They may be seriously wrong. Some contracts may be incompatible

---

54. Ibid. at 83, 90, 97; E. J. Weinrib, "Law as a Kantian Idea of Reason" (1987) 87 Colum. L. Rev. 472 at 483; E. J. Weinrib, "The Jurisprudence of Legal Formalism" (1993) 16 Harv. J. L. and Pub. Pol. 583 at 590.

55. As noted by S. R. Perry, "Professor Weinrib's Formalism: The Not-so-empty Sepulchre" (1993) 16 Harv. J. L. and Pub. Pol. 597 at 603.

56. K. Kress, "Coherence and Formalism," (1993) 16 Harv. J. L. and Pub. Pol. 639 at 682; L. Röckrath, "Umverteilung durch Privatrecht?" (1997) 83 Archiv für Rechts- und Sozialphilosophie 506 at 513.

57. E. J. Weinrib, "Formalism and Practical Reason, or How to Avoid Seeing Ghosts in the Empty Sepulchre" (1993) 16 Harv. J. L. and Pub. Pol. 683 at 695 [hereinafter "Formalism and Practical Reason"].

with a good life (for example, prostitution). Others may sacrifice something that is good to something of lesser value or no value. Some drugs dominate one's life; some working conditions expose it to too great a risk; some renunciations of one's freedom (such as selling oneself into slavery) are unlikely to be worth the price.

One might think that the problem, from an Aristotelian standpoint, is to explain why an individual's choices are trumped so rarely. Cass Sunstein thinks that one who has a "substantive conception of the good" must face the "theoretical task [of] generat[ing] an antiliberal theory of the good life that is to be imposed in the face of plural and conflicting conceptions on the part of private citizens" and the "institutional problem" of explaining "to what institution might we give power to implement decisions of this sort?"[58] He seems to think a "substantive conception of the good" is something like the ideology of a one-party state. Writers in the Aristotelian tradition did believe that, substantively, some choices are right and others wrong. As we have seen, however, they did not think that people know right from wrong by a theory, let alone an ideology. They know by prudence, which is the capacity each person has to see what contributes to a good life. It is true that when a person chooses imprudently, his contract does not serve the ultimate end of living such a life. In some cases, the law will not enforce it. Nevertheless, writers in the Aristotelian tradition agreed that the law should not refuse to enforce a contract merely because it was imprudent.[59] While they do not elaborate, there are several reasons why, from an Aristotelian standpoint, the law should respect decisions that are imprudent or even seriously wrong.

To begin with, in the Aristotelian tradition, the defining characteristic of a human being is that he acts through reason. Prudence is reason applied to action. Thus, even if a person will choose wrongly, it does not follow that he would be better off if the right choice were made for him. Quite the opposite. If all of his choices were made for him, he would no longer be living a human life.

Moreover, in the Aristotelian tradition, virtues such as prudence are acquired by practice. A person allowed to choose for himself will make mistakes just as he does in learning a sport or a foreign language. But if he does not choose for himself, he will never learn.

In addition, there are some right choices that one cannot make for a person who lacks certain virtues. Suppose a person does not value literature or music because he has imprudently devoted all his time to making money, not for the

---

58. C. R. Sunstein, "Disrupting Voluntary Choices" in S. W. Chapman and J. R. Pennock, eds., *Markets and Justice* (New York: New York University Press, 1989) 279 at 297.

59. Soto thought that a sufficiently imprudent promise was not binding, at least in conscience. Dominicus de Soto, *De iustitia et iure libri decem* lib. 4, q. 7, a. 1 (1553). Molina and Lessius believed that even such a promise was binding. Ludovicus Molina, *De iustitia et iure tractatus* disp. 271, no. 4 (1614); Leornardus Lessius, *De iustitia et iure, ceterique virtutibus cardinalis libri quatuor* lib. 2, cap. 18, dub. 6, no. 9 (1628).

good he can do with it, but for its own sake. To force him to acquire books or concert tickets would be pointless.[60]

Finally, in a democratic society, there is a special reason for allowing each person to choose for himself. To the extent that a society is democratic, virtue, or the capacity to make the right choices, does not entitle a person to make choices for others. If it did, the society would not be a democracy but an aristocracy, which, for Aristotle, means rule by the virtuous (not rule by the rich or well-born, which is oligarchy). "[T]wo principles are characteristic of democracy, the government of the majority and freedom."[61] Freedom, to the citizens of a democracy, means that "a man should live as he likes."[62] According to Aristotle, it would be mistake, and one that undermines democracy, to think that this principle means each person should live however he likes, whether virtuously or not.[63] But to say that people should be virtuous does not mean that the virtuous should rule. The principles of a democracy are that each person "should be ruled by none, if possible," and if not possible, then by the majority.[64]

Modern writers find it much harder to explain why the law does not enforce certain contracts. Bentham's explanation was that, while an individual was likely to know best what gave him pleasure or satisfaction, he might be wrong. A choice could be trumped when it was clear that some other choice would really give him more satisfaction. As before, that explanation depends on the idea that "satisfaction" or "pleasure" is an homogenous quantity for the sake of which choices are made. Most contemporary theorists who speak of preference satisfaction have rejected that idea. Having done so, they have difficulty explaining why preferences should ever be trumped. Posner says it is "puzzling from an economic standpoint" that a husband cannot burn himself to death on his wife's funeral pyre, that Shylock cannot enforce his contract with Antonio, and that a person cannot sell himself into slavery.[65]

Kant's position was more complicated. He said that people had a moral duty to cultivate their talents, curb their sexual desires, and so forth, because people should respect the purposes for which "nature" gave us our faculties. As mentioned earlier, most modern scholars find that idea inconsistent with the rest of his philosophy. Kant then claimed that the law should not require people to act morally because actions performed from fear of punishment are not free and therefore are not morally significant.[66] Then, for reasons that modern scholars

60. See Thomas' discussion of why it does not belong to human law to repress all vices, *Summa Theologiae, supra* note 13 at I–II, Q. 96, a. 2.
61. *Politics, supra* note 11 at V.ix 1310ᵃ 27–29.
62. Ibid. at V.ix 1310ᵃ 30–31; VI.ii 1317ᵇ 14–16.
63. Ibid. at V.ix 1310ᵃ 27–29.
64. Ibid. at VI.ii 1317ᵇ 14–16.
65. R. Posner, *Economic Analysis of Law,* 2nd ed. (Boston: Little Brown, 1977) at 187.
66. *Metaphysik der Sitten, supra* note 40 at 346–347.

find obscure,[67] he insisted that certain immoral actions such as prostitution and bestiality should be prohibited.[68] He therefore left his intellectual successors with no viable explanation of how to limit the principle that choices should be respected. According to Charles Fried, to tell a person that he may not do something is to "infantilize" him.[69] Yet the law sometimes does so.

Some writers in the utilitarian and Kantian traditions have concluded that the law should not trump people's choices. Others have tried to explain why sometimes it should. They typically discuss the process by which a person chooses. The process may or may not lead a person to choose what he truly prefers or enable him to make a genuinely free decision. A process that does is more consistent with preference satisfaction or autonomy.

One wants to ask: Is the process supposed to be better only because it helps a person to choose what he truly prefers (or to choose more freely)? Or is the process better because it leads to choices that are better – better because they have a normative value that is not due entirely to the fact that they are preferred or freely chosen? In the latter case, we seem to have returned to an Aristotelian world in which there are better and worse choices, and a distinctively human capacity, that cannot be reduced to deductive logic, to tell which are which.

Some contemporary writers are not clear on this point. Often, however, they hint, at the very least, that the process is of value, in part, because of the normative value of the outcomes to which it leads. According to Cass Sunstein, autonomy means, not merely choice, but choices made with full information and "a full vivid awareness of available opportunities."[70] While he regards such choices as more free, he does not seem to value them simply for that reason. He presumably would not think the choice of a rapist is of greater value if it is made with vivid awareness of available opportunities. Autonomous choices, he seems to think, will be more likely to reflect a higher type of welfare, welfare that is promoted "not by satisfying current preferences" but rather those "consonant with the best or highest conception of human happiness."[71]

Margaret Radin objects that if we value choice, whatever is chosen, we must assume implicitly that raping benefits rapists, which would be inconsistent with any sound conception of "human flourishing."[72] She argues for a "positive view of liberty that includes proper self-development as necessary for freedom."[73] It is not clear that her concept of self-development or flourishing is a substantive

---

67. See, for example, A. D. Rosen, *Kant's Theory of Justice* (Ithaca, NY: Cornell University Press, 1993) at 22.
68. *Metaphysik der Sitten, supra* note 40 at 445, 488.
69. Fried, *supra* note 45 at 21.
70. C. R. Sunstein, "Preferences and Politics" (1991) 20 Phil. and Pub. Aff. 3 at 11.
71. Ibid. at 9
72. M. J. Radin, "Market-Inalienability," (1987) 100 Harv. L. Rev. 1849 at 1884.
73. Ibid. at 1899.

one. She speaks about freedom, about "identity" in the sense of "the integrity and continuity of self," and about "contextuality" in the sense of "the necessity of self-constitution in relation to the environment of things and other people."[74] She is not so clear about what the self might value other than itself. Knowledge, beauty, love, service to others? If there is no intrinsic reason the self should value such things, then "self" seems an empty conception. If there is, she is moving toward a substantive idea of human flourishing.

Anthony Kronman believes that some paternalistic legislation protects people against their own bad judgment. Good judgment is not instrumental rationality which concerns the choice of means. It is "skill in [the] choice of ends."[75] According to Kronman, this skill requires deliberation, and therefore is different than the Aristotelian virtue of prudence by which one can see without deliberating that an end is worth pursuing.[76] One wonders how a person could deliberate about ends if he did not see, before doing so, that some ends were worthwhile. Be that as it may, Kronman, like Aristotle, seems to think that some ends are better than others, and that people have a capacity to know which are which.[77]

However it may be with these other writers, with Joseph Raz we truly seem to have reentered an older world. According to Raz, people "engage in what they do because they believe it to be a valuable, worthwhile activity."[78] That is a matter about which they may be right or wrong.[79] "To the extent that their valuation is misguided it affects the success of their life."[80] "A person who spends all his time gambling has, other things being equal, less successful a life, even if he is a successful gambler, than a live stock farmer busily minding his farm."[81] Consequently, the value of these goals is not due entirely to the fact that they are chosen. "People adopt and pursue goals because they believe in their independent value, that is, their value is believed to be at least in part independent of the fact that they were chosen and are pursued."[82] "[A] person's well-being

---

74. Ibid. at 1904.
75. A. T. Kronman, "Paternalism in the Law of Contracts," (1983) 92 Yale Law J. 763 at 790.
76. Ibid. at 790, 790 n. 87.
77. That being so, one wonders why Kronman explains only some paternalistic legislation as an effort to protect people against bad judgment: for example, laws that require a "cooling off" period or refuse to enforce the contracts of minors. In contrast, he says that a contract by which a person gives away too much of his liberty is unenforceable to protect him against a loss of self-respect if his goals should change. Ibid. 774–86. One wonders why the contract is not an instance of bad judgment if it is so threatening to one's self respect that it shouldn't be enforced. A warranty of habitability cannot be waived, according to Kronman, either because a tenant should buy such a warranty even if he prefers not to, or in order to redistribute wealth from landlords to tenants. Ibid. at 771–174. But in the first case, there again seems to be bad judgment, and in the second, merely an odd form of rent control.
78. J. Raz, *The Morality of Freedom* (New York: Oxford University Press, 1986) at 298–299.
79. "[T]he satisfaction of goals based on false reasons does not contribute to one's well-being. . . ." Ibid. at 302.
80. Ibid.   81. Ibid.
82. Ibid. at 308. Such goals have an "impersonal value" which is "their value judged independently of the fact that this agent does or can engage in them." Ibid. at 299. Such goals are pursued

depends on the value of his goals and pursuits."[83] Raz argues that a respect for "well-being" provides with stronger reasons than conventional liberalism for respecting "autonomy." Be that as it may, his theory is not voluntaristic in the sense described earlier. Choice matters, in part, because of the value of what is chosen. "[P]ursuit of the morally repugnant cannot be defended on the ground that being an autonomous choice endows it with any value."[84]

Indeed, once one becomes concerned with what people choose, as these writers are, it is hard to think that the normative value of a choice could depend entirely on whether it is what they truly prefer or whether they choose it freely. These writers are concerned because some people choose, for example, to use drugs, to buy or sell sex, to work under unsafe conditions, or to commit rape. It is hard to see how the process of choice is relevant to this concern unless the process should lead to different substantive results. It is hard to see how it could unless some results are substantively better, and the process helps people to choose rightly.

Moreover, the question to be answered is why the law sometimes trumps the parties' choices, for example, by prohibiting drugs, prostitution, or unsafe working conditions. Such laws are not enacted to help people to identify what they truly prefer or to help them choose freely. If they were, they would be useless except when prohibiting something leads people to reconsider why they want it. Lawmakers enact them, not to encourage reflective decision-making, but because they believe that drugs are harmful, sex should not be commercialized, and working conditions ought to be safe.

Still more fundamentally, if all that ultimately matters is what people prefer and whether they choose freely, there can be no criterion for what they ought to prefer or to choose. Absent any such criterion, it is hard to see how there could be better and worse processes for making a choice. Presumably, one should consider one's alternatives, taking everything relevant into account. But without a criterion, one could not tell what is relevant. If it doesn't matter what one does, thinking about what to do is pointless. Admittedly, the criterion for making a choice might be something one already wants or has previously chosen. One might choose to steal a car because one wants it, or choose not to steal it because one has decided never to steal. But the question then arises, why did one want the car, or decide not to steal? Was that a genuine preference or a truly free choice? And if that choice was also made on the basis of a previous choice, how was the previous choice made? Sooner or later one must arrive at a criterion or standard for choosing that is not itself a choice. That is the reason Thomas Aquinas gave why there must be an end for human choice which is not itself chosen but for the sake of which choices are made.[85] Otherwise the regress would be infinite.

---

for reasons that are believed to be "impersonal" which "means that they are judged inasmuch as they are reasons to all, regardless of their desires or goals." Ibid. at 299 n. 1.
83. Ibid. at 298.   84. Ibid. at 418.
85. *Summa theologiae, supra* note 13, at II–I, Q. 1, a. 4.

B. *Purchasing Power and the Virtue of Distributive Justice*

One condition, then, for contract to improve the way resources are allocated is that people must not only choose, but choose rightly. A second condition is that people have the amount of purchasing power that they should have. Writers in the Aristotelian tradition believed that it is possible for some people to have more and others less than they should, or to put it another way, for the distribution of purchasing power to be just or unjust. When they discussed distributive justice, they did not recommend a set of institutions that would ensure a fair distribution of wealth. They did discuss the principles that make a distribution fair or unfair.

The ultimate reason for caring about distribution of wealth, they tell us, is that people need external things if they are to live good lives. But that does not mean that resources are allocated by asking what particular things each person needs and assigning them to him. Hugo Grotius pointed out that such a system could work only if a society is very small and its members on quite good terms.[86] In any event, each person's own decision about what he most needs would then be subject to the judgment of an allocator rather than left to his own prudence. Most writers in the Aristotelian tradition do not even consider the possibility. For them, distributive justice is concerned with giving each person a proper share of resources.

Ideally, each citizen should receive a share that is proportional to his "merit" or "desert." There is, however, no single principle for appraising merit. Aristotle and Thomas Aquinas mention two different and conflicting ones and hint that there is some truth in both. According to one principle, which would be favored in a democracy, every person ideally should have the same amount. As we have seen, to the extent a society is democratic, greater virtue, meaning a greater capacity to make the right choices, does not entitle a person to make more choices. According to the other principle, which would be favored in an aristocracy, those who have a superior virtue should ideally have a larger share.[87]

Here, equality (or inequality) of resources should not be confused with equality (or inequality) of welfare as a utilitarian or a modern economist would imagine it. True welfare or happiness, in the Aristotelian tradition, is not defined in terms of utility or preference satisfaction but in terms of leading a good life. To say that resources are distributed equally in a democracy does not mean that people are equally able to lead such a life since, democracy or not, the virtuous are better able to make choices and will be able to live better. Equality means equal power to command resources, what we might call equal purchasing power. It is the sort of equality that Ronald Dworkin describes as "equality

---

86. H. Grotius, *De iure belli ac pacis libri tres,* ed. by B.J.A. de Kanter-van Hettinga Tromp (Leiden: E.J. Brill, 1939) at II.ii.2.
87. *Nicomachean Ethics, supra* note 8 at V.iv 1131^b–1132^b; *Summa theologiae, supra* note 13 at II–II, Q. 61, a. 2.

of resources" in contrast to "equality in welfare." As an illustration, he imagined shipwrecked sailors on an island dividing its resources equally by auction-
ing them off, all bids to be made in clam shells, and each sailor to start with an
equal number of shells.[88] My image in an earlier article was similar: heirs auc-
tioning the items in an estate by bidding in poker chips, each starting with an
equal number.[89]

Writers in the Aristotelian tradition made it clear that these two principles
are ideals. They did not propose that a democracy confiscate the wealth of rich
people, or even rich people of distinctly limited moral capacity, and divide it
equally. Aristotle warned against doing so.[90] We can see why if we consider his
objections – with which Thomas concurred – to Plato's proposal to abolish
private property. Do so, Aristotle said, and there will be endless quarrels, and
people will have no incentive to work and to take care of property.[91]

For Thomas Aquinas, this argument explained a conclusion reached by the
medieval canon lawyers. In one of their authoritative texts, St. Ambrose ad-
monished rich people who refused to help the poor: "Let no one call his own
what is common."[92] The canon lawyers interpreted this text to mean that that even
private property is common in the sense that one who has enough for himself
must assist others. Moreover, in a state of necessity, property becomes literally
common so that a starving person is entitled to take the property of another.[93]
Thomas concluded that all property would be held in common were it not for
the disadvantages of common ownership mentioned by Aristotle. But because
private ownership is instituted as a remedy, the rights of an owner are not absolute but extend only so far as necessary to effect a remedy. That is why the
canonists were right that those who have more than enough for their own needs
are obligated to give to others, and why, in a state of necessity, a person can take
what he needs to survive.[94]

These conclusions became staples of the Aristotelian tradition. They were
accepted by Soto, Molina, and Lessius, and then by natural lawyers such as
Grotius and Pufendorf. While these authors developed them in different ways,
they all say that by nature, or originally, or in principle, all things belong to
everyone. They all describe private ownership as instituted to overcome the

---

88. R. Dworkin, "What is Equality? Part 2: Equality of Resources" (1981) 10 Phil. and Pub. Aff.
283 at 283–290 [hereinafter "What is Equality?"].
89. J. Gordley, "Equality in Exchange" (1981) 69 Cal. L. Rev. 1587 at 1614–15.
90. *Politics, supra* note 11 at V.5 1304^b; V.9 1310^a; VI.3 1318^a 25–26; VI.5 1319^b–1320^a.
91. Ibid. at II.v; *Summa theologiae, supra* note 13 at II–II, Q. 66, a. 2.
92. *Decretum Gratiani* in E. Friedberg, ed., *Corpus iuris canonici,* Vol. 1(E. Friedberg, ed., 1876)
at D.47 c. 8.
93. *Glossa ordinaria* to *Decretum Gratiani,* D. 47 c. 8 to *commune* (1595). Similarly, ibid. to D. 1
c. 7, to *communis omnium; Glossa ordinaria* to *Decretales Gregorii IX,* 5.18.3 to *poenitaet*
(1595). The *Gloss* cited a Roman legal text which provided that all passengers had a right to
share the provisions on a ship if food ran short during a voyage. Dig. 14.2.2.2.
94. *Summa theologiae, supra* note 13 at Q. 66, a. 7.

disadvantages of common ownership, usually the ones mentioned by Aristotle and Thomas.[95] Therefore, they regarded the rights of a private owner as limited, usually in the ways mentioned by Thomas.[96]

Subject to these limitations, however, they agreed that one person could not deprive another of his property. The owner may have more than he ideally should since an incentive must be given to work and to manage. By establishing the incentives, the society has recognized that a person is entitled to the larger share than his work and good management brings him.

We can see, then, why they might not have been troubled by Robert Nozick's observation that voluntary transactions will necessarily conflict with a distribution of wealth based on citizenship or virtue or any similar characteristic. Nozick asked us to suppose that the distribution is just according to any such principle, and then to imagine that Wilt Chamberlin, a famous basketball player, agrees to play extra games in his spare time which are attended by a million people, each of whom pays him personally twenty-five cents for doing so. Nozick asked whether the distribution is now unjust, and if so why, since the original distribution was just, and each person was entitled to spend his money as he chose.[97] He is correct that the distribution will deviate from the ideal when people pay Chamberlin to induce him to play extra games. That is another way of saying, as the writers in the Aristotelian tradition recognized, that the ideal must be compromised to provide an incentive for people to work or to manage property effectively. It may therefore take "continual interference," as Nozick suggested, to prevent the ideal from being too severely compromised.[98] It doesn't follow that there is some logical contradiction between seeking justice and providing these incentives, or that Chamberlin has an absolute right to whatever he can charge.

Other modern writers have thought it strange that accidents or natural events are allowed to change a supposedly just distribution.[99] Writers in the Aristotelian tradition surely knew that they would. In Roman law, as in modern law, *res pereat domino:* The owner bears the loss if his property perishes. They recognized that a merchant must charge a price that reflects, not only his labor and expense, but the risks he assumes such as the risk that his goods will be de-

95. Soto, *De iustitia et iure, supra* note 59 at lib. 4, q. 3, a. 1; Molina, *De iustitia et iure, supra* note 59 at disp. 20; Lessius, *De iustitia et iure, supra* note 59 at lib. 2, cap. 5, dubs. 1–2; Grotius, *De iure belli ac pacis,* II.ii.2; S. Pufendorf, *De iure naturae et gentium libri octo* II.vi.5; IV.iv.4–7 (1688).

96. Soto, *De iustitia et iure, supra* note 59 at lib. 5, q. 3, a. 4; Molina, *De iustitia et iure, supra* note 59 at disp. 20; Lessius, *De iustitia et iure, supra* note 59 at lib. 2, cap. 12, dub. 12; Grotius, *De iure belli ac pacis, supra* note 86 at II.ii.6–7; Pufendorf, *De iure naturae et gentium, ibid.* at II.vi.5.

97. R. Nozick, *Anarchy, State and Utopia* (New York: Basic Books, 1974) at 161.

98. Ibid. at 163.

99. S. R. Perry, "The Moral Foundations of Tort Law" (1992) 77 Iowa L. Rev. 449 at 451 [hereinafter "Moral Foundations"]; E. J. Weinrib, "Corrective Justice" (1992) 77 Iowa L. Rev. 403 at 420 [hereinafter "Corrective Justice"].

stroyed accidentally.[100] Nevertheless, they do not explain why, if the point of distributive justice is to ensure that each citizen has a fair share of wealth, random events are allowed to change the distribution.

One answer, however, seems to be implicit in their account of private property. Private property is supposed to provide an incentive to work and to prevent quarrels. To eliminate chance gains and losses, a society would have to distinguish them from gains and losses that are the result of labor and care. It may not be possible to do so. Even if it were, the attempt might lead to so many charges of arbitrariness as to cause the quarrels that a system of private property is supposed to prevent.

Moreover, some resources are more vulnerable to chance destruction than others. Some decisions about what to produce or consume are more prone to error. If everyone were fully compensated when his property was destroyed or his decisions were thwarted by bad luck, those who had chosen to hold more vulnerable property or to embark on riskier projects would use up a greater share of resources than those who did not. A person who chose to live in a glass house, to pick an extreme example, might use up five or ten houses in the same time another person would use up one. Thus, rather than conserving a given distribution of wealth, such a system of compensation would transfer wealth from those whose property was less vulnerable to those whose property was more vulnerable, from those whose projects were more conservative those whose projects were more adventurous.

Writers in the Aristotelian tradition do not make these arguments expressly. They seem to assume that once one adopts a system of private property, one adopts along with it the rule, *res pereat domino*. But they may have had an understandable difficulty seeing how a system of private property was supposed to work without this rule.

In this tradition, then, there is a reason why people should have the amount of resources they do, even though the distribution is not ideal. Consequently, there is a reason why, when two people want something, it should go to the one who pays more. It is harder for modern theorists to find a reason.

1. THEORIES BASED ON PREFERENCE SATISFACTION. For a utilitarian, the point of acquiring things is not to live a good life but to obtain pleasure or satisfaction. Consequently, the optimal distribution of resources is the one that will maximize pleasure. Some utilitarians said that ideally, this distribution would be equal since spending an extra dollar presumably gives less satisfaction to a rich man than a poor one. Others said that some pleasures, such as the appreciation of art or music, are of a higher nature and therefore more satisfying than others such as drinking beer. Those capable of the higher pleasures should have more resources.

---

100. Molina, *De iustitia et iure, supra* note 59 at disp. 348.

As before, however, the test of a utilitarian theory is not whether, when a sufficient number of background conditions are satisfied, it can produce results which for thousands of years non-utilitarians regarded as fair. Someone who believed the theory only because it does, and would reject it if it does not, is really not committed to the theory. And, indeed, if we change the background conditions, the theory produces results that few would regard as normatively sound. Few would think a person who takes intense pleasure in watching movies about chain saw massacres, or in defacing or destroying works of art, or in causing pain to others, is, for that very reason, entitled to more resources than another person who takes moderate pleasure in good music or art or in relieving pain.

In any event, few people who subscribe to theories based on preference satisfaction still believe that there is something called satisfaction that accompanies all objects of choice, and that choices are made to obtain as much of it as possible. They do not claim one can compare the importance of one individual's preferences with those of another. Consequently, most of them have stopped making normative claims as to how resources should be initially distributed. The claim instead is that, given any initial distribution, one can explain why, normatively, a person who is willing to pay the most for something should get it. Only if he does can we arrive at a state in which it is impossible to make anyone better off, in terms of his own preferences, without making someone else worse off. Such a state is said to be "Pareto efficient."

To illustrate, suppose Ann has something she does not want for which Bob will pay $65 and Cara only $60. If Cara were to get it, it would still be possible to move to a state in which she and Bob will both be better off: She could resell to Bob. Only if Bob buys the object in question is a further improvement no longer possible.

This argument assumes that the mere fact that Bob has certain preferences doesn't make anyone else worse off. It may. As Trebilcock and Posner have noted, his preferences might drive up the price of something that others want.[101] In the example just given, if Ann sells directly to Bob, Cara will be worse off than if Bob hadn't wanted the object in question since she could then have bought it for $60. Moreover, the mere fact that a person gratifies his own preferences may distress others.[102] Even if Cara didn't want the object herself, she might not want Bob to have it because she hates or envies Bob or because the object is a rooster that Bob wants for cockfighting which she thinks is immoral.

These problems arise because the objective is to maximize preference satisfaction. From an Aristotelian standpoint, the objective is different. It is to enable each person to have the resources he needs to live a good life. As already

101. Trebilcock, *supra* note 27 at 58; R. Posner, "Utilitarianism, Economics and Legal Theory" (1979) 9 J. Leg. Stud. 103 at 114. A similar point is made by Dworkin, *supra* note 88 at 307–308.
102. Trebilcock, *supra* note 27 at 62–63, 243. See G. Calabresi, "The Pointlessness of Pareto: Carrying Coase Further," (1991) 100 Yale Law J. 1211 at 1216–1217.

explained, ideally, each person should have a share of purchasing power that reflects what he needs for such a life. To the extent that this ideal is realized, and that each person chooses rightly how to spend his share, goods and services move to their normatively best uses. That is so even though the particular goods and services each person can buy is affected by the choices of others.[103]

Moreover, from an Aristotelian standpoint, not all preferences should be gratified. If Cara hates or envies Bob, quite possibly her preference that he suffer, or not prosper, is wrong. So may be Bob's preference for cockfighting. If so, his preference harms him because he leads a less worthwhile life. Cara should be distressed if she cares about Bob. The difficulty is resolved to the extent that Bob and Cara prefer what they should. Because virtue is its own reward it is also what an economist might call a free lunch.

A further difficulty is that Bob may discover he really is worse off paying $65 for the object. Benson and Trebilcock have called this problem the "Paretian dilemma": A contract only makes both parties better off *ex ante,* and nothing in the theory explains why that is better than to make them better off *ex post.*[104] From an Aristotelian standpoint, one could ask whether the risk Bob runs of being worse off *ex post* is one that, for the reasons described earlier, a person should be allowed to take, and whether Bob was prudent to do so. To ask those questions, one needs to talk about prudence and distributive justice. As Guido Calabresi has noted, as long as there are *ex post* losers, "we will not be achieving an improvement according to the strict Pareto standard. . . . [W]e could say that we do not *care* about these losers, . . . but that lack of care implies a distributional theory that has all too conveniently been kept out of sight."[105]

A still more fundamental objection to attaching normative significance to Pareto efficiency is that the normative claim is circular. We are seeking a reason why it is normatively better that goods go to whomever will pay the most for them. Supposedly, the answer is that unless they are sold to that person, it will still be possible for a further transaction to make everyone better off and no one worse off. That transaction is possible, however, only if the rule of law is in force that a person can sell what he owns to whomever will pay most for it. To make a normative claim, one must not only assume this rule is in force but that it should be. But that is, in effect, to assume that goods should go to whomever will pay the most for them – which was the conclusion to be proven.

---

103. Consequently, a single rare stamp should command a high price if several people wanted it, although Trebilcock seems to think such a price would violate the theory of justice I am defending. Trebilcock, *supra* note 27 at 90.

104. P. Benson, "The Idea of a Public Basis of Justification for Contract" (1995) 33 Osgoode Hall Law J. 273 at 284–287; Trebilcock, *supra* note 27 at 244. See "Theory of Contracts," *supra* note 51 at ms. 86–87.

105. G. Calabresi, "The New Economic Analysis of Law: Scholarship, Sophistry or Self-indulgence?" (1983) 68 Proceedings of the British Academy 1982. 85 at 96 [hereinafter "The New Economic Analysis].

To illustrate, suppose we are in a society in which nearly everything is owned by a small group who live in decadence while the rest go hungry. Suppose Bob is one of the rich and will pay Ann $65 for a side of beef for which Cara, who is starving, cannot pay more than $1. Why would it be an "improvement" for Bob to have it? Many people might think it a definite improvement if someone like Robin Hood stole the meat and gave it to Cara. If Bob then offered to buy it back from her for $65, many people might think it a still further improvement if someone stole the $65 from Bob as well. These "improvements," of course, can only be made by violating the rule that Ann, who owns the beef, is free to sell it to Bob if he offers to pay more than anyone else. If we assume that rule will be followed, then, even if Cara owned the beef, both Cara and Bob will prefer for Bob to acquire it at a price that Cara will accept. But to conclude that it is normatively better for Bob to end up with the beef, we need to assume, not only that this rule will be followed but that, normatively, it should be. That is to assume the conclusion: People who are willing to pay the most for things ought to have them.

Moreover, the proposition assumed is far from obvious. As mentioned earlier, writers in the Aristotelian tradition claimed that a starving person had the right to take what he needed to live without the owner's permission. In time of war or famine, most governments ration goods rather than leave their allocation to the market. An economist might object that necessity, war, famine, and the extremely unjust society just described are aberrational cases. But that concedes the point. Whether a situation counts as aberrational depends upon one's theory of distributive justice. The Aristotelian writers thought the starving man could take what he needed because, according to their theory of distributive justice, people ought to have enough to live. An economist who claims to be agnostic about the justice of the initial distribution of resources cannot claim that a move to Pareto efficiency is an improvement.

Some writers make normative claims for what is called "Kaldor-Hicks" efficiency or for "wealth maximization," which Richard Posner admits is formally identical.[106] Goods are supposed to go to whomever would pay the most for them whether he actually has to pay or not. Since those who lose out are not compensated, the usual objection is that one cannot assume that the change is normatively for the better.[107] Suppose, Ronald Dworkin argues, that Derek's book is worth $2 to him and $3 to Amartya. Wealth would be maximized if somebody (an imaginary tyrant) forcibly transferred the book to Amartya who then does not need to pay for it. But there is no reason to think the transfer is an improve-

106. R. A. Posner, "The Value of Wealth: A Comment on Dworkin and Kronman," (1980) 9 J. Leg. Stud. 243 at 244 [hereinafter "The Value of Wealth"].

107. "The New Economic Analysis," *supra* note 105 at 89 ("who ever believed that wealth maximization without regard to its distribution could qualify as the goal of law in a just society?"); H. Collins, "Distributive Justice Through Contracts" (1992) 45 Current Legal Prob. 49 at 51 ("what is important is the ability of each individual to pursue a meaningful life, and the fulfillment of that aim involves some sacrifice of collective prosperity").

ment unless we assume, gratuitously, that the book will provide more satisfaction to Amartya than to Derek.[108]

Posner answered Dworkin by saying that the figures chosen are deceptive. The transfer "probably will increase the amount of happiness," meaning satisfaction, if the book were "worth $3,000 to Amartya and $2 to Derek."[109] He also said that wealth maximization is conducive, not only to satisfaction, but to freedom, self-expression and other uncontroversial goods.[110] That answer raises one of the graver problems with utilitarianism: we have to imagine that satisfaction or happiness is a quantity or "amount." Moreover, it seems that we have to imagine that there are amounts of freedom and self-expression. Then we must assume that these amounts are maximized (at least probably) when goods and services go to a person who will pay much more for them than others. And that assumption supposedly does not depend on any assumptions about the nature of his preferences or about how purchasing power is distributed.

In one essay, Posner defended wealth maximization, not on these grounds, but by claiming the results will be consistent with our moral intuitions. When wealth is maximized, people must benefit others to secure benefits for themselves, they will have "economic liberty," and they are likely to practice "traditional ('Calvinist' or 'Protestant') virtues."[111] According to Posner, the principle of wealth maximization also suggests that resources should be initially distributed in a way that answers to our moral intuitions. People should have the right to their own labor or to determine their own sex partners. Wealth will be maximized if they do by avoiding the transactions costs people would incur buying these rights back if they initially belonged to others.[112] Posner acknowledges that very poor people will not be entitled to support, and that those whose "net social product is negative" through no fault of their own may starve. That "grates on modern sensibilities" yet he "see[s] no escape from it" that is consistent with any major modern ethical theory.[113]

With that line of argument, we have come full circle. Three centuries ago, philosophers decided that our moral intuitions should not be the test of what is normatively good. That decision started them down the path to utilitarianism, and then to efficiency and wealth-maximization. In his fidelity to that tradition, Posner does not build his theory on our intuition that some preferences are normatively better than others. Yet in the end he wants our moral intuitions to vindicate the enterprise. Moreover, it seems that the point of the enterprise is to find amoral reasons, such as minimizing transactions costs, for conclusions that correspond to certain moral intuitions, for example, that we should not rape or enslave others, and that we should live by some traditional but selectively

---

108. Ronald M. Dworkin, "Is Wealth a Value?" (1980) 9 J. Leg. Stud. 191 at 197, 199.
109. "The Value of Wealth," *supra* note 106 at 245.
110. Ibid. 344.
111. "Utilitarianism, Economics and Legal Theory," *supra* note 101 at 122–124.
112. Ibid. at 126.   113. Ibid. at 128.

chosen platitudes. Why, one wonders, do we need amoral reasons for trusting our moral intuitions if, in the end, we have to trust them anyway? And if we are supposed to trust them, why should we ignore them, for example, by letting a person starve, when we cannot find an amoral reason in support? If this is journey's end, we ought to reconsider why we embarked on the journey.

My conclusion, again, is not that economics is false science or that its conclusions have no normative significance. On the contrary, we can now see the conditions under which, when resources go to whomever will pay the most, they will be allocated as they should be. The conditions are that members of society actually practice virtues of prudence, temperance, fortitude, and justice that economists never discuss.

2. THEORIES BASED ON AUTONOMY. As noted earlier, the starting point for Kant and Hegel was in one way like that of the utilitarians. They agreed that one cannot say that the purposes that people pursue are better or worse. All one can say is that people seek what they desire. Kant called the ability to satisfy one's desires without interference "external freedom." He contrasted it sharply with "internal freedom" which meant choosing without regard to what one desired.[114]

For Kant, as for the utilitarians, the satisfaction of one person's desires often means that those of another person cannot be satisfied. Given his principles, he had to find a normative solution that did not depend on the importance of the desires themselves. The importance of desires could not depend on the normative value of whatever is desired without returning to the Aristotelian idea that some purposes are normatively of greater value than others. It could not depend on the pleasure or satisfaction of gratifying them because, as we have seen, Kant did not ascribe normative significance to the gratification of a desire.

The answer, Kant claimed, is that each person should act so that his freedom can coexist with every other person's freedom according to a universal law.[115] The freedom he is speaking about here is "external freedom": gratifying one's desires without impediment. The "universal law," by Kant's principles, cannot depend on the importance of the desires gratified. Therefore, such a law must assign resources to people without regard to the importance of their desires, and then allow each to gratify his own desires only from his own resources.

Kant tried to derive rules for assigning resources from the idea of the will itself. He thought he could show that one had a right to one's body, to one's labor, and to appropriate anything that was not previously owned by someone else. People could alter these entitlements by consent, through exchange, gift or inheritance, but not without consent, through force or fraud.

The attempt is not convincing. For example, according to Kant, the will would pointlessly lose some of its freedom if a person could not appropriate some-

114. *Metaphysik der Sitten, supra* note 40 at 318.
115. Ibid. at 337.

thing that no one else owned or was using. Kant concludes that each person invariably has an unlimited right to do so. But the argument proves, at most, that the prior possessor should have some right to appropriate such a thing under some circumstances.[116] According to Kant, I have exclusive rights over my body, my labor, and the exploitation of my own abilities because otherwise I would be treated as a thing rather than a person.[117] But unless a person is completely deprived of all external freedom, why is he a "thing" rather than a person whose entitlements are minimal?

Hegel realized that more was necessary. As described earlier, he said that property exists because the free will, in order to be self-determining, must embody itself in something that is other than the will itself. Slavery rose and fell, he thought, because of some ultimately self-frustrating effort of the will to determine itself in relation to something that must be conceived as a thing and yet is not a thing.[118] As noted earlier, my problem is that while these arguments claim to be deductions, they are not deductive, and while they describe the will in terms of purposes, they are not functional in any ordinary sense.

With the exception of Peter Benson and Alan Brudner, few people who write in the Kantian and Hegelian tradition today try to get from the concept of will to rules for assigning resources. One reason is that they doubt it is possible to do so. But another is that, if the rules are derived in this way, people can have very different amounts of resources for reasons that seem arbitrary. People may have more than others if they are lucky enough to inherit more or first to appropriate a gold mine, a valley, or possibly a continent. John Rawls thinks it objectionable even to allow people to become wealthier because they have superior abilities since their superiority is a matter of chance.[119] Admittedly, any normative theory of the distribution of resources must recognise that, as a practical matter, chance is going to affect the distribution. In Kant's theory, however, the chance events are not random deviations from the ideal. They are the very operation of the rules that are said to assign resources justly.

We cannot escape from these difficulties unless we recognize that the purposes people pursue are normatively important and that, in relation to these purposes, one person may have more and another less that he should. Ernest Weinrib, who writes in the Kantian tradition, agrees that a theory of distributive justice must take the well-being of people into account.[120] But it is hard to see how to take account of well-being without considering the importance of the purposes people pursue, and then we have left the Kantian and Hegelian tradition behind. The difficulties are illustrated by the theory of John Rawls, which Weinrib believes to be compatible with his own ideas.[121]

---

116. Ibid. at 354.   117. Ibid. at 345–346.
118. *Grundlinien der Philosophie des Rechts, supra* note 42 at §§57, 356.
119. J. Rawls, *A Theory of Justice* (Cambridge, MA: Harvard University Press, 1971) at 101–102.
120. "Formalism and Practical Reason," *supra* note 57 at 684, 686.
121. Ibid. at 688–690.

According to Rawls, ideally, each person should have an equal share of resources. The reason is that people would agree on this principle if we imagine them deciding how to distribute resources without knowing the role they will occupy in society or the particular purposes they will choose to pursue. According to Rawls, if a person does not yet know whether he will be A pursuing A's purposes or B pursuing B's, he will want them each to have an equal share. He will not give B a greater share at A's expense lest he turn out to be A.[122]

The conclusion sounds like the principle of distributive justice that Aristotle said would be favored in a democracy. For Aristotle, however, the point of distributing resources is that people can use them rightly. The reason for distributing them equally is that in a democracy, as distinguished from an aristocracy, a greater capacity to make the right choices does not entitle a person to make more choices. When differences in capacity are set aside, each citizen counts merely as a person who needs resources to live well. He receives the same power to obtain them as anyone else.

In contrast, for Rawls, the distribution cannot proceed on the assumption that there are normatively better choices. The criterion is whether the distributor would equally prefer to be any of the persons to whom he has distributed resources, whatever the goals of each may be. That is really a criterion of preference satisfaction: what matters is what sort of life the distributor would prefer to have. But then, what is the criterion for preferring one life to another?

Suppose, first, that the distributor actually knew what goals A and B would actually pursue with their resources. He would have to distribute resources so that he would equally prefer to be A or to be B without passing a normative judgment on their goals. But then he would implicitly apply some standard of what makes a life preferable that does not call for a normative judgement. Rawls would not want that standard to be satisfaction, pleasure or something similar. If that were the standard, we would be back to a form of utilitarianism. Like Bentham, we would then have to imagine satisfaction or pleasure as an homogenous something which people obtain in varying but comparable quantities whatever goals they pursue. Moreover, if we wanted A and B to be equally satisfied, we would violate both the spirit of Rawl's project and our common sense notions of justice. The spoiled and arrogant person who can scarcely be made happy with a kingdom should not have more than a kingdom just because he is so hard to please.

Suppose, then, that the distributor is not allowed to know what A's and B's goals will actually be. He might then give them an equal share of purchasing power because there is then an equal chance that A's life will be as desirable as B's. That procedure merely dodges the question just raised. What does it mean for two lives to be equally preferable? It means nothing unless there is some standard by which two lives can be compared. This standard cannot depend on

---

122. *A Theory of Justice, supra* note 119 at 12, 18–19, 136–137.

a normative judgment of what goals are worth pursuing. As before, all that seems to be left is some notion of satisfaction or pleasure. But then again we are back to a form of utilitarianism with all its problems. Again, in principle, *A* should have more resources than *B* if they would make his life equally satisfying. That seems unfair. Strangest of all, if our objective is make *A*'s and *B*'s lives equally preferable, why is the distributor not allowed to know what their goals are?

III. The Content of a Contractual Obligation: Gift and Exchange

In the Aristotelian tradition, the parties' obligations depend, not only on their express will, but on the type of arrangement they enter into when they promise. There are two basic types of arrangements that the law should respect: exchange and gift.

In the *Nicomachean Ethics,* Aristotle described exchange as a type of commutative justice. While distributive justice secures for each citizen a fair share of whatever wealth and honor the society had to divide, commutative justice preserves the share he has.[123] Thus, according to Aristotle, each party to an exchange must give something equivalent in value to what he receives.[124] In another passage in the *Ethics,* Aristotle discussed the virtue of "liberality": the liberal person disposes of his money wisely, giving "to the right people the right amounts and at the right time."[125] Thomas Aquinas put these ideas together: when one person transfers a thing to another, either it is an act of commutative justice that requires an equivalent or it is an act of liberality.[126]

As I have described in detail elsewhere,[127] the late scholastics built a theory of contract on this groundplan that was then borrowed by the northern natural law school in the seventeenth century. According to the theory, a party, by expressing his will to be bound, might enter into either of these two basic types of arrangement.[128] Grotius and Pufendorf present elaborate schemes of classification in which they show how the contracts familiar in Roman law can be fitted into these two grand categories.[129] This classification means more than the tautology that a party either does or does not receive back something in return for what he gives. In a gratuitous contract, the donor must actually intend to benefit the other party, and if he does not, the contract is not a gratuitous contract whatever the document to which the parties subscribed may say.[130] In an onerous contract, a party must receive, not simply a counterperformance, but one of

---

123. *Nicomachean Ethics, supra* note 8 at V.ii.
124. Ibid. at V.iv–v.   125. See note 8, *supra.*
126. *Summa theologiae, supra* note 13 at II–II, Q. 61, a. 3.
127. *Philosophical Origins, supra* note 3 at 69–133.
128. Soto, *De iustitia et iure, supra* note 59 at lib. 3, q. 5, a.1; Molina, *De iustitia et iure, supra* note 59 at disp. 252; Lessius, *De iustitia et iure, supra* note 59 at lib. 2, cap. 17, dub. 1.
129. Grotius, *De iure belli ac pacis, supra* note 86 at II.xii.1–7; Pufendorf, *De iure naturae et gentium, supra* note 95 at V.ii.8–10.
130. Grotius, *De iure belli ac pacis, supra* note 86 at II.xii.11.1.

equivalent value. Writers in the Aristotelian tradition thought that the rules that govern the parties' obligations should depend on which sort of agreement they had entered into. The rules should ensure, so far as practicable, in the case of an exchange, that each party receives an equivalent, and in the case of a gratuitous contract, that the donor behaves sensibly.[131]

A. Gratuitous Contracts and the Virtue of Liberality

As we have seen, writers in the Aristotelian tradition typically said that private property was instituted to remedy the disadvantages of holding property in common: people would not have an incentive to work hard and manage property well. Therefore, rights to private property were not absolute but only as extensive as necessary to remedy these disadvantages. In particular, those who had more than they should were under an obligation to help those who had less. In doing so, they practiced the virtue of liberality.

Peter Benson has asked why liberality should be a virtue in a society in which each person has the amount that he should as a matter of distributive justice.[132] As we have seen, however, even if the distribution were as just as practicable, some people would still have more than they should and others less. Some discrepancies from the ideal are necessary if people are to have an incentive to work and manage property well. Others will arise by chance. When the state cannot remedy these discrepancies lest worse evils ensue, the remedy has to be left to private individuals acting without legal compulsion.

Benson has also objected that if liberality is a moral virtue, it is hard to see how it can be the basis of an obligation.[133] The late scholastics debated this point among themselves. No doubt, a person who broke such a promise has failed to practice, not only the virtue of liberality, but that of fidelity to his word. It was not obvious, however, that the promisee could demand as a matter of justice that the promise be kept. In the sixteenth century, in his commentary on Thomas Aquinas, Cajetan argued that the promisee could not. Commutative justice requires a party who takes or destroys what belongs to another to make compensation. But, Cajetan argued, one who makes and then breaks a gratuitous promise may have left the promisee no worse off.[134]

The leading late scholastics disagreed with Cajetan. Molina pointed out that if the donor had given something away outright and delivered it to the donee, it

---

131. For an argument that these considerations can explain the way American courts apply such doctrines as consideration, promissory reliance, waiver, and offer and acceptance, see J. Gordley, "Enforcing Promises" (1995) 83 California Law Review 547.
132. "Abstract Right," *supra* note 44 at 1194 n. 168.
133. "Contract," *supra* note 51 at 44.
134. Cajetan (Tomasso di Vio), *Commentaria* to Thomas Aquinas, *Summa theologica* II–II, Q. 88, a. 1; Q. 113, a. 1 (1698).

would belong to the donee. Under the Roman law of his time, the donor could not then take it back unless the donee was guilty of gross ingratitude.[135] But there is nothing magical about the moment of delivery. In principle, Molina argued, the donor ought to be able to transfer the right to a thing, or the right to claim it, in advance of delivery. If he did, then depriving him of that right by failing to perform is a denial of commutative justice.[136]

Lessius agreed that the question was one of intent, but he argued: "to promise is not merely to affirm that one will give or do something but beyond that to obligate oneself to another, and consequently to grant that person the right to require it."[137] By this definition, all promises conferred a right on the promisee and were therefore actionable as a matter of commutative justice. Grotius agreed with Molina, and later writers such as Pufendorf and Barbeyrac agreed with Grotius, although they were not always careful to distinguish Molina's position from that of Lessius.[138]

Under the Roman law of their day, however, not all promises to make gifts were enforceable, as they recognized. Although they never explained why, they seem unconcerned that Roman law sometimes deviates from their principle. In my view, there is no reason why they should have been concerned. Their theory offers the best explanation of why, though in principle promises of gifts should be enforceable, some are not enforced by their law or modern law.

There are two reasons. First, although the promisor has to judge for himself whether he is giving sensibly, the law might enforce such a promise only when he is particularly likely to have acted sensibly. Second, the law might enforce such a promise only when he is particularly likely to have wanted the promisee to be able to demand performance as a matter of right.

In Roman law, with certain exceptions, to make a binding promise of a large gift required a special formality called *insinuatio*. By the sixteenth century, this formality could be performed by registering a document that describes the gift with a court.[139] The rule that a formality is required passed into modern civil law. Typically, the formality is that the promisor subscribe to the promise

---

135. The rule is described by Lessius, *De iustitia et iure, supra* note 59 at lib. 2, cap. 18, dub. 8 no. 52; and Molina, *De iustitia et iure, supra* note 59 at disps. 272, 281.

136. Molina, *De iustitia et iure, supra* note 59 at disp. 262.

137. Lessius, *De iustitia et iure, supra* note 59 at lib. 2, cap. 18, dub. 8 no. 52.

138. Grotius, *De iure belli ac pacis, supra* note 86 at II.xi.1.3–4; Pufendorf, *De iure naturae et gentium, supra* note 95 at III.v.5–7; J. Barbeyrac, *Le Droit de la guerre et de la paix de Hugues Grotius* (1729) at n. 2 to II.xi.1; n. 1 to II.xi.3 [hereinafter Barbeyrac on Grotius]; J. Barbeyrac, *Le Droit de la nature et des gens . . . par le baron de Pufendorf* (1734) at n. 10 to III.v.9 [hereinafter Barbeyrac on Pufendorf].

139. Molina, *De iustitia et iure, supra* note 59 at disp. 278 no. 3; Lessius, *De iustitia et iure, supra* note 59 at lib. 2, cap. 18, dub. 13, no. 97. On the formality in the sixteenth century, see Alexandrinus Clarus, *Sententiarum receptarum liber quartus* (1595) at lib. 4, "Donatio" q. 15 no. 3; D. Antonius Gomez, *Variae resolutiones, iuris civilis, communis, et regii* (1759) at t. 2, cap. 4, no. 14.

before a member of the legal profession called a notary who is charged with preparing documents.[140]

At common law, absent reliance by the promisee, promises of gifts are supposed to be unenforceable because they lack consideration. But a person who tells his lawyer he wants to bind himself to make a gift will not be told it is impossible to do so. He will be told that he can achieve through a deed of gift or a trust what he cannot through the law of contract.[141] By a deed of gift, he can make an immediate gift of personal property. To do so, he executes a signed document declaring the intention to make a gift, and naming the donor, the donee, and the object given. By a trust, he can give away any type of property by declaring that he holds it in trust for the donee.[142] The trust is then irrevocable if he so declares, and the intention to create an irrevocable trust will usually be found even absent such a declaration.[143] While a deed of gift transfers the property right away, a person who wishes the gift to take effect in the future can create the trust at once by specifying that the property is reserved for his own use, or that income from the trust is to be paid to himself, for a certain period of time.[144] By using a trust, a person can thus give away anything he presently owns, though not property to be acquired in the future.[145] In practice, a lay person will always have the help of a lawyer to execute a deed of gift or establish a trust, even though there is no requirement that he do so. Consequently, at an operational level, the common law rules on contract and trust provide a safeguard like that of the older and more recent civil law. To make a gift enforceable, the promise must be formalized with the help of a member of the legal profession.

Such a rule makes sense if the objective of the law is to ensure that the promisor acts sensibly and wishes to confer a right to performance on the promisee. The promisor is less likely to act impetuously since he cannot bind himself on the spur of the moment, and may receive caution and advice from the legal professional he consults. As the late scholastics explained, the formality ensures deliberation.[146] It also shows that the donor meant to be legally bound.

The Roman law in force before codification also recognized certain exceptional cases in which a promise to make a gift was enforceable without a formality. One was a promise of a gift to a charitable cause (*ad causas pias*).[147]

---

140. See, for example, Code civil art. 931; Bürgerlichesgesetzbuch (BGB) art. 518.
141. See L. L. Fuller and M. A. Eisenberg, *Basic Contract Law*, 6th ed. (St. Paul, MN: West Pub. Co, 1996) at 7–8.
142. A. W. Scott and W. F. Fratcher, *The Law of Trusts*, vol. 1, 4th ed. (Toronto: Little, Brown, 1987) §28 at 310–312, n. 4.
143. Ibid. §29 at 315.
144. See ibid., vol. 1A, §57.6 at 188.
145. Ibid., vol. 1, §30 at 316.
146. Lessius, *De iustitia et iure, supra* note 59 at lib. 2, cap. 18., dubs. 2, 8; Molina, *De iustitia et iure, supra* note 59 at disp. 278, no. 5.
147. Lessius, *De iustitia et iure, supra* note 59 at lib. 2, cap. 18, dub. 13, no. 102; Molina, *De iustitia et iure, supra* note 59 at disp. 279 no. 2. On the exception in the sixteenth century, see

Typically, the modern codes did not preserve this exception. Supposedly, there never was one in common law. Nevertheless, in modern times, both civil and common law courts have stretched the law in order to enforce such promises.

French courts have sometimes done so by classifying promises to charities as exchanges on the grounds that the feeling of satisfaction or other intangible benefit the donor experiences is a recompense.[148] German courts have sometimes done so by holding that such a promise is not a gift because it does not enrich the charitable organization itself which is merely an intermediary between the promisor and the ultimate beneficiary.[149] My point here is not that French and German courts generally enforce promises to charities but that they have tried to find ways to do so.

Before the rise of promissory estoppel, American courts used fictions to find consideration for such promises. Consideration was found in commitments of other subscribers to donate money,[150] or in the commitment of a charity to name a fund after the donor,[151] to locate a college in a particular town,[152] or even to use the money for charitable purposes.[153] Under the doctrine of promissory estoppel, such promises are supposed to be enforceable without consideration provided that the promisee has relied on them. Yet, courts have not demanded proof of reliance.[154] In deference to the case law, the Second Restatement changed the language of Section 90 to provide that such promises are enforceable "without proof that the promise induced action or forbearance."[155] To

---

Clarus, *Sententarium receptarum, supra* note 139 at lib. 4, §Donatio, q. 17, no. 1; Gomez, *Variae resolutiones, supra* note 139 at t. 2, cap. 4, no. 10.

148. See, for example, Decision of July 19, 1894, Cass. civ. 1, 1895 D.P. I 125 (calling a promise of land to build a church a "contract subject to payment" rather than a donation requiring a formality, where promisor could expect benefits to himself and to the community); Decision of March 15, 1900, Trib. civ. de Langres, 1900 D.P. II 422 (finding an assignment of right of recovery to three priests not a pure act of liberality because assignor could receive consideration from feelings such as vanity, piety, or moral obligation). See also J. P. Dawson, *Gifts and Promises* (New Haven: Yale University Press, 1980) at 84–96 (arguing that French courts treat such contracts as commutative, made for the benefit of third parties and thus enforceable).

149. See, for example, Decision of May 7, 1909, Reichsgericht, 71 *Entscheidungen des Reichsgerichts in Zivilsachen* [RGZ] 140. See F. Fromholzer, *Consideration US-amerikanisches Recht im Vergleich zum deutschen* (Tübingen: Mohr-Siebeck, 1997) at 321–328.

150. *Congregation B'nai Sholom* v. *Martin*, 173 N.W.2d 504 at 510 (Mich. 1969); *First Presbyterian Church* v. *Dennis*, 161 N.W. 183 at 187–188 (Iowa 1917).

151. *Allegheny College* v. *National Chautauqua County Bank*, 159 N.E. 173 at 176 (N.Y. 1927).

152. *Rogers* v. *Galloway Female College*, 44 S.W. 454 at 455 (Ark. 1898).

153. *Nebraska Wesleyan University* v. *Griswold's Estate*, 202 N.W. 609 at 616 (Neb. 1925).

154. J. D. Calamari and J. M. Perillo, *The Law of Contract*, 3rd ed. (St. Paul, MN: West Pub. Co, 1987) at 280; R. E. Barnett and M. E. Becker, "Beyond Reliance: Promissory Estoppel, Contract Formalities and Misrepresentations" (1987) 15 Hofstra L. Rev. 443 at 451–453; C. L. Knapp, "Reliance in the Revised Restatement: The Proliferation of Promissory Estoppel" (1981) 81 Colum. L. Rev. 52 at 59–60. In a few exceptional cases, however, courts have refused enforcement because the charitable organization did not rely. See *Mount Sinai Hospital* v. *Jordan*, 290 So. 2d 484 at 487 (Fla. 1974); *Congregation Kadimah Toras-Moshe* v. *DeLeo*, 540 N.E. 2d 691 at 693 (Mass. 1989).

155. *Restatement (Second) of Contracts* §90(2) (1979).

dispense with proof of reliance is as much a fiction as to pretend a gift is really a bargain.[156]

Again, although the late scholastics did not explain why there should be such an exception, it makes sense from the standpoint of their theory. Promises to charitable causes are more likely to be sensible in that they change the distribution of wealth in a good direction. Thus, some American jurists now acknowledge that such promises are enforced because courts regard them as particularly meritorious.[157] As E. Allan Farnsworth has said, their enforcement is "particularly desirable as a means of allowing decisions about the distribution of wealth to be made at an individual level."[158] But then we are back to the idea that donative promises should be enforced because they allow people to make sensible changes in the distribution of wealth.

Of course, there are equally deserving promises that the law does not enforce: for example, to give a brilliant acquaintance the cash he needs to finish university; or to give money to family members who are in need. But in contrast to these, the promise to a charitable cause is impersonal. For that reason, the promisor's decision is less likely to be influenced by personal pressure or the emotions of the moment.

Moreover, because promises to charitable causes are impersonal, they are more likely to be meant as legal commitments. As Melvin Eisenberg has observed, often, to enable the promisee to demand performance as a matter of right would be inconsistent with the relationship of trust and affection that led the promisor to make the promise.[159] Moreover, often a donative promise is understood to be subject to conditions which are implicit. If a parent promises his son a new car, neither would expect the promise to be binding if the money were needed to pay for a grandparent's medical operation. Eisenberg has noted how hard it would be for a court to decide to what unexpressed conditions a donative promise is subject.[160] For that reason, the promisor might not want the promisee to have a legal right to performance. In an impersonal situation, however, the promisor is likely to spell out whatever conditions he wishes to attach to the promise because he cannot rely upon a promisee who is not a friend or family member and who is not familiar with his affairs to understand intuitively the implied conditions that might attach.

In the time of the late scholastics, another exceptional case in which a formality was not required was a promise to people about to marry (*propter*

156. See Calamari and Perillo, *supra* note 154 at 279–281.
157. See ibid. at 280; Knapp, *supra* note 154 at 60.
158. E. A. Farnsworth and W. F. Young, *Cases and Materials on Contracts,* 4th ed. (Westbury: Foundation Press, 1988) at 98.
159. "Theory of Contracts," *supra* note 51 at p. 230.
160. M. A. Eisenberg, "The World of Contract and the World of Gift" (1997) 85 Cal. L. Rev. 821 at 850 [hereinafter "World of Gift"].

nuptias).[161] In Germany today, such promises are enforceable under Section 1624 of the German Civil Code.[162] The civil codes of France, Italy and Spain do not contain such a rule, but one may not be as necessary since the custom of wealthy families has been to make such commitments formally and in writing before a marriage is celebrated.

In common law countries, where such promises are more likely to be made informally, courts have found ways to enforce them. Until the nineteenth century, courts said that the natural love and affection of a parent for a child was consideration.[163] Then, with the rise of the "bargain theory" of consideration, the forthcoming marriage was said to be the inducement for the parents' promise. Parents who might have begged their children not to marry were treated as though they had bribed them to do so.[164] The doctrine of promissory estoppel now makes that fiction unnecessary. The promise is supposed to be binding as long as the couple change their position in reliance upon it. But, as in the case of charitable subscriptions, courts do not ask whether the parties actually did so.[165] According to the Second Restatement, no proof of reliance is required.[166]

Again, one reason to enforce such promises more readily is that they are likely to be sensible. Moreover, even though the promise is personal, it is more likely that the promisor would want to confer a right to performance on the promisee. Particularly when the couple is promised a large amount of money, the promise was probably made to enable them to establish an independent household in which they could treat resources as their own. If so, to allow them to regard these resources as their own is not inconsistent with a relationship of love and trust. Indeed, the purpose of the promisor is to allow them to do so. Given that purpose, it is much less likely that the promisor wants his promise to be subject to unexpressed conditions.

All of these rules make sense only on the assumption that a person can behave sensibly or foolishly when he gives a gift. As Farnsworth put it, if the law

161. Molina, *De iustitia et iure, supra* note 59 at disp. 279 no. 7. On the exception in the sixteenth century, see Antonius de Gama, *Decisiones Supremi Senatus Lusitaniae Centuriae* (1622) at IV dec. 348, no. 5.
162. Section 1624 provides: "That which the father or mother accords to a child towards marriage, or towards obtaining an independent position in life, for founding or preserving the establishment of the position in life" does not count as a gift, and therefore is not subject to a formality, except to the extent it is immoderately large, given the parents' circumstances.
163. A. W. B. Simpson, *A History of the Common Law of Contract The Rise of the Action of Assumpsit* (Oxford: Clarendon Press, 1987) at 435–437.
164. Even then, in the famous case of *De Cicco v. Schweitzer,* 117 N.E. 807 (N.Y. 1917), it was hard to arrive at the desired result since the promise was made to a fiancé who, having already engaged himself to marry, was legally obligated to do so. Cardozo ingeniously observed that the affianced couple might still have given up their legal right to dissolve their engagement by mutual consent. 117 N.E. at 809–810. In effect, the parent's promise was treated as though it were made to induce them to marry should they no longer wish to do so.
165. See the sources cited Gordley *supra* note 131 at 576–77.
166. *Restatement (Second) of Contracts* §90(2) (1979).

enforced all donative promises, "what would limit your profligacy?"[167] Once we say, however, that gift-giving can be sensible or foolish, we are back to the Aristotelian idea of liberality whether we use that word or not.

For that reason, modern theories of contract based on preference satisfaction or autonomy cannot explain the law that governs gratuitous promises. Unless they incorporate something like the Aristotelian idea of liberality, all preferences or exercises of autonomy must count the same, not as wise or foolish.

Richard Posner, as well as scholars who are less committed to the law and economics movement,[168] has said that the law is reluctant to enforce a gift because it does not serve the same purpose as an exchange: "to facilitate the movement [of resources], by voluntary exchange, to their most valuable uses."[169] But if one is to judge matters solely from the standpoint of the preferences of the individual, as Posner wants to do, then whatever a person chooses must be valuable – whether to sell property, to give it away, or to destroy it. As Posner has observed elsewhere, such a promise "would not be made unless it conferred utility on the promisor."[170] If all that matters is preference satisfaction, why not enforce it?

Posner has proposed another solution. The law is reluctant to enforce a gratuitous promise because the social cost of doing so may exceed the utility the promisor gains by making a binding promise. Social cost includes the administrative costs of enforcement and the cost of making mistakes as to whether the promise was actually made.[171] According to Posner, one would expect courts to enforce promises only when the "stakes" are high so the administrative cost is worth it, and the promise is well evidenced so the chance of error is low.[172] If Posner were right, however, any well-evidenced donative promise would be enforced when the "stakes" are as high as in commercial litigation.

Neither can the law be explained by a theory based on autonomy. Kant and Hegel discussed gifts in formal terms which take no account of the purpose of the donor. Kant explained that that the loss of a right by one party and its acqui-

---

167. E. A. Farnsworth, "Promises to Make Gifts" (1995) 43 Am. J. Comp. L. 359 at 364.
168. See, for example, Farnsworth and Young, *supra* note 158 at 47 (suggesting that gifts are not productive); L. L. Fuller, "Consideration and Form," (1941) 41 Colum. L. Rev. 799 at 815 (referring to gifts as a "sterile transmission"); E. W. Patterson, "An Apology for Consideration," (1958) 58 Colum. L. Rev. 929 at 944–946 (preferring bargained-for promises over gifts as useful economic devices). Eisenberg speaks of the absence of independent social interests. The only one he identifies is the redistribution of wealth, and he discounts it because "[e]ven assuming . . . that the redistribution of wealth is an appropriate goal of contract law, the enforcement of donative promises would be a relatively trivial instrument for achieving that end." M. A. Eisenberg, "Donative Promises," (1979) 47 U. Chic. L. Rev. 1 at 4. As the objection indicates, he is not thinking about redistributing wealth to a particularly deserving person or charitable cause, but of achieving a more desirable distribution of wealth among the members of society generally.
169. R. A. Posner, *Economic Analysis of Law,* 4th ed. (Boston: Little, Brown and Co., 1992) at 69.
170. R. A. Posner, "Gratuitous Promises in Economics and Law," (1977) 6 J. Leg. Stud. 411 at 412.
171. Ibid. at 415.   172. Ibid. at 415, 426.

sition by the other are a single act that can only be performed by the intent of both parties outwardly declared.[173] A free being is able to perform such an act simply because he is a free being. Hegel said that this loss and acquisition occurs when "two wills are associated in an identity."[174] The transaction is a gift when "one of them has a negative moment – the alienation of a thing – and the other a positive moment – the appropriation of a thing."[175] For Hegel, however, this common will is formed because it is necessary for the self-determination of a free being. I must be able to alienate property "in order that thereby my will may become objective to me as determinately existent."[176] In his account, as in Kant's, the power to make a gift is explained without regard to the purposes for which one would want to make them, whether wise or foolish.

Charles Fried's theory faces the same difficulty. As already noted, while he claims to be following the Kantian tradition, unlike Kant and Hegel, he explains the institution of promising in terms of its purpose. The purpose, however, is to give each person's will "the greatest possible range" consistent with the will of others. Since a person who promises to make a gift has made a choice that is consistent with the freedom of others, by Fried's theory, all gratuitous promises should be enforceable. Indeed, Fried himself has rejected the common law doctrine of consideration as inconsistent with "the liberal principle that the free arrangements of rational persons should be respected."[177]

As Fried has admitted, that is not the law. Would anyone want it to be? As it turns out, not even Fried. Gifts, he has observed, should be made "rationally, deliberately" and should not frustrate the "legitimate interests of third parties." Paraphrasing Lon Fuller with approval, he has suggested that one benefit of the doctrine of consideration is to exclude "the more dubious and meretricious kinds of gifts in which strangers are promised the moon, to the prejudice of a spouse or children."[178] Apparently, the complaints of the spouse and children become legitimate just at the point when, to paraphrase Aristotle, the promisor gives the wrong amount to the wrong person at the wrong time. Sacrificing consistency to common sense, Fried has reintroduced something like the Aristotelian idea of liberality.

There is another problem with theories based on autonomy. According to these theories, a promise is morally binding simply because the promisor committed himself and without regard to the value of what he was trying to accomplish. But if we pay no attention to the value of what he was trying to accomplish, we cannot know whether he meant to commit himself. We also cannot know to what tacit conditions the promise is subject. Whether there are any such conditions depends upon the value of what the promisor was trying to accomplish.

---

173. *Metaphysik der Sitten, supra* note 40 at 78–81.
174. *Grundlinien der Philosophie des Rechts, supra* note 42 at §74.
175. Ibid. at §76.   176. Ibid. at §73.
177. Fried, *supra* note 45 at 35.
178. Ibid. at 38.

Surely, a parent's promise to buy his child a car is not binding morally, let alone legally, if he gets sick and the money is needed for an operation. Surely, no one would think his promise to take his child to the zoo committed him if he broke his leg.

Writers in the Aristotelian tradition explained why a promise must be subject to such tacit conditions by drawing on Arisotle's concept of equity. Since laws serve a purpose, circumstances can always arise in which the purpose will be thwarted if one obeys the law.[179] The lawmaker would not have wished the law to be binding under those circumstances. Thomas Aquinas concluded that an oath, vow, or promise is binding only under circumstances in which the promisor would have intended to be bound, had these circumstances been called to his attention.[180] He thus found an Aristotelian explanation for a doctrine the medieval canon lawyers had formulated: in every promise, "this condition is always understood: if matters remain in the same state."[181] The canon lawyers used that doctrine to explain one of their authoritative texts in which: St. Augustine had agreed with Cicero that a promise to return a person's sword was not binding if that person had become insane or had decided to use it for some evil purpose.[182] They thereby invented the doctrine of changed and unforeseen circumstances which was read into the civil law by the great medieval lawyer, Baldus degli Ubaldi.[183] The late scholastics adopted the doctrine along with its Aristotelian explanation, and the northern natural lawyers borrowed it from them.[184]

To apply the doctrine, one has to ask what the promisor was trying to accomplish and how important this objective was for him. Consequently, it is hard to square the doctrine with an autonomy theory in which the promisor is supposed to be bound simply because he committed himself, and without regard to his objectives and their importance. Indeed, if the promisor is bound simply because he chose to commit himself, it is hard to see how one can add or subtract from his commitment by asking what he would have done had he anticipated circumstances that he did not in fact consider. Charles Fried has said that the terms that courts read into a promise when the parties are silent are not really part of the promise. They do not correspond to any decision the promisor actually made. The court must ask what he "in all probability would have agreed but did not" or "what somebody else, say, the ordinary person would have intended by such words of agreement." It is "futile" to "attempt to bring these cases under the promise principle."[185] If that is so, then one cannot bring tacit conditions

---

179. *Nicomachean Ethics, supra* note 8 at V.x 1137ª–1137ᵇ.
180. *Summa theologiae, supra* note 13 at II–II, Q. 88, a. 10; Q. 89, a. 9.
181. *Glossa ordinaria* to *Decretum Gratiani* to *furens* to C. 22, q. 2, c. 14.
182. *Decretum Gratiani* C. 22, q. 2, c. 14.
183. Baldus degli Ubaldis, *Commentaria Corpus Iuris Civilis* to Dig. 12.4.8 (1577).
184. Lessius, *De iustitia et iure, supra* note 59 at lib. 2, cap. 18, dub. 10; Grotius, *De iure belli ac pacis, supra* note 86 at II.xvi.25.2; II.xxi.20.2; Pufendorf, *De iure naturae et gentium, supra* note 95 at III.vi.6; Barbeyrac on Pufendorf, *supra* note 138 at n. 3 to III.vi.6.
185. Fried, *supra* note 45 at 60, 61, 63, 69.

under the promise principle. Either one must say that a promise cannot be subject to tacit conditions, which seems wrong, or that the promise principle does not explain when a promise is binding.

B. *Contracts of Exchange and the Virtue of Commutative Justice*

We turn now to the other basic type of voluntary arrangement discussed by writers in the Aristotelian tradition: contracts of exchange. The parties to this type of arrangement exercise the virtue of commutative justice by exchanging resources that are equivalent in value. We will first discuss the relationship of commutative justice to distributive justice and then the principle of equality in exchange.

1. COMMUTATIVE AND DISTRIBUTIVE JUSTICE.

Distributive justice secures a fair share of purchasing power for each citizen. In voluntary transactions in which the parties exchange resources, commutative justice requires that the resources be equivalent in value so that the share of each party is preserved.

Anthony Kronman has said that the rules of contract law are "distributional" because they determine the sorts of advantage-taking in which the parties can engage.[186] Writers in the Aristotelian tradition would have agreed that contract law must be concerned with how a transaction affects the distribution of purchasing power between the parties. But they thought that, in normal circumstances, the rules governing exchange were merely concerned with preserving the pre-existing distribution.

Peter Benson has objected that if the point of commutative justice is to preserve the existing distribution of wealth, one must either take the existing distribution as given, whether it is fair or not – which is arbitrary – or one must insist that it be fair – in which case "the moral acceptability of a given transaction depends, not just on commutative justice, but on distributive justice."[187] If it does depend on distributive justice, Stephen Smith has objected that an exchange could be substantively fair "only in societies – unlike any we know of – which are already distributively just."[188]

I think that the moral acceptability of a transaction does depend on distributive as well as commutative justice. To say so, however, does not imply that wealth must be ideally distributed. As we have seen, a society must allow deviations from the ideal to provide incentives for people to work hard, to manage property well, and to assume risks which must fall on someone. Once society does so, it must recognize that people are entitled to what they have gained even

---

186. A. Kronman, "Contract Law and Distributive Justice" (1980) 89 Yale Law J. 472.
187. "Contract," *supra* note 51 at 44–45.
188. S. A. Smith, "In Defence of Substantive Fairness" (1996) 112 L. Q. Rev. 138 at 147.

if, ideally, they have more than they should. Moreover, if the distribution of wealth is unjust, it should be changed by a social decision, rather than by individuals who go about redistributing wealth on their own, and by a centrally made decision, rather than transaction by transaction.

Nevertheless, to the extent the distribution of wealth is unjust, transactions will be morally objectionable because they allocate resources to those who should not have them in preference to those who should. It is morally objectionable, in that sense, for some people to buy luxuries while others go hungry. One may have to put up with the situation, just as one has to put up with much that is morally objectionable in society. Still, in an extreme case, a person's need could be so serious that the ordinary rules of commutative justice no longer apply. As we have seen, writers in the Aristotelian tradition agreed that a starving man could take what he needs to survive without the owner's permission.

Ernest Weinrib and Peter Benson also object that if the point of corrective justice is to preserve a just distribution of resources, one can no longer distinguish it from distributive justice.[189] Stephen Perry agrees provided one holds a "simple patterned theory" of distributive justice.[190] Lessius, however, distinguished between distributive and commutative justice even in a very simple hypothetical case in which an academic authority must distribute fellowship money among scholars according either to their poverty or to their learning. He would violate distributive justice if he disregarded the principle of proportionality that was supposed to guide the distribution. He would violate the arithmetic equality of commutative justice if he gave a scholar less than the amount that had been determined to be due to him.[191] Lessius' example shows that while one can calculate an individual scholar's share in two different ways and arrive at the same answer, the knowledge required for each calculation is different, as is the moral principle one must respect. To do distributive justice, one must know the size of the fund, the qualifications of everyone who might be entitled to a share, and the distributive principle. One must be willing to apply that principle even-handedly. To do commutative justice, one needs to know that someone should receive a certain amount, however that amount may have been determined. One has to be willing to pay whatever is owed.

---

189. "Corrective Justice," *supra* note 99 at 420–21; Peter Benson, "The Basis of Corrective Justice and its Relation to Distributive Justice," (1992) 77 Iowa L. Rev. 515 at 530. The same objection is made by R. W. Wright, "Substantive Corrective Justice" (1992) 77 Iowa L. Rev. 625 at 705–706.

190. "Moral Foundations," *supra* note 99 at 451.

191. Lessius, *De iustitia et iure, supra* note 59 at lib. 2, cap. 1, dub. 4, no. 23. Molina, *De iustitia et iure,* had made a similar argument in response to the 14th century philosopher Buridan who claimed distributive and commutative justice were the same, since if the state refused to pay what was due someone as a matter of distributive justice, the failure to pay the amount due would be a violation of commutative justice. Molina, *De iustitia et iure, supra* note 59 at disp. 12, citing J. Buridan, *Quaestiones super decem libros Ethicorum Aristotelis ad Nicomachum* (1513) V, q. 7.

In any case, the Aristotelian tradition did not have a "simple patterned theory" in which each citizen is simply entitled to the share assigned by the prevailing principle of distributive justice. Private property was supposed to prevent quarrels and to provide incentives to work. Consequently, a citizen cannot demand more resources in a democracy simply because he has less than someone else or in an aristocracy simply because he has the same amount as someone less virtuous. To obtain the advantages of a system of private property, a society will have to tolerate some deviations from principle of distributive justice it regards as ideal.

Weinrib has also claimed that the rules of contract law cannot be shaped by any larger social purpose because, if they were, the pursuit of this purpose would have to favor one party over another and so violate commutative justice. Moreover, it would necessarily extend beyond the interaction of the two parties to the exchange which is all that matters from the standpoint of commutative justice.[192]

This problem arises because, although Weinrib defines commutative (or corrective) justice as Aristotle did, his disregard of purpose breaks fundamentally with the Aristotelian tradition. In that tradition one cannot understand the structure of a thing apart from its function, final cause, or end. Aristotle explained everything, be it a human being, an animal, or a political institution, by examining its parts, their purposes, and how these purposes were related to the end of the whole. His account of virtues such as commutative justice explained the contribution that each made to the ultimate end of living the life appropriate to a human being. Thomas Aquinas began his commentary on Aristotle's *Ethics* by explaining that there are two kinds of order: that of part to whole, and that of means to end, and the first is founded upon the second.[193]

Indeed, voluntary commutative justice is defined in terms of an end: Each party obtains something he wants by giving something of equivalent value in return. In the Aristotelian tradition, one can explain why that purpose should be respected in terms of higher purposes. Each party is enabled to obtain the goods and services he needs to live a good life while preserving a distribution of wealth that is just because it allows others to get what they need to live a good life. The purposes are functionally related like those of the organs of the body or the parts of a machine. The subordination of the purpose of the circulatory system or the brake to those of an organism or a car does not make the structure of these parts incoherent. Indeed, because they are functionally or teleologically ordered, one cannot understand their structure apart from this subordination.

It does follow that sometimes a lower level purpose must be sacrificed to a higher level one. As we have seen, in the Aristotelian account, if a person is starving the normal rules of commutative justice do not apply, and he can take

---

192. *Private Law, supra* note 52 at 212–213.
193. Thomas Aquinas, *In decem libros ethicorum Aristotelis ad Nicomachum expositio,* ed. by A. Pirotta (Taurini: Marietti, 1934) at lib. I, lectio i, no. 1 [hereinafter Thomas Aquinas, *In decem libros ethicorum expositio*].

what he needs. But the advantage of the Aristotelian account is that it allows us to see why that can sometimes happen. If the normal rules of commutative justice always applied, then, it would seem, a ship in distress could not tie up to another's pier, and a person drowning could not pull himself into another's boat, without the permission of the owner. But modern legal systems typically recognize that that, in cases of necessity, a person does have such a right.[194]

2. EQUALITY IN EXCHANGE. Commutative justice requires that the parties exchange resources of equivalent value. We will see how the principle of equality in exchange provided a standard for evaluating the fairness of the price term and the auxiliary terms of the contract. We will then see how it was used to explain the implied terms that a court reads into an agreement when the parties are silent.

a. The fairness of the price term. We will see how writers in the Aristotelian tradition conceived of a just price. Then we will see that their approach explains the relief that courts actually give when a price is unfair.

i. The meaning of a fair price. As modern scholars have noted,[195] writers in the Aristotelian tradition thought that normally, unless public authority set a price, the fair price was the market price under competitive conditions. They knew that this price varies from day to day and from region to region. It has puzzled scholars that these writers expected exchange at such a price to preserve equality.

A first step to understanding their viewpoint is to recognize that, like modern economists, they thought that the market price had to fluctuate to reflect factors that they called need, scarcity, and cost. Need meant the value people place on goods. It might be quite different than their intrinsic worth or usefulness. Scarcity meant the quantity available. Cost meant the labor, expenses, and risk entailed in producing them.[196]

These factors are like those that determine supply and demand in modern economic theory. Unlike modern economists, however, these writers did not

---

194. See on American law: *Ploof* v. *Putnam*, 71 A. 188 (Vt. 1908); *Vincent* v. *Lake Erie Transp. Co.*, 124 N.W. 221 (Minn. 1910); on German law: BGB §904; on French law: F. Terré, P. Simler, and Y. Lequette, *Droit civil: Les Obligations*, 5th ed.(1993) at §704; B. Starck, H. Roland, and L. Boyer, *Obligations 1. Responsabilité délictuelle*, 4th ed. (1991) at §§300–301; on Italian law: Codice civile §2045; A. Venchiarutti in 4 *Commentario al Codice civile*, ed. by P. Cendon (1991) at §2045 no. 1.

195. J. Noonan, *The Scholastic Analysis of Usury* (Cambridge, MA: Harvard University Press, 1957) at 82–88; R. de Roover, "The Concept of the Just Price and Economic Policy" (1958) 18 J. Econ. Hist. 418; Ambrosetti, "Diritto privato ed economia nella seconda scolastica," in P. Grossi, ed., *La seconda scolastica nella formazione del diritto privato moderno* (1973) 28.

196. Gordley, *Philosophical Origins, supra* note 3 at 94–102; Soto, *De iustitia et iure, supra* note 59 at lib. 6 q. 2 a. 3; Molina, *De iustitia et iure, supra* note 59 at disp. 348. All of these factors had been mentioned, albeit cryptically, by Thomas Aquinas, *In decem libros ethicorum expositio, supra* note 193 at lib. 5, lec. 9; *Summa theologiae, supra* note 13 at II–II, Q. 77 a. 3 ad 4. They were discussed by medieval commentators on Aristotle. O. Langholm, *Price and Value in the Aristotelian Tradition* (Bergen: Universitetsforlaget, 1979) at 61–143.

think of supply and demand as separate schedules that clear at a unique equilibrium price.[197] Their explanation of how the market responds to need, scarcity,
and cost was a simpler one. Buyers and sellers simply make a judgment of the
price that adequately reflects these factors. The market price is set by the common judgment (*communis aestimatio*). In their view, the common judgment could
be wrong. If the public authorities thought it was wrong, they might fix a different price at which everyone must trade. But unless they did so, the just price
was the market price which reflected the judgment of buyers and sellers generally.[198] Monopoly prices were unfair because they reflected, not the common
judgment, but the efforts of a small group to get rich.[199]

These writers merely discussed why prices change, not why a fluctuating
market price preserves equality. But the fact that they thought this explanation
sufficient suggests how they conceived of equality. Prices had to change to
reflect need, scarcity, and cost. When and if these fluctuations need not be tolerated, public authority could fix a price. If it does not, then the market price
preserves equality to the extent feasible. There is no need to tolerate the further
inequalities that arise when, as Lessius put it, one party took advantage of the
other's "ignorance" or "necessity" to sell to him for more than the market price
or to buy for less.[200]

Moreover, as Soto observed, a party who gains when prices change later
might well have lost. A merchant must bear his losses if "bad fortune buffets
him, for example, because an unexpected abundance of goods mounts up," and
he may sell for more if "fortune smiles on him and later there is an unexpected
scarcity of goods." "For as the business of buying and selling is subject to for-
tuitous events of many kinds, merchants ought to bear risks at their own expense,
and, on the other hand, they may wait for good fortune."[201] Similarly, Lessius
noted that "this is the condition of merchants, that as they may gain if they receive goods at small expense, so they lose if the expense was disproportionate
or extraordinary."[202]

Elsewhere, I have argued that these considerations explain why the market
price is normally a fair price.[203] If society has an interest in seeing that purchasing power is justly distributed, then it should try to preserve existing distribution
or to change it by a social decision. An exchange at the market price preserves

197. Langholm, *supra* note 196 at 116.
198. Soto, *De iustitia et iure, supra* note 59 at lib. 6 q. 2 a. 3; Molina, *De iustitia et iure, supra* note
      59 at disp. 348; Lessius, *De iustitia et iure, supra* note 59 at lib. 2 cap. 21 dub. 2; Grotius, *De
      iure belli ac pacis, supra* note 86 at II.xii.14 and 23; Pufendorf, *De iure naturae et gentium,
      supra* note 95 at V.i.8.
199. Soto, *De iustitia et iure, supra* note 59 at lib. 6, q. 2, a. 3; Lessius, *De iustitia et iure, supra*
      note 59 at lib. 2, cap. 21, dub. 21; Grotius, *De iure belli ac pacis, supra* note 86 at II.xii.16.
200. Lessius, *De iustitia et iure, supra* note 59 at lib. 2 cap. 21 dub. 4.
201. Soto, *De iustitia et iure, supra* note 59 at lib. 6 q. 2 a. 3.
202. Lessius, *De iustitia et iure, supra* note 59 at lib. 2, cap. 21, dub. 4.
203. Gordley, "Equality in Exchange," *supra* note 89

this distribution insofar as it is feasible to do so. It is true, of course, that the purchasing power a person commands depends on the market value of the resources he owns. It therefore changes when market prices change. We have already seen, however, that some chance events must be allowed to alter a person's share of purchasing power. One reason is that worse evils might ensue if society tried to compensate the owner for chance losses. Another is that the very effort to do so might redistribute purchasing power. So it is with losses caused by changes in market prices. To prevent them, we would have to freeze prices. If we did, we would confront the evils economists describe: unsold goods or queues of buyers. Moreover, if buyers queue up because the market doesn't clear, goods will no longer go to those who are willing to pay the most but to those who are ahead in line. We will thus have redistributed the power to obtain them from those who should be able to do so, if the initial distribution was just, to those who happen to queue up first. There are, then, certain changes in the distribution of purchasing power that we cannot prevent. That is not a reason for tolerating others. There is no reason for allowing one party to charge more by taking advantage of another's ignorance of the market price or inability to use the market.

Moreover, as Soto suggested, even though prices may change in the future, the party who loses might well have gained. If he contracts at the market price and markets work as economists say they do, either event will be equally likely. Therefore, a party is not poorer at the moment he contracts although the contract does change the risk that he will be poorer in the future.

Critics of my argument have sometimes missed the point that I am claiming that exchange at the market price preserves (so far a possible) each party's share of purchasing power. Of course, the personal value that each party places on the resources he receives will necessarily be greater than the value he places on the resources he gives. Otherwise he wouldn't exchange. As Aristotle said, the shoemaker does not exchange with another shoemaker but with the house builder.[204] I am not claiming that each party places the same personal value on what he gives and gets,[205] or that each party should place the same personal value on what he receives as the other party does,[206] or that each party should be guaranteed that he will obtain something that he personally values as much as what he gave.[207]

---

204. *Nicomachean Ethics, supra* note 8 at V.v 1133ᵃ.
205. At one point Trebilcock seems to think I am. He claims that I could not object "to an exchange coerced at gunpoint if the values exchanges were equivalent market values." Trebilcock, *supra* note 27 at 81. But I agree that the value of goods to the party who buys them should be higher than the market value, and that the decision to buy is up to him.
206. Trebilcock, *supra* note 27 at 115 ("Gordley's proposal holds that both parties should gain equally").
207. Collins, *supra* note 107 at 63 (who thinks I want to "prevent transactions which are not Pareto optimal").

Consequently, I am not claiming that the payment of an amount equal to the market price adequately compensates a person for parting with an object that is personally worth more to him. The point of preserving a person's share of purchasing power is so that he can acquire things which have greater personal value than what he pays for them. Writers in the Aristotelian tradition recognized that once he has done so, compensation for their loss is measured by their value to him, not their value on the market.[208] Michael Trebilcock has objected that unless a person is allowed to charge more than the market price, he will not sell an object that had a higher personal value to himself, such as a house to which he is attached for "family, sentimental, historical or locational reasons."[209] The late scholastics thought he could charge a price that would compensate him for this loss of personal value provided that the other party valued the object for a similar reason, or at least, that the other party was not led thorough his own ignorance to pay more than the amount for which he could acquire an object elsewhere that was equally valuable to him.[210] Otherwise, they said, the seller would suffer a loss. Another way to put it is that, as we have stressed, once purchasing power is fairly distributed, goods are supposed to go to whoever will pay the most. In Trebilcock's case, the owner is that person until he is offered a price at which he is willing to sell. It is like an auction in which the owner is, in effect, bidding more than anyone else until someone offers him an amount he will accept. Whether it is an exception to the rule that normally, the just price is the market price, depends on how one defines the market price. In any event, it is not an exception to the principle we have been discussing.

Trebilcock also objects that, if people must trade at the market price, the incentive will disappear "to search out undervalued assets with a view to moving them to higher valued uses as reflected in prevailing or evolving markets."[211] I can't see why. Soto, Lessius, and, for that matter, Thomas Aquinas, noted that merchants are free to buy goods where and when they can find them cheaply in hopes of a profit when they resell.

ii. Relief when a price is unfair. Writers in the Aristotelian tradition used the principle of equality to explain why the Roman law of their day gave relief for what was called *laesio enormis,* a deviation of more than one-half from the market price. Thomas Aquinas explained that, for practical reasons, a remedy was given only when the deviation was large.[212] Before Aristotle's *Ethics* was

---

208. De Soto, *De iustita et iure, supra* note 59 at lib. 4, q. 6, a. 5; Molina, *De iustitia et iure, supra* note 59 at disp. 315, 724; Lessius, *De iustitia et iure, supra* note 59 at lib. 2, cap. 12, dubs. 16, 18; cap. 20, dubs. 10–11. See Grotius, *De iure belli ac pacis, supra* note 86 at II.xvii.1–2; Pufendorf, *De iure naturae et gentium, supra* note 95 at III.1.3; Barbeyrac on Pufendorf, *supra* note 138 at n. 1 to III.i.3.

209. Trebilcock, *supra* note 27 at 116.

210. Molina, *De iustitia et iure, supra* note 59 at disp. 351; Lessius, *De iustitia et iure, supra* note 59 at lib. 2, cap. 21, dub. 4.

211. Trebilcock, *supra* note 27 at 81–82.

212. *Summa theologiae, supra* note 13 at II–II, Q. 77, a. 1, obj. 1 and ad 1.

read in the West, medieval jurists had created this remedy by generalizing a
Roman text that gave a relief to a person who sold land for less than half the
just price.[213] Like the writers in the Aristotelian tradition, the medieval jurists
identified the just price with a market price that changed from day to day and
region to region.[214] Unlike these writers, they had no theory of why the market
price was just. They seem to have identified the just price with the market price
simply because otherwise thousands of seemingly normal transactions would be
called into question.

Today, many legal scholars are in a position like that of the early medieval
jurists. Their legal systems give relief when a price is extremely unjust, and yet
they have no theory of how prices can be unjust.

In France, article 1674 of the Civil Code of 1804 preserved a remedy for
lésion for the sale of land at a low price. That was the only case in which French
customary law had traditionally permitted relief.[215] In the nineteenth and
twentieth centuries, special statutes were enacted which gave a remedy to those
who pay an excessive amount for fertilizer, seeds, and fodder,[216] or for a rescue at sea[217] or after an aviation accident.[218] Another statute gave a remedy to
those who receive too little when selling artistic or literary property.[219] In other
cases, courts have sometimes given relief by declaring the contract was procured
by fraud, duress, or mistake even though the victim had neither been told a lie
nor threatened, and his only mistake concerned the value of what he bought
or sold.[220]

In nineteenth-century Germany, although some local statutes limited relief,
the traditional remedy for *laesio enormis* was available wherever Roman law
remained in force. At the end of the century, the first draft of the German Civil
Code of 1900 abolished relief. But an amendment (now section 138 par. 2) re-
instated a remedy whenever one party obtained a "disproportionate advantage"

---

213. Cod. 4.44.2. The text was generalized soon after the rediscovery of Roman law. See *Brachylo-*
  gus III.xii.8 (1743); Hugolinus de Presbyteris, *Diversitates sive dissensiones dominorum super*
  toto corpore iure civilis, ed. by G. Haenel (1834) at §253.
214. *Glossa ordinaria* to Dig. 13.4.3 [vulg. 13.4.4] to *varia* (1581). As the great medieval jurist
  Accursius pointed out, one who bought something and later sold it for less than half the purchase price might not receive a remedy for "it could be . . . that when the sale of the object to
  him occurred, it was worth more than when he now sells." *Glossa ordinaria* to Cod. 4.44.4
  to *auctoritate iudicis.*
215. C. de Ferrière, *Dictionnaire de droit et de pratique* II.v "lézion d'outre moité de juste prix,"
  nouv. ed. (1769) 135 at 137; Honoré Lacombe de Prezel, *Dictionnaire portatif de jurispru-*
  dence et de pratique II.v. "lézion," (1763) 430.
216. Law of July 8, 1907.
217. Law of April 29, 1916, art. 7.
218. Law of May 31, 1925, art. 57.
219. Law of March 11, 1957.
220. Decision of April 27, 1887, Cass. req., *D.P.* 1988.I.263; Decision of Jan. 27, 1919, Cass. req.,
  S. 1920.I.198; Decision of Nov. 29, 1968, Cass. civ. *Gaz. Pal.* 1969.J.63; Decision of June 2,
  1930, Douai, *Jurisp. de la Cour d'appel de Douai* 1930.183; Decision of Jan. 22, 1953, Paris,
  Sem. jur. 1953.II.7435.

by exploiting the difficulties, indiscretion, or inexperience of the other party. Since 1936, German courts have been willing to give relief for a violation of "good morals" (German Civil Code § 138 par. 1) if the contract is sufficiently one-sided even if such a weakness were not exploited.[221]

In the United States, the courts of equity traditionally gave relief if a contract was "unconscionable." In the nineteenth century, they claimed to do so, not simply because a bargain was one-sided, but because its one-sidedness was evidence of fraud.[222] Nevertheless, they gave relief where no fraud was alleged. As I have shown elsewhere, they did so quite generously.[223] Today, section 2-203 of the Uniform Commercial Code allows a court to give relief in law or equity when a contract to sell goods is severely unfair. Section 208 of the Second Restatement of Contracts provides for similar relief in other types of contracts. American courts have held the price to be unconscionable when home appliances were sold for over three times their usual retail price[224] and homeowners were charged extravagant amounts for windows and sidewalls.[225]

The relief given in these cases is easy to explain in Aristotelian terms. For reasons already given, the market price is normally a fair one. It is hard to explain in any other way. Some American jurists have distinguished "substantive" from "procedural" unconscionability. Substantive unconscionability means the terms of the contract are unfair. Procedural unconscionability means that one party was at an unfair disadvantage in protecting himself. Some have said that relief should be given when a transaction is substantively unfair only if it is procedurally unfair as well.[226] Some have said that the reason relief should be given is because of procedural unfairness, for example, because of a disparity in bargaining power.[227]

It is true that no one will pay more or charge less than the market price if they know what the market price is and are physically able to use the market. If these types of ignorance and necessity count as "procedural unconscionability," then they will accompany every instance of substantive unfairness. It is also true that sometimes, a party is less able to protect himself for some additional reason such youth, age, or poor education. A court should pay attention to such disadvantages when there is doubt as to whether a transaction deviated from the

---

221. Decision of Mar. 13, 1936, Reichsgericht, *Entscheidungen des Reichsgerichts in Zivilsachen* [RGZ] 150, 1.
222. A. W. B. Simpson, "The Horwitz Thesis and the History of Contracts," (1979) 46 U. Chic. L. Rev. 533 at 569.
223. *Philosophical Origins, supra* note 3 at 154–158.
224. *Jones v. Star Credit Corp.,* 298 N.Y.S.2d 264 (Sup. Ct 1969); *Frostifresh v. Reynoso,* 274 N.Y.S. 2d 757 (Sup. Ct 1966), *rev'd as to damages,* 281 N.Y.S.2d 964 (App. 1967).
225. *American Home Improvement Co. v. MacIver,* 201 A.2d 886 (N.H. 1964).
226. R. Craswell, "Property Rules and Liability Rules in Unconscionability and Related Doctrines," (1993) 60 U. Chic. L. Rev. 1 at 17.
227. W. D. Slawson, *Binding Promises: The Late Twentieth Century Reformation of Contract Law* (Princeton: Princeton University Press, 1996) at 23, 38.

market price so severely as to warrant relief. The better able a party is to protect himself, the less likely it is that a severe deviation will happen. Nevertheless, the reason relief is given must be that the terms are substantively unfair. If they were not – if a consumer were paying the retail market price for an appliance – no one would care that a salesman could have taken advantage of him. Indeed, procedural unconscionability seems to mean nothing more than any circumstances that would enable the salesman to charge more than the market price. So we come back to the question of why the market price is normally a fair one. The Aristotelian tradition had an answer.

Posner and Landes have tried to explain relief by speaking about efficiency rather than fairness. Suppose a ship in distress promises a huge amount of money, vastly exceeding the costs of rescue, to the only possible rescuer. The promise is unenforceable in admiralty law, and the rescuer can receive only his costs plus a premium to give him an incentive to rescue ships in distress. The reason, according to Posner and Landes, is not that the price is unfair but that otherwise, ship owners would overinvest in safety equipment so that they would not find themselves in need of rescue.[228]

This is one of many instances in which scholars who do economic analysis of law have tried to add credibility to their approach by using it to explain what courts do. We ought to be careful. It is one thing to suggest that a judge saw a particular result was right but did not fully grasp the reason, or that he endorsed a certain principle but did not fully grasp its implications. It is quite another to suggest that his decisions can be "explained" by principles he is unlikely to have had even vaguely in mind. Such an "explanation" means that, by complete coincidence, a decision taken for one reason has turned out to be advantageous for another quite different one. If that is all that is meant, one should say so. One cannot explain the American seizure of the Philippines in the Spanish-American War by pointing out that it makes a good base for military aircraft.

In any event, if Posner and Landes were right, a court would give relief only when there is some possible safety precaution that a shipowner could have taken to avoid the need for a rescue. That is not the law.

Charles Fried, as we have seen, endorses "the liberal principle that the free arrangements of rational persons should be respected."[229] One might think that Fried would condemn the doctrine of unconscionability outright as he does that of consideration. Nevertheless, he concedes that "some bargains, though they meet all the tests I have set out so far, seem just too hard to enforce."[230] For example, a rescuer should not be able to charge too much to save the cargo of a

---

228. W. M. Landes and R. A. Posner, "Salvors, Finders, Good Samaritans and Other Rescuers: An Economic Study of Law and Altruism" (1978) 7 J. Leg. Stud. 83. The same explanation is given by F. H. Buckley "Three Theories of Substantive Fairness" (1990) 19 Hofstra L. Rev. 33 at 40–48 [hereinafter Buckley, "Substantive Fairness"].
229. Fried, *supra* note 45 at 35.
230. Ibid. at 109.

disabled ship. The reason, according to Fried, is that a random event has caused the breakdown of what Fried calls a "functioning social system" or "political system of social redistribution" within which exchange normally takes place.[231] Might one call it a system of commutative and distributive justice? At that point, instead of talking about "self-determination" it would be more consistent to acknowledge that while promise-keeping is a virtue, justice is a virtue as well.

Following Hegel, Peter Benson has tried to extract the requirement of equality in exchange from the concept of freedom. The realization of freedom is said to require that the wills of the parties become identical, which they supposedly do in a contract of exchange. Their wills would not be identical, however, unless they were directed to something that is the same, and since that cannot be the resources they exchange, it must be their value.[232] One of my problems, again, is that I don't understand why this sort of reasoning counts as reasoning, since it does not relate one concept to another deductively, as in mathematics, or functionally, as in biology or engineering. But, in any event, it seems impossible to get from equality in value as a concept in the mind of the parties to equality in market value as a criterion of fairness. As Benson himself notes, "Hegel's justification of a requirement of equivalence in exchange should be viewed as elucidating a postulate that goes to the intelligibility of contractual obligation rather than as establishing a rule that can be applied to particular cases."[233]

Finally, a few scholars have suggested that contract prices should be substantively fair. Their theories get into difficulties because they do not identify the fair price with the market price.

According to Michael Swygert and Katherine Yanes, one party ought not to receive "almost all of the surplus utility created by the transaction."[234] It seems intuitively wrong, however, that the fairness of a contract depends on the degree of personal advantage the parties derive from it. A beer might be barely worth the market price to one person and ten times that price to another but it is not unfair that they pay the same.[235] Moreover, the person who saves my life at a small cost to himself would not be receiving "almost all the surplus utility" if he demanded my life savings in return, but it seems unfair for him to do so.

According to Stephen Smith, prices are unfair when they are "abnormal," that is, when they deviate from what a person would normally expect. The reason is that such prices "harm individuals' abilities to plan and thereby to achieve

---

231. Ibid. at 109–110.
232. "Abstract Right," *supra* note 44 at 1192–93. Weinrib, citing Benson, seems to give a version of this argument when he says that "equal value is necessary if [the parties] are to count for each others as equals within the transaction." *Private Law, supra* note 52 at 138.
233. "Abstract Right," *supra* note 44 at 1104 n.168.
234. M. I. Swygert and K. E. Yanes, "A Unified Theory of Justice: The Integration of Fairness into Efficiency" (1998) 73 Wash. L. Rev. 249 at 262.
235. A point made by Buckley, "Substantive Fairness," *supra* note 228 at 36.

autonomous, fulfilling lives."[236] Again, that explanation intuitively seems wrong.
To rescue someone at small cost in return for his life savings seems unfair even
if he expected a rescuer would charge that much. To sell someone an appliance
for three times its retail price seems unfair even if the buyer had no expectations about what such an appliance might cost. Monopoly prices are unfair, but
as Smith notes, they may not be unexpected. Moreover, if prices become unexpectedly high on a competitive market, the reason must be that there was an
unexpected change in cost of production or in demand or in short term supply.
If the change is in cost, it would be odd to say a producer is acting unfairly because he refuses to sell at a loss. Moreover, his plans have been disrupted as
well. If the change is in demand or short-term supply, then someone's plans will
have to be disrupted. If prices do not rise, the market will not clear, and the person whose plans must change will be the one at the end of a queue.

    b. The fairness of auxiliary terms. For Thomas Aquinas, the late scholas-
tics, and natural lawyers, the types of exchanges into which the parties might
enter – for example, sale or lease – were all acts of commutative justice. The
terms appropriate to each type were those that would effectuate the parties' purposes while maintaining equality. An illustration is their explanation of why a
seller should be liable for defects in the goods he sold. If he were not liable, the
contract would be unequal since the buyer would have paid more than he
ought to for defective goods.[237] The parties could modify these terms in any
way that suited them provided they did not violate equality. According to Molina
and Jean Domat (a French jurist influenced by the natural law school), the seller
might disclaim liability for defects if he lowered his price to compensate the
buyer for the risk the goods would be defective.[238] Thus, risks and burdens
can fall on either party provided the price is set so as to compensate him fairly
for bearing them.

    In my view, this theory provides the best explanation of the cases in which
courts refuse to enforce unfair auxiliary terms. To see why, we must consider
the reason such a term might appear in a contract. As economists say, the parties would want to place risks and burdens on whichever party can bear them
most easily. As long as a party knew that he was to assume a risk or burden and
also knew the cost to himself of bearing it, he would agree to bear it only if the
price were adjusted in his favor by at least the amount of his cost. Consequently,
if both parties always had this knowledge, the terms would never be unfair. That
is so even if the market is noncompetitive for roughly the same reason that even
a monopolist will put leather upholstery in cars if people are willing to pay more
for it than his cost. Suppose the cost to one party of bearing a particular risk or

236. Smith, *supra* note 188 at 157.
237. *Summa theologiae, supra* note 13 at II–II, Q. 77, a. 2; Molina, *De iustitia et iure, supra* note 59
    at disp. 353.
238. Molina, *De iustitia et iure, supra* note 59 at disp. 353; J. Domat, *Les Loix civiles dans leur
    ordre naturel* (1713) at I.iv.2.

burden is $50, and it is $500 to the other. The parties would place the risk or burden on the first party and compensate him by at least $50. For any lesser amount, he would not agree to bear it. For any greater amount, he would want to do so. An economist would say that this allocation of risks and burdens is "efficient" because there is no way to change it in return for compensation so as to make both parties better off. The Aristotelian approach explains why it is not only efficient but fair. And indeed, Hugh Beale has noted that the terms that courts regard as fair do tend to be those which are "efficient" in the sense just described.[239]

Suppose, however, that a party does not know that the contract places a risk or burden on him or the cost of bearing it. Then the other party might place it on him without adjusting the price by the amount of his cost. Indeed, we can be sure the other party did not adjust the price by that amount if that party could have born the risk or burden more cheaply himself. A party who can bear the risk or burden for $50 will not throw it on the party who can bear it for $500 if he has to alter his price by $500.[240]

In fact, the terms that courts have held to be unfair are ones that place risks and burdens on a party who is unlikely to have been compensated for bearing them. Admittedly, it is often difficult for a court to estimate the size of a risk or burden and to determine whether a party has been fairly compensated. Courts tend to give relief in cases in which it is easier to see that he has not been.

Sometimes, a term is so onerous for one party and of such little significance for the other that it is clear by inspection that the advantaged party would not have paid fair compensation for inserting it in the contract. In a well-known American case, a farmer had agreed to sell his tomatoes to a soup manufacturer. If, for any reason, the soup manufacturer rejected the tomatoes, the farmer would not be paid and was forbidden to sell them to anyone else.[241] It is hard to imagine that the soup company gained an advantage by forbidding resale of tomatoes it did not want that was greater than the hardship this provision inflicted on the farmer. Therefore, it is hard to imagine the soup company actually compensated the farmer adequately for this hardship.

In other cases, it will be clear that a risk or burden is placed on the wrong party after considering the reasons why a party is better able to assume a risk or burden. He might be able to control the occurrence of some event at lesser

---

239. H. Beale, "Unfair Contracts in Britain and Europe" (1989) 42 Current Leg. Prob. 197 at 206.
240. Note that this argument does not assume that the first party keeps the $ 50 he has saved by shifting the risk or burden to the other. F. H. Buckley notes, quite correctly, that even if consumers cannot tell whether a term in a contract hurts them, and producers cannot compete by eliminating it, the producers may still compete by lowering prices. If so, they may lower their prices until the gain they make by including that term disappears. Buckley, "Substantive Fairness," *supra* note 228 at 62. Even so, the term will still place a risk or burden on the other party for which he is not adequately compensated. If the producer had to compensate him adequately, he would prefer to bear the risk or burden himself.
241. *Campbell Soup v. Wentz,* 172 F.2d 80 (3rd Cir. 1948).

cost. Even if he could not have prevented such an event, it might be hard to prove whether he could or not, and thus the cheapest solution might be for him to assume liability and raise his price by an amount that will compensate him for doing so. Even if the event is uncontrollable, he might be able to assume the risk of its occurrence most cheaply because he is better able to estimate its likelihood. If people are risk-averse, risks or burdens are smaller when they are easier to estimate. Or he might face the same risk or shoulder the same burden continually. A risk would then be easier to bear because, as in the case of an insurance company or a casino, outcomes are more predictable when the same risk is faced over and over.

If a court can see that, for these reasons, one party is better able to bear a risk or burden, it can conclude that the other party could not have been adequately compensated for assuming it. For example, modern courts have refused to enforce a waiver of the seller's liability for defects in factory new products. In *Henningsen v. Bloomfield Motors,*[242] an American court held it was unconscionable for a car manufacturer to disclaim liability for personal injury if the car is defective. According to Uniform Commercial Code §2–217, disclaimers of liability for personal injuries caused by defects are "*prima facie* unconscionable." Most American states reach the same result today by imposing strict liability in tort for product defects. European courts will reach similar results under a European Community directive governing product defects which was inspired by American law.[243]

In such cases, it hard to see how the consumer can be in a better position to bear the risk than the manufacturer. If the consumer by some reasonable precaution could have reduced the risk, he will be held to be comparatively negligent if he fails to do so. But otherwise, the manufacturer would have been in the best position to take any feasible precautions. The problems of proving whether he did can be severe. He will be best able to estimate the size of the risk. Moreover, the manufacturer who is held liable will face the same risk over and over. If, for these reasons, the manufacturer can best bear the risk, it is hard to think that he has reduced his price adequately to compensate consumers for bearing it.

In other cases, a court can conclude a term is unfair because it gives one of the parties control over the content of the contract or over whether he is bound by it. Such a contract may be one-sided despite any advantage it seems to offer the other party. Suppose, for example, that one party has a thirty-year option, for which he has paid nothing, to buy the other party's land at a set price; or the right, terminable whenever he wishes, to sell him a fixed quantity of goods each year at a set price; or the right to sell or buy any quantity of goods he chooses

---

242. 161 A.2d 69 (1960).
243. European Union Directive E. C. Directive Concerning Liability for Defective Products, Directive 85–374 EEC, O.J. 1985 L 210/29–33 1(a).

at a set price. The party with such a power can profit by exercising his option if the market price rises above the contract price; by terminating the contract if the market price rises above the contract price; or by buying (or selling) a huge amount if the market price falls below (or rises above) the contract price. Adjusting the contract price in the other party's favor can make these events less likely but it can never make the arrangement fair.

Understandably, modern courts have refused to enforce various arrangements of this type. Common law courts traditionally refused to enforce the ones just described on the grounds that they lacked consideration. As Eisenberg has noted, the fundamental problem was one of fairness.[244] The modern tendency is to ask directly whether they are fair. For example, the Uniform Commercial Code provides that if a merchant promises in writing not to revoke an offer to buy or sell goods, the promise is binding for up to three months.[245] An Official Comment notes that in an appropriate case, it could still be struck down under the doctrine of unconscionability.[246] The Second Restatement, with some support in the case law, will enforce an option when consideration is nominal – for example, one dollar – and the option is signed by the offeror and "proposes an exchange on fair terms within a reasonable time."[247] A requirements or output contract is enforceable but the quantity demanded must correspond to one's usual needs or production, and must be consistent with good faith.[248]

Some similar arrangements can be set aside under the law of continental countries which is now supplemented by a Directive on Abusive Contract Terms of the European Community. For example, under the Directive, a contract is deemed to be unfair if one party is bound while the obligations of the other depend on a condition whose fulfillment depends on that party's will alone.[249] It is unfair if one party alone has an option to terminate.[250] Under a German statute on standardized contract terms, an option to terminate is deemed unfair unless the contract states a reason for termination.[251] Under the European Directive, under French legislation passed in response to it, and under the German statute, it is deemed unfair for one party to be able to unilaterally alter the performance to be made.[252] According to the German statute, it is unfair for one party to be able to increase his price within four months.[253] According to the

---

244. M. Eisenberg, "The Principles of Consideration" (1982) 67 Cornell L. Rev. 640 at 649–655.
245. Uniform Commercial Code §2–205.
246. Uniform Commercial Code §2.205 cmt. 4.
247. *Restatement (Second) of Contracts* §87(1)(1979).
248. Uniform Commercial Code §2–306(1).
249. E.C. Directive on Unfair Contracts, Directive 93/13 EEC, O.J. 1993 L 95/29, Annex 1(c).
250. E.C. Directive on Unfair Contracts, Annex 1(f); see 1(p).
251. Allgemeinengeshäftsbedingungengesetz (AGBG) §10(3).
252. Decree of 24 March 1978, art. 3; ABGB §10(4); E.C. Directive on Unfair Contracts 1(k) (unfair to modify characteristics of a goods without reason).
253. ABGB §11(1)(prohibits a clause allowing a price increase within four months for goods to be delivered or services to be performed).

European Directive, it is unfair to allow one party to increase his price unless the other has the right to withdraw from the contract.[254] It is also unfair for one party to have the right to modify the terms except when a good reason is specified in the contract.[255]

In other cases, one can see that a term is unfair because, rather than shift a risk to a party who can better bear it, it amounts to a side bet concerning a risk that the parties are equally able to bear. Risk-averse parties do not gamble if they must pay the expected value of a bet. A court could conclude that a party would not insert such a clause in the contract if he had to adjust the price sufficiently to compensate the other party.

The clearest example is a clause that obligates a party in breach to pay a penalty that exceeds the harm that the other party suffers. The party to receive it would not have inserted such a clause merely to encourage the other party to perform. In fact, he will be better off if the other party fails to do so. Nor would he have inserted it if he had to compensate the other party adequately for the risk of having to pay this extra amount. The expected value of their bet is the extra amount times the probability of breach given the incentives not to breach created by the penalty clause. Since both parties are risk-averse, the party who risks paying the penalty is not adequately compensated unless he receives more than this expected value, and the party who stands to benefit will not insert such a clause if he had to pay that much.

It is understandable, then, that common law courts have traditionally refused to enforce such a clause. A contract can require a party in breach to pay an amount that is a reasonable estimate of the damages the other party will suffer. It cannot require him to pay more.[256] Civil law countries have moved in that direction. In France, a law of 1975 allowed the judge "to reduce or increase the penalty agreed upon if it is manifestly excessive or derisory" despite any "contrary stipulation" by the parties.[257] The German statute on standardized terms provides that, without a special showing of their reasonableness, contract penalties are void,[258] and terms prescribing the damages to be recovered in the event of breach must correspond to what one would expect in the normal course of events.[259] The European Community directive on abusive terms contains a similar provision.[260]

In still another type of case, the party who was benefitted by a clause might have been willing, if necessary, to compensate adequately the party burdened by

254. E.C. Directive on Unfair Contracts 1(l).
255. E.C. Directive on Unfair Contracts 1(j).
256. *Restatement (Second) of Contracts* §§355–356 (1979).
257. Law no. 75–597 of 9 July 1975, art. 1, now Code civil art. 1152.
258. AGBG 11(6).
259. AGBG §11(5). Other provisions prevent the drafter from achieving this result indirectly by imposing a charge for use of property or for expenses (§10(7)) or for late acceptance or withdrawal (§11(6)).
260. E.C. Directive on Unfair Contracts 1(e).

it. But he never made such an adjustment. A good example is the American case of *Williams* v. *Walker-Thomas Furniture Co.*[261] A woman made a series of purchases on credit from a store. A clause in the contracts she signed provided that all of her payments would be applied to the debt outstanding on all the items she purchased, so that if she defaulted, all the items could be repossessed by the store. The court held this clause unconscionable. Richard Epstein has pointed out that the clause could have served the useful purpose of providing the store with security for the loans it extended, and security of a kind it could easily verify since it knew which items it had already sold.[262] That is true. But Mrs. Williams, it seems, did not receive a mark-down of the price to compensate her for the added risk she incurred in order to provide the store with this security. For all the appears, she paid just the price charged people who had not previously bought anything that the store could repossess.

 c. The implied terms of a contract. Writers in the Aristotelian tradition used the principle of equality in exchange to explain, not only why courts sometimes disregard the express terms of a contract because they are unfair, but why they read other terms into the contract when the parties were silent. Much of the Roman law of sales, leases, and so forth, specified what these terms are. These writers explained why they should be read in. They were appropriate because they effectuated the purposes of the parties while maintaining equality.[263]

 In discussing unfair terms, enough has been said to show how one can analyze whether a term will maintain equality. As the law and economics scholars say, risks and burdens should be placed on the party who can bear them at least cost. The price should then be adjusted to compensate him for bearing them. As we have seen, the contract will be unfair if the party who can bear a risk at least cost succeeds in shifting it to the other party since the party shifting the risk would prefer to bear it himself if he had to compensate the other party fairly.

 In one way, then, this approach to determining the terms that belong in a contract is like that of the law and economics scholars. Risks and burdens are to be placed where they can be born at least cost. The difference is in the reason why. For the law and economics scholars, the rationale is efficiency. Unless risks and burdens are placed on the party that can bear them most cheaply, it is possible to alter the terms of the contract so as to make both parties better off by reassigning the risk or burden and altering the price. From an Aristotelian standpoint, the rationale is fairness: to avoid, so far as feasible, changes in the share of purchasing power that belongs to each party.

 The trouble with the economic rationale is that we are speaking of implied terms, terms that the parties did not set for themselves when they contracted but

---

261. 198 A.2d 914 (D.C., 1964).
262. R. A. Epstein, "Unconscionability: A Critical Reappraisal," (1975) 18 J. L. and Econ. 293 at 308–310.
263. *Philosophical Origins, supra* note 3 at 105–111.

which the court reads in later on. It is true that, had the parties considered the matter, they would place risks and burdens on the party who could bear them most cheaply and then adjust the price to compensate him. But they never did consider the matter. Therefore, it is hard to think that their decision to contract was affected by the way they expected these risks and burdens to be allocated. Quite possibly, the reason that terms later have to be read in is that these terms cover contingencies that are sufficiently remote that *ex ante* it was not worth the parties' time to decide how to deal with them. If so, then the way these risks and burdens are allocated *ex post* will not affect the value of the contract to the parties *ex ante* or their decision to enter into it. If it does not, then an economist has no reason for caring about what happens *ex post*. *Ex post,* a court's decision to place a risk or burden on one party rather than the other merely affects how much money each party has.[264]

One response might be that sometimes, a matter is sufficiently important to the parties that they would draft their own terms to deal with it. The law can spare them this trouble by providing a set of default rules that are like the ones that they would have drafted for themselves. The law should do so if it can at a lower cost than the parties would incur. According to this explanation, the advantage of placing risks and burdens on whoever can bear them the most cheaply is not that it is efficient to do so, but that it is efficient to spare the parties the trouble of doing so in the cases in which they care enough *ex ante* to trouble themselves. If so, the entire law of sales, leases, partnerships, and so forth exists for the sake of these people. One wonders how many there are. According to Jay Feinman and Melvin Eisenberg, most people don't know what terms the law will read into their contract.[265] That suggests they are not sufficiently interested *ex ante* to find out in order to adjust their prices to reflect the risks they are assuming. If so, it seems unlikely they would be drafting their own terms if the law provided different ones.

On Aristotelian principles, it is easier to see why the law should place a risk or burden on the party who can bear them the most easily. The reason is not to affect the parties' decision whether to contract. It is because the contract is fair when this party assumes the risk and is compensated for doing so. It is true that if the parties have not considered a risk or burden *ex ante* they will not have adjusted the price to compensate the party who assumes it. Nevertheless, it may

---

264. A response might be that *ex post* one party might be better able to bear a risk or burden than another. To allocate it to the party least able to bear it will necessitate another transaction: one in which the parties agree to transfer the risk to the party better able to do so in return for suitable compensation. One problem with that response is that the party who can best bear a risk or burden *ex post* is not necessarily the one could can best do so *ex ante*. Another problem is that then, we are merely talking about transactions costs which may be quite small, and considerably smaller than the efforts that courts, attorneys, and scholars have put into developing a law of sales, leases, corporations, and so forth.

265. J. Feinman, "The Significance of Contract Theory," (1990) 58 U. Cinn. L. Rev. 1283 at 1306; "The Theory of Contracts," *supra* note 51 at p. 249.

be that, without considering specific risks, they have set a fair price based on their general experience with contracts of that type. They may be trading at a market price that reflects costs for a given type of transaction in the industry, and these costs reflect the risks and burdens each party is assuming. It may be that no adjustment of the price is needed because, as in some of the cases discussed earlier, the risk or burden is insignificant for one party even though it is substantial for the other. Finally, even if the parties did not consider a risk or burden *ex ante,* the fact remains that one party can bear it at a lower cost than the other *ex post,* when the risk materializes or the burden has to be shouldered. If we want to preserve, so far as possible, the amount of purchasing power that each party controls, it is better for this party to bear the cost rather than the other party.

With the Aristotelian approach, in part, the justification for reading such terms into the contract is that they are fair. In part, the justification is that these are the terms that the parties themselves would have wished to govern their agreement had their intention been the one the law should respect: to exchange resources but not to alter the share of purchasing power that belongs to each. Writers in the Aristotelian tradition did not conceive of equality in exchange as a requirement foreign to the will of the parties and imposed on them, so to speak, from the outside. Had one of them wished to enrich the other party at his own expense, he would have made a gift rather than entering into an exchange. As Grotius said, "Nor is it enough for anyone to say that what the other party has promised more than equality is to be regarded as a gift. For such is not the intention of the contracting parties, as is not to be presumed so, except it appear."[266] Had one of the parties wanted to enrich himself at the other's expense without the other party's consent, he would have had an intention the law should not respect. That intention should not affect the content of his obligations any more than an undisclosed intention not to perform.

The implied terms were read into the parties' contract, then, because they effectuated the parties' legitimate purposes, and maintaining equality was regarded as one of these purposes. The parties wanted the implied terms in the sense – though only in the sense – that a person who buys a car wants a camshaft even though he has never heard of one: He wants whatever the car must have to make it do what it is supposed to do.

Writers in the Aristotelian tradition thereby avoided the difficulties of modern theorists who explain contractual obligations by autonomy or consent. The implied terms are obligations to which the parties never consciously consented. As Richard Craswell has pointed out, theories based on autonomy are not useful in explaining what these terms should be. Any set of them seems consistent with the parties' freedom to choose the terms to which they expressly consent.[267]

---

266. Grotius, *De iure belli ac pacis, supra* note 86 at II.xii.2.1.
267. "Philosophy of Promising," *supra* note 38 at 514–529.

Indeed, Charles Fried seems to concede as much. He claims that because a court reads them into the contract by asking what the parties might have done, or what reasonable people might have done, or what is fair, no one should make "the futile attempt to bring these cases under the promise principle."[268] As his critics have noted, his principle therefore cannot explain most of contract law.[269]

To do so, other writers have tried to stretch the idea of autonomy or consent to make it the source of implied terms. Conrad Johnson believes that autonomy merely requires that "the parties must have a fair opportunity to find out what risks they are accepting."[270] But to have such an opportunity merely means that the parties could have exercised their autonomy, not that they did.

Randy Barnett has admitted that by his theory, if parties have no subjective intent, then their intentions will be satisfied equally by any default rule. But he believes that the parties can have expectations that never come to consciousness. The parties "subjective consent" is most likely satisfied by a default rule that conforms to "commonsense or conventional expectations that likely are part of the tacit assumptions of particular parties."[271] But the body of law that determines what terms govern a contract is vast. It includes most of the law of leases, sales, partnerships, and so forth. As Feinman and Eisenberg have noted, most businessmen are ignorant of it.[272] This body of law may not contradict commonsense expectations, but to say it conforms to them is to imagine that the parties have implausibly precise expectations about matters that they never considered.

David Charny has also admitted that with implied terms, "the principle of autonomy that requires courts to honor parties' choice is simply not in play." He believes the court should consult other principles of "autonomy" such as "the fair sharing of gains and losses not allocated by prior agreement."[273] But at that point, the terms are said to be autonomous because they are fair, not because they are chosen autonomously.

With the Aristotelian approach there is no need to pretend the parties know law any more than the car buyer knows engineering. If the implied terms are a means to purposes which the parties have consciously in mind and which the law respects, then the parties would want them, just as a car buyer would want a camshaft even if he has never heard of one. But the reason for reading in the terms, or including the camshaft, is not to respect the will of the parties on a matter they have never considered. It is to help them achieve an end that they have considered.

---

268. Fried, *supra* note 45 at 60, 61, 63, 69.
269. "Theory of Contracts," *supra* note 51 at 279; Johnson, *supra* note 47 at 300.
270. Johnson, *supra* note 47 at 300–302.
271. R. E. Barnett, "The Sound of Silence: Default Rules and Contractual Consent," (1992) 78 Va. L. Rev. 821 at 876–877.
272. *Supra* note 265.
273. D. Charny, "Hypothetical Bargains: The Normative Structure of Contract Interpretation" (1991) 89 Mich. L. Rev. 1815 at 1833.

IV. Liability for Broken Promises

Our last question is the extent of the promisor's liability for breach of contract. As noted earlier, writers in the Aristotelian tradition saw two possibilities. He might only be liable for any harm the promisee had suffered by changing his position in reliance on the promise. Or he might be liable for the full value of the promised performance.

Cajetan took the first position. He acknowledged that it was wrong to break a promise. One who did so failed to exercise the virtue of fidelity. But commutative justice was violated only by diminishing the other party's resources. Therefore, a person who had been promised a gift was not entitled to it as a matter of commutative justice since, if he failed to receive it, he was no worse off than if the promise had never been made. He would have a claim only if he had become worse off by changing his position in reliance on the promise.[274]

Had this position been adopted, something like the modern American doctrine of promissory reliance would have passed into continental law centuries ago. As we saw, however, it was rejected by most of the late scholastics and then by the northern natural lawyers. Molina pointed out that the donor would violate commutative justice if he took back a gift after it had been delivered to the donee. He argued that the donor, if he wished, should be able to confer a right to the gift at the moment the promise was made rather than at the time of delivery.[275] Lessius argued that a promise, by definition, conferred such a right.[276]

Molina and Lessius were assuming, without argument, that the promisor might have a good reason for wanting to confer such a right on the promisee, a reason that the law would respect. Later we will discuss whether that assumption is correct. If it is, however, then they do seem to have detected the fallacy in Cajetan's argument. Cajetan assumed that the promisee did not acquire a right to the performance at the time the promise was made. If he did, the promisor who failed to perform would be depriving him of something to which he was already entitled.

Modern writers have often made the same assumption without presenting any more justification for it than Cajetan. Fuller and Perdue did so in what had been called the most important law review article of the twentieth century. It would be odd, they said, to speak of specific performance or expectation damages as "compensation for an injury" because then "we 'compensate' the plaintiff by giving him something he never had."[277] In the very steps of Cajetan, they argued:

In passing from compensation for change of position to compensation for loss of expectancy, we pass, to use Aristotle's terms . . . from the realm of corrective justice. . . .

---

274. Cajetan, *Commentaria to Summa theological, supra* note 134, at II–II, Q. 88, a. 1; Q. 113, a. 1.
275. See note 136, *supra.*   276. See note 137, *supra.*
277. Fuller and Perdue, *supra* note 9, at 211–212.

The law no longer seeks merely to heal a disturbed status quo but to bring into being a new situation. It ceases to act defensively, restoratively, and assumes a more active role.[278]

They thus assumed, like Cajetan, that the promisee had not already acquired the right to the performance of which he was deprived. They concluded, as he had, that protection of the promisee who had relied was the most easily intelligible objective the law might have. Nevertheless, they found other secondary or pragmatic reasons why the expectation interest might be protected.[279]

Similarly, Joseph Raz has argued that while the promisor does have an obligation to perform, it is a moral one: He is obligated in the sense that he has created a special bond with the promisee that excludes certain reasons he might otherwise have for refusing to perform.[280] But his failure to perform does not, in and of itself, harm the promisee. Therefore, to require him to perform would seem to violate the "harm principle, which holds that "the only proper purpose for imposing legal obligations on individuals is to prevent harm.[281] The reason the law should require him to perform is not to vindicate the rights of the promisee, but to prevent the "institutional harm" that results from the "erosion or debasement of the practice of undertaking voluntary obligations."[282] Again, the implicit assumption is that the promisee has not already acquired a right to the performance.

A similar assumption seems to underlie the "efficient breach" theory. Suppose A has sold B a painting and then discovers that C will pay a huge price for it – more than it is worth to B. B does not know that C will pay so much and will not find out unless A tells him. According to the theory, it is "efficient" for A to breach, compensate B, and sell the painting to C himself. He and C will be better off, and B will be no worse off.

One objection to this argument is that the result will be efficient even if A is not allowed to breach the contract and pay damages.[283] A will tell B about C, charging for the information, and B will sell C the painting. A and B will then incur the transaction costs of negotiating with B over the price of information, but they will avoid those of negotiating and possibly litigating over the value of the painting to B.

---

278. Ibid. at 215.
279. At one point, they consider the possibility that "the law" might consider that the promisee has something like a property right in his "expectancy." According to them, however, to say that the purpose of the law is to protect that right is to go in a circle because it is the law that confers that right: "A promise has present value, why? Because the law enforces it." Ibid. at 218. If, however, the purposes of the parties are best served by the creation of such a right, then we are out of the circle.
280. J. Raz, "Promises and Obligations," in P. M. S. Hacker and J. Raz, eds. *Law, Morality and society Essays in Honour of H. L. A. Hart* (Oxford: Clarendon Press, 1997), 210 at 226–8; J. Raz, "Promises in Morality and Law," 95 Harv. L. Rev. 916 at 927–9 (1982).
281. "Promises in Morality and Law," *supra* note 281 at 934.
282. Ibid. at 937.
283. D. Friedmann, "The Efficient Breach Fallacy" (1989) 18. J. Leg. Stud. 1 at 6–7.

The more fundamental objection, however, is that the argument assumes that *B* will be no worse off if *A* breaches and sells the painting to *C*. If he already is entitled to the painting, then he will be worse off. If he is, then as Daniel Friedmann has pointed out, it should not matter in principle whether *A* breaches the contract before delivery, or sneaks into *B*'s house afterwards, and steals the painting to sell it to *C*.[284]

Moreover, if the promisee has no right to the promised performance, it is hard to explain why the law treats him as though he does. In civil and common law jurisdictions, he normally receives what he was promised or its value. In the case of the painting, he would receive the painting itself. The rule seems too constant to be explained by the pragmatic considerations mentioned by Fuller or the prevention of "institutional harm" mentioned by Raz.

Consequently, modern writers such as Friedmann, Benson, Barnett, and Smith have taken a position like that of Molina and Lessius: the promisee does have a right to the performance which he was promised.[285] The question then, as Richard Craswell and Stephen Smith have observed, is why he should have such a right.[286] As Craswell noted, unless we can give a reason we are assuming our conclusion.[287]

Craswell rejected this conclusion because he could not find a reason. T. M. Scanlon and Stephen Smith have tried to give one. According to Scanlon, the promisor is bound to perform if he meant to give the promisee "assurance" that he would.[288] The reason the promisee wants this "assurance" is not simply to avoid unease about how things will be in the future. The promisee "want[s] these things actually to be the case."[289] But that seems to be much like saying the promisee has the right to performance because that is what he wants and what the promisor means to give him. Indeed, for Scanlon, if the promisee has received an "assurance," it immediately follows that he has such a right.[290] That does seem to assume the conclusion.

Drawing on Raz, Smith has suggested a different reason. As we have seen, according to Raz, a promise creates a special bond with the promisee which excludes certain reasons the promisor might otherwise have for refusing to perform. According to Smith, such a relationship in "intrinsically valuable," and could not be created if it were understood that promises could sometimes be

---

284. Ibid., 1–2.
285. D. Friedmann, "The Performance Interest in Contract Damages," (1995) 111 L.Q. Rev. 628; P. Benson, "The Unity of Contract Law," this book; Benson, "Contract," *supra* note 51, at 42; R.E. Barnett, "A Consent Theory of Contract," (1986) 86 Colum. L. Rev. 269 at 304; S. Smith, "Towards a Theory of Contract," in Jeremy Horder, ed., *Oxford Essays in Jurisprudence Fourth Series* (Oxford: Oxford Univ. Press, 2000) 107, at 126.
286. Craswell, "Against Fuller and Perdue" (2000) 67 U. Chi. L. Rev. 99 at 123–4; Stephen Smith, *supra*, note 285, at 126.
287. Craswell, *supra* note 286, at 124.
288. T. M. Scanlon, "Promises and Contracts," this book, pp. 93ff.
289. Ibid. at p. 95.   290. Ibid. at p. 97.

broken.[291] Therefore, the promisee has a right to the performance he was promised. But this explanation seems to assume that promises will lose their value unless the promisee has such a right. On the contrary, Eisenberg observed of donative promises that sometimes the very recognition of a legal right in the promisee is incompatible with the relationship of love and trust that led the promisor to promise.[292] Moreover, one cannot simply assume that a commercial relationship loses its value if the promisee merely has the right to recover reliance damages for a change in his position.

Scanlon and Smith were looking for a reason why any promisee should invariably acquire a right to performance. It would be better to ask why he would sometimes want such a right and why the promisor might wish him to have it. If they have a reason which the law should respect, then, in these cases, the law should recognize such a right. Then, if we wish, we can then confine the word "promise" to cases in which the law does recognize that right, or we can use it more generally to refer to any assurance made by the "promisor." It will merely be a matter of terminology.

When the matter is put that way, the question of why the promisee is sometimes entitled to performance becomes much more mysterious since surely there are good reasons why the parties would want him to have such a right. In the case of a gift, the promisor could have at least three good reasons for wishing to confer it. First, he may rightly believe that his present decision to make the gift is more likely to be correct than a future decision not to make it. His present decision is prudent, he may believe, and the future decision is more likely to reflect greed than prudence. Second, he may rightly believe that conferring a right on the promisee is more consistent with the kind of relationship he wants with him. Eisenberg has noted that to confer such a right may be inconsistent with a relationship of love and trust between the parties.[293] But the converse may be true. Parents might give their adult children a house or bonds rather than merely letting them live in a house or endorsing over interest payments seriatim because they want the children to be independent rather than always beholden to them. Parent can effectuate such a purpose only if the law permits them to create a right in the children which does not depend on whether the parents have changed their mind or the children have relied. Third, though less likely,[294] the promisor might know the promisee does not trust him to perform absent a legal obligation and may wish to set his mind at rest.

---

291. Smith, *supra* note 285, at 127–28.
292. "Theory of Contracts," *supra* note 51 at p. 230.
293. Ibid.
294. This motive is less likely, in my view, because people are less likely to commit themselves to make gifts to those whom they believe do not trust them. Moreover, when they do so, the reason may not be a desire to relieve the promisee's anxiety but an imprudent concern for their own self-esteem. If a promisor like Diamond Jim Brady announced through a bullhorn that he wants to give a car to every student enrolled at the University of California, he might want to be able to commit himself so that his promise will not look like an empty gesture. In Dougherty v. Salt,

In an exchange, the promisee may want the right to require performance in order to lock in a favorable bargain.[295] He may fear that the other party will renege, having changed his mind about whether he wishes to exchange or about the terms. If the other party was to build something, he may increase his bid; if he was to sell something, he may decide to keep it himself, or to sell to someone else, or the market price of such a thing might rise. The party who is afraid he will renege may induce him to relinquish the opportunity to do so by promising some benefit in return, which may or may not be the relinquishment of his own right to renege. Once the parties have made such an agreement, a party who reneges harms the other by withholding a performance to which he is entitled whether or not the promisee relies. It is like reneging on a bet the parties have made as to whether one of them will decide that his bid is too low; or that he may need an item himself; or that he may be able to sell it for more elsewhere.[296]

---

125 N. E. 94 (N.Y. 1919), an aunt signed a note to give her nephew money because she was goaded into it by a sister who accused her of wanting to "take it out in talk." (The court held the written promise lacked consideration.) Consequently, when the promisor commits himself because he knows the promisee distrusts his word, it is hard for a court to be sure whether his promise was made for a good reason or not. Therefore, this motive did not figure in my earlier discussion of which promises of gift a court should enforce, although the other two motives did.

Nevertheless, for members of the law and economics movement, the motive of relieving the promisee from anxiety is often assumed to be the only reason or at least the standard one for wanting a promise of gift to be binding. When they say that the promisor's motive is the well-being of the promisee, they usually mean that the promisor wants to get the promisee more of what the promisee wants. If the promisee doubts that the promisor will follow through, then his level of well-being will be less, according to Posner, because he will discount the value of the performance by the probability it will be kept, and according to Steven Shavell, because he will be unable to change position in reliance in ways that make him better off. Therefore, if the promisee has these doubts, the promisor will have to promise a larger sum to bring him to the same level of welfare. R. Posner, "Gratuitous Promises in Economics and Law" (1977) 6 J. Leg. Stud. 411; S. Shavell, "An Economic Analysis of Altruism and Deferred Gifts," 20 J. Leg. Stud. 401 (1991). This explanation assumes that the donor conceives of his welfare as an economist does: as enhancing his ability to get whatever he wants.

295. Eisenberg, "Theory of Contracts," *supra* note 51 at p. 279.

296. An economist should be the first to agree that if the parties want to make such a bet, they should be able to do so because they thereby place a risk where it can most cheaply be borne. Yet, although Richard Craswell mentions Barnett's claim that making a promise confers a right on the promisee, this claim does not fit easily within either of the two economic theories he presents for the enforcement of promises. The first theory ("promise as performance") is that "enforcing the promise is efficient just in case performing the promised actions would be efficient." "For example, if *A* has promised to sell her car to *B* for $6,000, this theory rests the efficiency of enforcing *A*'s promise on the efficiency (or likely efficiency) of actually exchanging *A*'s car for *B*'s $6,000." Richard Craswell, "Two Economic Theories of Enforcing Promises," this volume, p. 20. What this analysis misses is that the initial promises may be, not merely a car for $6,000, but a car for $6,000 neither party having a right to renege. If the latter, then the initial exchange can be efficient – or, as I would prefer to put it, prudent – even though, at the time of performance, one party loses by it and the other wins. The second theory is concerned with incentives: "enforcing the promise is efficient just in case the new set of incentives is, on balance, efficient." Ibid. at p. 20. What that theory misses is that, for reasons just discussed, the parties may have mutually transferred to each other their right to renege, independently of whether by doing so, they provided the right incentives.

These considerations explain why, as we have seen, the law should enforce promises of gifts only when the promisor wished to confer a right to performance on the promisee, and why, if he did, the law should enforce the promise to its full extent. They also explain the remedies the law gives when a party breaches a contract to exchange. As just described, the reason the promisee may have received the right to require performance may have been to enable him to lock in a favorable bargain. If that is so, then, if the performance is unique, he will get what he bargained for only if he receives the very performance he was promised. If the promise concerned goods that are fungible or a service that any qualified person can make, then he will get what he bargained for as long as he receives goods or services that are the same in quality or kind. It does not matter whether the promisor performs himself or assigns the duty to someone else or pays the promisee an amount sufficient to obtain the performance on terms as favorable as those initially agreed.

It is understandable, then, that common and civil law courts require the promisor to perform personally when the goods or services promised are unique. They do so even though the doctrines they apply sound very different. In common law jurisdictions, specific performance is granted, in principle, only if a damage remedy is inadequate.[297] In Germany, in principle, the plaintiff always has the right to insist that the defendant perform.[298] In France, he can only demand damages.[299] Nevertheless, when goods and services are unique, courts in common law jurisdictions grant specific performance because a damage remedy is inadequate. German courts simply order the defendant to perform. French courts force him to perform by *astreinte,* that is, by threating to award large damages if he does not.[300]

If goods or services are not unique, courts in common law jurisdictions say that a damage remedy is adequate.[301] While, technically, a German plaintiff has the right to demand that the defendant perform, when the goods or services are not unique, there is no difference in practice. A defendant who performs simply pays the same amount of money to a third party to deliver the goods or perform the services that he otherwise would pay in damages.[302] Typically, the plaintiff accepts a payment from the defendant rather than insisting that he do so. French courts simply award damages.

---

297. *See Restatement (Second) of Contract,* §359(1) (1979).
298. BGB §241. Section 243 says that he must do so even when the performance is generic goods.
299. This is said to be the effect of Code civil art. 1142 ("Toute obligation de faire ou de ne pas faire se résout en dommages et intérêts en cas d'inexécution de la part du débiteur").
300. Statutory authorization for this traditional practice was finally provided by the Law of July 5, 1972, now superceded by the Law of July, 9, 1991. See, generally, Terré, Simler, and Lequette, *Droit civil: Les Obligations* §§ 1024–31.
301. *See Restatement (Second) of Contracts* §360(b) (1979).
302. He is entitled to have such a service performed by a third party. BGB §267.

V. Conclusion

The Aristotelian approach to contract was a synthesis of two intellectual traditions that profoundly affected the West: Greek philosophy and Roman law. The writers we have discussed brought the two traditions closer than they had ever been before or were to be again. As we have seen, these writers addressed a wide range of problems that are still with us. They did so, however, with a comparatively small stock of closely related ideas.

At the pinnacle, as we have seen, was the idea that human beings have an end, a manner of life in which their human potentialities are realized. The particular purposes they pursue are worthwhile to the extent they contribute to this ultimate end. It is therefore possible to say that people spend their money in better or worse ways, and that there are better and worse distributions of purchasing power. Consequently, one can explain how contract can improve the way resources are allocated. There will be an improvement to the extent that people use their purchasing power to acquire the resources they should, and each person has the purchasing power he should have to acquire resources. In Aristotelian terminology, contract improves the allocation of resources to the extent people exercise the virtues of prudence and distributive justice.

Even if the distribution were as just as practicable, some people would still have more than they should and others less. When private people use their own resources to help those who have less than they should, they practice the virtue of liberality. To the extent that the distribution of purchasing power is just, however, it is worth preserving. When people exchange at a price and on terms that preserve their respective shares of purchasing power, so far as practicable, they exercise the virtue of commutative justice. There are, then, two basic types of arrangements the law should respect: those based on liberality and those based on commutative justice. As we have seen, the rules of modern law serve the purposes of these types of arrangements. Those concerning promises of gifts try to ensure that the gift is made sensibly. Those concerning exchange try to ensure that neither party enriches the other at his own expense.

For a contract to serve these purposes, there must be some point at which the arrangement becomes final so that the promisor cannot change his mind. That point, however, depends on the purposes of the parties. As we have seen, there are several reasons why sometimes, the parties would want the promisor to be committed at the very moment he makes the promise. If so, as of that moment, the promisee acquires a right to the performance that it would be unjust to take away. To deprive him of it is a violation of commutative justice.

According to this approach, the details of contract law must be understood in terms of the purposes served by contract which must themselves be understood in terms of the ends of society and of human life itself. Historically, one reason the approach was discredited was that modern philosophers became sceptical about whether one could talk about an end of human life for the sake of which choices are made. If not, then it was impossible to talk about virtues in the Aristotelian sense, since a virtue is an acquired capacity to choose what contributes to a good life. Today, there are signs of change. Few contemporary scholars are committed to the ideas that initially made the utilitarian and Kantian traditions seem plausible: that choices are made to maximize a quantity of pleasure or satisfaction, or that freedom means choice without regard to one's own inclination or purposes. Some are saying – at least almost – that the value of a choice depends in part on the value of what is chosen. It is a short step to talking about virtue once again. If we do, we may find old law books worth reading.[303]

303. I would like to thank Peter Benson, Melvin Eisenberg, Scott FitzGibbon, Christopher Kutz, Ariel Porat, and Stephen Smith for their comments.

Index